THE
GREAT
RIVALRY

BOOKS BY ED LINN

The Eternal Kid
Veeck — As in Wreck, with Bill Veeck
The Last Loud Roar, with Bob Cousy
The Hustler's Handbook, with Bill Veeck
Koufax, with Sandy Koufax
Masque of Honor, a novel
Thirty Tons a Day, with Bill Veeck
The Adversaries, a novel
Big Julie of Vegas
Out of the Fire, with Ernst Papanek
Nice Guys Finish Last, with Leo Durocher
Where the Money Was, with Willie Sutton
Inside the Yankees: The Championship Season
Steinbrenner's Yankees
A Great Connection
The Great Rivalry

THE
GREAT
RIVALRY

*The Yankees
and the Red Sox
1901–1990*

ED LINN

Ticknor & Fields • New York • 1991

For information about permission to reproduce selections
from this book, write to Permissions, Ticknor & Fields,
Houghton Mifflin Company, 2 Park Street,
Boston, Massachusetts 02108.

Library of Congress Cataloging-in-Publication Data

Linn, Edward.
The great rivalry : the Yankees and the Red Sox, 1901–1990
/ Ed Linn.
p.   cm.
Includes index.
ISBN 0-89919-917-8
1. New York Yankees (Baseball team) — History.   2. Boston Red Sox
(Baseball team) — History.   I. Title.
GV875.N4L55   1991   91-7592
796.357'64'09747'1 — dc20   CIP

Printed in the United States of America

MAP 10 9 8 7 6 5 4 3 2 1

The quotations opening Chapters 3 and 4 are from
The Glory of Our Times by Lawrence Ritter.

To Michael Linn
Did I ever tell you you're my hero . . .

Contents

Contents

Introduction to the Rivalry

I don't care what anybody says, there is no rivalry on the face of the earth that can compare with the Yankees vs. the Red Sox. Something special happens when these two teams meet — a certain shiver in the air as the home team comes racing out onto the field that turns their uniforms whiter against the greener grass.

It's everything a rivalry ought to be. US AGAINST THEM. It's not only New York City against Boston. It's New York against New England. The canyons of Wall Street and the caverns of Madison Avenue vs. the White Hills of New Hampshire and the Green Mountains of Vermont.

We the People vs. the Barons of Entrenched Privilege.

And, as appropriate battlefields, the spacious expanse of Yankee Stadium against the looming monster of Fenway Park.

Don't think it doesn't communicate itself to the players on the field. "It's different," they will tell you. "You can feel the excitement from the moment 'The Star-Spangled Banner' begins to play." The action seems crisper, the fielding sharper; the ball comes off the bat with the fresh, clean sound of the first day of spring training. Baseball becomes again what baseball is supposed to be, a game of shifting fortunes within a series of steadily rising climaxes. A happening. An Event!

There is a tradition here, a rich history that speaks of ancient heroes and sleeping giants.

Joe DiMaggio, Ted Williams, Carl Yastrzemski, and Reggie Jackson coming off the bench in the final innings of crucial games to do what the greatest of stars are supposed to do — win the game with a home run.

Old dog-eared Casey Stengel pulling his first pennant out of a hat by beating Joe McCarthy, the ringmaster of the previous Yankee dynasty. McCarthy bringing his team down to the final game not once but two years in a row and, in another year, departing from Boston empty-handed.

A young Joe DiMaggio and a younger Ted Williams pitting their greatest year against each other, and when it was over — the year was 1941 — not knowing, for none of us could have known, that no matter what they would ever do again, they had posted the feats they would forevermore be identified with. Nor could any of us have known back in 1941 that neither they nor we would ever be able to look upon those white uniforms and green fields with quite the same innocence.

This is a rivalry that goes back to the beginning of the century. Boston came into the American League as a charter member in 1901; New York joined up in 1903, and the following year the two teams fought it out over the last five games of the season after passing the lead back and forth for a month.

Tradition is a product of time and proximity. Boston and New York are close enough to allow the supporters of either team to travel back and forth with comparative ease. In the early days the trip meant eight hours on the Old Post Road, or six hours of revelry between South Station and Grand Central. In a time of turnpikes and air travel, it takes just three hours on the road or an hour by plane.

The fans have been known to affect the outcome of a game, both directly and indirectly. In 1939, the Red Sox had a seven-game winning streak against the Yankees going into their final meeting of the season, a streak that included a never-to-be-forgotten five-game sweep at Yankee Stadium. The streak came to an end, on a forfeit, after the Boston fans had expressed their irreconcilable differences with the umpiring crew by bombarding the field with so much garbage that the visiting New Yorkers were moved to wonder whether Bostonians brought their garbage into the park with them or purchased it from an independent contractor.

Jump to 1977, the first year of free agency and the beginning of the two most turbulent years of the rivalry. A New York fan sitting in the front row of the left-field bleachers will affect the outcome of the most important game of the season by turning a spectacular Carl Yastrzemski catch into a Yankee home run by plucking the ball right out of his glove.

·   ·   ·

But let's not kid ourselves. In order to have a Classic Rivalry, you have to have an Ancient Grievance. This one goes back to 1920, when Harry Frazee, who rates right up there in Boston's Hall of Infamy with King George III and tax stamps, sold Babe Ruth to the Yankees for $125,000. Harry Frazee, who was himself a New Yorker, a producer of Broadway musicals and a close friend of the mayor of New York, the effulgent Jimmy Walker.

In truth, the sale of Babe Ruth was only the most devastating transaction in what was to become such a complete transfer of players as to take a three-time pennant winner and sentence it to a decade in the dungeon.

A dozen years passed before a 32-year-old millionaire named Tom Yawkey came along to give them hope that they could overtake the swaggering New Yorkers.

After that it became a battle of star names. Cronin-Foxx-Grove vs. Gehrig-Lazzeri-Gomez-Ruffing. Then, in the Golden Age of Baseball, the Forties and Fifties, it became Joe DiMaggio-Berra-Rizzuto-Henrich against Williams-Doerr-Pesky-Dom DiMaggio, with the Red Sox pitting a pair of aces, Mel Parnell and Ellis Kinder, against the Yankee threesome of Vic Raschi, Allie Reynolds, and Eddie Lopat, and the big guy out of the bullpen, Joe Page.

Then onward and upward to the late seventies, when free agency came along to give the deck a shuffle with Jackson-Munson-Nettles-Rivers vs. Yastrzemski-Rice-Lynn-Evans-Fisk.

And, of course, those members of the chorus who had their one great moment in the sun: Bucky Dent, Jerry Coleman, Johnny Lindell, Roy White, Al Zarilla, Billy Rohr, Bill Campbell. And maybe we'll come up with a surprise or two along the way.

The rivalry has a resonance that carries beyond the local precincts and suburbs. The New York Yankees and the Boston Red Sox are national teams, as Frank Bloss, who now covers the Red Sox for the *Providence Journal,* discovered at the time of the 1978 play-off game. Bloss was breaking in as the sports editor for a suburban newspaper in the Houston area. He completed his assignment just in time to duck into a restaurant-bar where he suspected there would be a television set. "The name of the place was Thank God It's Friday. I'll never forget it." To his astonishment he found that the place was packed. "It was like sitting across the street from Fenway Park. They were screaming at each other on every pitch, the New York rooters on one side and the Bostons on the other." And while a certain number of them were transplanted Bostonians and New Yorkers, the vast majority, he discovered, was composed of people who had relocated from all over the country to work in Houston's then-booming oil industry.

Haywood Sullivan, the general partner and chief executive officer of the Red Sox, came to the Red Sox originally in 1955 as a bonus-boy catcher fresh out of college. "The Red Sox and the Yankees are the two national teams," he says. "They are the greatest gate attractions everywhere." A not unmixed blessing, Sullivan has come to believe.

As the expansions of the Sixties and the Seventies added six new teams to the American League, the 22-game series that had set the pace and rhythm of the rivalry for almost 60 years was nibbled away at until it dwindled to 13.

The Sox and Yankees got snookered, says Sullivan. "The western clubs outnumber us, eight to six, and they were very, very cagey in setting up the schedule to help themselves. Right now we play more games in the other division than in our own division, which makes no sense. George [Steinbrenner] and I would talk about it every time we went into a scheduling meeting and whenever we'd get together to talk about reorganization or expansion. Every year we say that something has to be done, and nobody knows how to do it." The western teams have the votes, and as much as they may sympathize with the arguments put forth by the Yankees and the Red Sox, they are not willing to give up a single game against them.

"To be honest," Sullivan says, "I think it's going to take an expansion of four clubs — and it's going to happen — so that we can split the league into three divisions. There's going to have to be movement somewhere along the line. Whenever we play the Yankees we fill the park. It's the greatest rivalry in sports."

The hotbed of Yankee fandom versus Red Sox fandom isn't in either Boston or New York. It's in western Connecticut, along a line that runs between New Haven and Waterbury. East Waterbury and all points east is Red Sox territory. West Waterbury on into New York state belongs to the Yankees.

Rumor has it that it was in Waterbury where, in the aftermath of the Red Sox's elimination of the Yankees in 1986, one local official drove through the west side of town mooning the Yankee fans as he went. His resignation the next day was voluntary, it was said.

There are also cities such as Worcester and Pittsfield in Massachusetts and Providence, Rhode Island, where a large segment of the population began to turn toward the Yankees out of ethnic pride in the days of Tony Lazzeri and Frank Crosetti and became solid with the arrival of Joe DiMaggio.

Rich Gedman, the Red Sox catcher from 1981 to 1989, grew up in Worcester dreaming of playing for the Red Sox and hating everything that was even remotely connected with the Yankees. Gedman is a man who thinks so carefully about what he is going to say that you are constantly left with the feeling that he has decided not to answer at all. "Whether you come from New England or not," he says, finally, "you have to be aware that when you play the Yankees, you are a part of history. But even more so, as a kid growing up in the Worcester area, knowing what the rivalry means in Boston and New York, an extra special feeling forms. The thing I remember most is that when sitting down and watching Red Sox games with my Dad, I'd say, 'I hope the Red Sox win today.' He'd say, 'I wouldn't bet on it.' And it was like he was saying, 'My heart's with the Red Sox but my money's with the Yankees.' "

To a young Rich Gedman, that said it all. "It was always the Yankee tradition and the great clubs they'd had over the years. And then, because of where I lived, it seemed like the guys on my high school team were split, some for the Yankees, some for the Red Sox, and always it was the Red Sox playing second fiddle. When I finally got down here to play, that's the only thing that was in the back of my mind: I don't want to play second fiddle anymore."

His first big chance came in the split season of 1981. "It didn't matter so much that we didn't win. The season series meant more to me. They won the pennant, and we won the season series seven games to six. That meant a lot to me because even if they won, we won too."

Is there anybody else in the whole wide world who would remember that in 1981 the Red Sox won the season series from the Yankees, 7–6?

After Gedman had been around for a few years and got to know a few of the New York players, he no longer hated them. "Now I get a feeling of, I like the New York players but I can't stand the Yankees."

There is a camaraderie among ballplayers that comes and goes according to the times. Roger ("Doc") Cramer, the great center fielder of the early Yawkey years, was always the most convivial of men, a great kidder and practical joker. "It was very competitive on the field," Doc says. "But there was great camaraderie after the game. Hell, we'd go out to dinner together afterwards, some of us." Cramer is now in his eighties, and he does not recall the rivalry as being that intense among the players ("Except Joe Cronin, and he was the manager"). But, then, Cramer had been purchased from Philadelphia, and his relationships were already established. Almost all of the Boston players of his era were veteran players who had been brought over from other teams. "There was more excitement in the crowd itself. It was the fans. The whole town, they'd go crazy. They'd always applaud a good play by a Yankee player, though. Boston was always like that. New York not so much."

Joe Cronin, the Red Sox player-manager, hated the Yankees with a passion all his life, and yet, as competitive as he was, he was always willing to make an exception for a fellow Californian. Lefty Gomez, scheduled to pitch against the Red Sox, took a stroll through the Fens behind Fenway Park and saw some kids playing ball. "Let me hit, son," he said. Gomez couldn't hit worth a damn, but he always had a dozen bets spread around the locker room about how many hits he was going to get, and now he saw a chance to sharpen his eye.

Result: He fouled one off his foot, limped back to the ball park on a rapidly swelling ankle, and went in to tell his tale of woe to Joe Cronin. "Joe," he said, "we Californians got to stick together. Will you tell Joe McCarthy I fell down your dugout steps?"

"Certainly," said Cronin. Otherwise, as Joe would say in telling the story, McCarthy would probably have killed Gomez on the spot. Of course, he would then chuckle, he didn't mind that he wasn't going to have to hit against Lefty that day. "Old Lefty was always as tough on me as anybody I ever faced."

Through the early part of the Casey Stengel era, when the two teams seemed to be fighting for the pennant in every game, there was a professional correctness between the players. Jerry Coleman was a rookie in 1949, Stengel's first year. "We never talked to the opposing players the way they do now," Coleman says. "In all the years I played against the Red Sox, I said hello to one person and that was all I said, Hello, and that was to Bobby Doerr. I didn't want to. They were there, and we were here." Joe DiMaggio would have dinner with his brother Dom on occasion, but that was about it, says Coleman. "I never talked to Dominic DiMaggio until he retired. Ever. Tebbetts would talk to us. Not so much *to* us as *at* us. 'Well, I think we'll throw this kid a curve ball,' that kind of thing. Birdie was like that. But he was also cussing his pitcher out more than he was talking to me."

In the seventies a real hostility took hold between the players.

Mike Torrez, who pitched for the Yankees in 1977 and the Red Sox in 1978, was in the best of all positions to see it. "The Yankees hated certain of the Red Sox players," is the way he sums it up. "The Red Sox hated the Yankees."

When Jerry Remy came to Boston in 1978, that was the first thing that struck him. The second thing that struck him was how much the New York fans hated the Red Sox. "We'd come out after the game and they'd be lined up four deep at the bus to curse us. The biggest ovation I ever got was at Yankee Stadium. I messed up my knee and walked out of the stadium with a cast all the way up my leg. These people were out there yelling and screaming, 'Hey, you bleep, way to go! Way to get hurt, ya bum!' "

Remy loved it. "Every minute of it," he says. "Even though it could get hairy. I had a few tomatoes thrown at me at second base, but that was nothing like what Dwight Evans had to endure. He had everything thrown at him in right field."

The same thing would happen to Mickey Rivers in Fenway Park. Each of them would have to stop the game, at times, and run back to the dugout for a helmet. Bottles. Bolts. Sharp pieces of metal. Anything and everything.

Carlton Fisk was always a prime target, too. Fisk went to the Chicago White Sox in 1981 after the Red Sox fouled up his contract. The first time the White Sox played in New York, the bus pulled up to Yankee Stadium, and nobody was there. "I couldn't get over it. When we went with the Red Sox, there'd be a mob waiting for us. They'd be screaming at us and spitting and throwing things. I thought it was always that way."

Coming or going, that's how it remained for the Red Sox. Jack Rogers, the team's 70-year-old traveling secretary, was crossing the field after the final game of the 1968 World Series when he was hit on the head by an unopened beer can and knocked cold. His skull was fractured. An ambulance had to be called. It wasn't Yankee Stadium, but as far as the Red Sox were concerned, they were the same New York fans in a different setting.

Earlier that same season Dave Henderson had come to Boston in a trade with Seattle, and he had no idea what the fuss was all about. Nor, given his sunny view of life, did he care. "There was a fight every two or three minutes in the bleachers right behind me. I'd be looking around — you know me. I'm California mellow. I'm messing around a lot out there. The special police come down, they drag out thirty guys. Thirty other guys rush down to take their seats before the cops are out of sight, and you hope they aren't Yankee fans because there will be another fight and I've got a ball game going on."

Inevitably there have been some pretty good brawls between the players through the years. Joe Cronin and Jake Powell had a classic punchout on the pitcher's mound. Jimmy Piersall and Billy Martin went under the stands to slug it out after Piersall had thrown out a challenge during fielding practice. A beanball battle in the wonderful year of 1967 escalated into a full-scale donnybrook.

Given the hostility of the seventies, it should come as no surprise that a couple of fights broke out. Or that Thurman Munson and Carlton Fisk were involved. Munson and Fisk hated each other. So did Billy Martin and Bill Lee. To Martin, Bill Lee was "the Lady," he was "the Fag," he was . . . well, you get the idea.

To Lee, Billy Martin was a storm trooper, a bit of a lout — and an irresistible target. "I could get Martin's goat in a heartbeat," Lee says. "With Billy, it was psychiatric and alcoholic. It was his liver talking back."

When Billy was managing the Texas Rangers, prior to coming to New York, Lee had played such a dissonant tune on Martin's head that he had Billy swinging from the dugout roof, pointing at Lee and scratching his armpits like a chimpanzee. "Two days later he was fired. I like to think I had something to do with it."

But at the core of the enmity were the catchers, Munson and Fisk. Both were easy men to dislike if you happened to be playing against them. Fisk had a slow and stately way of moving that drove opposing teams crazy. He was also maddeningly slow and deliberate in giving his signs to the pitcher. The Yankees would yell at him to stop playing with himself in terms — how to put this? — that would have been more appropriately applied to a woman.

Both had come to the majors in 1969. Both had been through their team's system, and both had a strong sense of loyalty. Fisk had been the greatest all-around athlete in the history of New Hampshire. Munson had been the greatest athlete in the Akron-Canton area. Fisk was stubborn and austere. Munson delighted in being rough and crude.

Neither of them had ever been known to take a backward step.

Fisk came out of New Hampshire steeped in Red Sox tradition. The Yankees had the first draft choice in his year, and the only reason they didn't select him was that he had already let everyone know he would not sign with any team except the Red Sox.

Munson was a truck driver's son out of Akron and he had a truck driver's code. He wanted the part of the road that belonged to him. In his heart he believed that he was superior to Fisk in every way. Fisk was getting hits off the wall at Fenway Park, while he was hitting 400-foot fly balls to the deep caverns of Yankee Stadium. Every year the fans would vote Fisk to the All-Star team. Fisk was big and handsome (6 feet 2 inches, 210 pounds) and looked like a catcher. Munson was a solid 5 foot 11, 195 pounds, but he looked round and dumpy in his uniform.

Munson hated Fisk, and because Munson hated him, the hard core of the Yankee ball club hated him too.

Sparky Lyle once came in from the bullpen after Graig Nettles had been hit by a pitched ball, threw his jacket down on the bench, and announced, "The first one is right in his throat." They knew he was talking about Fisk, and that he was saying it as much for Munson's benefit as for Nettles's. He threw the first pitch in back of Fisk and hit him in the arm with the second.

The opportunity for Munson came in 1973 when Gene Michael missed the ball completely on a suicide squeeze with the score tied in the ninth inning.

Michael had the best view in the park. "Bill Lee threw a slider down and in, and I bunted over it, and Munson is roaring down, and I'm standing in front of Fisk. Fisk shoved me away and I knew what was going to happen. He hits into Fisk like a steamroller, and they both go flying, and Thurman gets up and starts back, and Fisk flips him over on his back again. There's a pile and this and that. Fisk is standing over him, smiling, and this and that. So I hit him. Everybody else is being held by somebody, but nobody still had me. So, what the hell, I hit him again."

Fisk and Munson got thrown out of the game. Michael escaped scot-free. "I'm standing at the plate. I got two strikes on me. The umpire, I think, was Joe Brinkman. I say, 'How come you didn't throw me out? I was the only one who hit anybody.' He says, 'When I go to a three-ring circus, I always watch the wrong ring.'"

Bill Lee was pitching the next time there was a fight at home plate. To his eternal sorrow. The brawl ended with a torn ligament in Lee's pitching shoulder. He was disabled for nearly two months, and his fast ball was never quite the same again.

This one occurred during the Red Sox's first trip to Yankee Stadium in 1976, when Lou Piniella tried to score from second on Dwight Evans's arm and was out by 10 feet. The only thing he could do was try to knock the ball out of Fisk's glove. Or kick it out. In the tangle of arms and legs, he kicked Fisk instead.

Whereupon Fisk decided to tag him a second time just to make sure. On the head. Hard.

Out streamed the players from both benches. Bill Lee, who had been backing up the plate, was grabbed, spun around, and belted in the head from behind by Mickey Rivers. As Lee was trying to clear his head, Nettles picked him up and threw him down on his shoulder. When Lee got up, holding onto his pitching arm, he realized that his season was probably over. "You sonofabitch!" he screamed at Nettles. "How could you do this to me? How could you be such an asshole?"

By way of explanation, Nettles belted him flush in the eye, knocking him down and giving him a shiner to go with his crippled arm.

There is no symmetry. The Yankees championships piled up upon each other with such regularity that they blend together in the mind, distinguishable only by the name of each World Series's particular hero.

There is the Johnny Lindell Series, the Charlie Keller Series, the Joe Gordon Series, the Jerry Coleman Series, the Phil Rizzuto Series, the Billy Martin Series, the Bob Turley Series, the Ralph Terry Series, the Hank Bauer Series, the Whitey Ford Series, the Bobby Richardson Series, the Elston Howard Series. Am I leaving anybody out?

The Yankees had the Organization. From the time of Jake Ruppert down through the ownership of Dan Topping and Del Webb, the Yankees had tough owners and even tougher general managers. It was produce or take a hike. And when it came to signing their contract, the players were reminded that part of their salary came in the form of their annual World Series check.

Tom Yawkey idolized his players, pampered them, and frequently undercut his managers' authority. The Organization, such as it was, was filled with old Yawkey retainers. The general manager was usually an old Yawkey crony.

The Red Sox were always one starting pitcher short, forever lacking a left-handed reliever, and frequently without a pinch-hitter when one was needed. In 1949, the year the Red Sox needed to win only one of the final two games at Yankee Stadium, they'd had nobody on the bench all season who could buy a pinch-hit. But the Yankees? The Yankees had such a depth of talent that they were platooning everybody except Rizzuto and DiMaggio (and DiMaggio was out half the season).

They had the pitching and they had the depth and, if need be, they would buttress their roster at the end of the season by buying a veteran player to fill a perceived weakness. Johnny Mize. Johnny Hopp. Johnny Sain. Sometimes it didn't even seem to matter who. "Put a guy in a Yankee uniform . . . ," they would say.

Frank Malzone was the Red Sox All-Star third baseman through the early Sixties. He is currently their superscout. "The Yankees knew how to play the game," he says. "All of them. You go out on Old Timers' Day, and it's one great player after another being introduced. You see them there and you begin to wonder how the Red Sox even came close."

You go to Yankee Stadium and there are all those retired numbers staring down at you.

But if the Red Sox didn't win often, they had a way of winning when they were least expected to. "No New York pennants have been talked about like ours in 1967 and 1975," says Haywood Sullivan.

Sullivan is right.

Red Sox pennants come so rarely that you can recite the significant dates and details the way schoolchildren recite the dates and details of the great events of American history.

Listen, my children, and you shall hear of the wondrous year of 1967, when the Red Sox came from last place (well, almost) to first to win the pennant in what was being called the Impossible Dream. And of 1975, when they made every fan's springtime fantasy come true by coming up with not one but *two* great rookies, Fred Lynn and Jim Rice.

It is no great secret that the Red Sox are the team with the fatal flaw. It is because they are perceived as the team with the fatal flaw that they have become the darlings of the literati — and not only the literati. Of all the tests that can be given to divine the true nature of a man, no test is more revealing than the one that separates the Yankee fan from the Red Sox fan. The Yankees have always been the team that carries the stamp of success. To become a Yankee rooter was to enlarge oneself effortlessly. The Red Sox are the team that must be loved, cherished, and, in the end, forgiven. "Fenway Park is a religious shrine," Bill Lee once said. "People go there to worship." And if it is a bit much to say that rooting for the Red Sox is a religious obligation, it is fair to say that anybody who had been a Red Sox fan over a full lifetime should be granted absolution from any other form of penance.

There is a Hand, to paraphrase a local poet named James Russell Lowell, that bends the Red Sox to mightier misfortunes than should be rightfully borne.

In addition to not being able to beat the Yankees in the game that has to be won — goes the mythology — the Red Sox are the team that has participated in the only two play-off games in the history of the American League, played them both in their home park, where they are supposed to be all but unbeatable, and lost them both. In 1949 they also lost the final game of the season to the Yankees, in what amounted to a play-off game.

They are the team that cannot win the seventh game of a World Series, and always under circumstances that are meant to try the patience, if not the soul, of any dedicated Red Sox fan.

Boston's own Seventh Commandment decrees: Thou Shalt Not Win the Seventh Game!

There have been four Red Sox World Series, and four seventh games. In 1946 there was Ted Williams, hurting from a bruised elbow because of a ridiculously misconceived exhibition game; Dom DiMaggio twisting his ankle going into second base and being forced to leave the game under circumstances that proved to be fatal; and

Johnny Pesky holding the ball a split second too long before throwing to the plate.

In 1975 their leading slugger, Jim Rice, fractured his wrist a week before the Series opened; Bill Lee could not resist the temptation to throw his blooper pitch to Tony Perez, the best off-speed hitter in baseball; and the cover actually came off the ball, turning what should have been an inning-ending double play into a tie game.

More than anything else, though, the damnest pitchers have held the fate of the Red Sox in their hands in those games. In 1946 Joe Cronin called upon a 38-year-old relief pitcher named Bob Klinger to pitch the final inning. Klinger had just come back from a three-week leave because of sickness in his family. In the year of the Impossible Dream, Jim Lonborg was forced to start the seventh game with only two days' rest since he was not only their best pitcher but their only pitcher. Lonborg didn't have it. Everybody knew he didn't have it. Dick Williams, the manager, was told he didn't have it. "I know Dick Williams well enough to say that he pitched Lonborg so that he wouldn't be second-guessed by the press," Frank Malzone says.

In 1975 they ended with a left-hander named Jim Burton, who had a total of 53 innings in the major leagues and had won only one game.

When you run down the list, you find Denny Galehouse, a mediocre pitcher in the sunset of his career, starting the play-off game in 1948; sore-armed, seldom-used Tex Hughson being called out of the bullpen in the final inning of the final game of the 1949 season; Bobby Sprowl, just up from the minors, being asked to pitch the final game of the Boston Massacre of 1978, as the Yankees were knocking the Red Sox out of first place.

Hughson never pitched another game. Galehouse never started another, and pitched only two innings the next year in relief. Sprowl never pitched again for the Red Sox, and never won a game for anyone. Jim Burton pitched all of 2⅔ innings in relief two years later. In the case of Burton and Sprowl, the careers of two promising young pitchers were destroyed forever.

And, finally, there came the One Strike Away nightmare of the 1986 World Series. It was not enough to get to the seventh game for the fourth straight time; it was necessary to get to the final batter and the final strike — four times to that final strike — and still lose. Whether that was the final descent into the lower regions or the final blow that had to be endured before, at last, triumph — well, only the future can tell. But it is almost needless to say that for any Red Sox fan — for any baseball fan — there is the sense of a future that has already been determined. By such a reckoning Bill Buckner had no choice but to let that ball go through his legs. He was no more than an instrument of destiny.

There is even a certain bittersweet pleasure to being a Red Sox fan which the ball club has been able to turn to its advantage. Lives there a Red Sox fan anywhere in New England who has never said, "Before I die I want to see the Red Sox win a World Series"? In New England, the Great Come and Get It Day still lies tantalizing, offshore, just beyond the three-mile limit, somewhere over the horizon.

In the meantime the fans can develop a protective coloration. They can hope and they can dream, but they are always going to be expecting the worst. And this is something that a newcomer on the scene doesn't always understand.

Rick Cerone, a hard-bitten veteran of New York's Steinbrenner Wars, helped the Red Sox win their division in 1988. No thanks, Cerone would say, to the Boston sports writers. "The press here expects you to lose big games in September. They expected us to lose. They *wanted* us to lose."

Dave Henderson, who was wholly innocent of Red Sox lore, and Rich Gedman, who carried the history in the marrow of his bones, found the consistently negative attitudes of the Boston press equally incomprehensible. "Even when we were seven games up," Henderson says of the 1986 season, "we still had four games to go with the Yankees and somehow it was going to come to the last series and they were going to beat us out. That's what they were writing, and I could see that some of the players were taking it seriously."

We'll never know. By the time of the final series the Red Sox had already clinched the division. Says Henderson: "The batting championship was the only thing left for Boston to lose — Mattingly or Boggs — so that became the big issue. They were hoping Wade did lose the batting title to the Yankees. They've got to find something in that town that you have to lose."

Gedman puts it even more bluntly: "You get the feeling that the press would rather the Yankees beat the hell out of the Red Sox so they can say, 'Oh, here it is again. History repeated itself.' No doubt in my mind."

·   ·   ·

Lou Gorman, the man who put that 1986 team together, is another New Englander, out of Rhode Island. Lou has been a Red Sox fan all his life, and for one brief shining moment there he thought he had led the Red Sox to that elusive goal, a world championship. Three runs ahead, and one strike to go? Who wouldn't? "I was sitting with Mrs. Yawkey and [John] McNamara's wife and my wife. We and Haywood Sullivan, we were right by the commissioner and the American League president. And so we were starting to go down the aisle to go through the dugout and into the clubhouse to accept the trophy. The others didn't want to speak, so I was going to accept the trophy for the ball club. I was trying to think in my mind, *What thought can I have to say? Here's the first one in 74 years. This is for the fans of New England. I know exactly how much this means to you, because I grew up as a Red Sox fan myself.* And all of a sudden, boom . . . boom . . . boom. And I sit down again.

"It was deigned to be that we weren't going to win that game. Just weren't going to win it. After the game was over, in the clubhouse, of course, the clubhouse was devastated. They knew they'd blown it. They knew they'd had the world championship and blown it. And we were underdogs to the Mets. The Mets were heavily favored to win. All of a sudden, our guys had the World Series in their hands, and it's gone. Right down the goddamn chute. There wasn't a sound in that clubhouse excepting the reporters talking and the cameras and so forth.

"I rode the bus back with them, and you could hear the tires on the bus it was so quiet. Generally they're raising hell on the bus. Or chattering away. I thought to myself, *Jesus, what kind of a game will we play tomorrow? We'll be so horseshit tomorrow, we probably shouldn't show up.* I was sitting next to McNamara, and Mac was completely devastated. I knew that the last thing he wanted to do was talk. I didn't feel much like talking anyway. So we drove along like that and all you could hear was the tires on the bus going *galoomph, galoomph, galoomph.*"

Chapter One

1978 Play-Off

It all came down, in that final closing scene, to the old man with the stick and the young man with the arm. Pity it could not have been frozen and suspended there — this scene in Fenway Park, never to unfold — perhaps encased in glass in a corner of Cooperstown devoted to all those who write endings of their own.

— Bill Nack, *Long Island Newsday*

DON Zimmer is speaking:
    "All anybody remembers is the Bucky Dent home run, but so many things happened in that game that I'll never realize how we lost it. We're leading. 2–0. Guidry is still pitching. Sixth inning. We got two men on, two men out. Fred Lynn at bat. One thing about Fenway Park. You defensed everybody to give them both lines, because the fences were short down both lines. So what you did, you closed up the outfield so they couldn't hit a triple in the gap. With Guidry pitching you give them even more line because he throws so hard. There weren't many guys who pulled Guidry, especially left-handers.
    "I'm sitting in that dugout, and you got to remember you can't see the right-field line from the Fenway dugout. The way that wall comes out you can't see much past first base. Two men on, two men out. Piniella playing right and Fred Lynn gets around on the ball and nails it down the right-field line. You know it's going to be hooking, and I said, *Godamighty, that's two more runs. I know it's two more runs,* and as you jump up on the top step you still can't see, and you kind of hear — *hoomph* — a kind of groan as the crowd noise goes flat. Piniella catches it. Now, how could that be? How the hell could he catch a hooking line drive off Fred Lynn? Hit off Guidry?"

After the game, Zimmer sat around for about an hour and a half taking on the press, answering questions. "And then four or five of the Yankees came over. I know Piniella from Tampa. I'd spent some time with him over the winter. I said to him, 'They're going to be talking about this game forever. But there's one thing they're not going to talk about and it's the thing that bothers me. Explain to me how the hell you could be playing Fred Lynn to pull the ball off of Guidry.' He says, 'I'll tell you, I just didn't think Guidry had his real good stuff today, and I just went over and I cheated five or six steps to my left.'

"I thought, *Well, that's just the knowledge of a guy who knows how to play the game.* And you have to tip your hat to him. They can talk about all the other things, but it was the catch on Freddie Lynn's drive in the sixth inning that did it. Because that would have busted the game wide open."

Never mind what anybody might say now. You think back on the 1978 season today, and all you're going to remember is that the Yankees were the team that came from 14 games out in July to beat the Red Sox in the greatest comeback of all time. But that doesn't even begin to tell the story. There were two great comebacks that season. In point of fact, the Yankees didn't only make up those 14 games, they actually gained 17½. With 15 games left to play, the Yankees had pulled ahead by 3½ games and were clearly going to run away with the division. That was where the Red Sox pulled up their sox and won 12 of their last 14 games. With eight games remaining, they were able to cut the lead down to one. The Yankees thereupon won seven straight to hold on to their lead. Another way of putting that — if you happened to be sitting in Boston — was to say that the Red Sox won seven straight games in the last week of the season and gained nothing.

In order to force a play-off, the Red Sox had to make it eight straight on the last day of the season, and the Yankees had to lose. Each team had its old pro going — Luis Tiant and Catfish Hunter. Hunter hadn't simply made a second-half comeback; the Cat had come back from the dead. Without Hunter's return to life, the Yankees would never have been in the pennant hunt. So what happened? Tiant shut out Toronto, while Hunter, who was coming off an eight-game victory streak, was battered by Cleveland.

The Yankees were either going to go down as the team that had made the greatest comeback in baseball history or as the team that had pulled ahead by 3½ games with only two weeks to go, and then blown it all in the last two games.

The Yankee players had been so confident that few of them had paid any attention when the Red Sox won the toss that would put the play-off game in their home park in the event of a tie. "We were walking up the tunnel after we'd got beat," says Bucky Dent, "and they told us we lost the coin flip and had to go to Boston. *Oh, shit! We played 162 games and we lose a toss and now we got to go up and play at Fenway?*"

Instead of flying to Kansas City, as they had planned, for the opening of the American League play-offs, they had to catch a bus to Boston for the one game that was going to settle it all. "This is the right way for it to end," Lou Piniella told Thurman Munson as they were preparing to leave. "We'll settle it head to head."

"I would just as soon," said Munson the realist, "that we had settled it today."

Amen to that, Reggie Jackson would have said. Jackson, always a man to let his emotions run free, did not try to disguise his feelings. "The season starts tomorrow," he said. "In Boston." And then, from the heart, "I don't want to go there. I don't want to play this game in Boston. If we lose tomorrow, the season's over."

There had been three seasons that year. The first was typified when the Yankees came into Boston in June with five pitchers on the injured list and the entire middle defense wiped out. Willie Randolph's leg was in a splint, Rivers's hand was broken. Dent had a pulled hamstring, and Munson's leg was so bad he couldn't run.

The second season began on the last scheduled game before the All-Star break, when Rick Burleson, Boston's indispensable shortstop, sprained his ankle sliding into second. No sooner had Burleson come back than Jerry Remy, his second baseman, broke his wrist. Carlton Fisk cracked a rib diving for a foul ball, altered his throwing so that he could stay in the line-up, and ended up with bone chips in his throwing elbow. That made two of them. Butch Hobson, the third baseman, had so many floating bone chips in his elbow that you could hear them rattle when he threw. Dwight Evans got beaned in Seattle, tried to come back too early, and was helpless both at bat and in the field. Carl Yastrzemski, the 39-year-old wonder, was being bandaged from head to foot before every game. Freddie Lynn was playing on two bad ankles. And, oh yeah, the starting pitching broke down completely.

The second season achieved a crashing climax when the Yankees not only caught the Sox by sweeping a four-game series in Fenway Park but humiliated them so thoroughly — when the Red Sox weren't humiliating themselves — as to be identified, immediately and forevermore, as the Boston Massacre.

The combined line score, as entered into the Red Sox Book of Horrors, tells it all:

Yankees 42–49–4
Red Sox 9–16–11

That's right, the Red Sox had more errors than runs.

The third season took place over the final two weeks when both teams were healthy and doing nothing but winning.

Except for Evans, who had been beaned so badly that he was still suffering from dizzy spells, all the Red Sox players were back in time for the play-off game. As if to keep things even, Willie Randolph was out of action too, having gone down with another leg injury two days before the end of the season.

Dent: "Once it set in and you knew you had to go up there, everything else just kind of goes out of your mind. You just said, 'Here we're playing the Red Sox, we got one game and it's for all the marbles. We got Guidry pitching. To heck with them. If they beat us, they beat our best.' "

Rick Burleson, his opposite number on the Red Sox, basically agreed with him. "We've got the home park," he said. "And we've got the momentum and we've got Jim Rice. But they've got Guidry."

Ron Guidry had just completed the greatest season in modern baseball history, 24–3, running his streak since the second half of the previous season to 34–5. Guidry was going with three days' rest. After the loss to Cleveland he had walked into manager Bob Lemon's office and told him, "I'm pitching tomorrow." Not very often did anybody start a left-handed pitcher in Fenway Park on purpose. Guidry had pitched there only once. The last time the Yankees had been in, he had been touched for two singles in the first inning and pitched hitless ball the rest of the way. Although he liked to have at least four days off between starts, it wasn't so much a question of what he liked at this stage of the season as what was needed.

The Yankees were not that confident a team. Piniella, seeking to keep things as normal as possible, had decided to do what he usually did in Boston. He took himself to Daisy Buchanan's, a popular watering hole on Newbury Street, a block from the hotel, to relax over a couple of drinks. Before the night was over, he found himself joined by half a dozen teammates.

Bucky Dent was not among them: "I usually drop in at Daisy's when we're in Boston. But I had my wife with me, so we just spent the night in the hotel and relaxed." A little irony music in the background, Professor. A new and wholly reconstituted Bucky Dent would be coming back to the hotel the next night. One swing of the bat would change his life, and that change was going to wreck his marriage.

Ray Negron, the Yankee clubhouse man, had been with the organization for six years. "It was the only time I ever saw the Yankees where they didn't expect to win," he says flatly. One of the reasons — the principal reason, really — was Mickey Rivers. "Mickey Rivers was the soul and spirit of that club," Negron explains. "Any of the players on those three pennant-winning teams will tell you that."

Mickey was the guy who loosened everybody up with his antics. "Even the pitchers, they'd go to Mickey, they'd rub him, whatever they felt they had to do. Everything about Mickey tickled them. During a game, Mickey would strike out and come back and ask, 'Did my horse come in in the third? You hear anything about that?' and then go back and make a phone call to find out.

"I never saw a player so well liked. The guys didn't even understand what he's saying half the time, he had that mush-mouth way of talking, and everybody would break into a laugh regardless, because they know it's supposed to be a funny line. That's the way he was. They thought he was crazy, but they loved him." And even Mickey, crazy as he was, knew how important this game was. "That morning in the clubhouse, those guys turned to Mickey, and Mickey had nothing to say. And that's when you knew that with all the big, big games these guys had played, and as tough as these guys were, this was going to be a game unlike any other game. Because Mickey was the key. Mickey was the guy. Not Reggie. Not

Thurman. Mickey. And because Mickey was tight, the whole team was tight."

Don Fitzpatrick, the clubhouse man for the visiting team at Fenway Park, saw it, too, and was perhaps even more surprised. For Fitzie, it was his thirty-third year on the job; he had been there when the Red Sox lost the only other play-off game in American League history. He had seen so many Yankee teams come swaggering in that he had developed the typical Boston attitude about them, an attitude consisting in equal parts of weariness, resignation, and admiration. "Even Yogi," Fitzie recalls. "I had never seen Yogi looking tense before. Not even when he was the manager." And Yogi was now only a coach.

They remained tight and tense through the first six innings of the game. "Until they went ahead, they were very quiet. Even humble. Then they got ahead and WOW, it was, 'Hold 'em! Hold 'em!' On every pitch." Some of the players were so nervous they couldn't sit still. They'd come running into the clubhouse to watch a batter or two on TV, and then go dashing back out to the dugout.

The Red Sox, finding themselves in the play-off after everybody had written them off, seemed to be remarkably loose. That is how, at any rate, they impressed Lou Piniella. After jawing with some of them around the batting cage before the game, Piniella came back to tell his teammates that this was not the same team they had massacred three weeks earlier. "This is a different bunch of guys now," he told them. "This is going to be a tough one."

Their main hope, they kept telling one another before the game, was Mike Torrez. Mike Torrez had played for the Yankees in 1977. They had faced him four times during the current season and had beaten him three times.

Mike Torrez, they kept saying, was not the kind of pitcher who was going to beat them in this kind of a game.

Why they should have held their former teammate in such low esteem remains a mystery. In that first year of free agency, with the Yankee pitching staff decimated, it had been Mike Torrez who had kept the Yankees within striking distance of the Red Sox by pitching seven straight complete-game victories. *Complete games!* Do you know what that means to an overworked bullpen? Go ask Sparky Lyle. Sparky had come over to Mike's locker after every one of those games to thank him personally.

In the final game of the championship series against Kansas City it had been Mike Torrez who had come out of the bullpen to shut the Royals down, and, having pitched the Yankees into the World Series, went on to beat Los Angeles twice. A pitcher who wins two games in the World Series would usually be MVP, but that second win had come in the game where Reggie Jackson hit his three home runs.

And yet, there had been a game toward the end of the season that nobody on the Yankees had ever been able to forget — the last game, as it happened, between the Yankees and the Red Sox that year, too. Pleading an inability to get his shoulder loose, Mike had asked out of the game in the fourth inning with the score tied, 1–1. "Did you ever see such a choke-up?" one player had growled to a reporter. "Here we had a chance to finish them off, and that sonofabitch gave them a life."

Even after Mike had put the Yanks into the World Series, George Steinbrenner was asking sports writers whether they thought this guy Torrez had any guts. But Torrez had a reason. He had been traded to the Yankees during the season because he was playing out his option in Oakland, and, with the season almost over, his agent — who was also Reggie's agent — had not been able to get Steinbrenner to discuss terms for the next year's contract. Given those conditions, Mike had already made the decision to find out what he was worth on the free agent market. *What was he supposed to do?* Torrez was asking himself. *Risk an injury that might prevent him from making the first real money of his life?*

Whatever the Yankees might have felt, Torrez had always seen himself as a big-game pitcher. "From the time I knew I'd be pitching against my former teammates for all the marbles, I had the same feeling I had before those two World Series wins. I don't know what some of the others might say, but for myself, that was a quiet but confident bunch of guys we had in the clubhouse that day."

But if the Red Sox weren't visibly tense, the Boston crowd was. The game was played in a strange and almost disorienting silence until Carl Yastrzemski, the money player, did what Yaz always seemed to do when everything was on the line: led off the bottom of the second by hammering a Guidry fast ball into the right-field stands to give the home team a 1–0 lead.

The third inning was noteworthy not so much for what happened as for what didn't happen. What didn't happen was that Mickey Rivers did not put on his sunglasses, and the Red Sox did not score.

George Scott (a .233 hitter on the year) led off with a double to the bottom of the center-field fence, a ball that Rivers quite probably would have caught if he had been wearing his sunglasses. The reason he wasn't wearing his sunglasses was that the sun hadn't come out until shortly before the ball was hit. Very significant. As we shall see, the sun was going to play a crucial role in this game.

For the moment, Scott was bunted over to third by Jack Brohamer. With the chance to bring in a second run, Rick Burleson tapped weakly to third base. Those are the lost runs, as all baseball people know, that are going to come back to haunt you.

In the sixth inning Burleson atoned by pulling a double past third and scored on Jim Rice's line single to left to make it 2–0. Rice went to second on Yaz's ground ball to first, and with first base open and two men out, Carlton Fisk was given an intentional base on balls.

And that was how Fred Lynn came to the plate with two on and two out.

After Yaz had pulled Guidry's fast ball into the stands, Piniella had talked things over with Munson on the bench. It was clear to both of them that Guidry, going on three days' rest, did not have his overpowering fast ball, and without a really good fast ball, his slider, which was his strikeout pitch, did not have its accustomed bite. They had therefore agreed that the fast ball was going to have to be used sparingly against the right-handed hitters. And they had also decided that Fred Lynn, who would normally have been looking to slap Guidry's slider to left field at Fenway Park, would be able to pull the kind of breaking pitch that Guidry was throwing that day. And so when the sign was flashed to Piniella that a slider was coming up, Piniella moved toward the foul line and signaled Rivers in center to move with him.

Fred Lynn: "I figured it was either a three-run homer or a two-run double. I couldn't believe it when I saw him make the catch. Piniella was 20 yards out of position. I don't hit five balls into that corner a year. The man's just a gambler."

Gambler or not, the catch was even better than it appeared to be. As Don Zimmer was racing up the dugout steps to see whether Lynn had hit a homer or only a double, Piniella was taking the ball over his shoulder while shielding his eyes from the midafternoon sun. Dwight Evans, master of those right-field gardens, had come up the dugout steps alongside Zimmer. As they looked at each other in disbelief,

Evans told him that Lou had made the catch in the toughest part of the field at the brightest time of the day.

As it happened, Evans's pronouncement came an inning too soon. When Piniella got back to the bench after the seventh inning, he told Bob Lemon that he hoped the Sox wouldn't hit any more balls out to him. "The sun's got so bad that I can't see." He was not going to get his wish. A ball was going to be hit to him, and that ball and that sun were going to combine to create one of the most memorable moments in the Great Rivalry. But that wasn't going to happen for a couple of more innings. And by then, the home run that would turn the game around had already been hit.

How often does it happen that a team that has just escaped from a dangerous situation comes back immediately to score?

Mike Torrez was taking a two-hitter into the top of the seventh. He was not only outpitching Guidry, he was pitching the game of his life. On Mike's best days his fast ball had been clocked as high as 97 or 98 miles per hour. On a good day he'd be consistently in the low nineties.

"I had great stuff that day. Nasty sinker, good slider. Fast ball consistently 93–94. And I never gave in to anybody."

It was the supporting cast, the guys at the bottom of the line-up, who did him in. It began with the two quiet men, Chris Chambliss and Roy White. Chris Chambliss, the unobtrusive, noncharismatic first baseman, and Roy White, the oldest living Yankee, the little guy who always seemed to be in the middle of any important rally. They both singled.

Two men on, one out, and now Bucky Dent steps over to the bat rack to keep his appointment with destiny. Bucky Dent, hitless in his last 13 times at bat. Bucky Dent, .243 hitter on the year, with four home runs and 37 RBIs.

Why, then, is Bucky batting in this situation? Because with Willie Randolph injured, Brian Doyle, who had been brought up from the minors to replace him, was taken out for a pinch-hitter just before Bucky came to bat. Fred Stanley is the only remaining infielder, and Stanley is going to be replacing Doyle at second base. Bucky Dent is being allowed to bat only because there is nobody left to play shortstop. He takes a strike, then fouls the next pitch off his foot and goes hopping up and down in pain. Out comes the trainer, Gene Monahan, to spray a freezing compound on his leg. And now comes a scene we will be returning to a little later. Mickey Rivers, who has been waiting in the batter's circle, comes over to tell Bucky that he is hitting with a cracked bat. Without giving it any particular thought, Bucky takes the new bat that is being pressed on him by the batboy.

Through it all, Carlton Fisk, who clearly hadn't expected such a long delay, was peering at the Yankee bench, apparently looking to see whether Lemon was going to send up a pinch-hitter. And that was out of character, too. Fisk is usually all over his pitchers, bawling them out, keeping after them. Especially in such a crucial situation.

Torrez: "I wish I had thrown some more off the mound. I wish I had called out to Carlton. I threw a couple to the infielders while all this was going on. But I wish I would have thrown a couple of warm-up pitches to get a little rhythm. I felt my timing, my concentration on that one pitch, the very next pitch, may have been different."

But if Torrez had lost his concentration, Bucky Dent hadn't. "I was so involved in what I was trying to do. I was crouching in the on-deck circle when [Jim] Spencer was hitting for Doyle, and I knew that if Willie Randolph was playing, Spencer would have been hitting for me. I went up to the plate thinking, 'I've been given another chance. Here's my chance to show them.' " Probably his last chance of the year.

"I really was more into getting a ball I could drive. Torrez had good stuff, but I knew I'd had a couple of good swings earlier. First time up he threw me a high fast ball and I flied out. I felt like I had a pretty good swing at it, just missed it. The second time he did the same thing, and I had another good swing. Just got under it and popped it up. That time I was just looking pretty much in the same area for him to go after me with another fast ball, up and in. But he just made a mistake and didn't get it in enough."

The delay — the fortuitous, as it turns out, injury to his foot — had broken Torrez's rhythm.

Torrez: "It wasn't a hanging slider, as some writers say. It was a fast ball. It wasn't a bad pitch. I got it in, not as far in as I thought or as I wanted. It was the way he swung. He jerked back and gave the ball a kind of uppercut. I thought it was an out."

Off the bat it looked like a routine fly ball. And when the ball dropped into the net a few feet inside the foul line, the park went absolutely silent in what seemed to be utter disbelief.

Dent: "When I hit the ball I hit it pretty good. I didn't know how high it was. I knew it took off, and I didn't know if it was high enough to get out."

The tombstone quiet in the park didn't hit him right away. "I was around first base when I saw the umpire giving the home run sign, and it wasn't until I was rounding second base that I realized there wasn't a sound anywhere. Not a sound."

Zimmer: "You have to remember it had turned into a beautiful day. Usually it would be cold that time of year, and when it's cold in Fenway the wind blows in. When it's warm the wind blows out. It was a beautiful fall day where it had got warm enough so that the wind was blowing out. "When he hit the ball, I said, *That's an out.* Usually I can tell in Fenway when a ball's a home run, whether the wind is blowing in or out. You have a knack from being in a ball park enough times to know. And to see Yaz backing up, backing up, backing up, and all of a sudden I see him looking up and I said, *That ain't the worst thing, it's off the wall,* and as he looks up, it went into the net."

Torrez: "When Dent hit it, I thought it was just a fly ball. To myself I said, *I'm out of the inning.* I was already walking off the mound and Yaz is popping his glove, right there, and backpedaling and backpedaling as the ball is coming down, and all of a sudden he's almost against the wall. I was going toward the dugout, looking over my shoulder and saying: *Goddam, come on down, ball, willya! Catch it, Yaz, catch it!* And all of a sudden the ball is hanging right there. The ball just kept kind of carrying and carrying and went out, and I went: *Oh-oh, I can't believe that.* And that's when everybody and everything went quiet."

Carlton Fisk didn't think it was a good pitch, or even an approximation. Fisk let out a sigh of relief. "We got away with a mistake pitch, I thought. I almost screamed at Mike. I didn't think it was hit good enough. Then I saw Yaz looking up."

Yaz never dreamed that it was going out either: "I kept going back and back, and then I made a decision it was going to hit the wall. I turned around to play it for a single." When he saw the ball disappear, his knees grew so weak that he thought his legs were going to give way under him.

Torrez would pitch to one more batter. "I walked Mickey Rivers after he fouled off five or six pitches on the 3–2 count. I ended up walking him on a borderline pitch on which I really felt the umpire could have gone either way. So the next hitter is Thurman. I said, *O.K., it's 3–2, man on first. All right, I've got to tighten my belt.* I had Thurman's number this day. I had struck him out three straight times. I had him all confused. I had some great sliders and sinkers. Up and in on the fast ball, slider down and away. He didn't know which pattern I was going to use.

"And I see here comes Zimmer, and I see him bring his arm down toward the bullpen. He's already called for [Bob] Stanley. And I was kind of pissed off. I was wondering what his thinking could be because Thurman hadn't fouled off a ball the whole game. I was going to ask him, 'Zim, why aren't you going with the guy on the mound? Let me at least have one more hitter to finish him off, then bring in somebody to start the eighth.'

"He'd already called for Stanley, so I just thought, *Hell, I pitched a great game. Hopefully Bob can hold them.*"

For Bob Stanley, in his second year in the majors, the season had been pure joy. His record was 15–2. The first time Zimmer had heard his name was when the Red Sox farm people had insisted on protecting this kid from Class AA in the expansion draft. In the spring Zimmer had pitched him in the first intersquad game and had seen a big right-hander, built like a buffalo, who threw a heavy ball that both sank and moved away from a right-handed hitter. That early in the spring the hitters couldn't touch him. "If he can pitch like that," said Zimmer after the game, "I've got to keep him. He's got relief pitcher written all over him."

They had used him as a starter, they had used him in relief, used him in middle relief and used him to close. How valuable is a pitcher who can be used like that? Well, he was freeing up at least one other place on the roster, and all he seemed to do was win, win, win.

During the final game of the season Stanley had led the cheering against the Yankees from the bullpen, relaying the score to the bleacher fans inning by inning. He had come to the game with high expectations, but it was not going to be his day. Stanley pitched to three hitters and got only one of them out.

On the first pitch he threw, Mickey Rivers stole second. Easily. The second pitch was a strike, which Munson lined to the fence in left-center to score the speedy Rivers.

To Dick Bresciani, the Red Sox publicity director, that stolen base is one of the overlooked keys to the game. "Because," he says, "it allowed Rivers to score with two out, and gave the Yankees a two-run cushion."

In the eighth Stanley threw only one pitch, a fast ball that Reggie

Jackson deposited into the center-field bleachers, three rows up. The score was 5–2.

But, you know, the ball didn't look that good coming off Reggie's bat. Like Bucky Dent's drive, it just seemed to be carried along on Yankee wings. In the configuration of Fenway Park, the baseball always did seem to carry very well to straightaway center field.

Bob Stanley: "Truthfully, I didn't think it was hit that good. Nobody was more surprised than I was when it carried into the center-field bleachers. In fact, it just did get in."

Reggie was in the second year of that psychodrama that was being played out between him and Billy Martin and George Steinbrenner. In the course of the season he had been benched, he had been relegated to the role of designated hitter against right-handed pitching only, and he had been suspended for bunting against his manager's orders.

Leave it to Reggie. "It didn't mean anything at the time," he said of the homer with uncharacteristic modesty. Don't kid yourself. Reggie had a one-liner coming up: "We needed an insurance run, so I hit it to the Prudential building." The Prudential building is a skyscraper that dominates the Boston skyline beyond the ball park. You didn't have to be an insurance salesman to know by then that the insurance run had paid off by becoming the winning run.

Because the Red Sox came back.

Guidry had come out for the seventh with mixed feelings. He was grateful for the 4–2 lead. But if the long inning had given him a chance to rest his tiring arm, it had also given the arm a chance to tighten up on him.

One hit was all that was needed. And not much of a hit at that. George Scott snuck a ground ball through the infield, Zimmer sent in a right-handed pinch-hitter, Bob Bailey, and that brought Goose Gossage into the game. Why not? Guidry had done what only the great ones do. He was winning a huge ball game without his good stuff. In Gossage the Yankees had the best relief pitcher in baseball. He was in a little early, sure, but this was no ordinary game.

Once the Yankees had the two-run lead, Lemon was determined not to give Guidry a chance to become the losing pitcher. As soon as a man got on base, he had told his coaches, Guidry was coming out. In one way it was a decision from the heart. As an old pitcher himself, he did not want to put Guidry in a position where he could possibly tarnish his incredible season and his even more incredible record. To get right down to it, though, that's what Gossage was there for. He was the clutch guy. He was the guy they wanted in there to close it down. And he'd been doing just that for them all year. To see him come stalking in, wild-eyed and menacing, was to fill his teammates with confidence.

Bob Bailey was simply overpowered. Three fast balls and he never took his bat off his shoulder.

The booing that ensued was directed not so much at Bob Bailey as at Don Zimmer, whose faith in Bailey surpassed all understanding as far as the Red Sox fans were concerned. It went even beyond that, though. It went to Zimmer's relationship with Bernie Carbo and Bill Lee. It went to the psychedelic drama that had been boiling in the Boston clubhouse for two years over the old values versus the counterculture. Bernie Carbo (what Red Sox fan can ever forget?) had pinch-hit the three-run homer that had tied the sixth game of the 1975 World Series and set the stage for Carlton Fisk's winning blast off the foul pole. Bernie Carbo's record as a pinch-hitter had, in fact, been superseded only by his record of total irresponsibility. The Red Sox had sent him on his way at the June 15 trading deadline — if giving him away could be called a trade — and Bill Lee, his buddy and mentor, had expressed his displeasure by throwing a temper tantrum all over Haywood Sullivan's carpet and quitting the club for about 15 minutes.

The luck of the Red Sox. No sooner had Carbo been shipped away than the Red Sox outfielders began to go down, and the pinch-hitters, as exemplified by Bob Bailey, had ranged from pitiful to helpless.

Even more than that, Bill Lee, the long-time darling of Boston fandom, had either been removed from the pitching rotation as a form of punishment — that was his version — or been pulled because he couldn't get anybody out. That was Zimmer's version. The record would seem to bear Zimmer out. Bill Lee had started 10 games since June 15. By the time he was taken out of the starting rotation he had lost seven straight.

Of course, pitchers, like hitters, have their cycles. Bill Lee was a great competitor. He owned the third-best record against the Yankees of any left-hander in history, behind only Babe Ruth and Dickie Kerr. Before the last game of the Boston Massacre, with the Red

Sox totally bereft of pitchers, Lee had gone to Zimmer and begged to be allowed to pitch. Every player on the ball club wanted him in there. So, in fact, did most of the Red Sox officials. No dice.

Bill Lee: "When Bob Bailey struck out on three pitches, that was God's revenge on Sullivan and Zimmer for giving Carbo away. That was a spot that was made in heaven for Bernie. Bernie Carbo was the best fast-ball hitter in baseball, and Gossage was a dead fast-ball pitcher."

At his best Gossage had no idea where the ball was going. He just threw every pitch as hard as he could and tried to keep the ball somewhere around the plate. What difference did it make? Gossage's fast ball was so explosive that he didn't know how it was going to break anyway.

But not today.

Although Gossage had been able to overpower Bailey, this was not the same wild-eyed, ferocious figure whose very presence on the mound had always filled his teammates with optimism. On the contrary. His face was red and he was breathing so heavily that he seemed to be laboring. "After 162 games it was all coming down to this," says Gossage, the most honest of men. "I had never faced that kind of pressure. I didn't know how to react. I was overthrowing the ball, trying to throw too hard." One of the things that happens when you overthrow is that you lose the action on your fast ball. "It's like facing any kind of crucial situation. If you panic when you're driving a car, you end up in a wreck. I was saying to myself, *Just stay within yourself, be yourself. Don't let the pressure bother you.* It's easier said than done."

He had got out of the seventh all right, but in the eighth and ninth innings Gossage was fighting to stay out of a car wreck.

Jerry Remy, who was about to take center stage, opened the eighth by doubling over first base and scored on Yaz's line single to center. Two hits for Yaz, two runs batted in. It was Carlton Fisk, however, who alerted the Boston writers that Gossage wasn't Gossage by fouling off a succession of 3–2 pitches and then rocketing an inside fast ball into left.

When Fisk was healthy, he was as dangerous on an inside fast ball as any hitter alive. With that damaged elbow of his, though, he hadn't pulled a fast ball in weeks. Nor, for that matter, had he been able to do much of anything in these clutch situations.

Fred Lynn slapped a single to left, a typical Freddie Lynn hit. The score was 5–4, two men on, and the batters were Hobson and Scott. The recapitulation of the season again. There were writers in the press box who had been keeping a balance sheet on Hobson's RBIs versus his errors. A complete wash, they were saying: 100 runs batted in and 100 runs let in. He had made 44 errors when he came to Zimmer with two weeks remaining in the season and asked to be taken out of the line-up before he destroyed the ball club completely. As for George Scott, he had been the best-fielding first baseman in baseball. Once upon a time. Maybe the best first baseman ever. But not in 1978. With the Red Sox defenses crumbling, Scott had made errors on balls he would normally have gobbled up. As a hitter he had become a certified rally killer, the great disaster in the Red Sox line-up.

With the tying and winning runs on base, Hobson popped up and Scott did what he had been doing in that spot all year. He struck out. End of rally. The score was still 5–4.

One inning remained. It would go down as one of the great innings in the rich and star-studded history of the rivalry. The magic names are Piniella, Remy, Gossage, Burleson. And Carl Yastrzemski.

Dwight Evans opened the bottom of the ninth by hitting for Frank Duffy, who had replaced Brohamer at third. Boston had played the 1975 World Series without Rice, and they were playing the deciding game of 1978 without Evans. Dewey Evans, one of the great out-fielders of his time, could not go after a fly ball without becoming woozy. He sent an easy fly to center field.

But then Gossage walked Burleson. He still hadn't got his act to-gether. In giving up the walk he had put the tying run on base, turned each subsequent batter into the potential winning run, and all but guaranteed that Jim Rice, the major-league leader in home runs, would be coming to bat.

Jerry Remy, Jim Rice, and, before we are done, Carl Yastrzemski. No, this ball game is not over.

Remy: "My only thought was that I didn't want to hit into a double play. Because if I hit into a double play, I'd be the guy who ended the ball game and the season." And deprived Jim Rice of the opportunity to end his glorious season gloriously.

And Jerry Remy came damn near to ending the ball game in a way that would have brought fame, glory, and immortality to the name of Jerry Remy. Not with a long drive into the distant stands. No. Jerry

Remy was not that kind of hitter. Jerry's game was speed. Jerry Remy hit a line drive into right field — hit well enough, but an out off the bat. Let's be clear about that. A routine out.

But then, all of a sudden you could see — and when *could* you see it, that was the thing — that Piniella didn't know where the ball was. Either he had been unable to pick it up coming off the bat or he had lost it in the sun. You could see it as he began to retreat backwards to buy himself a little time and give himself the widest possible angle within which to react. There is no panic in this guy, that is the amazing thing. If the ball gets by him and rolls to the fence, then Jerry Remy, who can fly, is going to be around the bases with the winning run. At the very least he will be on third with one out and the Boston power coming to bat.

Just before the ball hits the ground, or so it seems, Piniella stretches his arms wide to alert Mickey Rivers that he is in trouble and — let's not kid ourselves — to let everybody know that if the ball gets by him, it isn't his fault.

The ball hits the grass about eight feet in front of him. It hits the ground, and takes a big hop, and Piniella throws his glove out in the general direction . . . and the ball is there.

It was luck and it wasn't luck. How do you define luck, anyway? Where does the luck begin?

If Piniella hadn't spread his arms out, he wouldn't have had a chance to make the play. The ball was on his left, the glove was on his left hand, the bounce was shoulder high. He saw it at the last split second, made his lunge, "and the good Lord put it there."

One other thing: Piniella had sat out the last couple of games of the season with a slightly wrenched foot. If Reggie Jackson — who was DH-ing — had been in right field, his glove would have been on the wrong hand.

But look at it this way. The Red Sox were lucky that the ball was hit into the sun. Otherwise it would have been a routine out. Sure, leave it to the Red Sox to get half a break. But, O.K., half a break is better than none.

Rick Cerone was in the ball park. In two more years he would be catching for the Yankees, and in another eight he would be catching for the Red Sox. But Cerone was in the park that day as a spectator, the only time he had ever watched a game as a fan in his life.

"I was with Toronto that year, and when Tiant beat us the last game of the season to force the play-off I decided to stay in Boston because I didn't want to miss that game. It was a great game for a fan. A super game. I really got caught up in it that day. I enjoyed watching it as a ballplayer, but I was a fan.

"I was sitting down the right-field line so I had a very good angle on Yaz's homer and a pretty good angle on Piniella's play. The way I saw it he never saw the ball until it hit the ground and then he just flung out his glove and the ball stuck. Looking at it as a ballplayer, the great thing was the way he immediately whipped the ball to third."

Piniella: "It was the best throw I ever made in my life. If God made the ball stick in my glove, then God was with me on the throw. Because I never had that kind of an arm."

Eddie Yost, the third-base coach, was waving for the runner to come around, but Burleson, who did not have as good an angle as Yost, was playing it safe. His thinking in that first split second was not very different from Remy's: if Piniella did make the catch and doubled him off first, the game and the season would be over.

Now Jim Rice and Carl Yastrzemski are coming to bat, the number-three and -four hitters. The new monster and the old champ.

Roy White: "When they had one out in the ninth with Rice and Yaz coming up, I was just holding my breath. You want to close your eyes and not see them swing. The wind was blowing out, and I could feel that Green Monster creeping in closer."

Bucky Dent: "When those guys came up, Rice and Yaz, I could feel it trickling down my back. Rice has done it all year and Yaz had done it all day. Heck, all his career."

Entering the game, Jim Rice was only four short of Joe DiMaggio's greatest season in total bases. If Guidry had still been in there, this would have been the confrontation of the generation: the top pitcher versus the top hitter. With or without Guidry, there was the sense that this was where the real MVP of the 1978 season was going to be determined.

It had been a career season for Rice. In 1975, his freshman year, he had been overshadowed by Fred Lynn, even though it was Rice who had been the headliner in the minors. To make matters worse, his wrist had been fractured by a pitched ball in the final week of the season, and he had missed the entire World Series.

The single in the fourth inning was his 213th hit of the season, the RBI was number 139. He was the major-league leader in hits, triples, home runs, runs batted in, and total bases, and was second in runs scored.

He was, moreover, the first player to lead the league in both hits and home runs since Yaz had done it in 1967. There were only three other players who had ever accomplished that feat before, and we're talking tall timber here: Napoleon Lajoie, Ty Cobb, and Lou Gehrig. Also, in a kind of freak category, Rice was the first player ever to lead either league in home runs, triples, and runs batted in. The triples are, of course, the odd category here, and they stood as testimony to his power alley in right-center.

Putting statistics aside, 30 of his home runs had either tied the game or put his team ahead. This was Jim Rice's year, and here was his Moment. There is a rule of life that says the wheel comes around to the great ones in these situations. And the great ones seize the moment and make it a part of their legend. The single in the fourth inning had brought his total bases to 406 and his RBIs to 139. A home run here and he could take the season of 1978, stamp his name on it, and set it up in his trophy case for future generations to gaze upon forever.

But maybe you have to be lucky, too. Rice got a pitch and drove it deep, albeit somewhat to the right of his right-center power alley. As it left the bat, Bob Ryan of the *Boston Globe* jumped up in the press box and shouted, "It's out of here!" He was not the only one who thought so. One inning earlier Reggie's drive had kept carrying. From the press box Rice's drive just seemed to die. Or maybe it only looked that way if you were rooting for the Red Sox.

Gossage: "He hit it well, but he didn't crush it. I never thought, *Shit, it's out of here.* My thought was, *It's in the park.*"

After the catch, Burleson went to third base.

Nobody has ever talked about the play-off game of 1978 without saying that if Burleson had gone to third on Remy's hit, he would have scored on Rice's long fly. But if Burleson had gone to third, the entire game would have changed. Every game is in a constant state of flux; every variation changes everything. Never mind. Since we can't make these judgments based on all the things that didn't get a chance to happen, we can only play the game of "would have/should have" with what we've got.

The possibility that Burleson might not have been able to make it to third is never brought into the equation, either. And yet, if all things had remained the same, if Piniella, throwing the ball into an actual base runner had made the same play, there is every possibility that Burleson would have been out.

And now it was all up to Yaz, the man of a hundred moments. The hero of 1967. Put Yaz in a pennant race and he surpasses himself. How could you not be thinking of the final game of 1967, against Minnesota (which amounted to a play-off game), when Yaz had practically picked the Red Sox up by the scruff of the neck and carried them to the pennant?

Gossage and Yaz became the matchup that we remember. It was a matchup with charisma. The electricity was so palpable that you could all but hear the sizzle.

Back in the trainer's room, Ron Guidry was sitting with his arm in an ice bucket and his eyes on the television screen. The trainer's room is the baseball player's sanctuary, and so Don Fitzpatrick was in there with him ready to shoo any intruder away. As Yaz came up to bat they turned to each other. "I know who you're pulling for," said Guidry. "I understand." But, of course, if Guidry was letting Fitzie know that he was free to root for his guy, he was also giving the same permission to himself. "C-o-o-o-o-m-e *on*, Goose!" he shouted. "Yaz . . . you've done enough today!"

After all the games, over the long season, it had come down to this. To the final out in the final inning of a play-off game, with the Red Sox one run behind, the tying run 90 feet away, and the winning run on first. There is a rhythm to a baseball game that communicates itself to the dugout, the playing field, and the stands. The Yankees expected Yaz to hit it out. The momentum of the game was tending that way. The players on the bench looked to the bullpen, where Sparky Lyle, last year's Cy Young winner, was warming up. Lemon was sitting still. He was going to live or die with Gossage.

Gossage, the fast-ball pitcher, and Yaz, the dead fast-ball hitter who had already taken Guidry's fast ball out of the park. And if Guidry's fast ball hadn't been a bolt of Louisiana lightnin' this day, neither, as had become abundantly clear, was Gossage's.

Up till now.

During the most difficult moments of the eighth and ninth innings Gossage had found his mind flashing back to his home in the cool Rocky Mountains of Colorado. No matter what happened, he had been telling himself, he wouldn't end up so bad. "If we won, I'd be going to Kansas City and on to the World Series. If we lost, I'd be going to my beautiful Colorado home. Exactly what you shouldn't be thinking at a time like that."

And so if it was Yaz's moment, it was Goose's moment too. And in that moment the Goose remembered who he was. "Something just came over me. Something inside me finally said, *This is stupid to be thinking like that. Be yourself.* That pitch I threw to Yaz was the only good pitch I threw all day."

With Chambliss holding Remy on at first, there was a big hole at second. Yaz was hoping for a slider. "The way Gossage throws, it's sure tougher to hit a fast ball than a slider. All I was trying to do was get the bat out there and hit a ground ball through the hole and tie the score."

He was hoping for a slider, but he was looking for a fast ball. "When I saw a fast ball coming, I thought, *This is just what I wanted, right where I want it. A fast ball on the inside corner.* As he swung, the ball exploded in on him. When Yaz swings, there is no holding back. He knew he was in trouble before the ball hit the bat.

It was over with a wrenching suddenness, on a high foul pop that left you feeling cheated. You wanted to say, "Hey, something's gone wrong here." You wanted to say, "Now wait a minute, let's rewind the camera, have everybody go back to their marks, and run this over again. And this time let's get it right."

You wanted to say, "How about making it the best two out of three?"

It was, everybody agreed, the season in microcosm. The Red Sox jumping off to an early lead, the Yankees coming back in the middle innings to pass them, only to have the Red Sox come fighting back as time was running out. Except that this time they fell, just barely, short.

The count should have gone down to 3–2. Or at the very least there should have been a split second as the ball went rocketing off the bat when your heart leaped in momentary hope. Better if Yaz had taken one of his nothing-held-back swings and missed.

Instead, the ball went squirting off high above third base. Yaz threw his bat to the ground and took a couple of automatic steps toward first base, mumbling to himself.

Nettles: "I was thinking, *Hit another fly ball,* and then I thought,

Jeez, not to me." Don't believe it. Nettles was the team wit, and that was a characteristic Nettles line.

As Nettles camped under the little fly ball, Bucky Dent began to leap in the air, and as he did, he felt something crawling under his arm. Instinctively his hand shot inside his shirt to squash the bug he thought was there. Instead, he discovered that the gold chain he wore around his neck had broken and crumbled under his armpit. "That's why you don't see me in any of the pictures of the guys jumping on Gossage. I should have been there at the same time as Munson. But I never actually did see the final out."

The Boston fans were in shock. Eddie Yost, crossing the diamond toward the Red Sox dugout, had the impression of looking at a painted canvas. "Nobody had moved. They all seemed to be sitting there with their mouths frozen open."

The Red Sox players felt that way too. Jerry Remy, standing on first base, could not believe that it was over. Some of the other players wandered back to the bench and sat there awhile, as if they were waiting to be called back onto the field to finish the game.

As for the Yankees, it seemed no more than a matter of seconds after the ball had been caught before the players came charging into the locker room like a herd of buffalo, trampling everything in sight. Munson came roaring into the trainer's room to grab Guidry and pull him out into the clubhouse. The veterans had ordered that the door be locked against everybody, including the club officials. Including George Steinbrenner. The veteran players wanted 20 minutes for themselves, just to savor their victory before celebrating it. To Don Fitzpatrick — who was, in a way, the lone outsider there — it seemed as if they needed a minute or two to affirm to each other that they had won. To believe it. And when they did, the call went up for beer. And then they went wild.

Mickey Rivers, who was at the center of the celebration, as always, was trying to give everybody credit for the Bucky Dent home run. "Yeah," he said, pointing to the trainer, Gene Monahan. "He gave me the idea of giving him the bat." And then giggling and pointing to various players in turn, "He told me . . . He told me . . . No, it was him. He told me."

Even Yogi Berra, who held all the records for World Series appearances and World Series victories, was acting as if there had never been a win as sweet as this one.

For the Red Sox there had never been so bitter a defeat. There was one row of lockers where Yaz, Remy, Burleson, and Hobson dressed, and they sat there with eyes downcast, not wanting to look at each other. "It ended so fast," Remy says. "It wasn't until the press came in and they began to talk to us about it that we absorbed the significance of defeat."

Yaz sat there and took all the questions, repeating his description of what had happened over and over again. And when the last reporter had left, he went into the trainer's room and cried. He was, after all, 39 years old, and he seemed to know that he would never play in a World Series again, would never know what it was to wear a world championship ring.

Jerry Remy had taken all the questions too, but the questions were mostly directed at whether he felt Burleson should have gone to third. Remy had had a magnificent game: two hits, a perfect bunt, and a diving catch in the field. With a little luck from the Big Guy in the sky, Dent's day could have been Remy's day, and Yankee fans could have been cursing his name.

"The hardest part was leaving the clubhouse, once you got over the way you felt. Now you got to go over and pick your bags back up and drive home with the luggage you brought in that morning expecting to go to Kansas City. You drive home and the bags are sitting there, taking up more and more space.

"The next day you put the TV on, and there's New York playing in Kansas City. You feel like shit because you're supposed to be there. Then to watch them go through the rest of the play-offs and World Series. We felt we were just as good as they were and it should have been us. That's how I felt. Never knowing if that opportunity would come up again. And it never did for me. But at the time when you're still playing you don't realize. . . . There's always next year, and those years run out, and you look back and you say, "God, that was the year it should have been."

On his way back to Tampa, Don Zimmer suddenly stopped his car in the middle of nowhere, got out by the side of the road, and screamed into the empty air, "Bucky . . . Fucking . . . Dent!"

Now that the game has entered the mythology, you will hear people say, "Everybody forgets that it was Jackson's home run . . ." or "The thing that nobody remembers is that if Burleson had gone to third . . ." Pay no attention to the "Everybody forgets" and "Nobody remembers." Bucky Dent has been given credit for hitting the home run that won the game because it was Bucky Dent's home run that won it. First, because it was the turning point, and second, because it was Bucky Dent who hit it.

Up until then, the Yankees were a dead and listless ball club. Nobody on the Yankee bench was thinking home run with Dent at bat. They were hoping for a base hit. When they got a three-run homer, it was — as Don Fitzpatrick says — Christmas and New Year's Eve all at once. Both on the bench and in the clubhouse.

If the Yankees had lost that game, says Haywood Sullivan, George Steinbrenner was going to break up that team. "I was convinced of that from the talks I'd had with him. And we've talked about it often since."

In a way, it happened anyhow. The following spring Gossage was injured in a wrestling match with Cliff Johnson, and Ron Guidry, in one of the most selfless acts imaginable, volunteered to go back to the bullpen, where he had started.

Later in the season Thurman Munson was killed in a plane crash. Mickey Rivers was traded after a noisy argument with a Yankee official.

Roy White came back to the locker room at the end of the season and found his pink slip sitting in his locker.

Billy Martin returned to manage and was soon gone again. Lemon replaced him and was soon gone too.

The Red Sox got rid of Bill Lee at the end of the season, and for reasons that are inexplicable they did not re-sign Luis Tiant, who was as much the soul of the Red Sox as Rivers was of the Yanks.

Munson and Martin and Fisk and Lee had been at the center of the storm. Munson hated Fisk with the fierce hatred that only jealousy can ignite, and Fisk was perfectly willing to hate him right back. Billy Martin loathed and despised Bill Lee, and because he hated him so loudly and so visibly, the inner core of Yankee players hated Lee too. Bill Lee loathed and despised Billy Martin and Graig Nettles and anybody else who wore a Yankee uniform.

The Yankees won the Series that year and went on to win a division championship in 1980 and a league championship in the split season of 1981. Carlton Fisk, Fred Lynn, and Rick Burleson were lost to the Red Sox in a contract fiasco in 1981. When Reggie Jackson was handed his release at the end of that same season, the last vestiges of the great years that had followed immediately upon the free-agency revolution were gone.

There is this about a classic baseball game: it takes on its own portraiture with the passage of time. The Dent home run is always painted as a windblown fly ball that wouldn't have been a home run in any other ball park.

How true is that, though? There is one Boston writer who enters a stiff demurrer — Will McDonough of the *Globe,* the same Will McDonough you see on the pregame panel of the NFL football telecasts.

"Torrez pitched a sensational game," McDonough says. "But what bothers me is that everyone says it was just a fly ball. In almost any other ball park in the American League, that's a home run. Look it up and see in how many parks the left-field foul pole is only 300–310 feet. You'll be surprised."

And if the wind was blowing out, so what? That's part of playing at Fenway Park, too.

Bucky's time had come. Under the impetus of his fly ball that dropped into the net, Bucky Dent, the nonhitting shortstop, went on to win the MVP in the World Series with a .417 batting average and seven runs batted in. He became an overnight celebrity, and it almost destroyed him.

Bucky's great value as a shortstop was that he was so dependable. Not much range, the book on him said, but will field anything he can get to, and will never make an error that will cost you the game. But Bucky had always been a maze of insecurities. His parents were divorced before he was born, and he was in his teens before he discovered that the woman he thought was his mother was really his aunt. He had searched for years before he found his father.

In Chicago he had been the star on a terrible team. In New York, Billy Martin was pinch-hitting for him whenever the Yankees were behind in the late innings. At times even earlier. And why shouldn't he, with all those good hitters he had sitting on the bench? Bucky took it so personally that he would go around from player to player saying, "I hope Billy likes me . . . I've never done anything that he shouldn't, have I? . . . I'm just trying to play . . . Gee, I hope he does like me and that we can get along."

When Bob Lemon, who likes everybody, came in and did the same thing, Bucky was reduced to asking, "Why does he do that to me when no other shortstop in the league gets it done to them?"

And then all of a sudden he was a celebrity, a merchandisable commodity. Baby-faced and good-looking, he became the darling of the teenagers, and what had seemed to be a perfect marriage to a beautiful wife went *kaput*.

When the next season started, he was still taking his celebrity status so big that his teammates began to call him Little Reggie, and his best friend on the club, the always good-natured Goose Gossage, became just about fed up with him.

By the time he came back to himself and made a desperate attempt to save his marriage, it was too late.

In his final two years with the Yankees, Bucky would go into the Nautilus room at Yankee Stadium with a baseball priest, known as Father Joe, to get himself mentally prepared to play. They'd spend an hour together before every game, and then Bucky would go out and play the steady brand of shortstop for which he was noted.

Mike Torrez played out five more years on his Red Sox contract and was released with a year to go. His experience over those five years was painful. "They chastised me there. If this had happened in New York, no big deal. In Boston they wanted a whipping boy, and I was the whipping boy for losing that game."

The great thing about Mike Torrez is that he never permitted that one pitch to affect his life. Mike Torrez's attitude is that if you can't make it unhappen, you can at least develop a philosophy to deal with it. And Mike Torrez has developed a philosophy that's hard to beat. "You've got to be a man about it," he says. "Anybody who knows baseball knows I pitched a great game." And then he leans in closer and all but laughs. "I'm happy it did happen. If I'll always be remembered as the guy who threw the home run ball to Bucky Dent, then I'll always be remembered, won't I?"

Bucky Dent has a baseball camp in Deland, Florida, and over a period of years he built a replica of the left-field wall. When it came time for the grand opening in the spring of 1989, he invited Torrez and Rivers down to reenact his great day. Torrez accepted without a second's thought.

.   .   .

But what about that cracked bat? Was it really cracked? And if it was, how bad? What happened was this: Toward the end of the season, Bucky Dent had decided to go to a lighter bat, the popular Roy White model. The same bat that Mickey Rivers used. By the time they went into Boston, they were down to just two bats between them, and because the season was coming to an end, they had not placed a new order.

After taking batting practice, Bucky had noticed a little hairline crack that started just above the knob and disappeared under the tape that was wound around the handle — a tiny, almost imperceptible crack no more than an inch long at the very bottom of the bat. (Although most fans don't realize it, the batter is allowed to use a specified amount of tape or pine tar to afford himself a better grip.) Immediately Bucky had shown the bat to Rivers, and they had agreed that for all practical purposes they were down to one bat.

The two bats were side by side in the bat rack, and in going to the plate in the seventh, Bucky had inadvertently grabbed the wrong one.

Rivers was batting right behind Bucky. As Bucky stepped to the plate, Mickey went to the bat rack and realized at once that if the uncracked bat was still there, Bucky must be using the cracked one.

Rivers took the good bat to the batter's circle with him, and while the trainer was spraying the freezing compound on Bucky's leg, he seized the opportunity to effect the change. "Mickey came up to me and said, 'Hey, that bat you're using is the cracked one. You're using the wrong bat.' Actually it wasn't Mickey who gave it to me. Mickey gave the bat to the bat boy and told the bat boy to hand it to me."

A few years ago, during an Old-Timers' game, Dent and Rivers were dressing at adjoining lockers. The accusations of corked bats being much in the news at the time, Bucky said, "Hey, maybe we should say that the bat you gave me was corked."

"Yeah," Mickey said. "Yeah . . . yeah . . . yeah."

They laughed about it, Bucky says now. "But I guess we were laughing so much that the people around us overheard us. But that's all it was, a dumb joke."

And yet, if the Yankees did have a corked bat, what better time to force it upon the batter? Joke or not, conjecture becomes irresistible. Especially when you consider the way that ball kept carrying. And how Rivers had been so anxious to credit almost everyone else with the idea. The bat, after all, wasn't *that* cracked. What difference did it make if there was a little hairline crack down near the handle? The way Bucky choked up on the bat, it didn't matter at all.

The Yankees did use corked bats — Graig Nettles for one. (Nettles was caught red-handed a couple of years later when he hit a ball and the cork came squirting out.)

The only thing wrong with that scenario is that Ray Negron says it couldn't possibly have happened. "We didn't have any corked bats in 1978," Negron says. "I can tell you that for a fact, because when we did start to cork them, I was the guy who did the corking."

O.K., it probably didn't happen. And yet . . .

Chapter Two

Down to the Wire in 1904: Cy Young and Jack Chesbro

When New York met Boston for the last time on Monday then came the tug of war. If New York had won both games, both championships would have come hither. But, alas. . . . The margin was very narrow, not even a percentage, we believe, but only a permillage. But 'tis enough; 'twill serve. Though the metropolitan fan may be temporarily distressed and even impoverished, the metropolitan philosopher will be ashamed to grudge Boston one championship out of two. Her necessity is greater than ours.

— *New York Times* editorial, October 12, 1904

THE first time the rivalry went down to the last day of the season was back in old Hilltop Park in New York, with an overflow crowd spilling onto the field and upwards of a thousand Boston fans — complete with their own band, theme song, and assorted noisemakers — taking over the reserved section behind the Boston bench.

The year was 1904. The game, which marks the final shootout in the first great American League pennant race, was the first one to come down to us with a tag line attached to the score: "The pennant that was lost on Jack Chesbro's wild pitch."

It could just as easily, and perhaps even more aptly, have been "The pennant that was lost through the stupidity of the Yankee front office."

The opposing pitchers on that final day were Happy Jack Chesbro and Big Bill Dinneen, a most fortuitous pairing. Dinneen had defeated the Yankees, 6–2, the first time the two teams met. That was on May 7, 1903, at the Huntington Avenue Grounds in Boston. A day later the Yankees came back behind Chesbro to beat Boston, 6–1.

Three weeks later, in the first game ever played between the Yankees and the Red Sox in New York, it was Dinneen who defeated Chesbro, 2–0, on two home runs by Buck Freeman, the Boston first baseman. Freeman was entitled. In 1899 (hardly a man is now alive) he had hit 25 home runs for the Washington club of the National League, the record that Babe Ruth would eventually break as a member of the Boston Red Sox. (If we want to carry these cross-country linkages further, it was Dinneen, who took to umpiring when he retired, who was behind the plate the day Ruth hit his sixtieth home run.)

There is an even more direct linkage between the starting Yankee pitchers in those historic games in 1904 and in 1978. In 1978 Ron Guidry broke the New York Yankee strikeout record, which had been set by Jack Chesbro 74 years earlier. He did not break Chesbro's record for season victories. Nothing to be ashamed of there. Nobody in baseball ever has. And until they go back to pitching with beanbags, nobody ever will. In the game that cost the Yankees the pennant, Chesbro was going for his forty-second victory. Poor guy. He had to settle for a record of 41–12.

By 1904 Bill Dinneen had already established a record that has been tied but never broken. In 1903, when the Red Sox defeated the Pittsburgh Pirates in the first World Series ever played, Bill Dinneen was the winning pitcher in three of those games. Not that Chesbro was any stranger to these crucial situations. In the two years before joining the Yankees, Happy Jack had been the leading pitcher in the National League for two successive pennant-winning teams.

Neither of them, however, had ever been involved in anything to approach the final week in 1904. After a dogfight of a pennant race, in which the lead changed hands five times in the final month, the Red Sox and Yankees (né Pilgrims and Highlanders) arrived in New York for a five-game series that was going to determine the American League championship. The fact that the Red Sox were half a game ahead meant nothing. Whichever team won three of those five games was going to win the pennant.

And that would seem to suggest that the Yankees, with their home-field advantage, were sitting pretty. Except that they weren't. In order to pick up a few extra bucks, the Yankee ownership had committed an error of such monumental proportions that two of those games — a Saturday double-header right in the middle of the series — had been shifted to Boston.

Let's go back and excavate the relevant history.

It is always written that the American League was "the brainchild of Ban Johnson." And so it was. Ban Johnson's vision was to take four teams from the old Western Association, of which he was president, and graft them onto four new franchises in the more populous eastern cities to create a second major league. In that respect he was the spiritual godfather of both the Yankees and the Red Sox. Ban Johnson founded the league, awarded the franchises, and very carefully stocked the teams in an attempt to build winners. The man was so brilliant that he was his own Rotisserie League a century or so early.

Boston and New York were the two cities where he felt it would be absolutely essential for the American League, if it were to have any credibility, to take on the National League.

They were also the most difficult cities. The problem in New York was that Johnson was stymied at every turn by the New York Giants' big-time connections at Tammany Hall. The problem in Boston was that he was unable to find any local ownership that was willing to buck the very popular Boston club in the National League — the Beaneaters they were called. (It could have been worse. They could have been called the Codpieces.)

With time running out, he turned the franchise over to Charles Somers, a financier and lumber magnate who already had financial interests in three of the other new teams. Somers was the principal owner of the Cleveland franchise, and he had put up the money to back both Connie Mack in Philadelphia and Charles Comiskey in Chicago. Armed with Somers's money, Connie Mack hurried up to Boston and leased the Huntington Avenue Grounds. The stands were constructed in three weeks flat, just in time for the opening of the season.

To stock the teams, Johnson and his owners did what any new league does. They raided the older, established league. In this instance it could not have been easier. The National League had imposed a miserly salary cap of $2,400 that turned their players into sitting ducks. In 1901, the first year of operation for the American League, 111 of the 182 players on its rosters had been spirited away from the National League.

.   .   .

The Pilgrims (and for the sake of ease and clarity we are going to call them the Red Sox from now on) were able to acquire instant local identification by raiding the Beaneaters. Jimmy Collins, the premier third baseman in baseball, was lured away with an offer to become the manager and captain. They also grabbed Buck Freeman, the home run king, and Chick Stahl, a fleet, hard-hitting center fielder.

And then came the greatest coup of all. To that core of local heroes Ban Johnson was able to add the great Cy Young and his catcher, Lou Criger. Cy Young was not exactly coming fresh-faced off the farm. He was 34 years old when he arrived in Boston and he had already won 286 games.

As always seems to happen in these things, old Cy was clobbered in his first two starts and was just about to be written off as a has-been when he turned himself around. He finished the season with a league-leading record of 33–10. The next year the team found a worthy partner for him by stealing away the Beaneaters' star pitcher, Bill Dinneen.

To stop the hemorrhaging, the National League sued for peace. Which is to say they acceded to Ban Johnson's nonnegotiable demand to put a team in New York. To protect himself against Tammany Hall, which was threatening to run a city street right through their ball park, Johnson delivered the franchise to a couple of well-connected pols, Big Bill Devery and Frank Farrell. Farrell was a professional gambler and pool shark who was in the process of building the city's poshest gambling house. Devery was a former police chief, which means that he was corrupt to the core. An ex-Tammany police chief and the city's leading gambling tycoon. In other words, these guys had done business together before.

They established the team in a hastily constructed wooden park, seating 15,000, at Broadway and 168th Street. Because the park was situated at the very top of Washington Heights, it was known as Hilltop Park. The team itself became known as the Highlanders, partly because of the topography but mostly because the name of the club president, Joseph W. Gordon, inspired the more internationally oriented sports writers to make the obvious connection with the Gordon Highlanders, a famous unit of the British army. Which only shows how far Farrell and Devery had strayed from their origins. The biggest support for baseball came from New York's Irish, who were hardly clamoring for an identification with the British military. And so, while the Highlanders remained the team's official name until they moved to the Polo Grounds ten years later, to most of their fans, and indeed most of the writers, they had been either the Hill-toppers or the Yankees from the very beginning. The *New York Times,* great bastion of conservatism that it is, never called them anything except the Greater New Yorkers, which was a contraction of their corporate name.

Just as in Boston, the name of the game was Names. As manager, Ban Johnson was able to install Clark Griffith, who not only had managed the White Sox to the American League's first championship but, at the age of 34, was still a pretty good pitcher. Johnson had prevailed upon his old friend Charles Comiskey to surrender Griffith by telling him, "We need the best that we have in New York."

The major star and gate attraction was Wee Willie Keeler, whom Ban Johnson had plucked from Brooklyn across the river. Wee Willie goes down in history as "Hit 'Em Where They Ain't," which only means that he hit 'em where they weren't better than anybody else. While playing for the old Baltimore Orioles in 1897, Willie had hit safely in 44 straight games, a record that would not be revived — and never mind that artificial respiration would be necessary — until Joe DiMaggio's record-breaking streak in 1941.

Wee Willie stood 5 feet 4 inches and weighed 140 pounds. He choked his bat almost halfway up, pecked, poked, or slapped at the ball, and went flying down to first base. Willie had a mischievous little leprechaun look about him. And a laughing little leprechaun was what he was. There can be no doubt, from the recollections of the players of that era, that he was the most popular player in the game.

The park had been constructed so hastily that there was still a ravine out in deep right field. In the opening game Wee Willie almost went tumbling down into that ravine, never to be seen again, while chasing the first ball that was hit. Not to worry. There was a crew of workmen out there, complete with dirt and shovels, immediately after the game.

Since pitching was what the game was all about in those days when Wee Willie and "inside baseball" reigned supreme, Ban Johnson delivered unto the Highlanders the two pitchers who had taken the Pittsburgh Pirates to the National League pennant in the previous two years — the right-handed Jack Chesbro, and the left-handed Jesse Tannehill. Don't bother to cry for Pittsburgh, though. Why do you think they were called the Pirates?

•   •   •

Changes were taking place in Boston, too. Somers was dispatched to Cleveland to take personal charge of the league's other failing franchise. The new owner was Henry J. Killilea, a Milwaukee attorney who had been another of Johnson's associates in the Western Association. Killilea was around for only one year, but it was some year. It was attorney Killilea who, as Ban Johnson's surrogate, negotiated the fine-tuning of the peace treaty with Barney Dreyfuss, the owner of the Pittsburgh Pirates.

That wasn't all. By the end of 1903 the sports writers and fans were beginning to press for a championship series between the winners of each league. By coincidence, the pennant winners turned out to be Boston and Pittsburgh, and because of the relationship that had been formed during those treaty negotiations, Dreyfuss and Killilea had no difficulty in working out an agreement to play a nine-game World Series.

The Series proved to be Killilea's undoing. There were rumors of ticket scalping out of the Red Sox office, and they were clearly more than rumors. Betting was rampant. The agreement, as worked out by the two club owners, defined the split of the gate receipts. Killilea kept the club's share for himself while Dreyfuss, who was known as a players' owner, threw his share back into the pot. Killilea can be said to be one of the founding fathers of the World Series, and he was also the owner of the first World Series winner. By the time it was over, he was so universally despised and reviled that there was little for him to do except sell the club and return to Milwaukee.

Needless to say, there was no dearth of Boston interests eager to buy into the team now. Leading the list were the two fiercely competing political factions of the Democratic party. Ban Johnson, who was quite an operator, finessed that one very neatly by selling the club to General Charles Henry Taylor, the owner of the *Boston Globe*. In addition to being the publisher of one of the great Boston newspapers, General Taylor was a Civil War hero and a renowned figure in local political and social life. His son, John I. Taylor, a renowned playboy, was the leading sportsman of the city, a polo-playing, tennis-playing, golfing fool. He also drank a little. General Taylor bought the club for his wayward son, as fathers will, in the fond hope that it would keep him out of trouble.

John I. Taylor became an important figure in the history of the Red Sox. Like Killilea, he won a championship first crack out of the barrel.

His first year was so full of drama that it may have been almost as exciting as playing polo in Cohasset.

In their maiden season the Yankees had finished a respectable fourth, which was not exactly what Ban Johnson had in mind. To turn them into contenders he now had to do some shuffling within the American League. So New York added two of the top defensive players at their positions, catcher Red Kleinow and shortstop Kid Elberfeld. To strengthen the pitching he brought in Jack (Red) Powell, a consistent 20-game winner. And when it became clear during the season that the Yankees needed more hitting, he had young Taylor send over Boston's best hitter and most popular player, Patsy Dougherty. In addition to having led the Sox in five different offensive categories during the previous season, Dougherty had won a permanent place in their hearts by belting two home runs in the second game of the World Series.

The uproar out of Boston would have been even greater if Johnson hadn't already arranged a deal, during the course of his preseason shuffling, that brought Jesse Tannehill to Boston in a trade for Long Tom Hughes. As originally formulated, the trade was supposed to turn New York into an instant contender. Long Tom had been the number-three pitcher for the world champions, behind Cy Young and Bill Dinneen, a 20-game winner at the age of 26. Tannehill had been no better than a .500 pitcher for New York, a terrific disappointment. The best-laid plans can not only go awry; they have a way of biting you in the neck. By the time Patsy Dougherty was sent to New York, Tannehill was the leading Red Sox pitcher, and Hughes was about to be shipped to the minors. In Boston, Tannehill would have seasons of 21–11 and 22–9 and pitch a no-hit game.

Jesse Tannehill was the first player ever traded between the two clubs. When you consider the luck the Red Sox were to have in future dealings with the Yankees, he may well have been the best. Until Tannehill injured his arm with 20 games left in the season, he was Boston's winningest pitcher. After that, the 38-year-old Cy Young reestablished himself as the ace of the staff by pitching every second day.

When the Sox boarded the train in Chicago for that final series in New York, Cy had just pitched his second straight shutout while the Yankees were splitting a double-header in St. Louis to give his team that slender half-game lead. Not that Bill Dinneen's contribution can be overlooked, either. From the time of Tannehill's injury, Dinneen went on to win six of his seven starts, bringing his final record up to 23–14 against old Cy's 26–16.

The Yankees were coming back to New York by overnight train from St. Louis. They arrived only three hours before the game and took the field in their blue traveling uniforms to the cheers of 10,000 waiting fans.

There had never been any doubt whatsoever as to who was the ace of the Yankee staff. Without Jack Chesbro and his spitball, the Yankees would not have been within spitting distance of the pennant race. In addition to establishing the won-loss record that has remained unsurpassed in the twentieth century, his 14 consecutive victories remained a Yankee record until Whitey Ford tied it in 1961. He struck out 239 batters, and that too remained a Yankee record until Ron Guidry struck out 248 in 1978. In winning those 41 games he completed 48 of 51 starts.

Happy Jack's nickname came from the deadly scowl of his game face. But there was little reason for him to be scowling by the time the game was over. He pitched the Yankees back into first place with a 3–2 win and was carried back to the clubhouse in center field on the shoulders of his exultant fans.

The reports of the game don't inspire overwhelming regard for the talents of the turn-of-the-century ballplayer.

Each team scored a run in the third inning. The Red Sox scored with two men out on an infield hit, a passed ball, and what was described as "a high ball to the outfield which Anderson tried hard to catch." That was Honest John Anderson, the center fielder, another well-traveled player who had been shuffled over to the Yankees at the beginning of the year.

The tying run scored, "after Keeler had surprisingly struck out," when Kid Elberfeld, the Yankee shortstop, was hit by a pitched ball and scored on a two-out fly by Anderson "which dropped on the left-field foul line for two bases."

New York's other two runs were scored by Patsy Dougherty. In the fifth inning the ex-Soxer got himself a hit on the kind of pop fly that would be called a Texas Leaguer as soon as there was a Texas League around to call it after. He reached third when Candy La-Chance, Boston's mustachioed first baseman, dropped the throw from Jimmy Collins, and he scored on a fly to right. The winning run came in two innings later on another error by LaChance, a base on balls, and a single by the Yankee second baseman, Jimmy Williams. (Williams, the hero of the first game along with Chesbro, was going to become the goat — along with Chesbro — in the game that cost the Yankees the pennant.)

Boston got one of the runs back in the eighth. Kip Selbach, the left fielder, walked and was called out when he ran into the second baseman on Freddy Parent's ground ball. This was the age of "inside baseball," and there is always the possibility that he ran into Williams to prevent a double play. There is also the possibility that he was just being clumsy. Parent then went to second on a base hit, moved to third on a groundout, and scored — turnabout is fair play — when Elberfeld fumbled LaChance's grounder.

Candy LaChance is a name that has a boulevardier ring to it. There was, alas, no more to the nickname than meets the eye, tongue, and sweet tooth. The mustachioed LaChance was addicted to striped peppermint candy.

All the Yankees needed now was a split in the final four games. The original schedule had called for a single game on Friday, a double-header on Saturday, and, since there was no Sunday baseball, a final double-header on Monday. But there is a rule in life — remember the wind and sun of '78 — which dictates that all good fortune falls upon the certified winner. The Bostons had caught a break. Frank Farrell, who was clearly not blessed with the gift of prophecy, to say nothing of the optimistic spirit one might expect to find in a gambler, had arranged to pick up a couple of extra bucks by renting Hilltop Park to Columbia University for their titantic autumnal struggle against the footballers from Rutgers. And, in the process, he had transferred the Saturday double-header to Boston.

With Chesbro out of the way after the first game, and two of the four remaining games in Boston, winning three out of four was hardly out of the question for the Red Sox.

Having just traveled a full day on the train from St. Louis and pitched a full ball game, Jack Chesbro would seem to have had little need to jump back on a train to Boston for one day and then again the next day for the trip home to New York. Let alone to go to Boston and pitch. But Chesbro had not won 41 games by sitting in a hotel room or loitering in front of a bench.

There are two versions of the ill-considered odyssey of Jack Chesbro. The first version has him screaming at Clark Griffith upon discovering that his name has been left off the traveling list. "What's the matter," he supposedly rails, "don't I work for this team anymore?"

"You just pitched," Griffith protests. "Do you want to pitch them all?"

"Do you want to win the pennant?" asks Chesbro.

The other, and probably more accurate version is that Griffith saw Chesbro looking so forlorn as he was watching his teammates board the train out of Grand Central that he took pity on him and invited him to come along for the ride. Once he was in Boston, Chesbro had insisted on pitching the first game of the Saturday double-header against his old rival Bill Dinneen.

Playing any game in Boston at that time was no picnic for the visiting team, and playing such an important game could be downright intimidating. The Red Sox had a wild and raucous gang of supporters who called themselves the Royal Rooters. The Rooters had evolved out of the Winter League, a group of Boston businessmen who would rush out to the Huntington Avenue grounds after work, take off their hats, and play baseball until it became too dark to see. The president of the Winter League, John Stephen Dooley, was a wealthy cotton broker, and since Boston is a city of tradition, Dooley's daughter, Lib, reigns today as the Number One Red Sox fan. The beneficiary of a permanent box seat at Fenway Park, courtesy of Mrs. Jean Yawkey.

The political leader was John F. ("Honey Fitz") Fitzgerald, who used to be identified as a former mayor of Boston but will slide through history forevermore as John F. Kennedy's grandfather.

The spiritual leader was a saloon keeper with the lovely old name — a period piece of a name really — of Mike (" 'Nuf Sed") McGreevy. McGreevy did not exactly run a corner bar. He was a pol himself, and he conducted a lavish establishment that was as much a salon as a saloon. It was the meeting place for politicians and sports figures and that not inconsiderable segment of Boston society that was intimately involved with politics and sports. McGreevy was the final arbiter of all disputes, and once he had handed down his opinion, that was it. 'Nuf sed.

The Royal Rooters roamed around the field before the game, and sometimes during it. They would come running onto the field during the game to give a player a piece of their mind or to argue with the umpire.

For the double-header that Saturday 30,000 wild fans mobbed the Huntington Grounds, and another 10,000, many of whom had been turned away from the ball park, gathered along Newspaper Row in downtown Boston to catch the bulletins as they were being posted.

Every reserved seat had been sold out for a week. The bleacher seats were gone an hour and a half before the game. When the fans stormed the park, temporary seats had to be placed in front of the grandstand to coax them away from the base lines. Beyond that, the overflow crowd was roped off in the outfield. What this meant was that any ball hit into the crowd became a double — a considerable asset for the home team. The leading members of the Rooters held the rope. When one of the Sox hit a fly ball that had a chance of carrying into the crowd, the distinguished citizens holding the rope would all move forward in unison. Need we say in which direction they would move when the ball was hit by an opposing player?

In the middle of that madhouse Jack Chesbro put the first nine hitters down in order, while Dougherty did his usual thing by opening the game with a base hit and eventually scoring. In the fourth inning all those games and innings fell in on Chesbro. Also the roof. Six hits, a walk, and two errors, and there were six runs across the plate before he was willing to admit that maybe he should have stayed in New York.

It was the worst beating Chesbro had taken all year, and only the third time he had been knocked out of a game in 50 starts.

The Red Sox kept hitting, and the final score was 13–2.

The second game immediately became the critical game in the series. If New York won, the Red Sox would have to sweep the double-header back in New York. If Boston won, it would be the Yankees who had to sweep.

Cy Young had reestablished his primacy on the pitching staff after a slow beginning by winning eight of his last nine games. Over that stretch he had pitched four shutouts. Against him the Yankees sent Jack Powell, no stiff. Powell's record was 23–18 as he went out to pitch the most important game of his life.

Red Powell outpitched the great Young, but the great Young won, as the great ones do, 1–0, his third straight shutout. The lone run was scored in the fifth inning on an infield hit over second base by the weak-hitting Boston second baseman Hobe Ferris, a sacrifice, and — here we go again — an error. The error occurred when Ferris took off for third after Cy Young had sent a long fly to center field. Harry Anderson's strong throw got by Wid Conroy in the gathering dusk, and Ferris came in with the only run "amidst deafening cheers," according to the next day's *Times*.

The game was called after seven innings because of darkness. Young had scattered seven hits over those seven innings, and had been kept out of trouble by some brilliant play in his infield. Except for that one unearned run, Powell had never been in trouble.

So back they went to New York for the double-header on Monday that was going to decide it all. Taking the mound for New York, as we know, was our old friend Jack Chesbro. And his opponent, once again, was going to be Bill Dinneen.

But this time, of course, the New Yorks would have the benefit of the home crowd. Well, not necessarily. By going to Boston on Saturday, New York had put the Royal Rooters into play. The Rooters were accustomed to traveling with the ball club for the big games. They rode with them on the same train, and they stayed with them in the same hotel, and in anticipation of just such a finale they had already reserved a whole section of the grandstand in New York, right behind the visitors' bench.

Anybody who doubted the effectiveness, enthusiasm, and sheer lung power of the Royal Rooters had only to consult the Pittsburgh Pirates. In 1903 Pittsburgh had won its third straight pennant and had gone into the Series as the heavy favorite. The first three games were played in Boston, and when the Pirates evened the Series by winning the fourth game at home, they were confident of closing it out before they had to go back.

"And then," as Tommy Leach, the Pirates' great third baseman, related in *The Glory of Their Times*, "they began to sing that damned 'Tessie' song." A rather obscure love song of days gone by, with words that were both simpering and banal:

> Tessie, you make me feel so badly,
> Why don't you turn around,
> Tessie, you know I love you madly,
> Babe, my heart weighs about a pound.

The fans had begun to sing it, apparently, as a love song to their ball club. As soon as they started to sing, the Red Sox scored, and so they kept on singing. In the following days they developed lyrics to fit every player on both sides. And every time the air was filled with the strains of "Tessie," the Red Sox would be ignited. "I think the Boston fans actually won that series for them," Tommy Leach said, "with that damn Tessie song."

Well, a couple of hundred Royal Rooters were on hand in New York, including Honey Fitz and 'Nuf Sed and their brass band. They wore big red badges with the emblem "World Champions" pinned to their coats. By common agreement, they were all carrying the same suitcases and satchels they had brought to Pittsburgh the previous year. Also the same megaphones, tin horns, and cowbells.

On Sunday night they roamed through downtown, making pests of themselves, and on Monday they gathered in front of the hotel so they could infuriate the New York fans even further by marching to the ball park behind their band.

Jack Chesbro was pitching in the first game — his third start in four days. The Boston fans had been telling New York fans that Chesbro had shot his bolt when he chose to make the trip to Boston and then taken such a drubbing.

They should not have been so confident. After six innings Chesbro had a 2–0 lead, in part through the hitting of that ex-Boston slugger Patsy Dougherty.

In a way it was as if the 1978 play-off game had been placed in a time capsule and shifted into reverse. In 1904 it was New York, not Boston, that did all the hitting in the early innings and kept blowing its chances to put the game away. And it was Boston, not New York, that was the recipient of every break.

The Yankees' great opportunity occurred in the fifth inning. The bases were loaded twice; there were three straight hits and two bases on balls. Out of it all the Yanks, incredibly, were able to score only two runs.

As the inning had got under way, Jack Chesbro owned the only hit for his ball club. He had tripled to the gate in center field with two out in the third, not necessarily a great idea for a pitcher going out there for the third time in four days.

As he came to the plate in the fifth, with a man on first and two out, the game was halted so that a delegation of fans could come marching onto the field to present him with a handsome fur-lined coat and cap. Here you had the most important game the Yankees had ever played, and they were holding it up for a presentation; they did that in those days. After Chesbro had been taken care of, a delegation of players came off the New York bench to present the club secretary with a gold watch and diamond-studded fob in appreciation of everything he had done for them.

When play was resumed, Chesbro showed his appreciation by rapping out a single. Dougherty followed with another hit to knock in the first run, and the second run came in on a bases-loaded walk.

After all that huffing and puffing by New York, Boston tied the score in the seventh on one solitary infield hit and a couple of errors by the unfortunate Jimmy Williams. His first error came on a ground ball by Hobe Ferris. The second and truly disastrous error came with runners on second and third, one out and the infield drawn in. Bill Dinneen hit an easy ground ball. Williams had the runner cold at the plate, but his throw came in very low, skipped past the catcher, Red Kleinow, and rolled to the backstop. Both runs scored.

The Red Sox had tied the game on two unearned runs. The next wild throw Kleinow saw was going to come from the weary old arm of Jack Chesbro.

In the eighth inning the Red Sox actually rapped out three solid hits, but on the third hit Johnny Anderson threw the pesky Ferris out at the plate. This was not a day when Boston was going to win on solid base hits. This was a day when they were going to win on unearned runs. (If you go back, you will see that the only earned runs the Red Sox scored in the whole series came in the game in which they had clobbered Chesbro.)

In the top of the ninth, with the Royal Rooters filling the air with the sound of music, Lou Criger, who couldn't hit much and couldn't run at all, beat out an infield hit, giving Dinneen a chance to bunt him over to second. Kip Selbach, the left fielder, came to bat, and it looked as if a great story might be in the making. Selbach had started the season with Washington and had been shipped to Boston by Ban Johnson to offset the shuffle that had sent Patsy Dougherty to New York. While he was in Washington, he had led off the opening game of the season by singling sharply off Chesbro, and Chesbro had gone on to set the next 27 men down in order.

Get the picture? Kip Selbach had started the season by spoiling what might have been a perfect game for Chesbro, and he could end it, on his final time at bat, by sending him to his most bitter defeat.

It didn't happen. Selbach grounded out, and Lou Criger went to third.

Slow runner on third, two out, and Chesbro gets two quick strikes on little Freddy Parent. And it is right here, with a count of 0–2 on the batter, that Jack Chesbro unleashes one of the wildest pitches of his generation. Chesbro's spitter goes squirting up into the sky, far over Red Kleinow's head, and Lou Criger comes loping in with the run that is going to win the ball game.

But not yet. The game didn't end on Chesbro's wild pitch any more than the 1978 play-off ended with Bucky Dent's home run. Dougherty, who had been a real pain in the ass to his erstwhile teammates throughout the series, came up to bat in the last of the ninth with two men on — they had both walked — and two out.

Another story in the making. Patsy Dougherty, the one-time Boston favorite who had been handed over to the enemy earlier in the season, was up with the tying and winning runs on base. Like Selbach, he had become a powerful force with his new club. Even more than Selbach, he had been having a powerful series.

Big Bill Dinneen struck him out.

New York won the meaningless nightcap, 1–0, in a 10-inning game that was played in one hour and 10 minutes. Fair enough. Otherwise Boston would have won the pennant by 3½ games, which would hardly have presented a true picture of the season. The game-and-a-half margin was just about right.

It is always written that John T. Brush, the owner of the New York Giants, rejected Boston's challenge to resume the World Series because he felt they were "a bunch of bush leaguers." That doesn't really tell the story.

Brush had purchased the Giants only two months before his fellow owners gave in to Ban Johnson's demands and forced an American League rival down his throat. To Brush the upstarts weren't the Highlanders, the Hilltoppers, or the Yankees. To Brush they were the Invaders.

What made the situation even more galling for him was that he and Ban Johnson were old enemies. When first their paths had crossed, Brush had been the owner of the Cincinnati ball club, and Johnson was a Cincinnati sports writer who was constantly excoriating him as a tightwad, pinch penny, and all-around fool.

And now Brush was in New York. His Giants had won with such ridiculous ease that they had clinched the pennant with a month to go. Very gratifying, to be sure, but hardly an unmixed blessing. The National League pennant race ended so early that all attention had turned to the thrilling battle that was being waged in the American League. The New York sports writers had been drumming up the prospects of the pitching matchups: Chesbro vs. Christy Mathewson (33–12). Powell vs. Joe McGinnity (35–8).

The initial challenge had therefore come not from the Red Sox but from the Yankees, the hated Invaders, and it had come at a time when the Yankees had nosed into first place.

It wasn't until the eve of that final five-game series, two weeks later, that the Giants had felt called upon to respond. And even then, Brush, claiming illness as the reason for the long delay, turned the matter over to his manager, John McGraw. McGraw's statement had the fingerprints of lawyers all over it and was remarkable for its sheer stupidity.

McGraw took upon himself all responsibility "for protecting the honor" of his championship. He reminded the fans of the city that in less than three years he had taken the Giants from last place to first. "Now that the New York team has won this honor, I for one will not stand to see it tossed away like a rag. It is the first I have ever won. It means something to our players and they are with me in my stand." He pointed out that the team had clinched the pennant early, incurring great financial loss. "If we didn't sacrifice our own race to the box office we are certainly not going to put in jeopardy the highest honor in baseball simply for the box office inducements."

And then he added, "If the National League should see fit to place postseason games on the same plane as championship games and surround them with the same protections and safeguards for square sports as championship games then, and not until then, will I ever take part in them."

What was the man saying? John McGraw was a guy who ran with gamblers. Was he saying that the 1903 World Series had come under suspicion? And that Devery and Farrell had a reputation that would not stand close scrutiny. If he wasn't saying that, what *was* he saying?

Immediately after the Sox won the pennant, John I. Taylor issued a statement through the press in which he was careful to give Brush an escape route by declaring that he was not issuing a challenge to the National League champions, but merely making an offer to play a series of games against the New York Giants, with all the receipts to go to the players.

What could Brush do? Having said so emphatically that he would not accede to the wishes of the New York press and fans and play the Yankees, he could hardly agree to play the Red Sox. The Red Sox became the "World Champions by default," and that made them world champions for two straight years.

Brush, having made himself ridiculous, was, well, ridiculed. Especially when his players, in flat contradiction to McGraw's public proclamation of their support, formally petitioned that the Series be allowed to proceed.

The Giants won again the next year, and Brush, in an obvious response to McGraw's earlier call for "protections and safeguards," drew up a list of World Series rules and regulations, including the split in the gate receipts, which are the same rules and regulations that are still in force today.

The Red Sox were the world champions. But they did not in fact play what would have been their second World Series. They would not play in another World Series for eight years.

Within two years they would suffer such a complete collapse that in 1906 they finished dead last, 45½ games behind the leader. The Yankees had done their part in sending them to the cellar by sweeping the opening series. Not that New York was doing much better. For the Yankees, that one year of heightened competition, the year of Chesbro's 41 wins, was almost an abberation. After one more run up to second place in the year of the Red Sox collapse, they fell rapidly out of contention and were never a factor again in what may be referred to as the pre-Ruth era.

There is one highlight during that time, however, that should not pass unnoticed. In 1908 the 41-year-old Cy Young pitched a no-hitter against the Yankees in New York, the third no-hitter of his glorious career.

Nor was it the final flare-up of a career in decline. Pitching for a fifth-place club that year, Cy had a record of 21–11.

At the end of the season the Red Sox traded him to Cleveland.

In 1909, at the age of 42, Cy Young won 19 games for the Indians.

To prove that gross lack of sentiment was not restricted to the Boston side of the rivalry, New York gave Chesbro his release a year after the Red Sox bade goodbye to Cy Young.

The Red Sox, with an eye toward the box office possibilities, picked him up immediately so that they could pitch him against the Yankees in the final game of the season.

His old teammates knocked him out of the box.

Sayonara, Jack, and keep smiling.

Chapter Three

The Babe. The Sultan of Swat. The Big Ape

You know, I saw it all happen, from beginning to end but sometimes I still can't believe what I saw. A 19-year-old kid, crude and poorly educated, only lightly brushed by the social veneer we call civilization gradually transformed into the idol of American youth, and the symbol of Baseball the world over — a man loved by more people and with an intensity of feeling that perhaps has never been equaled before or since.

I saw a man transformed from a human being into something pretty close to a God.

—Harry Hooper, captain of the Boston Red Sox

WHEN Don Mattingly came to Yankee Stadium for the first time, he was greeted by that paragon of clubhouse men, that prince of fellows, Pete Sheehy. "Well, kid," said Pete, "you're in the house that Ruth built." And with Mattingly looking at him rather quizzically, he said, "That was Babe Ruth's locker right over there."

"You mean there really was a Babe Ruth?" Mattingly asked. "I always thought that Babe Ruth was a character in a book. You know, a fictional character."

Asked about that now, Don says, "Yup. I did say that. That's what I thought. Pretty dumb, huh?"

Nope. Don Mattingly was righter than he thinks. If Babe Ruth wasn't a fictional character, it's only because nobody would have dared to make him up. He was a character right out of Dickens. Tossed into an orphanage–reform school at the age of seven, he emerged 12 years later as a big (6 feet 2 inches), unhandsome innocent who had been deprived of everything except an all-conquering talent and a vast, unquenchable appetite for life.

You have to go back and research him to comprehend that no matter how overwhelming a figure you thought he was, you didn't know the half of it. He was a great outfielder with a strong and accurate arm. He was a wild and aggressive base runner who stole 123 bases over his career. He stole home 10 times. As a hitter, he was a new wind sweeping clean.

I don't want to go overboard on this, but there has never been anything quite like him on the American scene.

• In 1920 he hit 54 home runs. George Sisler was runner-up with 19.

• In 1921, which may have been his greatest year, his slugging percentage was .846. Harry Heilmann, the runner-up, was at .606.

• In that same year he scored 177 runs. The runner-up, Jack Tobin of St. Louis, had 132.

Each of those marks represents the greatest differential between the leader and the runner-up in the history of major league baseball.

He wasn't merely ahead of the power curve, he *was* the power curve.

• In 1927, the year he hit 60 home runs, he had more homers all by himself than the total number hit by any other single team.

• When he retired with 714, he had more than twice as many home runs as the next man on the list.

• From 1918 to 1934 he led the league in home runs 12 times. The only years he didn't were those when he was out of action for a considerable part of the season.

Not only did he have the longest home runs ever hit in every park, he also seemed to hit "the longest home run ever hit" in every park two or three times a season. The only plausible explanation is that he would hit them so hard and they would go so far that every time the sports writers saw one disappear from sight, they would tell themselves that nobody could have hit a ball that far before.

In 1930, the first year Sunday baseball was permitted in Boston, the Red Sox were forced to play their Sunday games at Braves Field because of Fenway Park's proximity to a church. In the one game Babe played at Braves Field as a Yankee, he hit the longest home run ever hit there. Well, that's not entirely true. He also pitched the final game of the season against the Red Sox that year — Babe always loved to put on a show in Boston — and that game was played on Sunday, too. Babe didn't get any hits during the game itself, but on his first swing in batting practice he hit the only ball that was ever — *ever* — hit completely out of Braves Field in dead center field.

He was 35 years old at the time.

Nobody seems to be able to write about Babe Ruth these days without saying, "Everybody forgets it now, but in his younger days he was the best left-handed pitcher in baseball." Actually, nobody can forget it, if only because the writers keep reminding us.

• Here's how good he was. In 1916 he was 23–12 with a 1.75 ERA and nine shutouts. In 1917 it was 24–13 with a 2.01 ERA and six shutouts. He really had seven shutouts that year. He threw one away on his last appearance in New York, and he did it for a laugh.

A special day was being held for the military, and the ball park was packed with soldiers. Babe was their unofficial pinup boy as the result of a home run show he had put on during a tour of army camps. It didn't matter to them that he was breezing along with a two-hitter; they were screaming for a home run every time he came to bat. When he did hit one for them in the ninth inning, they went crazy.

Babe came out to pitch the ninth with an 8–0 lead, but he was having too much fun to let it end. He signaled the cheering soldiers that he was going to let the Yankees hit. And he did. He lobbed the ball up to five straight batters. Five straight batters lashed out base hits. The soldiers were roaring. Babe was prancing around like a performing monkey, grinning and bowing and saluting.

With three runs in and two runners on base, he signaled the soldiers that it was time to go back to work. The next three hitters were set down with ease.

Take away those three runs and his ERA would have been 1.93.

• In 1918, his conversion year, he tied for the home run crown and pitched his team to two wins in the World Series while setting a record for consecutive scoreless innings that lasted for 43 years. More remarkable still, he pitched the final game with a badly bruised and swollen knuckle on the middle finger of his pitching hand — the finger a pitcher needs for both his spin and his control.

Babe Ruth straddled two eras. He was the best left-handed pitcher in the days of "inside" defensive baseball, and he was the greatest hitter in a time when the hitter was king.

He was, Don Mattingly, the stuff that fiction is made of.

• In 1930 Babe hit three home runs in one game against the Philadelphia A's, and with a chance to become the first player in modern baseball to hit four, he went up to the plate right-handed.

• After having been jailed by a New York judge for speeding, he rushed out through a cheering crowd to a waiting limousine, was sped through the streets of New York behind a police motorcycle escort, and came running into Yankee Stadium through the centerfield entrance in the fifth inning to take his place in the line-up.

It would be nice to say that he stepped up to the plate and hit a home run. But, listen, not even the Babe batted .1000. Still, we can say that he might have inspired his teammates to equally grand deeds, because they promptly put on a winning rally.

He defied authority. He defied his managers. He defied the commissioner. He defied the umpires.

• When he was with the Red Sox, he jumped the club after a fight with his manager, Ed Barrow, and signed to play for a shipyard baseball team in Pennsylvania. Two contracts didn't bother him. What the hell, there was a war on, wasn't there? Once he had cooled off, and the lawyers had done their thing, he returned to Boston, wasn't put in the line-up immediately, and jumped again.

• Babe fought with the umpires. Not squabbled with them; fought with them. As a pitcher for the Red Sox he once walked the Washington lead-off man on four straight balls, bitching after every call. When the umpire, Brick Owens, threatened to throw him out of the game, the Babe responded by threatening to punch Owens on the nose. Whereupon Owens did. Whereupon Babe did. Whereupon Babe had to be pulled off the umpire by his teammates and escorted off the field by a policeman.

It is an escapade that has gone down in the record books, not because Babe was the only player to hit or be hit by an umpire in those rowdy days, but because Ernie Shore, who had to come off the bench cold, went out and pitched a perfect game. Ernie Shore became known as the guy who pitched a perfect game after Babe Ruth got thrown out. And Brick Owens was identified for the rest of a long and not unmeritorious career as the umpire whom Babe Ruth had socked in the nose.

• While with the Yankees, he was suspended five times in a single season. The first suspension was for six weeks for going out on a barnstorming tour in flat defiance of the new commissioner's orders. (Babe was right about that one, for a change. It was a silly rule, inartfully written.) The other four suspensions came for using such unreasonable methods of persuasion on umpires as throwing dirt in their face, going for their throat, and threatening to kill them.

His return from the long suspension was treated as a second Opening Day. A Second Coming, almost. Never a man to let a Second Coming pass unnoticed, Babe arrived at the park in a rented limousine and stepped to the plate — amid a thunderous ovation — swinging a big green shillelagh.

• He was always jumping into the stands after abusive fans. In his first spring training with the Yankees, the fan he was going after pulled a knife on him, and his new teammates had to come piling over the dugout roof to rescue him. Leading the rescue operation was the Yankees' big, ungainly co-owner, Colonel Tillinghast L'Hommedieu Huston, whose name alone should have been enough to frighten the guy off.

• There was another time when a handsome woman chased him through the team train. She was wielding a wicked-looking knife at the time. It was, as everybody immediately observed, the only time in his life Babe had ever been known to run away from a woman.

It has become customary to say that the sports writers of the day protected Ruth by not letting their readers know what a drunk and a womanizer he was. Absolute nonsense. The Roaring Twenties were not a time when the citizenry shook a trembling finger of indignation to hear of pleasure's name. Babe Ruth loved the limelight as much as the limelight loved him. He lived in the headlines.

He was uncivilized. He had been in a cage for 12 years, and he came out ready to eat up the world. His teammates called him the Big Ape and the Big Baboon. At lust and gluttony he had few peers, although — one cannot deny it — King Henry VIII does come irresistibly to mind.

• Babe gobbled food. Throughout his life, he stuffed food into his mouth. He ate double portions of everything. He discovered hot dogs

and soda pop on his first day of spring training and he never undis-
covered them. Eddie Bennett, the Yankee bat boy, said later that
one of his duties was to have three or four hot dogs ready for Babe
when he came into the clubhouse and then hand him a glass of bicarbonate of soda at the start of every game. "Got my milk ready?"
Babe would grin. After he had gulped down the bicarbonate and
burped a couple of times, Babe was ready to play.

The bellyache heard 'round the world: was it from overeating, as
the doctors said, or did he have a venereal disease, as was widely
rumored?

• There were stories, which are probably not exaggerated, that
Babe would rent a bordello for a night and sample all the merchandise. During his remarkably brief recuperative periods, the girls
would pour champagne over his head. If they didn't also put a toga
on him and pop rich, ripe grapes into his mouth, it could only have
been because neither he nor they were that well versed in the more
languid practices of ancient Rome.

• When Earle Combs came to Boston in the late Forties as a coach,
he told the Boston writers how Ruth had ordered him to stay on in
the big city for a week at the end of his rookie season with the Yankees. Combs was a very religious young man from Kentucky, a complete teatotaler. While his teammates were out carousing, Combs
would be in his hotel room reading the Bible. Nobody in baseball was
more anxious to get home.

"I want you to do something, kid," the Babe said to him.

"Yes, sir," said Combs.

He gave Combs an address in the market district and instructed
him to buy a couple of dozen pheasant, a couple of deer, and a few
small animals. At the end of the week Earle was to attach them to
the hood of Ruth's big open touring car. That, he told the rookie with
a wink, was when he was due to return from his hunting trip to North
Carolina.

The Babe had two babes in an apartment room. His plans were to
lock himself up with them for three days, and then take on a new pair
for three more. Upon emerging, he posed for the newspapers with
the trophies of the hunt festooned all over his car. The whole charade, of course, was aimed at an audience of one — his wife, Claire,
with whom he was engaged in an unending and apparently mutually
satisfying game of deceit.

"Good job, kid," said the Babe.

"Can I go home now?" asked Combs.

He was a showman. He was there to play and he was there to win, but he was also there to entertain and have fun.

• If there was a big crowd, with a lot of kids in the bleachers, he would trot over to the railing in foul territory between innings and sign autographs during the Yankees' turn at bat.

• Reasonably ambidextrous — he wrote with his right hand — he would entertain the fans, particularly on the road, by warming up the pitcher right-handed. Bob Meusel, who is generally acknowledged to have possessed the greatest throwing arm ever hung on mortal man, was also ambidextrous, and they would occasionally entertain the home crowd by warming up in the outfield with Babe firing the ball across the field with his right hand and Meusel firing it back left-handed.

Batting right-handed was also a lark he indulged in at times. It served another purpose, too. He started doing it in 1923, the year he was walked 177 times (still a world's record). He would do it most often when he knew he was going to be walked. But not always.

On the day he hit the three home runs in Philadelphia, a different kind of showmanship was at play. In dead center field of the Baker Bowl there was a narrow metal ladder leading up the top of the flagpole. When Ruth came up for the fourth time, outfielder Al Simmons, who had spent the day watching baseballs fly over his head and out of the park, called time, strolled over to center field, sat himself down on the second rung of the ladder in mock surrender, and signaled for the game to proceed.

With the chance to become the first batter in modern baseball to hit four home runs in a single game, the Babe stepped across to the right-hand side of the batting box. And struck out.

But that was all right. Everybody had a good chuckle and — more important still — Babe Ruth hadn't been upstaged.

The first time he hit right-handed, as far as can be determined, he did it out of sheer devilment. It could hardly have been a coincidence that the pitcher was Sherrod Smith, the Cleveland Indians' left-hander. Seven years earlier Babe had pitched his first World Series victory against Smith, then with Brooklyn, a 14-inning thriller hailed for years as the greatest World Series game ever played. Now, batting right-handed, Babe took one strike and then jumped back to the left side as Smith got ready to pitch, forcing the Cleveland defense to go scurrying back into the Ruth shift. They needn't have bothered. Babe walloped the next pitch into the right-field bleachers.

Usually he'd jump over to the other side as a way of daring them to pitch to him. Almost always they walked him anyway.

• He did it later in that same year, 1923, after he had hit two home runs off Ray Kolp of the St. Louis Browns to bring the Yankees back from an 8–0 deficit. Now, Ray Kolp is not a name to ring chimes in the mind of the ordinary baseball fan. To baseball players, however, Ray Kolp is known as the most wicked bench jockey who ever lived. If you don't believe it, ask Leo Durocher. Leo was a teammate of Kolp's for three years in Cincinnati, and he always spoke in awe of his powers of both invective and inventiveness.

Since Babe was a ferocious bench jockey himself, one can only surmise the brilliance of the repartee that was being flung back and forth. It was, of course, no contest. Kolp may have been quicker with the tongue, especially while he was holding his big lead, but Babe Ruth, in the end, let his bat do his talking for him.

In extra innings he came to bat twice against Elam Vangilder, the ace of the Browns' staff. Both times there were two men on base. Both times he stepped into the box right-handed and challenged Vangilder to pitch to him. Both times Vangilder put him on intentionally.

Immediately following the second walk, Bob Meusel singled to win the game. That happened a lot, too. But they were not going to let the Babe beat them.

• Did he or didn't he call that home run in the 1932 World Series? It was, of course, the vicious bench jockeying centering on Babe that provided the background to that one, too.

Did he point? Well, the count was 0–2, and Charley Root, the Cubs' pitcher, always said, with what seems to be unassailable logic, that if Babe had pointed, he'd have ended up on his ass. Except that we all know what happens to logic when passion walks in the door. One might ask, with equal logic, what Root was doing giving Babe Ruth a pitch he could hit into the center-field bleachers on an 0–2 count.

What probably happened was that Babe held up two fingers and said, "I've still got one left." He had done that a hundred, nay, a thousand times before. And sometimes he hit it out, and sometimes he struck out, and sometimes he accomplished one of the 93 variations that were possible in between.

My own feeling is that if he had really pointed, there wouldn't be any dispute about it, would there?

Whether he pointed or not is irrelevant. He had called his shot on home runs countless times. He did it in exhibition games, he did it during the regular season, and he did it — certifiably — against the St. Louis Cardinals in the 1928 World Series.

Despite an injured ankle that had him limping through the 1928 Series, Ruth established another of those marks that has never been equaled by hitting .625, and rapping out 10 hits in a four-game sweep.

In the fourth game the Cardinals, trying hard to stay alive, took a 2–1 lead into the seventh, the one run being a homer Babe had hit off Willie Sherdel, their tough little lefty.

In the seventh Sherdel got two quick strikes by him, and as Babe turned his head to exchange a few jibes with the catcher, little Willie quick-pitched him. If they had been playing by National League rules, Babe would have struck out. They were, however, playing by American League rules, something, apparently, that nobody had bothered to let Sherdel and his pals in on.

During the tumultuous argument that ensued, Babe stood by with a huge grin on his face, and, when it was over, sent Sherdel up the wall by ostentatiously applauding him and his teammates for the spirited argument they had put up.

Sherdel shouted something at him. Babe shouted something back. They continued to go back and forth as the count went to 2–2. At which point Babe leveled his bat across the plate and said, "Put it right here and I'll knock one out of the park for you."

Sherdel came close enough so that Babe knocked it out of the park to tie the game, and went laughing around the bases, waving his hat at the suddenly silenced crowd. Two innings later he got up again against Grover Cleveland Alexander and made it three home runs in a row.

• Next to the home run off Sherdel in the World Series, the Babe's own favorite was the home run he called against an abusive fan in Boston, a real leather lung, as they were always called. Every city had one. In Boston it was a fan named Conway. Conway was ripping Ruth so mercilessly this one day that Babe stepped out of the box,

leveled a finger directly at him, pointed to the right-field bleachers —
and hit the next pitch out of sight. As he was crossing home plate,
Ruth stopped dead, turned to Conway, and made a low, deep bow.

He was always doing that, too. Or snapping off a series of precise
military salutes to the opposing bench or bleachers.

What is generally forgotten in the passage of time is what a complete
ballplayer he was. He was a superb outfielder. The accounts of a
remarkable number of games report on his great game-saving
catches. What is not so surprising is that he had a great arm. And an
extremely accurate one. You did not go to third base on balls hit
down the right-field line at Yankee Stadium. He and Bob Meusel
would sometimes entertain early arrivals by laying a towel down in
front of the plate and seeing how often they could hit it with a throw
from the outfield. (Babe played right field in Yankee Stadium in order
to protect his eyes from the wicked sun in left field, and left field
everywhere else.)

He was an excellent bunter and a smart hitter. When you picture
Ruth, you see that twirling bat and that powerful swing, and the long
fly ball arching high into the right-field stands. Actually, the Babe hit
to left more often than anybody seems to remember. When he was
in a slump, he'd choke up a little on the bat, shorten his swing, and
practice hitting to left. He'd also pitch early batting practice and
sometimes even put on the catching tools and go behind the plate to
enable himself to get back the feel and rhythm of the thing.

The usual explanation for his frequent problems with his legs was
that he swung so hard that he would sometimes wrench his knee or
twist an ankle. One eminent scientist, in seeking to explain to the
populace how Ruth was able to generate so much power, wrote that
with his broad and heavy upper body and his relatively thin legs, he
would set in motion the same centrifugal force that made a top spin.
And, indeed, the sports cartoonists, who loved to demonstrate how
Babe had set the crowd afire by striking out, would draw his legs
braided together like a corkscrew.

In truth, he was forever being carried off the field with leg injuries
after running into walls or bowling over infielders. To think of Babe
Ruth as a potbellied, spindly-legged old guy who took that big, bay-
windowed, wind-around swing and went tippy-toeing around the
bases is to have no sense of his speed. Until the lightning-fast Earle

Combs joined the team, nobody on the Yankees went from first to third quicker than the Babe. He was a wild and aggressive base runner. He was a leading exponent of the hook slide, but it sometimes seemed that given any choice at all, he preferred to go barreling into a fielder.

In the opening inning of the opening game of the 1931 season at Fenway Park, as a portly old gentleman of 36, he came roaring home on a short fly to right field and looked dead at the plate until he bowled into Charlie Berry, a former All-American football player, and knocked the ball out of his glove. Then he went out into left field, collapsed while running after a fly ball, and had to be carried off the field.

He was carried off the field so often, only to arise and be back in action again the next day, that he was sometimes accused of putting on an act. Not so, said Babe. "I heal quickly."

He was simply a phenomenon. All the physical attributes that go into the making of a baseball player were combined in this one big guy. There never was such a player; there never was such an entertainer.

• He was a photographer's delight. There are pictures of him wearing every kind of headgear known to butcher, baker, and of course Indian chief. Especially Indian chief. Indian headgear was a big thing in the twenties, and the Babe actually went to bat wearing an Indian headdress more than once. Derbies suited him, too. Perch a derby atop those porcine features and shove the omnipresent cigar into his mouth, and he looked like every big-city politician who ever lived.

He posed in cowboy hats and chaps, and he posed in high hat and tails. There are pictures of him in the uniform of a deputy police chief of almost every town he ever visited, and he is pictured wearing every kind of crown and royal headgear while being honored as the Sultan of this or the King of that.

He also got the idea somewhere that if he kept a cabbage leaf on top of his head during a hotspell, it would keep him cool. The public discovered this when he absent-mindedly doffed his cap to the suddenly tickled crowd.

He posed in boxing trunks exchanging punches with the likes of Jack Dempsey, and in full football regalia with whatever All-American was in town. There is a picture of him with Knute Rockne, in which Rockne is wearing civilian clothes and Babe is wearing a Notre Dame uniform. You could catch him in full flight off a diving board, or in full swing on the golf course.

He posed with gorillas, with chimpanzees, and with lions. He posed riding horses and heifers. Well, the horses were for real. Herb Pennock, whom he admired when they were teammates in Boston, came from a fox-hunting family in Pennsylvania, and, talk about the original Odd Couple, Pennock took Babe home with him and taught him to ride to hounds. One suspects that if Herb had been able to anticipate the girth his protegé would one day achieve, he would not have done that to a generation of horses yet unborn.

He posed with leading musicians, blowing whatever musical instrument was shoved at him.

He posed aiming a rifle, playing pool, drinking booze. He posed with everybody, and he endorsed almost everything.

He was everywhere. Red Sox fans could open up the paper almost every day and see what they had lost when Harry Frazee, whose name will forever live in infamy in Boston, sold him to their greatest rival.

Chapter Four

The Babe in Boston: 1914–1919

He played by instinct. Sheer instinct. He was like a damn animal. They know when it's going to rain. Nature, that was Ruth.

— Rube Bressler, pitcher for the Philadelphia Athletics

H E bestrode the playing fields of America. He invaded the Red Sox–Yankee rivalry from both sides for 20 years.

His story, like the story of all legendary figures, is the stuff of wonderment. Born in the waterfront section of Baltimore, George Herman Ruth, Jr., was sent to St. Mary's Industrial School for Boys, a Jesuit institution, at the age of seven as an incorrigible child. School meaning reform school. He was no orphan. His parents didn't die on him; they gave him away. The way Babe told it, he was a rotten kid. Hung around bars, stole fruit from pushcarts, chewed tobacco, and drank. "Incorrigible" was the word, all right, according to Babe.

He told Grantland Rice that when he was six years old he stole a dollar out of the till at his father's bar and bought ice cream for all the kids on the block, and when his father beat the hell out of him, he did it again just to show the old man.

Yet that has the sound of a story dreamed up to allow him to admit he was a bad kid while at the same time saying that he wasn't — not really.

How bad, after all, could a seven-year-old be? From the independent evidence that can be adduced, it seems more likely that his mother, who had suffered through seven miscarriages before she gave birth to George Junior — always pregnant, always sick — was simply incapable of coping with such a spirited child. During the eight subsequent years of her life, she would plead for George to be sent home to her, and in short order she would be whacking him around again and shipping him back. What we have here, quite clearly, is a classic case of an emotional disorder. Anybody running a home for juvenile delinquents or disturbed children would find the profile very familiar.

When he was turned over to the Baltimore Orioles at the age of 19, he would say that getting out of St. Mary's was like getting out of a cage. His second wife, Claire, who was the only person he ever felt free to be totally honest with, never referred to St. Mary's as anything except "that jail."

Well, if you want to get technical about it, that's what it was. Young George was there under court order. One of the other kids who grew up in St. Mary's with the Babe became known professionally around the racetracks as Clocker Lawton, the purveyor of a tip sheet that always had six or seven winners — not when you were entering the track, you understand, but when you were leaving. According to Clocker Lawton, the school was literally a jail, down to "guards with guns on the walls."

Still, it couldn't have been all that bad. The Jesuit brothers taught the kids a trade. George was trained to be a shirtmaker with a specialty in turning collars. One of the most affecting passages in Claire Ruth's book occurs when she talks about how the Babe, the most profligate of spenders, that nonparagon of thrift, would turn the collars of all his expensive new shirts, commenting all the while about the shoddy work being done by the younger generation of shirtmakers.

The best thing that ever happened to him, certainly, was Brother Mathias, a father figure. "The greatest man I ever knew" was the way Babe always referred to him. The first time young George saw Brother Mathias, he saw a huge man, dressed in the flowing garments of his calling, swinging a fungo bat one-handed and hitting mammoth fly balls to the outfield. So George was imprinted from an early age with the image of a baseball being driven up into the high blue yonder.

Brother Mathias was so shy that he gave only one interview in his life. That interview was given to Tom Shehan of the *Boston Evening Transcript* at the time of Babe's signing with the Boston Braves at the very end of his career. Shehan was able to pull off his coup, with the intercession of higher authorities, because he was an active alumnus of St. John's Prep in Danvers, Massachusetts, the Jesuit institution to which Brother Mathias was assigned in his final years. The first thing Shehan noted — talk about revealing — was that Brother Mathias had the same mincing pitter-patter way of walking as Babe Ruth. Or, to put it the other way around, little Georgie Ruth had, consciously or unconsciously, mimicked his mentor's gait.

The old Jesuit wanted it understood from the beginning that George Herman Ruth, Jr., had always been the best ball player in the home. "I had nothing to do with that," he told Shehan. "I don't want you to say that I did." Babe had started out as a left-handed catcher, a species far more common in the days before all the experts came along to explain why a left-hander would be performing under a terrible handicap. Brother Mathias described for Shehan how George would tuck the right-handed mitt under his arm and rifle the ball down to second to catch anybody who was trying to steal.

In explaining how Babe became a pitcher, Brother Mathias confirmed, with only minor variations, the rather unlikely story Babe himself had always told.

"One day our star pitcher was batted out of the box and the other team hit every pitcher we sent against them. Babe, as you know, is a man who has always had a strange sense of humor. Instead of being upset about the licking we were taking, he thought it was funny. 'If you're so smart,' I told him, 'Let's see how well you can do.' " They didn't get a hit off him, and he was St. Mary's pitcher from then on.

Eventually, George Herman Ruth of St. Mary's Industrial School for Boys played all positions. Wherever he played, he continued to hit a baseball farther than anybody had thought possible.

It wasn't Brother Mathias who told Jack Dunn about George Ruth. (Jack Dunn was the owner of the Baltimore Orioles in the Triple-A International League.) As a member of the Xaverian order, Brother Mathias was forsworn from having any contact with the outside world. Dunn's story, which you can believe if you want to, was that he was tipped off by a Brother from another order who was trying to discourage Dunn from signing his own star pitcher. According to Dunn, he arrived at St. Mary's in February 1914, just around the time of Ruth's nineteenth birthday, and saw a big, overgrown kid dressed in overalls sliding on the ice. "Until he put on a uniform at my Fayetteville, North Carolina, training camp a few weeks later, I never had seen him play ball. I was amazed at the way he hit in batting practice, but at the time we considered him only as a left-handed pitcher."

From the first he was a sensation. As a pitcher he dazzled the three major league teams Dunn sent him against. As a hitter he was hammering the ball so far that there is still a plaque in Fayetteville commemorating the prodigious home run he hit in his first exhibition game.

There are two stories about how he was christened "Babe." The first one is that he followed Dunn around the field so slavishly in his first couple of days that someone said, "Here comes Dunnie and his new babe." It makes sense. In order to release Babe from St. Mary's, the Jesuits had to parole him to Dunn. Legally, Dunn was his guardian.

The second story makes sense, too. Having spent his whole life behind walls, the big, overgrown kid was seeing the world fresh. "Why, he's just a babe in the woods," somebody was supposed to have said, as Babe was spending his first evening in the Fayetteville hotel riding up and down in the elevator.

His first official game was against Buffalo on April 22, 1914. He pitched a six-hit shutout. On his first time at bat he singled, one of the two hits he would have on the day.

There were some stop-you-dead names in the line-ups. The second batter he faced was a light-hitting second baseman named Joe McCarthy. Yeah, *that* Joe McCarthy. The catcher for the Bisons was Paul Krichell, who would go on to become the greatest of all Yankee scouts. Nine years later Krichell would be sending a telegram to the Yankees saying, "I think I've found another Babe Ruth." The player was Lou Gehrig. Close enough.

The Babe's third baseman, if you're looking for a tie-in to the Red Sox, was Freddy Parent, the little shortstop who had been at bat when Chesbro unloosed his wild pitch. His shortstop was Neal Ball — the same Neal Ball who had pulled off the first unassisted triple play. More important to Babe on that day, Ball pulled off a sparkling play that got the rookie left-hander out of a very nervous first inning.

By midseason Ruth had won 14 games, Baltimore was 17 games ahead, and Dunn was broke, done in by the newly formed Federal League.

In the parlance of organized baseball the Federal League was an "outlaw" league, but it called itself a major league and, of equal importance, the Baltimore franchise was owned and managed by Ned Hanlon, who had been the manager of the championship Baltimore teams of the 1890s, the fabled Old Orioles of Willie Keeler, John McGraw, and Wilbert Robinson. The fans of Baltimore, who looked upon themselves as major leaguers, flocked to their park while the Orioles, for all their success, were playing before gatherings that sometimes numbered as few as a dozen paying customers.

Although the Federal League lasted only two years, it was to exert a tremendous influence over the career of Babe Ruth and, indeed, over all of baseball. If it had not been for the damage inflicted upon Dunn, Babe Ruth would have been sold, in the passage of time, to Dunn's usual customers, Connie Mack or John McGraw.

The Babe was sold to the Red Sox (along with the Orioles' other great pitcher, Ernie Shore, and their catcher, Ben Egan) because Joe Lannin, the new Red Sox owner, had been keeping the hard-pressed International League going by financing two of its teams and lending money to a couple of others.

"I owed it to him," Dunn explained to the enraged McGraw.

Four months after George Herman Ruth, Jr., had walked out of the gates of St. Mary's, Babe Ruth was on a train to Boston to pitch in the big leagues.

It was a strange and remarkable season. He spent the first half pitching Baltimore to what seemed to be a runaway pennant and was back in the International League over the last three weeks helping to pitch the Providence Grays, one of the two teams owned by Joe Lannin, to the pennant over Dunn's dismantled and demoralized Orioles. His combined record with Baltimore and Providence was 23–8. For the Red Sox it was 2–1, giving him an overall record for the season of 25–9, despite 25 consecutive days on the Boston bench before being sent to Providence.

The second win in a Red Sox uniform, little noted at the time, came after he had been recalled to Boston on the completion of the International League season. And while it was an inartistic 11–5 win, it came in his first appearance against the New York Yankees, the same game in which he had his first major league hit, a double off Leonard ("King") Cole.

·   ·   ·

The team he joined in 1915 had most of the same personnel as the great 1912 team, which had won 106 games, a record that would last until it was broken by the 1927 Yankees. The 1912 Red Sox had defeated the Yankees in the season series, 19–2, the largest spread in history.

The great outfield of Speaker, Hooper, and Lewis was still in place. Tris Speaker, the center fielder, played so shallow that he would get involved in rundown plays, but would still be able to turn his back and outrun long flies to center field. Harry Hooper was the closest thing around to being his equal. In the 1912 World Series, Hooper had robbed the Giants' Larry Doyle of a home run by what was always regarded in his generation as the greatest catch ever made. Turned halfway around as his back hit the low bleacher railing, his feet cut completely out from under him, he had reached up and caught the ball with his bare hand as he was disappearing into the crowd.

Duffy Lewis, overshadowed though he was by Speaker and Hooper, was a great clutch hitter and a superb fielder. There was a steep incline in front of the left-field wall at Fenway Park, and he played that incline with such perfection that it continued to be called Duffy's Cliff long after he was gone.

Larry Gardner was still at third base. Everett ("Deacon") Scott had taken over at shortstop. If you were called Deacon, it meant that you either wore glasses or were unusually quiet, and there were no active players then wearing glasses. Whatever he was called, nobody could make the play in the hole like Everett Scott, because nobody else had both his range and his arm. ("Scott's trolley-line arm," manager Wilbert Robinson moaned after his Brooklyn Dodgers had lost the 1916 World Series. "Every time we thought we had a key hit, we lost it on the trolley line.") Early in the season, Jack Barry, who had been the shortstop for Connie Mack's $100,000 infield, was sold to the Red Sox, and although Barry had been considered the top defensive shortstop for years, he was more than willing to tip his cap to Scott and move over to second base.

Bill ("Rough") Carrigan, the manager, was also the best defensive catcher in the game, a man who was famous for his ability to block the plate. And also for his skill in handling pitchers.

Babe Ruth always said that the 1915 Boston Red Sox were the best defensive team he ever saw. They had to be. The Red Sox won

101 games; Ty Cobb's Detroit Tigers won 100. That 101st victory was pitched by George Herman Ruth.

Years later, when Ty Cobb was reminiscing with Babe about that bitterly contested season, Cobb told him that he did not believe there had ever been a team that could field with the 1915 Red Sox. "You guys would get off to a lead," said Ty, "and hold on like grim death. Time after time we'd think we had a rally going in the late innings only to have Scottie or Gardner come up with great stops. Or Spoke, Duffy, or Hooper pull one of their circus catches in the outfield."

Gardner, in particular, drove Cobb crazy with what seemed to be an uncanny ability to anticipate when he was going to bunt. In later years, when it no longer mattered, Gardner let Cobb know that he had tipped him off by gritting his teeth just before he brought the bat down.

With pitching you could have an argument. The great unbeatable pitcher versus the solid five-man staff. For the Red Sox 1912 had been the year of Smoky Joe Wood. Joe Wood was out of Kansas City. He had started his career — are you ready for this? — as a member of the Bloomer Girls. (The Bloomer Girls were exactly what you think they were, a barnstorming team of young women — except that some of them weren't.) Joe Wood, at the age of 22, had put together the greatest season any Red Sox pitcher has ever had. He won 16 straight games. His record was 34–5, with 10 shutouts. He went on to win three games in the World Series.

And he was a certified Yankee killer. A year earlier, at the age of 21, Smoky Joe had beaten the Yankees five times and shut them out in all three starts at the Polo Grounds.

In place of the one dominating pitcher, the 1915 Red Sox had what was perhaps the most solid pitching staff ever assembled. Joe Wood (15–5), Rube Foster (19–8), Ernie Shore (19–8), and Babe Ruth (18–8) finished one, two, three, four in winning percentage. The other starting pitcher was Dutch Leonard, and he just barely missed making the top five with a hardly disgraceful 15–7.

Joe Wood, no longer Smoky Joe, led the American League in both winning percentage and ERA with an arm so sore that he had to be used pretty much as a spot pitcher. What made it even more remarkable was that he was never able to win another game.

But there was something else about that team. It was never any secret that the Red Sox were split into two cliques. Carrigan, Heinie

Wagner, and Duffy Lewis were at the head of one clique. Speaker, Wood, and Larry Gardner headed the other. Bill Carrigan and Tris Speaker, the manager and his greatest star, detested each other. Just a conflict of personalities, it was said. You know how these things are. Uh-huh.

Duffy Lewis and Tris Speaker, two-thirds of the great outfield, had not spoken for years. The genesis of the feud, it was generally acknowledged, occurred after Lewis had shaved his head during one of those hellish heat waves in St. Louis. To his chagrin, the hair never grew back. To his further chagrin, Speaker kept sneaking up behind him after they returned to Boston so that he could snatch Lewis's cap off and expose his glistening pate. "Do that again," Duffy Lewis warned him, "and I'll kill you." Speaker showed how unintimidated he was by doing it again. Duffy showed how serious he was by slamming his bat across Speaker's shin so hard that he had to be carried off the field.

Does that have the sound of two normally friendly teammates horsing around? Or does it sound as if there was a deep underlying hostility at work there?

To those feuds was very shortly added a new one — Babe Ruth and Joe Wood. Or, if you want to take in the whole entry, Babe Ruth versus Joe Wood and Tris Speaker.

The way Babe always told it, a ball had got past Wood while he was warming up, and when Smoky Joe called out to Babe to stop it, Babe playfully spread his legs apart and allowed the ball to roll on through. A few choice expletives were exchanged, a few blunt challenges were hurled, and the two great pitchers were on their way to the clubhouse to duke it out when Bill Carrigan came running over to break it up.

The way Babe told the story, Speaker and Wood were such great friends — the word always used to describe them was *inseparable* — that any enemy of Smoky Joe's automatically became an enemy of Tris's.

But there has to have been more to it than that.

The Speaker-Wood faction had ridiculed and abused Babe from the beginning. Babe Ruth, remember, had come out of St. Mary's newborn. He knew nothing about such elementary amenities of civilization as personal hygiene. He wolfed his food like an animal. He got drunk every night. They called him the Big Pig as well as the Big Baboon. They called him Niggerlips. The nicest thing they called him was Tarzan the Ape Man. Things got so bad that Babe finally turned on his tormenters in the clubhouse and offered to take them all on.

But — again — wasn't there more to it than that?

In 1961 the Red Sox brought the surviving members of the great 1915 team back to Boston for a reunion. During the banquet that was being held for them at the Kenmore Hotel, Jack Barry, who had taken over as manager after Carrigan's departure in 1916, told Red Sox publicity man Bill Crowley that he'd better be careful about whom he selected to throw out the first ball in the next day's festivities at the ball park.

Crowley couldn't see why there should be any difficulty about that. Bill Carrigan, as the manager of that team, seemed to be an obvious enough choice.

Barry shook his head. The Masons wouldn't like that. "Don't sit the Catholics and the Masons together tonight, either," Barry cautioned him, "or you're going to have trouble."

And, you know, Crowley had the background to understand exactly what Barry was telling him. Bill's own father had come over from Ireland shortly after the turn of the century, and he had regaled his son with stories about the APA (American Protective Association), which was the native American organization behind the "No Irish Need Apply" signs.

What broke the feud wide open, as Barry told the story, was the burning down of a convent in Charlestown. Not that the Masons on the club were happy to see the nuns thrown out into the cold, he wanted Crowley to understand. It had simply been the incident that had brought the steaming hostility to a head.

Forty-six years later the hostility was still so strongly ingrained that without any help at all from Crowley, the two camps had automatically separated themselves out at the two tables.

The belated discovery cleared up a lot of questions. Once the basic conflict had been spelled out, you could see that the two cliques had formed strictly along religious lines. No wonder nobody had wanted to talk about it.

Babe Ruth, coming out of the Catholic boys' home, had automatically attached himself to the Catholics. The near fight over a loose ball had come as a reaction to the division within the club rather than the other way around.

·   ·   ·

Well, it was not the first championship club that was wracked by dissension. You can make a pretty good case that dissension can help a team. You can make an equally good case that it can only hurt. Since the case is usually made after the fact, we can say with confidence that it didn't hurt the Red Sox. And it sure didn't bother Babe Ruth.

He was a huge success from the beginning. And there was nobody he was more successful against than the New York Yankees — so much so that he still owns the best winning percentage against them (17–5) of any left-hander in history. The first reaction upon hearing that is to think: *Gee, Babe Ruth. I guess he was some pitcher at that.* The second reaction, if you have any historical perspective, is to say: *Well, yeah, but . . .* Remember, he wasn't pitching against the Yankees as we later came to think of them. The Yankees of Murderers' Row. He was pitching for a championship Boston team against a second-division Yankee club.

Yet, when you check the records you find something that reminds you, once again, of the joys of research. You find that those second-division Yankee teams gave the championship team fits. During Babe's five years in Boston, the Yankees won 52 games and the Red Sox won 50. Take away the Babe's 17–5 and it becomes 47 for the Yankees and 33 for the Sox.

Let's fool around with that a little. In 1912, when the Red Sox won their 106 games, they wiped out the Yankees, 19 games to two. In 1915 the Red Sox won 101 games but lost the season series to the Yankees, 10 games to 12. Babe Ruth, the rookie, was credited with four of the 10 wins. Nobody else on that wondrous pitching staff beat them more than twice.

He dominated the Yankees from the pitching mound, and he also terrorized them with his bat.

Let's go back to the beginning.

In Babe's first visit to New York to play the Yankees in the Polo Grounds, he lost in 13 innings. He also hit his first major league home run. The date was May 6, 1915. During his few appearances with the Red Sox in 1914, Babe Ruth had been to bat 10 times. So far in 1915 he had batted seven times. All he had to show for those 17 times at bat was three doubles and a single.

Now he came to bat against the Yankees for the first time, leading off the third inning. The pitcher was Jack Warhop, a veteran submarine pitcher. With that name, you can bet that he was called Chief.

You could even say that anybody named Jack Warhop was born to be called Chief (except that he was actually born to be called John *Wau-hop*).

Jack Warhop will live forever as the pitcher who threw the ball that Ruth hit out of the park for his first major league home run.

Paul Shannon, who covered the Sox for the *Boston Post,* was still telling the New York writers seated around him that he had never seen anybody who could hit the ball as far as this big kid when the Babe hit Warhop's first pitch into the second tier of the right-field stands, a wallop so prodigious that some anonymous reporter went over to record that it had landed in seat 26 of section 3.

Among the hardly anonymous sports writers covering that game were Damon Runyon, writing for the *New York American,* Heywood Broun of the *New York Tribune,* and Fred Lieb of the *New York Press.* Runyon would go on, of course, to become a leading literary figure; Broun would become a powerhouse political columnist; and Fred Lieb would become the biographer of both Babe Ruth and the New York Yankees. Through the eyes of this trio of gifted writers, we are afforded the opportunity of seeing the Babe as if for the first time.

Take the name itself. Babe Ruth. The first time any of us heard that name, it had already taken on the resonance of the man's power, accomplishments, and personality. Consider, though, how the name might have struck you if you were hearing it without the history and the packaging.

Wrote Runyon:

> Fanning this Ruth is not as easy as the name and occupation might indicate. In the third inning Ruth knocked the slat out of one of Jack Warhop's underhand subterfuges, and put the baseball in the right-field stands.
>
> Ruth was discovered by Jack Dunn in a Baltimore reform school a year ago where he had not attained his left-handed majority and was adopted and adapted by Jack for use of the Orioles. He is now quite a demon pitcher and demon hitter — when he connects.

Heywood Broun was a bit more informative about the ball game:

> Ruth was put in the reform school at an early age, but seemingly he quit too soon to be completely reformed. He is still flagrantly left-

handed. Babe (he was christened George) deserved something better than a defeat. It was his home run which gave the Red Sox their first run, and later he singled twice. He missed a chance to strike a telling blow in the 11th inning, for, with a runner on first and third with only one out, he was fanned by [relief pitcher] Pieh.

Fred Lieb, who would later become the mainstay of the *Sporting News,* displayed the research and perspective for which he was noted:

> George Ruth, the sensational kid who set the International League grass on fire last season, went the entire thirteen rounds for the crimson hose and but for his support would have registered a win in regulation rounds. Warhop cooled off in the second and then Paul Shannon began to lecture on Babe Ruth's ability as a smiter. It was an illustrated lecture, as Babe illustrated Paul's remarks by lifting the pill far up in the upstairs section of the right-field stand for a merry-go-round trip.

The best copy was produced by Wilmot E. Giffin of the *Evening Journal.* Giffin was fascinated by a pitcher who could display such power. Giffin himself displays a nice little talent for prescience.

> This Ruthless Ruth, the stem-winder, is some hurler. A pitcher who is so versatile that he can not only shoot all sorts of deliveries from the port turret, but can besides all this hit a home run and a couple of incidental singles in one game is some asset, ladies and gentlemen, some asset indeed. When he is not pitching, they can use him for an outfielder and pinch-hitter. In these days of efficiency he is the ideal player. It was a genuine home run that Ruth swatted the first time up, landing in the upper tier of the south grandstand with a thump. Mr. Warhop looked reproachfully at the opposing pitcher who was so unclubby as to do a thing like that to one of his own trade. But Ruthless Ruth seemed to think that all was fair in the matter of fattening a batting average.

The unclubbiness of it all affected Giffin so deeply that he illustrated it the next day with a dollop of poetry. Poetry was the "in" thing within the sports-writing fraternity in those days, especially in those twin cultural centers of the newspaper game, New York and Chicago. To Giffin, Ruth had committed "A Social Error."

When a pitcher meets a pitcher,
  Should a pitcher clout?
When a pitcher meets a pitcher,
  Shouldn't he fan out?
When a pitcher slams a pitcher,
  Lifts it from the lot,
You would call the gink unclubby,
  Very, would you not?

"Pitcher Warhop," wrote Giffin, "has not yet recovered from the great mental anguish he suffered when a player in the same line of endeavor took one of his nicest twists and just naturally lifted it out of the lot. Warhop probably will appeal to the other pitchers to ostracize Ruth over the violation of etiquette."

If so, Pitcher Warhop was soon enough provided with Exhibit B to attach to his indictment.

Four weeks later the Red Sox are back in the Polo Grounds. The date is June 2. Once again Ruth steps up against Warhop for the first time in the game. This time it's the second inning, with two out, and a man on first. This time the ball lands in seat 31 of section 3, more than ten feet farther. This time Babe wins, 7–1, limiting the Yankees to five hits.

He has his first two home runs. There are only 712 to go.

For the moment, it was his second victory as a pitcher that was pivotal. He had come into the Polo Grounds with four straight losses. The victory in New York launched him on a six-game winning streak, and he was never going to be on the losing side of the ledger again. It was against the Yankees at Fenway Park that he won the game that put him permanently in the black, and he came back four days later to beat them again before they left town. You will remember that the Red Sox took the pennant by winning 101 games while the Detroit Tigers were winning 100. When Babe Ruth won the 101st game, he won it against the Yankees in the Polo Grounds.

That home run on the first pitch ever thrown to him in New York may not have been pivotal, in the true meaning of the word, but it certainly was a harbinger of things to come.

Nineteen eighteen was a year of transition for Babe Ruth, for the Red Sox, for the Yankees, and for the rivalry.

For the Red Sox it was going to mean a world championship for one final time. For Babe it was a year in which the best left-handed pitcher of his time began to merge with the home run king. You think his first year out of St. Mary's was something? Try this.

In 1918, with a war-shortened schedule of 126 games, he tied for the home run lead, won 13 games, and capped his pitching career by completing 29⅓ innings of consecutive shutout innings in World Series competition. In later years he would say that the record he was most proud of was that string of scoreless innings as a World Series pitcher. And yet the record came in a year when he no longer wanted to pitch.

For the Yankees, the change in their fortunes was signaled by the arrival of a new manager, Miller Huggins. Although Huggins's first team finished in fourth place, three games below .500 and 13½ games behind Boston, little Miller Huggins was able to establish a feeling of confidence that better times were a-coming.

During the first week of May, the Red Sox came strutting into the Polo Grounds with a record of 12 wins in 15 games. The Red Sox had welcomed Huggins into the American League by taking four games out of five at Fenway Park. Babe Ruth's victory in that series had brought his three-year record against the Yankees to 15–3.

The Yankees took 10 of the remaining 12 games and won the season series, 11–6.

In that three-game series in the Polo Grounds, where so much that was vital to his career occurred, the once and future careers of Babe Ruth converged, intersected, and started to unfold before our very eyes.

Babe pitched the middle game and played in the field for the first time in the finale. In both of those games there were eerie echoes of that first visit in his rookie year.

Just as in the Warhop game, he hit a home run and he was the losing pitcher. And was nonetheless the dominant player in the game.

The next day the headline read:

Babe Ruth Is Hero Though Yanks Win

Sturdy Red Sox Twirler Bears
Burden of Bunting Attack Bravely

WIELDS A VICIOUS CUDGEL

Bangs out a Double and a Home Run
and Fields Busily but Huggins
Clan is victor, 5 to 4

The reason for all that bunting was that Ruth had messed up two sacrifice bunts in a row — a routine sacrifice he had allowed to go through his legs, and then a nicely placed bunt down the third-base line, by Home Run Baker of all people, on which the Babe made an off-balance throw that hit Baker in the back of the neck. (You know what's really going on here don't you? Or are you going to tell me that Huggins hadn't been tipped off by his spy at the hotel that Babe had come in at the break of dawn, falling down drunk?)

Huggins, figuring that he might have the big fellow on the run, kept bunting. Ruth ended up with nine assists and two putouts, and was running and diving all over the place. Far from being worn out, Ruth got stronger as the game went on, both on the mound and at the plate.

The only Yankee run after the third inning came in the eighth without the benefit of a base hit when Stuffy McInnis, playing out of position at third base, threw another of those Yankee bunts away.

At the plate Babe Ruth knocked in three runs in his last two times at bat.

In the seventh he hit the ball out of the park on two successive swings. On his first swing the ball landed high up in the right-field bleachers, barely foul. The next pitch ended up even higher and considerably fairer, scoring two runs.

In the ninth inning he hit a drive to the deepest part of right-center that scored one run and — in the words of the *Times* correspondent — left the Babe "perched on second base, begging Harry Hooper to supply a single that might send him in with the tying score." Why not? Hooper already had a single, double, and triple and had also made another of those spectacular barehanded catches. But that was going to be it. "Hooper missed fire this time and the Yankees breathed easy for the first time all afternoon."

But if Hooper failed to supply the game-tying single in that one ball game, he was about to achieve something of far more lasting value. With all their left-handed–hitting outfielders off in the service, Hooper had been campaigning to get Ruth's booming bat into the line-up on a regular basis.

In the third game of the series Babe Ruth appeared in a major league game for the first time as part of the regular line-up. He was playing first base and batting sixth. First base was fortuitous. The ostensible reason was that Sox first baseman Dick Hoblitzell had a sore finger. In point of fact, Hoblitzell hadn't had a hit all week and was about to go into the army anyway. Babe always fooled around at first during fielding practice. He was quick and he was fancy. In the ballad of what-might-have-been, Ruth might very well have ended up at first if Frazee hadn't already bought the nifty-fielding Stuffy Mc-Innis from the A's in anticipation of Hoblitzell's departure.

The date was May 6, 1918, three years to the day from Babe's first home run off Jack Warhop.

The Yankee pitcher was George Mogridge. A year earlier Mogridge had pitched a no-hit game against the Red Sox at Fenway Park. What made that performance of more than usual significance was not that a left-hander had pitched a no-hitter at Fenway Park — the lively ball had not yet made its appearance — but that Mogridge remained the only Yankee left-hander to pitch a no-hitter anywhere, against anybody, until Dave Righetti did it on July 4, 1983. And did it against the Boston Red Sox.

"Ruth can cover first just as well as he can pitch," said the *Times,* "and he can bat just as well as a first baseman as he can as a pitcher."

Sure could. He had a home run and a single. The home run knocked in the first two runs of the game, and it looked as if he was going to be the story of the game again. Colonel Jake Ruppert, who was watching the game with Harry Frazee, turned to the Red Sox owner and offered to buy Ruth from him on the spot. Frazee laughed it off, but the seed had been sown.

For Ruth there would be more and more time in the field and less and less time on the pitching mound. When the Red Sox returned to the Polo Grounds at the end of June, he was leading the league with eight home runs and had become so committed to his hitting that he was refusing to do any pitching at all.

Given Babe's record against the Yankees, however, Ed Barrow had him down to pitch the opening game. Who could argue with that? Well, Babe Ruth could. That knee he had twisted sliding into second in Philadelphia, he told Barrow, he could play on it all right but it was still far too tender to withstand the rigors of pitching. Oh yeah? If it was too tender for him to pitch, barked Barrow, it was too tender for him to play. And so what you had here was the absurdity of Babe

Ruth sitting on the bench at his favorite ball park, relegated to remain there until he was willing to pitch.

But, as we know, good things always happened to Babe Ruth in the Polo Grounds. Just as the second game was about to start, Amos Strunk twisted his ankle so badly that he had to be carried off the field. Babe replaced him in center field, hit another home run — and how were you going to keep him out of the line-up?

So how did he come to pitch two games in the World Series? For the same reason that he had gone to the outfield in the first place — the thinness of talent in wartime baseball. With the Red Sox down to three worn and overworked starting pitchers, he had agreed to go back into the pitching rotation, first to help out in double-headers and then, as the pennant race quickened, to take his regular turn on the mound. During a double-header he would pitch one game and play the outfield in the other. Either way he would be batting fourth. Over the last month of the season he won seven out of nine games, including the pennant clincher, to carry the Red Sox to their third pennant in four years.

Overall, Babe took part in 95 of the 126 games, hitting an even .300. In addition to his 11 home runs, he had 11 triples and 26 doubles — 48 of his 95 hits were for extra bases. As a pitcher his record was 13–7.

The next year he electrified the country by hitting an unheard-of 29 home runs.

Having set a record for pitching in the World Series, he would spend his final year in Boston setting a home run record that was supposed to last forever.

As always, a goodly share of the excitement took place against the Yankees.

He hit his first home run of the year at the Polo Grounds on the opening day of the season, and broke the record in the last game he was ever going to play there in a Red Sox uniform. Actually, he broke the home run record at the Polo Grounds twice.

An explanation is clearly in order.

The American League record of 16 was held by Socks Seybold of the Philadelphia A's. Then came the 24 home runs hit by Gavvy Cravath of the Phillies, a twentieth-century landmark on the way to Buck Freeman's record of 25.

The American League record fell in August, Cravath's record went on Labor Day, and a week later Babe hit his twenty-sixth at the Polo Grounds to break Freeman's record. Except that some spoilsport dug through the dusty archives and came up with a guy named Ned Williamson who had hit 27 for Cap Anson's Chicago White Stockings in 1884.

How is it possible to own a home run record that nobody had ever heard of? Easy. The mystery of Ned Williamson was cleared up when it was discovered that the White Stockings had played that year in a park where the right-field fence was only 200 feet from home plate. Also, if Williamson was not listed in the pantheon of home run hitters it was because this was the first time he had hit more than three. Not to mention that he had been hitting under rules in which a foul ball didn't count as a strike and the batter was allowed to designate whether he wanted the ball thrown high or low.

Still, a home run record is a home run record, and the chase was too flavorsome to let go. There is a question that could be asked here, back across the long corridor of time. What would have happened, one wonders, if Ruth had fallen short. Would the resurrected Williamson have been listed as the home run king, or would the collective wisdom of the sports fraternity have called out in unison: "Never mind!"

The great thing about rooting for Babe, as that same sports fraternity had already discovered, was that he could be counted on to come through for you. Probably in the most dramatic way possible.

The Red Sox were ending their home season with a double-header against the Chicago White Sox, who were on their way to winning the pennant and — this is 1919, remember — throwing the World Series.

The Red Sox had designated that final day as Babe Ruth Day to honor his stupendous season, and, in order to make the day even more attractive to the paying customers, Babe had agreed to pitch the first game.

The capacity crowd that packed the park had even more than the usual reason to believe that Babe would not disappoint them. He had gone back to the pitching mound three weeks earlier to help out the financially strapped owner in the Labor Day double-header. On that day he had pitched and batted the Sox to a 2–1 win and had then made the day unforgettable by hitting the home run that tied Gavvy Cravath's record.

It was, as we now know, the last game he would ever pitch for the Red Sox. And the last game he would be playing in Boston in a Red Sox uniform. The opposing pitcher was Lefty Williams, going after his twenty-fourth win of the season.

The Babe pitched an unspectacular six innings, went out to left field with the score tied, 3–3, and won the game in the ninth inning with a line drive that still seemed to be rising when it cleared the left-field wall. A left-handed hitter was not supposed to have that kind of power to left field, and most certainly not against a top left-handed pitcher like Lefty Williams. Between games, Buck Weaver, the great Chicago third baseman, came over to the Red Sox bench to say, "That was the most unbelievable poke I ever saw."

Having tied the record, the Babe had five games left to break it, a double-header in New York followed by a three-game series in Washington. If Buck Weaver was an aficionado of the "unbelievable poke," he should have accompanied the Red Sox to New York.

Just as in Boston, the crowd stood and cheered every time the mighty Babe came to the plate. In the first game Waite Hoyt, the 19-year-old Red Sox rookie, shut out the Yankees, but Babe Ruth was shut out by the 43-year-old Jack Quinn. In the second game the Yankees' 20-game winner, Bob Shawkey, was beating the Red Sox, 1–0, going into the ninth inning.

Normally Ruth murdered Shawkey. He had already hit four home runs off him during the season. In the sixth inning he had hit a long drive to the wall in right-center, and the way Babe went tearing around the bases, it looked as if the record breaker was going to be an inside-the-park home run. In the end, the ball was handled so cleanly that he had to hold up at third. Not that it mattered. In his eagerness to break the record he had cut second base by a couple of feet, and he was called out and given credit for only a single.

Into the ninth. One last chance. The first two batters went out. Unless the score was tied, it was going to be the last time Babe would be batting in the Polo Grounds all year.

And so he hit — all together now — "the longest home run ever hit in the Polo Grounds." You want to argue? Listen to the writeup in the *New York Times:*

"Ruth stood firmly on his sturdy legs like the Colossus of Rhodes and, taking a mighty swing at the second ball pitched to him, catapulted the pill for a new altitude and distance record. . . . Ruth's glorious smash cleared the right-field grandstand by many yards and went over the woods into Manhattan Field."

No ball had ever been hit over the roof before, let alone hit into the adjoining lot.

The next year he hit another home run over the roof and into Manhattan Field. And this one, incredibly, went even farther. It was the first home run he hit while wearing a Yankee uniform. He hit it off his old buddy, the master of the hounds, Herb Pennock, on the Red Sox's first trip to New York.

But we're getting ahead of ourselves. Over two years in Boston Babe Ruth had set the record for consecutive scoreless innings in the World Series and had established an all-time home run record.

Of the two, it was the home run record that was thought to be untouchable. Baseball was still, after all, a pitcher's game, not a hitter's game.

The pitching record lasted until 1961, when it was surpassed by another Yankee left-hander, Whitey Ford.

The home run record didn't last another year. In 1920 Babe Ruth not only broke his own unbreakable record but shattered it into little pieces. He didn't quite double it, however. That was going to have to wait for one more year. In 1920 the Babe had to settle for 54.

But by then he was setting it not for the Boston Red Sox but for the New York Yankees. Harry Frazee, the sixth owner of the Red Sox, had taken care of that.

Chapter Five

Harry Frazee,
Man of Infamy

*The Ruth thing was passed on from father to son, back to
two and three generations. The story goes, and I don't think
it's apocryphal, that years later a taxi driver who was taking
Harry Frazee from the train station to the Copley Plaza recognized him. Said, "Aren't you Harry Frazee, the guy who
sold Babe Ruth?" He said he was, and the guy hit him right
in the mouth. That could well be true. We had a bunch of
tough Irishmen in this town, and they don't forgive.*

> —Bob Holbrook, former sports writer
> for the *Boston Globe*

THE dismantling of the best team in baseball did not begin with
Harry Frazee, nor did it end with Babe Ruth. The first member
of that team to be traded was its greatest player, Tris Speaker. Joe
Lannin had sold Speaker to Cleveland for $50,000 plus a couple of
throw-ins in a salary dispute which had followed the folding of the
Federal League. One of the throw-ins, Sad Sam Jones, developed
into such an outstanding pitcher that Frazee, once he got going, was
able to put him in a package for delivery to the Yankees.

Harry H. Frazee had bought a team that had won two straight
world championships. In his first year the club finished second to the
Chicago White Sox. In his second year he won a world championship.
To give him his due, he was not afraid to spend it when he had it.
Which is a way of saying that he would not have won his one cham-
pionship if he had not been willing to put up the money to buy four of
Connie Mack's top players: Joe Bush, Wally Schang, Stuffy McInnis,
and Amos Strunk.

Frazee was a theatrical producer. He was a freewheeling entrepreneur, a gambler, a con man — the quintessential Broadway hustler. Even back when he was riding high, he had not been able to buy the club outright. Joe Lannin took a note for $350,000, and it was when that note was called up following a string of theatrical reversals that Frazee was left with little choice but to sell the club or sell Babe Ruth. Better that he had sold the club.

The first players to go to the Yankees were the returning servicemen Ernie Shore, Duffy Lewis, and Dutch Leonard, for $50,000 and four marginal players. Leonard refused to report to New York and was sold to Detroit. Which was kind of a shame, for if Leonard hadn't been so uncooperative, Jake Ruppert would have ended up with the entire Red Sox pitching staff.

Taken by itself, it wasn't such a bad deal. Shore and Lewis were never the same players they had been before the war. Neither, for that matter, was Leonard. But then, the Red Sox were never the same team again, either. By 1919, when the first of the killing deals was made, the Yankees' arrow was clearly pointing up and the Red Sox arrow was already pointing down.

The first crippling sale, the deal that started the Sox down the chute, was the sale of Carl Mays. It was a sale that was going to have repercussions not only for Boston and for New York but for the American League and all of organized baseball as well. For it was the sale of Carl Mays that led, in a manner not so very indirect, to the demise of Ban Johnson and the appointment of Judge Kenesaw Mountain Landis as the sole commissioner of baseball.

Carl Mays tends to be a forgotten figure when the talk gets around to the great Boston and New York pitching staffs of that era — probably because he was the kind of guy you'd like to forget. To call Carl Mays a lying, cheating churl with paranoid tendencies would be to give him the benefit of the doubt. To call him a great pitcher but a miserable human being gets it just about right.

For nine years the careers of Carl Mays and Babe Ruth ran on a parallel course. Mays had been the star pitcher with the Providence Grays when Babe joined the team at the end of 1914, and together they had pitched the Grays to the championship, Mays with 25 wins and Ruth with his nine wins in a couple of weeks. He came to the Red Sox with Ruth in 1915, moved into the starting rotation the next season, and had a record of 61–35 over the next three years. When

Babe Ruth went to the outfield in the war-shortened season of 1918, Carl Mays replaced him as the ace of the staff, won 21 games, and went on to win the two World Series games that Babe Ruth didn't win, both by scores of 2–1.

He was the last of the submarine pitchers, a tall, long-armed right-hander who came from so far down under that he would sometimes scrape his knuckles on the mound. To make him even more fun to watch, he delivered the ball with a loud grunt. "Spectators not only can see him pitch," according to a write-up of the day, "but they can hear him pitch. With every toss of the ball he makes a noise as if he were getting a tooth pulled."

Given the strength of the Red Sox pitching staff, and the unorthodoxy of Mays's delivery, Bill Carrigan had put him out in the bullpen in his first season and brought him in to relieve in 32 games. This almost certainly makes Carl Mays the first relief specialist in baseball, if only for that one year. (Firpo Marberry, who is generally credited with being the first career relief specialist, didn't begin to come out of the bullpen until a full nine years later.)

But Carl Mays has a far greater claim on the hearts and minds of Red Sox historians. It was Carl Mays — and his place in the Red Sox Hall of Fame should be secure for this alone — who pitched a three-hitter to clinch the last world championship the Boston Red Sox were going to win for . . . well, for seven decades and counting.

It was also the last good thing that was going to happen to him in Boston. In 1919 Babe Ruth was breaking the home run record and the Red Sox were in collapse. Carl Mays was pitching as well as ever, but the team wasn't scoring for him. By June his record had fallen to 3–8. In four of his losses the Red Sox had been shut out, and, pleasant fellow that he was, he was cursing out his teammates for lack of support. When, at last, he demanded to pitch both ends of a double-header in New York, there was a suspicion that he wanted to showcase himself to Ruppert. He won the first game, 3–0, after suffering through another scoreless game into the eighth inning, but lost the second, 4–1, to his old teammate Ernie Shore.

In that second game Babe came up in the seventh inning with the tying runs on base. He had already hit seven home runs by then and was by far the best-publicized player in the game. New York fans had become pretty much resigned to having Babe Ruth beat them — he had already knocked in the winning runs for Mays in the first game —

and so when Bob Shawkey came in from the bullpen and struck him out, the Polo Grounds erupted into a wild celebration during which thousands of straw hats and scorecards were hurled out onto the field. Two days later Babe faced Shawkey again with the bases loaded and hit a grand slam home run. A lot of good that did Carl Mays.

Next time out, with the Sox being shut out behind him again in St. Louis, he fired a ball at a heckler in the stands. Ban Johnson slapped him with a $100 fine. Mays announced that he was not going to pay it.

The final blowup came on July 13 as he was pitching against the first-place Chicago White Sox. A day earlier the Red Sox had scored 12 runs for Herb Pennock, who had replaced Mays as the ace of the staff. For Mays they were doing their usual nothing. After two innings he was losing, 5–0, and as if that wasn't bad enough, Wally Schang had fired the ball so low in an attempt to catch a base stealer that he had clipped the crouching Mays on the side of the head. Mays went stalking into the clubhouse at the end of the inning, changed into his street clothes, and told Sad Sam Jones, who had been sent to fetch him, "Just tell 'em I've gone fishing."

During the next two weeks, as the Mays case became a cause célèbre, the phrase "I'm going fishing" passed into the language to mean going AWOL as a way of removing oneself temporarily from an uncomfortable situation.

A temporary vacation was not what Mays had in mind, though. Upon reaching Boston, he wired manager Ed Barrow that he hated the city and would never pitch for the Red Sox again. Ban Johnson ordered Frazee to suspend him, and warned the other teams that no deal would be approved until Mays had returned to his original club.

Fat chance. There was a hot four-team pennant race going on, and all four contenders were eager to get in on the bidding. Fat chance for three of them. Harry Frazee had already put in a call to Jake Ruppert.

On July 24 the Yankees came to Boston on the last stop of a dreadful road trip which had seen them tumble from first place to fourth. The Red Sox made it even more dreadful by taking three games out of four, with the only Yankee victory occurring when Babe Ruth, who was playing left field, killed a rally by overrunning second base. But that was all right. The Yankee owners, Colonel Ruppert and Colonel Huston, were in Boston, too, and they had already seen Babe win the opener with a two-run homer off his dearly beloved Bob Shawkey, and then take over Carl Mays's vacated spot in the pitching rotation to beat them again.

It was the last time he was ever going to pitch against the Yankees. As rusty as he was, he had managed to hold on for a not very artistic 8–6 win.

The Yankee owners stayed on in Boston for a day after the Yankees left. The morning after their departure, there were two stories vying for the headlines in the Boston press. The on-field story was that Babe Ruth had hit his sixteenth home run to tie the American League record. The off-field story was that Carl Mays had been sold to the Yankees for $40,000, plus a mediocre pitcher named Allan Russell. That $40,000 was no small price. Only Eddie Collins and Tris Speaker (at $50,000) had gone for more.

The repercussions were enormous. Ban Johnson barred Mays from the line-up, and Ruppert went into court for an injunction. Since it is a rule of American jurisprudence, long held to be inviolate, that no athletic team can ever lose a legal battle on its own home court, Ruppert won. And then he won an even bigger victory, in the post-season showdown, after Johnson had moved to invalidate everything about the deal, including the six games Mays had won for the Yankees.

The upshot to the Mays affair was that Jake Ruppert (with Harry Frazee in tow) joined Charles Comiskey, who had become Johnson's mortal enemy, to give the National League owners the additional votes they needed to elect Judge Landis over the violent and, in the end, self-destructive opposition of Ban Johnson.

Which may be why Judge Landis, stern jurist though he was reputed to be, did not kick Harry Frazee out of baseball two years later when Frazee not only completed the transfer of Boston's championship talent to New York, but did it by achieving heights of shamelessness previously undreamed of.

The Mays case was still being fought out in court when Babe Ruth was sold. And it was Harry Frazee who made the initial approach, not the other way around. He did it by sending a letter to his drinking buddy, the spectacularly named Colonel Tillinghast L'Hommedieu

Huston, offering Ruth for $125,000 plus a loan in the form of a $350,000 mortage on Fenway Park. The story goes that when Ruppert brought the offer to Miller Huggins, the little manager leaped up into the air and exclaimed, "He's cheap at twice the price. Grab him."

Although the final negotiations were completed in late December, the deal wasn't closed until Ruppert, careful businessman that he was, had Ruth's signature on a three-year contract.

The sale of Babe Ruth was announced on January 5, 1920. In Boston the shock waves would have shot right off the tape of any seismograph machine. The citizenry reacted as if a civic treasure had been stolen away. FOR SALE signs appeared on Faneuil Hall, the Boston Public Library, and most of the other historic sites of Old Boston. If Frazee had been a bag of tea, he'd have been trundled onto a frigate and thrown into Boston Harbor.

Frazee had always hung the playbills for his shows at the entrance to the ball park. His upcoming play — another flop — was named *My Lady Friends*. Across the poster somebody had scrawled: THOSE ARE THE ONLY FRIENDS HE HAS LEFT.

The irony of a showman selling off the greatest gate attraction the world of sports had ever known did not go unremarked on, either. But if Frazee's instincts as a showman had failed him, his instincts for self-preservation, mixed generously with sheer gall, remained relatively unimpaired. "It would have been impossible to start next season with Ruth and have a smooth working machine," his announcement read. Ruth had become simply impossible, the statement went on, and the Boston club could no longer put up with his eccentricities. "I think the Yankees are taking a gamble. While Ruth is undoubtedly the greatest hitter the game has ever seen, he is likewise one of the most selfish and inconsiderate men ever to put on a uniform."

In private he was trying to mollify the Royal Rooters and their satellites by telling them that Ruth was a drunk and a skirt chaser, an indictment that would have perhaps been more compelling, Lib Dooley recalls, if Frazee had not been such a notorious drunk and skirt chaser himself. "My father and his friends knew that the police were picking Babe up out of the gutter almost every night. I suspect that most people in Boston were aware of that." But since when had drunken ballplayers been regarded as a stain upon the city? "Rabbit

Maranville was playing for the Braves at the same time, and my father used to take him home to the beach house every Friday to keep
him sober."

At the end of the 1920 season, Ed Barrow followed Ruth to the Yankees as business manager. Nor did he exactly stalk away from Frazee in disgust. Frazee had recommended him to his Broadway buddies. In a way it kept things kind of chummy. Despite Ruth's 54 home
runs and Mays's 26 victories, the Yankees had finished three games
off the lead. Barrow knew exactly what was needed to make up that
deficit, and, practically speaking, he knew exactly where he could go
to get it.

   Less than two months later Boston "traded" pitcher Waite Hoyt
and catcher Wally Schang to New York, along with a couple of throw-
ins, pitcher Harry Harper and infielder Mike McNally. In return, Barrow gave the Red Sox $50,000, plus catcher Muddy Ruel and second
baseman Del Pratt. Hoyt was a 21-year-old jewel who would win
clutch games for the Yankees for years to come. Schang was a jewel
of a different kind, a wise old head behind the plate. He had handled
a superb Philadelphia pitching staff through two pennant races, and
had then come to Boston to coax and bully the thin Red Sox staff to
their last world championship.

To be scrupulously fair about this, Barrow was not giving Boston a
couple of stiffs. Del Pratt was a good-hitting second baseman with a
reputation for being particularly tough in the clutch. As for Muddy
Ruel, he was an excellent young prospect, on his way to becoming a
star. Unfortunately, he was going to be in Washington by the time he
became one. The Red Sox practically gave him away.

   Hoyt began to pay off immediately by winning 19 games to go with
Carl Mays's 27. Babe Ruth hit 59 home runs and led the world in
everything. The Yankees won their first pennant but lost out in the
World Series because Babe Ruth was forced to sit out the final three
games with an infected elbow.

   Ruppert had his pennant, but he did not have his world championship, and so what would be more natural than for Ed Barrow to go to
Boston to see what bargains might be picked up at Filene's Basement
and Fenway Park.

   That takes us to the star-crossed year of 1922, the year in which

Harry Frazee did for the New York Yankees what no other owner has ever done for another team. He gave them the pitchers they needed to round off their staff, gave them his shortstop, gave them a third baseman in the middle of the season, and on the final day of the season, with the Yankees staggering and in danger of being caught, went down to the locker room and changed his manager's pitching selection.

Under their new manager, Hughie Duffy, the Red Sox had finished 1921 in fifth place, only four games below .500, owing mostly to the pitching of Sad Sam Jones (23–16) and Joe Bush (16–9), and the always brilliant play of their shortstop, Everett ("Deacon") Scott.

Deacon Scott, if you think hard enough, was the man whose consecutive-game record was broken by Lou Gehrig. By the time he was traded to the Yankees after the 1921 season, he had 832 games under his belt and went on to run the total to 1,307.

Everett Scott is a sadly neglected player. The Red Sox were a team that won on pitching and defense, which are, of course, inseparable. The quiet little shortstop had anchored the Boston infield through three world championships. The Yankees would go on to win two pennants and a world championship as soon as he arrived. What was true then is still true today: great-fielding shortstops are what hold a championship team together, and great-fielding shortstops are quickly forgotten.

In addition to the customary $50,000, the Red Sox got Roger Peckinpaugh, a shortstop whom the Yankees had soured on, and pitchers Rip Collins and Jack Quinn. Peckinpaugh was sent to Washington immediately in a three-team deal that brought Jumping Joe Dugan from Philadelphia. Joe Dugan was not only an excellent third baseman, but he also had a little pop in his bat.

The Red Sox, stripped bare, were henceforth to answer to the description of the "lowly Red Sox" and the "cellar-dwelling Red Sox." In the next nine years they would be in that cellar eight times. Until the coming of Tom Yawkey, they would finish last nine times in 11 years and never lift their heads out of the lower depths of the second division.

That's the bad news. The good news is that while the lowly Red Sox couldn't beat anybody else in 1922, they were able to beat the Yankees so consistently as to almost prevent them from winning the pennant.

The Yankees were in a tight race throughout the season with the

St. Louis Browns, who were led by the incomparable George Sisler. This was the year that Sisler hit in 41 straight games and batted .420. Ken Williams, having a career season, was beating Ruth out for the home run title. Also having the season of his life was a second base-man named Marty McManus. (McManus has a certain serendipitous value for us here in that he would become the manager of the last last-place Red Sox team of the post-Frazee era.)

The Browns had one other thing going for them: the Boston Red Sox. The same Red Sox team that kept rising from the Valley of the Living Dead to take the season series from the Yankees, 13–9, lost 19 of their 22 games with the Browns, a swing of ten games. Turn it around and the Yankees, for all their other problems, would have won the thing laughing.

The Yankees had Babe Ruth and five great pitchers. Their only weakness was that the five pitchers were all right-handed, and Ruth kept getting himself suspended. For the Babe it was a tortured sea-son. With all those suspensions, he never really got in shape. He was gambling so heavily on the horses that there were bookies traveling with the team. The players were having fist fights on the bench. On top of everything else, Ruth and his playmates were breaking training with such enthusiasm and vigor that Judge Landis met them in Bos-ton, in the middle of the season, to deliver a lecture on the evils of gambling, women, and booze.

The lowly Red Sox thereupon beat them in four straight to knock them into second place, 2½ games behind the St. Louis Browns.

St. Louis was agog. Cardinal fans were accustomed to being agog, but the Browns had never won anything. (And they were not going to win anything until the bottom-of-the-barrel war year of 1944, when they took a meaningless pennant with a team that was so bad that it hurt the eyes to watch.)

Not only was Ruth not hitting like the mighty Babe, but the Yan-kees had sprung a noticeable leak at third base, where Mike Mc-Nally, whom Barrow had plucked from the Red Sox as the putative successor to Home Run Baker, was not getting the job done. Well, Boston had one of the best in Joe Dugan, and that was practically the same thing, wasn't it? Of course it was. Harry Frazee was no longer even bothering to show up in Boston. He was working, quite openly, out of the Yankee offices in New York.

On July 23, with the Yankees two games behind, Joe Dugan was sold to them for $50,000 plus four highly disposable players. That wasn't what the announcement said, you understand. The announcement said, as always, that there had been "no cash consideration involved."

Howls of outrage went up in St. Louis. Indignation on behalf of the poor little Brownies was felt everywhere. Commissioner Landis, having only recently established his power to do anything "for the good of baseball" by barring the Black Sox players for life, retreated into a strict reading of the rule and announced that, outrageous as the deal had been, there was nothing he could do about it. (Since Judge Landis was not a man to countenance an outrage after it no longer mattered, he laid down a June 15 trading deadline after the season was over.)

To rub the noses of the Brownies in it even further, Dugan had changed locker rooms in New York just in time to accompany his new teammates to St. Louis. With their new third baseman leading the way, the Yankees took three out of four and left St. Louis with a half-game lead. It was the first time they had been in first place in six weeks.

Through the rest of the season the deal for Dugan hung over the race like a dark cloud — a dark cloud that was going to come very close to precipitating a tragedy.

The Yankees arrived in St. Louis in mid-September, still leading the Browns by half a game. It was to be one of the great series in Yankee history. And for as long as the beloved little Brownies existed, it was THE series in the barren book that was written by the St. Louis Browns.

Passions were still running so high in St. Louis that a mob was waiting at the railroad station on Friday night to give vent to some righteous indignation and — as long as they were up so late — shower Babe Ruth with invective and spittle.

For the Saturday game an overflow crowd of 33,000 somewhat overwrought fans, the largest in the history of the franchise, overran the ball field. Before the day was over, there would be mounted policemen and rioting fans on the field. Also blood. Actually, the blood came first.

It happened in the eighth inning, with the Browns leading, 1–0. Whitey Witt and Bob Meusel were converging on a fly ball when a bottle thrown from the bleachers hit Witt right between the eyes, opening up a gash on his forehead down to the bone and knocking him cold.

That was when the emotions of the fans in the roped-off outfield erupted. "We got Witt!" they screamed as they came after Meusel. "Now we're going to get you!" The rioting came to a stop only when they saw the still unconscious Witt being carried off the field, looking more dead than alive. A blood-soaked towel covered his head. The concussion had knocked the bottom out of the bottle.

For as long as the franchise existed, there was a tradition in St. Louis that the idiot bottle thrower had lost the pennant for the greatest Browns team of all time. The infuriated Yankees, having recaptured the moral high ground, came roaring back in the ninth to beat the shaken and rather shamefaced Browns. Although St. Louis recovered to win the second game, the Yankees took the crucial final game when — action, drama, roll 'em — Whitey Witt came off the bench in the ninth inning, still heavily bandaged, to knock in the tying and winning runs.

But it still wasn't completely over. When the first-place Yankees came to Boston at the end of the season, they still needed one win over the last-place Red Sox to clinch the pennant. Common sense, the law of averages, and the wisdom of the ages seemed to dictate that the Yankees would not only take the game they needed but would probably sweep the series and come out of the season competition with an even split.

In the first game the ex-Yankee Rip Collins beat them, 3–1. In the second game ex-Yankee Jack Quinn beat them, 1–0. Waiting in the wings to bring down the curtain was Herb Pennock, who had already beaten them three straight times.

Harry Frazee came into the clubhouse before the game and ordered Hugh Duffy to pitch Alex Ferguson, an undistinguished right-hander whom the Red Sox had picked up from the Yankees during the season on waivers. Not only had the Yankees defeated Ferguson the previous two times they had faced him, they had clobbered him.

Ferguson never got a man out. Witt and Dugan singled. Babe Ruth, who was in a terrible slump, beat out a bunt to fill the bases. Wally Pipp knocked in two runs with a line single, and, after Pennock had been rushed into the game, Ruth scored on a long fly. Over the rest of the game Pennock stopped the Yankees cold on two hits. The

Red Sox threatened and threatened against Waite Hoyt and Joe Bush but could score only one run.

You are never going to guess who Pennock was pitching for the following year. Well, the Yankees needed a left-hander to go with those five righty starters, didn't they?

In lamenting the Dugan deal as "another disgusting trade between the Red Sox and the Yankees," the *Boston Herald* had called Joe Dugan "the last outstanding player left of all the great Boston players who once wore the red hose." With the sale of Pennock, the cupboard was stripped completely bare.

Completely. Down in Columbia, South Carolina, the Red Sox had a big right-handed pitcher named George Pipgras, who was striking everybody out. Pipgras was sold to the Yankees, too.

In 1923, when the Yankees won their first world championship, 11 of the 24 players on their roster had come from the Red Sox. It was Ernie Shore, who had been the first to go, who put it best: "The Yankee dynasty," he said, "was the Red Sox dynasty in Yankee uniforms."

Harry Frazee was gone by then. He had stuck around just long enough to help his New York benefactors celebrate the opening of Yankee Stadium. He marched to the flagpole with Ruppert and Huston behind John Philip Sousa and the Seventh Regiment Band. He sat in the owners' box with Ruppert and watched Babe Ruth hit a three-run homer to beat the Red Sox, 4–1. ("I'd give a year of my life if I could hit a home run today," Babe had said before the game.)

No sooner had he sold the Red Sox than his luck changed. In 1925 he regained his fortune and stature by producing one of the great musical hits of the twenties, *No, No, Nanette*. When he died four years later, his best friend, Mayor Jimmy Walker, was at his bedside. Dapper, debonaire Jimmy Walker, the living symbol of New York.

All of Boston did not mourn.

On pitchers alone, here's what Harry Frazee did.

For three consecutive years the American League leaders in winning percentage were:

1921   Carl Mays, 27–9

1922   Joe Bush, 26–7

1923   Herb Pennock, 19–6 (followed by Sam Jones, 21–8, and Waite Hoyt, 17–9)

In 1927 it was Waite Hoyt, at 22–7.

In 1928 George Pipgras was the winningest pitcher at 24–18.

Except for Bob Shawkey, the Red Sox alumni pitched every one of the Yankees' World Series victories from 1921 to 1926. And, as you can see from the following summation, they started practically every game up to 1932. (The underlined name connotes the winning pitcher. Names in capital letters are former Red Sox players.)

1921: MAYS and HOYT pitched shutouts in the first two Series games. They were followed by Shawkey, MAYS, HOYT, HARPER, MAYS, HOYT.

The Yankees lost the last two games of the Series when Mays was beaten, 2–1, and Hoyt, 1–0.

In 1922 it was BUSH, Shawkey, HOYT, MAYS, BUSH.

With the Yankees' troubles continuing into the World Series, the Giants defeated them in a sweep. (There were five games because Game 2 was a 10-inning tie.)

1923: HOYT, PENNOCK, JONES, Shawkey (save by PENNOCK), BUSH, PENNOCK.

Only one game not started by a Red Sox transfer, and Pennock finished that game in relief.

SAM JONES lost his one World Series start, 1–0, on Casey Stengel's famous nose-thumbing home run.

1926: PENNOCK, Shocker, Ruether, HOYT, PENNOCK, Shawkey, HOYT.

Waite Hoyt lost the final game, 3–2, on three unearned runs.

1927: HOYT, PIPGRAS, PENNOCK, Wilcy Moore.

1928: HOYT, PIPGRAS, Zachary, HOYT.

In 1932 PIPGRAS won another game and PENNOCK had two saves.

To sum up, Hoyt had six World Series wins, Pennock five, Pipgras three, Mays one, and Bush one.

What made it all especially galling was that the pitchers were relatively young and generally long-lived. Here are the ages of the pitchers when they were sold, and the number of victories they won after they left Boston.

Carl Mays	28 years old	132 wins
Waite Hoyt	22 years old	227 wins
Sam Jones	29 years old	161 wins
Joe Bush	28 years old	87 wins
Herb Pennock	26 years old	164 wins
George Pipgras	23 years old	102 wins

Add it up and you get 873 victories that went elsewhere.

In 1930 the Yankees bought Charlie Ruffing. Ruffing was a fast-ball pitcher who had consistently led the league in losses while he was in Boston. Clubhouse man Bill Giffin told Ed Walton, the Red Sox historian, that Ruffing, who was apparently a student of Carl Mays, had deliberately dogged it in order to get himself traded to the Yankees.

Be that as it may, Charlie Ruffing, the big loser for the Red Sox, became Red Ruffing, the huge winner and Hall of Fame pitcher for the Yankees.

Add Ruffing to the roster and you get seven more World Series victories and 234 more wins.

That's a lot of lost victories over a lot of years. But it wasn't the pitchers who were a wound to the heart. It was the Babe. THE BABE. You could look at the pitchers, recognize that they were professional baseball players, and almost forget after a while that they had once toiled in Fenway Park.

Babe Ruth was different. The Babe was never looked upon as an enemy player in Boston. He was looked upon as a blood relative whom the gypsies had stolen away.

Babe understood that. So did the New York sports writers. In New York he reigned on the sports pages. In Boston he was always front-page news.

With no World Series to play in 1930, he agreed to help the Red Sox draw some extra people — and have a little fun for himself —

by pitching the final game of the season. A wholly meaningless affair between a perennial last-place club and a Yankee team that had finished a disappointing third. In Boston that was a front-page story — and in the biggest, blackest type.

BABE RUTH AGAIN
STARS AS HURLER

Returns to Box After 12 Years and Beats Red Sox 9–3; Blanks Old Mates for First Five Innings

When he made the decision to retire, he waited until the Yankees came into Boston before making his announcement. The first thing that happened was that the Red Sox declared Sunday to be Farewell to Babe Day. The second thing that happened was the largest crowd in Red Sox history came charging into Tom Yawkey's newly enlarged park to pay him homage.

John Drebinger was covering the game for the *New York Times:* "A crowd of 48,000 jammed its way into Fenway Park. It was the largest crowd ever to see the Red Sox play in this city and its enthusiasm overflowed all bounds. It also overflowed on the playing field in a solid mass from the right-field foul lines to the center-field flagpole, while outside the portals of the park some 15,000 more stormed and fumed in the streets because they could get no nearer to the scene."

There was a time, wrote Drebinger, when you could have guaranteed that the Babe would celebrate such an occasion by giving the fans the home run they were screaming for. The best he could do was a single and a double.

The Babe was growing old.

Chapter Six

The Rubaiyat of Babe's Sixty: 1927

Most Bostonians go to Yankee–Red Sox games to give the glad hand to Babe Ruth. The local fans hold the Babe in more affection and esteem than those of any other city, not excluding New York. It was here that the Bambino started his unique career, and he always will be considered a home town product.

— Herb Allen, *New York Post*

THE 1927 edition of the New York Yankees won 110 games, breaking the record set by the 1912 Red Sox. By general agreement they were the Greatest Team of All Time.

The *team* average was .307. Earle Combs, the lead-off man, hit .356 and set a Yankee record with 231 base hits. The combined batting average of the outfield — Combs (.356), Ruth (.356), and Meusel (.337) — has never been equaled. Four members of the starting line-up knocked in more than 100 runs: Gehrig (175), Ruth (164), Meusel (103), and Lazzeri (102). Lou Gehrig hit .373 and Tony Lazzeri hit .309.

More than anything else, as well we know, 1927 is the year in which was writ the *Rubaiyat* of the Babe's 60 home runs. The REAL home run record. Don't tell me about that other guy. There is something so round and right about the Babe's 60, so cylindrical; as complete and inevitable as a circle, as mystical as a crystal ball.

In hitting 60 home runs that year Babe Ruth hit more homers all by himself than any other entire team in the American League.

Add Lou Gehrig's 47 home runs, and between them they hit just short of 25 percent of all homers hit in the league.

The Red Sox? Well, for the first half of the season the Boston Red

Sox were the worst team in the history of baseball, unless you can dig up some other club that came up to July 4 with a worse record than 15 wins and 54 losses.

• The Yankees won their first six games and were never out of first place.
• The Red Sox lost their first six games and were never out of the cellar.
• The Yankees won the season series, 18–4, their largest spread ever, and yet the Red Sox could point to two famous victories at Fenway Park.
• In three of the four Red Sox victories, the winning pitcher was a young left-hander named Hal ("Pinky") Wiltse.
• Despite the Yankee runaway, the whole country became captivated by the home run derby between Babe Ruth and Lou Gehrig. Babe and Lou went head to head for 129 games, in what started as a race against each other and escalated into a run at the Babe's record of 59.
• The battle between Ruth and Gehrig was joined in a five-game series at Fenway Park in June, and was settled in a five-game series at Fenway Park in September.
• In that battle, to a remarkable degree the showdown kept occurring in the 22 games against their poor relatives, the Boston Red Sox.
• Each of them — Ruth and Gehrig — had his greatest day of the season at Fenway Park.
• Each of them hit 11 home runs against the Red Sox.
• Twelve of the 22 games were played at Fenway Park. If you want to know why, stick around.

Although the Yankees had come back from a disastrous seventh-place finish in the year of Babe Ruth's "bellyache" to win a narrow upset victory in 1926, they were very far from being the favorite to repeat. For one thing, they had been upset by the underdog St. Louis Cardinals in the World Series. For another, Connie Mack had a rising young team in Philadelphia led by Lefty Grove, who was just coming into his own, and Jimmy Foxx, Mickey Cochrane, Al Simmons, and Jimmy Dykes, plus two remarkable graybeard additions in Ty Cobb and Eddie Collins.

   An Associated Press poll of 100 players showed the Athletics as an overwhelming favorite. Professional odds makers listed the A's at

2–1, with the Yankees at 3–1 and Washington at 7–2. The New York beat writers, who presumably knew the ball club better than anybody else, were picking them no better than third or fourth. Even Fred Lieb, who had achieved some degree of fame as the only writer to have picked the Yankees to win in 1926, was giving them almost no chance to repeat.

The Red Sox's hopes were buoyed for about a minute and a half by the return of manager Bill Carrigan, who had been coaxed back from his banking interests in Maine. Which kind of made you wonder. Nine years earlier Miller Huggins had been hired by the Yankees only after Carrigan had turned the job down. Turning down the Yankees could be defended. Coming back with the Red Sox of 1927 said a great deal for Carrigan's bravery, loyalty, and sterling New England character. It also cast grave doubts on his sanity.

The manager for the preceding three years had been Lee Fohl, otherwise known as Dr. Hope, or the Doctor of Hopeless Causes. With even more justification he could also have been called the Master of Unluck. As the manager of the Cleveland Indians, he had moved the club up from seventh to sixth to second, and was making a serious run at the pennant in 1919, when he ran headlong into Babe Ruth.

It was a classic situation. Bases loaded, two out, last of the ninth, and the Indians leading the Red Sox by three runs. Fohl brought in a left-handed relief pitcher named Fritz Coumbe. The Babe crushed the first pitch into the right-field stands, and Fohl returned to the hotel just in time to discover that he had been fired. The next year the Indians won the pennant and the World Series for Tris Speaker.

In 1921 Lee Fohl was hired to manage the St. Louis Browns. Same bad luck. The combination of the Dugan trade, the bottle bounced off Witt's head, and Frazee's visit to the Boston clubhouse conspired to beat him out of the 1922 pennant. Halfway through the following season he was fired.

Just the man, as anybody should have been able to see, to work his magic upon the dismal Red Sox. Don't laugh. It was Lee Fohl who brought them out of the dungeon and up to seventh place, a scant 25 games behind the Indians.

But that was it. They spent the next two years back in the familiar surroundings of the cellar and doing worse than ever, losing 105 and 107 games. So long, Dr. Hope. Hello, Bill Carrigan.

(Lee Fohl, out of baseball, lost all his money in the 1929 market crash — Wall Street's equivalent of the Boston Red Sox — and ended his life pumping gas at a Cleveland filling station. The Red Sox of the 1920s could do that to you.)

As for the Babe, he had hit his record-setting 59 home runs in 1921 and hadn't hit as many as 50 since. In view of his travails over those six intervening years, nobody expected him to come close again. Including Babe himself. His body had turned to fat, his features had become gross. His only remaining ambition, he confided on his first visit to Boston, was to finish with 500 home runs. "A pretty big assignment," he was willing to concede, "considering that I'm 33 and I only have 359 so far."

For Babe Ruth, the season with which he was going to become perpetually identified could not have started more ignominiously. Miller Huggins pulled him out of the opening game for a pinch-hitter after the Babe had struck out twice with men on base.

Huggins's explanation was that Babe was suffering from a bilious attack that had rendered him blind, and if his story was greeted with a certain skepticism, it could have been because in the private language of the world of sports, "bilious" has always been a code word for "drunk."

Some of the New York writers were so unkind as to suggest that he had been blinded not by anything he had eaten or imbibed but by Lefty Grove's fast balls.

Whatever the reason, the first time the Red Sox came to New York, Babe was still in such a terrible slump that when Pinky Wiltse pitched the Sox to their first victory of the season, Babe Ruth was the best thing he had going for him. Two timēs the Yankees had Wiltse hanging on the ropes, and on both occasions Babe had given him new hope and sustenance by hitting back to the box for a double play.

When he came to Boston for the first meeting at the end of April, Babe had only three home runs and three runs batted in. Gehrig, who had got off smoking, had four homers and had knocked in 21 runs.

The Babe loved to hit in Fenway Park. But, then, so did Lou Gehrig. Lou had hit his first major league home run at Fenway — in the first game he ever played in Boston — after he had been called up as a 19-year-old kid at the end of the 1923 season. His first two home runs in the current season had been hit against the Red Sox in New York.

In hitting, as in all things, Ruth and Gehrig were perfectly orchestrated. Babe's power came from a sweeping, full-bodied swing. Gehrig spread himself across the batter's box and attacked the ball like a woodsman chopping down a tree. A typical Gehrig home run shot out of the park on a line, and it could just as easily leave the park in left field as in right field — or anywhere in between.

Babe Ruth announced that he was feeling "hitterish" as 30,000 fans showed up at the park. First time up he hit a home run into the right-field stands. Second time he doubled high off the wall in left — "high" meaning that the ball touched down on the very top of the wall and spun back onto the field. He also had a single and a walk, his first big day of the season.

Home had come the Babe.

Before the Yankees left town, they suffered the humiliation of losing to the Red Sox for a second time. Once again their nemesis was little Pinky Wiltse. To make it even more humiliating, the Yankees were breezing along with a 2–0 lead as the Red Sox came up in the ninth. And then, suddenly, the bases were loaded with nobody out. Jack Rothrock, a young infielder, was sent up as a pinch-hitter. Rothrock doubled in two runs to tie the score and then scored the winning run himself on a wild pitch to Fred Haney.

(Jack Rothrock was going to pop up again in the record books as the hard-hitting right-fielder for the Gashouse Gang in St. Louis, the one member of that fabled ball club whose name nobody could ever seem to remember. And Fred Haney is the same Fred Haney who would manage Milwaukee to a world championship over the Yankees in 1957.)

For the Red Sox, it was only their third victory in 12 games, and two of them were against the Yankees. For the Yankees, the loss had dropped them into a tie with the Philadelphia A's, the only day in the entire season when they would not hold undisputed possession of first place.

It looked as though Wiltse was going to make it three straight when his teammates gave him a 5–0 lead on a one-day stopover in Yankee Stadium at the end of May. But then the Yankees, led by Ruth, caught up with him. Babe hit a slicing drive over the left-field fence and was off on a home run rampage that had him leading Gehrig, 22–17, by the time the Yankees came to Boston for their five-game series in June.

There being no Sunday baseball in Boston, the series was scheduled to open on a Monday, and in those circumstances it had become the custom for fans to come in by train or bus from all over New England to spend the weekend in the big city and stay over to see the Babe.

The Monday game was rained out, so now there would be a double-header on Tuesday, a double-header on Wednesday, and a single game on Thursday.

A dinner honoring the Yankees' slugging second baseman Tony Lazzeri was held on the night of the rained-out game. During that dinner Ruth answered the inevitable question by reminding his audience, as he always did, that he wasn't being pitched to often enough to break his home run record. He had then added gratuitously, and perhaps generously, that the only player who did have a chance was Lou Gehrig.

Tony Lazzeri had become the idol of Italian fans everywhere following a tremendous freshman year. His 18 home runs were third, behind Ruth's 47 and Al Simmons's 19, and he had tied for second (114) in runs batted in. As the 1927 season began, Lazzeri was being rated pretty much on a par with Lou Gehrig as the great young power hitter of the future.

The newspapers referred to him as "Tony the Wop," "the Walloping Wop," "the Foremost Spaghetti Farmer." Obviously everybody was more relaxed about these things in those days, including Lazzeri himself. Among his fellow players he was known, not without affection, as "Poosh 'Em Up Tony," and when he was asked how he had got that nickname, he answered, "Well, when I was in San Francisco, there were these old wops who used to sit together in the bleachers and they didn't speak English very well and . . ."

Between the Italians who came out to honor Lazzeri and the out-of-towners who had stayed over yet another day to see the Babe, there were 16,000 people in the stands for the Tuesday double-header. Pitching for the Yankees were Herb Pennock and Waite

Hoyt, an inopportune pairing that inspired the *Boston Post* sports cartoonist to draw Pennock and Hoyt strolling out to the pitching mound together, dragging a couple of bedraggled little Red Sox dolls behind them. "You made us what we are today," they were singing in a paraphrase of a popular song of the day. "We hope you're satisfied."

The crowd was there, as the accounts of the game made clear, in the hope of seeing Babe Ruth hit at least one home run.

The headline on Paul Shannon's story in the *Boston Post* read:

Yanks Hand Sox
Double Licking

Babe Just Misses Homer
Has a double and two singles

The "near miss" wasn't that near. It was a long foul ball that would have gone completely unnoticed if anybody else had hit it.

The Babe was, however, playing on a bad ankle, which he had twisted in the batter's box during an exhibition game in Springfield. And while the two days' rest had undoubtedly been helpful, it had not been helpful enough. "He nearly swung himself off his feet several times," wrote Shannon, "in his efforts to drive the ball out of the park."

There was also the usual giddy commentary about one of Babe's mile-high flies, "lifted so high in the air that Ira Flagstead [the Sox center-fielder] nearly became dizzy waiting for it to drop."

You have to read halfway through Shannon's account before you discover that there had been a Yankee home run after all. "This was secured by Lou Gehrig who registered his eighteenth of the season and now stands but four behind the Babe."

It was, for the curious, a rising line drive over the wall in deep left-center. In other words, a blast.

For Wednesday's double-header there were 15,000 people in the park. And this time they were amply rewarded.

Two For Bam as Yanks Take Pair

Mighty Drives at Fenway Park

Yes, siree. "Big Babe Ruth, still the Colossus of Swat, in spite of ambitious rivals, did his stuff," wrote Shannon, "not only once but twice, and in a way that brought joy to the thousands who root just as loyally for him now as when he wore the livery of the Red Sox."

For five innings Hal Wiltse had been doing it to them again. Even unto striking Ruth out in the first inning with a big sweeping curve. The Babe tied it in the fifth with two out: "A tremendous swat which cleared the left-field fence, far down the flag pole opening, the ball crossing the street and colliding violently with a building on the opposite side."

The Red Sox handed the lead back to Wiltse in the seventh, Babe Ruth took it back in the eighth.

> Meeting the ball squarely at the end of his tremendous swing, he drove it far into the air and far out of bounds, the hit being, in the opinion of veteran fans, the hardest he had ever made at Fenway Park. The ball sailed away to right center. It shot like a rocket between the center-field seats and the right-field stands, landing down in the alley that divides these bleachers and hitting the brick garage that lies beyond on the third bound. The drive easily carried more than 500 feet.

He had previously saved the game, as James C. O'Leary of the *Globe* took care to inform his readers, with a pair of great running catches. And, as O'Leary also reported, he gave all the kids in the crowd a thrill by striking out on his final time at bat "on three air-shattering swings."

With the fifth and final game of the series being played on Thursday, the Boston fans were duly alerted that it was going to be their last chance to see Babe Ruth until the Yankees returned on Labor Day, a full 10 weeks — and 68 games — down the road.

They came out in force to see Babe Ruth, and they stayed to watch Lou Gehrig have a day that not even a Boston headline writer could ignore.

Gehrig Hits Three Homers for Yanks

Close to Babe's Track Now with 21

Babe Ruth had never hit three home runs in a regularly scheduled game. He had done it twice in World Series games, but never during the season. Two weeks earlier Tony Lazzeri, who would have some enormous days with the bat over the course of his career, had become the first Yankee ever to do it. Gehrig's day in Boston, therefore, carried a double message, one on behalf of the team and the other on behalf of himself.

This Yankee offense, it announced, was fearsome beyond anything that had ever been seen before. And Lou Gehrig, it said, was here to stay. Only a week earlier Lou had fallen as many as seven homers behind the Babe. Not only had he come back to cut that deficit by more than half, but he had achieved a personal high with the season not yet half over.

Even more dramatic was the way he did it. "Take them blow for blow," said James Harrison of the *New York Times,* "and they were three blows as handsome and as far as any man has ever hit in one game. Nearly every one was as far flung as Ruth's second home run in the first game yesterday."

The first one was over the wall in left-center, almost in the same spot where both he and Ruth had hit them in the previous games. The others were even longer. The second was a line drive that landed in the center-field seats, the third a booming fly ball that went high and deep into those same center-field bleachers. It was the first time anybody had ever hit two home runs into those bleachers in the same game.

The first time anybody had ever . . . Hey, what was going on here? Babe Ruth was supposed to have the patent on that one.

The Home Run was no longer a wholly owned subsidiary of Babe Ruth, Inc. That was the real message coming out of Gehrig's great day in Boston.

A week later, with the Red Sox in New York for three games, Lou caught him and went ahead. In the opening game he hit one of Wiltse's slow curves halfway up into the right-field bleachers to put the Yankees ahead to stay.

The next day both Gehrig and Ruth hit their twenty-fifth off Slim Harriss, the closest thing the Red Sox had to an ace. In the first inning Gehrig hit a 2–0 pitch into the stands with Ruth on base to move ahead of him for the first time in seven weeks. Three innings later Babe hit a 2–0 pitch into the same stands and they were tied again. And that told you something, too. In the days of "inside" or pre-Ruthian baseball, nobody swung at a 2–0 or 3–1 pitch. As part of the revolution he had wrought, Ruth was allowed to swing at the cripple, and by 1927 a few other well-established power hitters were also being given the green light. Lou Gehrig had entered that august company.

On the third day Lou Gehrig hit his twenty-sixth to pull into the lead. Nine of Lou's 26 had been hit against Boston versus five of the Babe's 25. But that was O.K. The season was still only about half over. And Babe had an appointment to keep at Fenway Park in September.

By then the Yankees would have played a home-and-home series against every other team in the American League, with a second western swing thrown in for good luck.

While the Boston fans were waiting, they could follow the progress of what was shaping up as the most tingling head-to-head home run competition ever seen.

Before the Yankees headed west, however, there was a game to be played in Washington against the suddenly red-hot Senators and then a quick jump back to New York for a Fourth of July double-header.

Before a near-sellout crowd in Washington, Ruth tied Gehrig by hitting "the longest home run ever hit into the center-field bleachers at Griffith Stadium," a drive that traveled well over 450 feet.

The next day back in New York, the largest crowd in the history of Yankee Stadium, 72,641, stormed the park, filling every aisle and crevice and screaming every time Ruth or Gehrig came to bat. It was Gehrig, not the Babe, who gave them reason to keep on screaming. In the opener he had a three-run homer off Walter Johnson. In the second game he hit a grand slam, high into the right-center-field bleachers.

Lou Gehrig was leading Ruth, 28–26, as the Yankees embarked on a 15-game road trip through the West the likes of which had never been seen before.

The spotlight had been turned on Gehrig. "Just one colossus is straddling the baseball world this pleasant morning," wrote George C. Daley of the *New York World*. "Mr. Henri Louis Gehrig, named for two kings and a king in his own right."

Dan Daniel of the *World-Telegram* was ready to celebrate the coronation of a new home run king, too. "It seems to be slightly better than an even bet that Lou Gehrig will beat Babe Ruth in the great Home Run Derby of 1927. While it does not appear likely that Lou will excel the Babe's record of 59 homers, even that is not without the plane of probability."

Writers are slaves to the story. For seven years everything written about the Yankees had been pinwheeling around Babe Ruth. Here, dropped into the reporters' laps, was fresh copy. They'd have given Gehrig the full treatment regardless. As it happened, they were more than ready to embrace a new star, not just as an offset to the Babe but as a club to beat Babe Ruth over the head with.

Just before the Red Sox came to town for the series that was going to push Gehrig front and center, a wire-service story out of Washington reported that George Herman Ruth, Jr., had filed an income tax appeal with the Treasury Department in which he was claiming that during 1924 he had "expended the sum of $9,000 for the purpose of establishing and maintaining good will to the extent of entertaining sports writers, press agents, and others similarly situated in order to constantly keep himself before the public."

Oh, come on. Babe Ruth had to pay for publicity? Obviously this was lawyers' business. You don't have to read much between the lines to realize that a $9,000 "deficiency assessment" had been posted against Ruth and that the people who handled such matters for him had found something in the tax code that allowed them to claim that kind of a deduction. In all probability the phraseology had come right out of the code itself.

But who knew anything about income taxes in 1927, except that they were something that the filthy rich had to pay?

The writers, who probably were not happy to find themselves coupled with press agents to begin with, were most sensitive to any suggestion that they were on the take, especially since they were. Those were the days when New York sports writers — and we're talking about the best of them — lined up outside fight promoter Tex Rickard's office for their envelopes. Looming on the immediate horizon, as it happened, for both Rickard and the objects of his largesse were a couple of prospective gold mines, Dempsey versus Sharkey, and the rematch of Dempsey and Tunney.

And there was this about it, too: $9,000 was not exactly a couple of dinners at the Plaza. Lou Gehrig's entire salary for the year came to only $7,500.

So the New York writers turned their brightest spotlight on Gehrig, and discovered that there was nothing there. At first glance

Jess Tannehill was the first player to be traded between the Yankees and the Red Sox. He won 21 games in 1904 to help the Red Sox to their first pennant. *(National Baseball Library, Cooperstown, N.Y.)*

Elston Howard's transfer to the Red Sox in August 1967 gave the Red Sox the wise old head needed to pull off the Impossible Dream. *(Courtesy of the Boston Red Sox)*

Traded to the Yankees in 1972, Sparky Lyle won the most valuable player award in 1977 and was a major contributor to three straight Yankee pennants. *(Courtesy of the Boston Red Sox)*

Traded to the Red Sox in 1986, Don Baylor knocked in 91 runs as the Red Sox won their first pennant in eleven years. *(Courtesy of the Boston Red Sox)*

Joe Cronin and Joe McCarthy, a couple of lantern-jawed Irishmen going chin to chin at the time of Cronin's first visit to Yankee Stadium as the manager of the Red Sox. *(National Baseball Library, Cooperstown, N.Y.)*

May 30, 1938: Decoration Day double-header before the largest crowd in the history of the Rivalry. Joe Cronin is ready to decorate Yankee outfielder Jake Powell with that cocked right fist. Number 14 is Boston pitcher Archie McKain, who started it all by plunking Powell on the noggin, possibly at Cronin's suggestion. The Yankee coach tugging at Cronin's sleeve is Art Fletcher. Number 1 is another shortstop out of San Francisco, Frank Crosetti. *(AP/Wide World Photos)*

Is he safe? The dispute that has reverberated down through the decades. Johnny Pesky is sliding home on a squeeze play with the run that puts the Red Sox ahead of the Yankees for the first time in the 1949 season. Against the evidence of the photos, umpire Bill Grieve *(bottom)* rules that Pesky has slid under rookie catcher Ralph Houk's tag. Number 2 is Al Zarilla. *(AP/Wide World Photos)*

Ellis Kinder, who preserved the lead by setting down six straight Yankee batters following the Pesky run, is being congratulated by his pal Arthur Richman of the *New York Daily Mirror.* A week later Kinder would pitch the most famous game in the history of the Rivalry after an all-night drinking session with Richman. Richman is now a senior vice president of the Yankees. *(Courtesy of Arthur Richman)*

Before and after the collision. Thurman Munson, caught at the plate on an unsuccessful squeeze attempt, is about to come barreling into his archenemy, Carlton Fisk. *(Courtesy of Dick Johnson)*

Carlton Fisk, bridged over the plate, is about to tag out archenemy Thurman Munson, who is trying to scramble back over the bridge. *(Courtesy of the Boston Red Sox)*

Billy Martin and Reggie Jackson clowning for the camera during the off day before Game 3 of the 1977 World Series. The big joke here is that everyone knows that Billy and Reggie hate each other's guts. *(Photo by Walter Iooss, Jr., © Time, Inc.)*

RICH GOSSAGE
Pitcher
1983

Goose Gossage: A friendly Goose smiles good-naturedly from the sidelines, and a wild-eyed, distinctly unfriendly Goose comes flying at the batter from the mound at Yankee Stadium. *(National Baseball Library, Cooperstown, N.Y.)*

Bucky Dent's final leap into immortality, October 2, 1978. Notice how many of the fans in the background are still looking out toward the left-field screen in disbelief. The happy teammates greeting the happier Dent are Roy White and Chris Chambliss. *(UPI)*

Luis Tiant, the soul of the Boston Red Sox through the Seventies. *(Courtesy of Dick Johnson)*

Top: The heart of the Yankee line-up in the late Forties and early Fifties. Allie Reynolds, Bobby Brown, Joe DiMaggio, Gene Woodling, and Jerry Coleman *(AP/Wide World Photos); bottom:* Hank Bauer, Yogi Berra, Billy Martin, and Joe Collins *(National Baseball Library, Cooperstown, N.Y.).*

you'd have thought he'd be a natural. Pleasantly handsome, with curly blondish hair and an extremely attractive smile, complete with dimples that you could have lost Shirley Temple in. Unfortunately, you could have lost his personality in there too. With Ruth, the writers had had to tone it down. With Gehrig, they not only had to beef it up, they had to make it up.

In earlier stories Gehrig had been treated with an amusement bordering on disdain. He was, as even the dullest reader could not help but discern, a mama's boy. "He takes his car after the game, on hot summer evenings, calls for his mother, and then spins down to Rockaway for a session at the hook and line." He was always home and in bed by 10:30. "There are no girls in his life as yet. The letters he receives at the hotels on the road are all from his mother."

And cheap? At a time when baseball players were guys who split a 50-cent taxi ride five ways, Gehrig qualified as the cheapest of the cheapskates. "Frugal" was the word most often used to describe him, and you could almost hear the writers clear their throats as they typed it out. Claire Ruth, when she finally got around to writing her memoirs, approached the matter gingerly. "Babe's $5 tips when 50 cents would have been generous were ridiculous," she wrote. "But Lou's ten-cent tips were ridiculous too."

He remained so . . . frugal . . . even after he had become one of the highest-paid players in the game that clubhouse men all around the American League hated to see him coming.

The New York writers faced the problem without flinching. How, they had to ask themselves, could they tie the mother's boy image and the German frugality together to give the guy some semblance of a personality?

How about this: he derived his power from his mother's pickled eels.

They also did their level best to sell him as a better fielder than he really was. In fact Gehrig's reactions were so slow that the Yankees were losing a lot of outs on ground balls hit down to him as he tried to decide whether to wait for the pitcher to cover first base or make the out himself.

But, what the hell, first base is a position where old outfielders go to die. Instead of burdening Lou with instructions, Huggins decided to leave it up to the Gehrig work ethic to get the job done. And through much effort over the years Gehrig did become an acceptable major league first baseman. Acceptable. Nothing more.

But, boy, could he hit.

The Yankees headed west, and it was Home Run Mania everywhere. Detroit, Cleveland, St. Louis, Chicago. Attendance records toppled everywhere they went.

Navin Field in Detroit had the most distant fences in the American League, and a seating capacity of only 30,000.

Friday's double-header drew the largest weekday crowd in history. "They came to see the performing home run twins, Babe Ruth and Lou Gehrig do their stuff," wrote Harry Bullion of the *Detroit Free Press*. Ruth obliged them by legging out an inside-the-park home run on a drive that hit the wall in center field, 478 feet away, and rebounded right back to Heinie Manush. Any kind of decent throw to the plate probably would have had him, but the throw was so far up the line that Babe was able to score standing up. It was the only inside-the-park homer either he or Gehrig hit all year.

For the Saturday double-header, temporary stands were installed in center field, and still the outfield had to be roped off to accommodate the overflow. If a ball went into the roped-off area, it was a ground-rule double. If it went into the temporary stands, it was a home run.

Babe hit two home runs into those center-field stands. It still took a mighty drive, of course, but take away those temporary stands and Ruth would have had only 58 homers on the year.

For Gehrig, there was one home run before he left Detroit to tie the Babe again briefly, and then another string of homerless games in Cleveland.

The first order of the day for the sports writers had been to find the guy a nickname to go with the Babe's. They tried various combinations. They tried Slam: Slam and Bam. They tried Slambino: Slambino and Bambino. They even tried Biff: the Biffer and the Babe. At length they settled on Buster. The Buster and the Babe. "Buster" has a kind of apple-cheeked innocence to it. Also a touch of condescension. "He's a real buster, isn't he?" That's what you say about a husky little kid. But, then, I don't suppose anybody called Babe was taken seriously before, either.

Ford Frick, a surprisingly colorful writer, came up with "Bam 'Em

Babe and Bust 'Em Lou," which permitted the future commissioner such locutions as "Bam 'Em Babe was a bust yesterday, but Bust 'Em Lou came through with a bam."

Unhappily, Gehrig went into a home run dearth right after the spotlight hit him, with only one home run in 12 games. The immediate challenge, therefore, was to explain why Bust 'Em Lou wasn't busting them. The new story — known hereinafter as Revision A — was that he had become convinced that he would be unable to get his power back until the team reached St. Louis, where "a delicatessen near the hotel" specialized in pickled eels.

Damned if he didn't get to St. Louis and hit a couple. Given that kind of cooperation the writers went back to the drawing board and came up with Revision B. Forget the delicatessen. Who needs a middle man? The new story — let me tell you, they had giants striding across the press box in those days — was that Lou had sent his mother a telegram from Cleveland pleading with her to rush the eels to him before it was too late.

It came right out of the plot of Babe Ruth's latest movie. You don't have to read this if you don't want to, but the plot went like this. Babe stops chewing tobacco because his girl friend, obviously a finicky sort, can't abide all that chawing and spitting. Deprived of his tobacco (should we get biblical about this and say "shorn"?), Babe sinks into a dreadful slump in which he cannot do anything except strike out. At the critical moment of the Big Game, his girl friend — who isn't really a bad kid, just misguided — slips him a chaw as he's going up to the plate, and guess what? Aw, you must have seen the picture.

Babe's chaw of tobacco became Lou's pickled eels. "The eels arrived just before the game on Sunday. Lou took a bite and immediately socked one into the center-field bleachers. Yesterday, he decorated another to go ahead of the Babe."

Question: Did the readers of the twenties really believe that kind of twaddle? Answer: Who knows? The only thing we can say for sure is that Lou's teammates knew him far too well to believe that he would have sprung for a telegram.

Think of yourself as a baseball fan in the summer of 1927. Every day you're waiting for the latest report. Two players on the same team, hitting back to back. "There has never been anything like it," wrote Paul Gallico. "Even as these lines are batted out on the office typewriter, youths dash out of the AP and UP ticker room every two or three minutes shouting, 'Ruth just hit one! Gehrig just hit another one!' "

The Great Home Run Derby was everywhere. And not only in New York and Boston. It was part of the pulse beat of the nation. Throughout the country, the latest news was in the air, passed by word of mouth in elevators, schoolyards, factories, and offices.

With a day off between St. Louis and Chicago, the Yankees — always looking to pick up a few extra bucks — had scheduled an exhibition game in St. Paul. And one of the most astonishing things took place. At every railroad station between St. Louis and St. Paul, through the night and into the early morning hours, there would be people waiting for the Yankee train to pass. Ruth would come out to the platform and make a little speech, and then drag poor Gehrig out to mumble a few words.

On July 24 the Yankees were in Chicago. A full month had passed since they had left Boston, and there would be another five weeks before their eagerly anticipated return on Labor Day. Comiskey Park had been rebuilt that year, with the fences moved back and double-decked bleachers installed. The architect had guaranteed the White Sox owner, Charles Comiskey, that no mere mortal would ever be able to hit a baseball clear out of the park.

First time in, Babe had done it in batting practice, but that was only a curiosity. Especially since Gehrig had won the game with a grand slam home run. Now, with the Home Run Derby on, 50,000 Chicagoans mobbed the South Side park.

In his first at bat Babe Ruth hit the longest drive ever hit inside the park, a three-bagger that went to the fence in dead center. Next time up he hit the longest home run ever hit inside the state of Illinois, a line drive that rocketed into the upper-right-field stands, where neither man nor beast had ever hit a ball before. Now, we know that Babe was always being credited with the longest ball ever hit. But this drive at Comiskey has always been included whenever people sing a medley of his truly greatest hits.

Then again, maybe they were singing about the home run he hit when the Yankees came back to Chicago less than a month later and (come on, you knew this was coming, didn't you?) he hit the damn ball completely out of the damn park and so ignited the crowd that the police had to rescue him from the fans who engulfed him before he was able to complete his tour around the bases.

The next day the park was packed with Chicagoans hoping to see him do it again. Instead, they discovered anew why Carl Sandburg or some other local poet had been inspired to label Chicago "the Windy City." So fierce was the wind blowing in from the lake that Babe shortened up on his bat and tried to drive the ball back through the pitcher's mound. Instead, he hit a line drive that cut through the wind and carried into the center-field bleachers to tie Lou Gehrig at 38, forcing the New York writers to perform another rapid rewrite.

Why? Because back in Yankee Stadium, between those two western trips, Gehrig had gone off on a tear that had pulled him ahead by three home runs. Once again, the New York press had begun to call him "the uncrowned home run King," and announce that the reign of Babe Ruth was drawing to a close. Even Paul Gallico, an unrepentant admirer of Babe Ruth, was ready to concede that Lou Gehrig was now "the cock of the walk" and would reign supreme until the next great home run hitter came along.

They should have known better. On that second swing through the West, the home runs had come with a seesawing regularity. Ruth caught up at 38 (that was the choked-up drive through the wind in Chicago). Gehrig went back ahead the next day at 39, but Ruth pulled even the day after that. Then it was Ruth back out in front at 40, with Gehrig catching him two days later. Then came a two-game drought, and in rapid succession on the last stop in St. Louis, it was Ruth 41, Ruth 42, and Gehrig — could it have been the pickled eels? — 41.

Coming off the second road trip, the Yanks were scheduled to meet the Red Sox in a two-game series in New York, after which they were going to Philadelphia for a couple of games before the long-awaited Labor Day double-header in Boston. In the opening game at Yankee Stadium, Ruth went ahead by two with another monster of a drive off Tony Welzer. At first it seemed as if the ball was going to go clear out of the stadium. As it was, the shot cleared the heads of the fans sitting in the upper stands and went rattling around in the top couple of aisles.

And then came what may have been a great stroke of fortune for the Babe. The second game of the series was rained out and tacked onto the coming series in Boston.

But first Buster and the Babe went to Philadelphia, where they upped the ante.

With two out in the first inning, Ruth went three ahead with his

400th career home run. Gehrig shook Babe's hand as he crossed the plate and then hit the first pitch on a line over everything, including the roof of the house across the street. They were both up again in the second inning. Ruth hit a high fly that was caught against the fence in right field. Gehrig followed with a high fly that went about two feet farther and dropped into the stands.

Buster and the Babe were on their way to Boston with Ruth's lead back down to one home run.

They were going to be playing five games in three days. In those five games the Gehrig-Ruth duel would be settled. The Red Sox took two of the games, but who cared? Gehrig had two home runs — he even got the lead back briefly — but that wasn't even close to being good enough.

For what it's worth — and it isn't worth much — the Yankees were facing a better Red Sox team than they had faced in June. Without going overboard on this, Carrigan had the Sox playing pretty good ball, all things considered. They had actually put together a streak of 12 out of 15 during their most recent home stand against the western teams.

The fans of New England not only mobbed the park, they literally broke down the fences.

An hour before the game the crowd stretched from the ball park down into Kenmore Square. Traffic was at a standstill. Announcements were being made at the subway and train stations warning anybody heading for the park without a ticket to turn around and go home.

The paid attendance of 34,385 exceeded the ball park's capacity, and that wasn't counting the illegals and the undocumented, who had rushed the turnstiles, broken through the outfield fences in two separate places, and overrun the outfield. Another 30,000 had been turned away, according to the official estimates, and there was no way of knowing how many others had heeded the announcements at the transit points or given up in the face of the traffic jam.

And, son of a gun, if they didn't witness one of the classic games of the rivalry, as the Red Sox won the opener, 12–11, in 18 innings.

Paul Shannon's report in the *Post* awoke the echoes of the glories that had once been theirs. "The spike-worn turf at Fenway Park has formed the stage for many an epic struggle. Four different pennants have been won in this theatre by Boston teams and three times the winning of a world championship was achieved on the same field. But seldom have the fans been enthused to the verge of frenzy as they were in the grim 18-inning duel yesterday." It was, he said — and you could see the pennants wave — "the hardest and most bitterly fought struggle that the famous home of former champions has ever staged."

The Red Sox scored three in the first. The Yankees went ahead with four in the third. The Red Sox matched their four on their next turn at bat. The Yankees got two of them back immediately, and the Red Sox made it 8–6 with a run in the fifth. And that was how the game remained until Earle Combs doubled with two out in the ninth to tie the score and send the game into extra innings. The Yankees scored three in the seventeenth; the Red Sox came right back with three of their own and then won it in the eighteenth.

Charlie Ruffing, a fast and wild young pitcher in his days with the Red Sox, pitched 15 innings and struck out 12. He also walked 11. He struck out Tony Lazzeri twice with the bases loaded. Ruth went down on strikes twice and was walked twice. He also tried to beat out a bunt and was thrown out.

Lou Gehrig hit his forty-fourth home run to tie Ruth, but for once that was only a footnote to the story. The star of the game for the Yankees was Earle Combs, the fleet center fielder, who was being all but overlooked as he was having his greatest season. After tying the game in the ninth, he kept the Yanks alive by pulling off a miraculous catch in the fourteenth and then drove in the tie-breaking run in the seventeenth with his fifth hit.

Hal Wiltse pitched three innings, allowed five hits, walked three, committed an error, and gave up three runs. One of the runs came in, if you can imagine it, when he flubbed the return toss from the catcher. With it all, Wiltse became the only pitcher to beat the Yankees three times in this, their finest season.

The hero of the game, in the end, was a seldom-used third-string catcher, Billy Moore.

The Sox came to bat in the last of the seventeenth, trailing by three runs. Wilcy Moore, who had come on in the ninth after Combs had tied the score, had throttled the Sox over eight innings with one hit. In the twinkling of an eye, everything changed. A double and a single brought in one run, and also brought Waite Hoyt onto the scene. Not today, Waite. He gave up a double on his first pitch, putting the tying run on second. One run scored on a groundout. At this point Carrigan called his second-string catcher back from the plate and sent in Billy Moore, the only left-handed hitter he had left.

Hoyt whipped two quick strikes by him, and Moore lined the next pitch to deep right field for a double that tied the score. It was his first extra-base hit of the year, and only his second run batted in.

"The roar from the crowd," said the *Post,* "could be heard all the way to the Back Bay station."

To make Billy's day complete, he ran back to the dugout, strapped on his catching equipment, and brought an incipient Yankee rally to a sudden end by making an absolutely perfect throw to nail Bob Meusel, who was trying to steal.

The Red Sox won in the eighteenth on doubles by Buddy Myer and Ira Flagstead. The Red Sox had Myer only briefly before trading him away to Washington. Buddy Myer (who won the batting title in 1935 and played in two World Series) is, along with Tony Lazzeri and Joe Gordon, the best second baseman never elected to the Hall of Fame. He wasn't a second baseman, though, when he was with the Red Sox. He split third base with Billy Rogell and played a little shortstop.

If they had traded Myer away to the Yankees, Boston fans would have added his name to their list of grievances. As it was, he left behind only a vague memory that, oh yeah, he was the kid who once played with us, wasn't he?

Having emerged from that first game with a very, very lucky win, Pinky Wiltse was sent back out to pitch the second game, which clearly wasn't going to go more than five innings. Wiltse pitched somewhat better than he had in the first game and lost.

Never mind. After making his mark as the only pitcher to beat the 1927 Yankees three times, Wiltse, a 10-game winner on the season, developed a bad arm the following year, pitched two games, and was a memory.

Billy Moore didn't even last that long. He was let go at the end of the year. In his entire career he came to bat only 87 times, knocked in just four runs, and threw out only that one base runner.

But in that one game, in those 15 minutes out of his life, Billy Moore had managed to take away the headlines from Babe Ruth and carve out a place for himself as part of the Red Sox–Yankee rivalry.

·   ·   ·

For the rest of the series Babe Ruth was going to take the headlines back. Starting with the double-header on Tuesday.

The second game was the rescheduled meeting that had been washed out in New York. From now on, the games would be reported under big, black three-column heads on the front page of both the *Post* and the *Globe*.

Ruth Reels Off Three Home Runs

First Wallop Is Longest on Record
Trails Gehrig for an Inning
Then It Reads 47–46

Gehrig hit his forty-fifth home run in the first inning. It was the last time that season he would be ahead. Ruth came up in the third, and, just like it says in the subhead, hit yet again what may well have been the longest home run ever hit in Boston. "He had many a long drive," the *Globe*'s O'Leary wrote. "This long one yesterday was the daddy of all others. The ball was still climbing when it went high over the highest part of the high fence in center field, just to the left of the flagpole. Nobody at the park could tell where it landed, but when it disappeared from view it was headed for the Charles River basin."

Gehrig had gone ahead of Ruth for about 20 minutes. He was going to remain tied for about the same length of time. For the twenty-first time that season the two were tied. It would also be the last. The next time up Ruth hit a 3–0 pitch — *unheard* of — into the right-field stands to take the lead.

The third home run was hit in the ninth inning of the second game, a booming drive that traveled high into the center-field bleachers. "Only the fresh memory of No. 45," wrote Burt Whitman of the *Boston Herald*, "prevented the enthusiastic fans from labeling No. 47 the greatest ever."

The next day Babe was back on the front pages.

Babe Drives Out Two More Homers

Boosts his standing
to 49 — Four Ahead
of Gehrig

Practically Beats
Boston All Alone

Yanks Triumph 12–10
Overcome 7-run
Lead of Sox

In the first inning Ruth hit a towering drive high over the left-field wall. The second homer was a line shot that went into the right-field bleachers "with the speed of a bullet."

The game itself was a reversal of the 12–11 opener. The Red Sox scored eight runs in the fourth, their biggest inning of the year, to gain an 8–1 lead. But with a chance to actually take a series from the mighty Yankees, they suddenly remembered who they were, committed three errors at the worst possible times and handed the lead back to the guys who knew what to do with it.

For Babe Ruth the tally was five homers in three games played over two days. Both records. More significant, it was the first time either the Babe or Lou had been that far in front since Gehrig had closed the gap with the three home runs at Fenway Park in June.

The Babe was leading, 49–45, and the contest was over. For Gehrig, it was as if the air had gone out of his balloon. He didn't hit another home run for 22 days. For Babe, the race was on against his own record. "The first time I felt I had a chance," he would say after it was over, "was when I hit those two home runs in the last game in Boston."

When he left Boston, he needed 11 home runs in 25 games.

Numbers 51 and 52 came in a double-header against Cleveland as the Yankees were clinching the pennant. Now he needed eight, with 14 games to go.

When the Yankees won their 105th victory to tie the record of the 1912 Red Sox, Ruth hit a two-run home run, his fifty-sixth, in the ninth inning to turn a 7–6 defeat into an 8–7 victory. Since the game was over the moment he hit the ball, he also took the elementary precaution of carrying his bat around the bases with him. Good thinking. A kid came running out as Babe was rounding third and — who else would this happen to? — grabbed the bat. And Babe — who else would do this? — dragged boy and bat across the plate with him.

Oh, one more thing. Earlier in the game Lou Gehrig had knocked in two runs with a triple and a single, giving Buster 172 RBIs to break the Bam's record of 170. Hardly anybody noticed, and almost nobody cared.

With four games left, Babe still needed four home runs.

No problem. He picked up number 57 against Lefty Grove, the pitcher who had humiliated him in the opening game. You want to talk about settling old scores? The Babe did it with a grand slammer that won the game.

The next day he hit numbers 58 and 59 against Washington. The record-tying fifty-ninth was a grand slam home run, his second in two days, against a kid named Paul Hopkins who had been brought up to finish out the season.

Number 60 came on Saturday in his last at bat against Tom Zachary, an excellent pitcher, to break a 2–2 tie. Zachary had served notice that he had no intention of allowing Babe to hit the record breaker against him by walking him on four straight pitches his first time at bat. Subsequently, Babe had stroked two singles and scored both Yankee runs. On a 1–1 count, he golfed a curving drive that landed a few feet fair halfway up in the bleachers.

Zachary came off the mound, screaming that the ball was foul, as a smiling, cap-waving Babe went jogging around the bases to the ear-splitting cheers of 10,000 fans.

Lou Gehrig hit his forty-seventh home run on the final day of the season.

Chapter Seven

Tom Yawkey to the Rescue:
1933

*My main purpose in buying the Red Sox is beating the Yan-
kees.*

— Tom Yawkey, February 25, 1935

OR the Yankees, the succession was seamless. On the same day
that Ruth did or did not point to the center-field bleachers during
the 1932 World Series, a lanky 18-year-old kid, listed as J. De Maggio in the box score, was playing his first game for the San Francisco
Seals of the Pacific Coast League. Back in New York, a 29-year-old
millionaire was casting around for a ball club to buy. His name was
Thomas Austin Yawkey.

Tom Yawkey had grown up around baseball. After his own father
had died, he had been brought up, and eventually adopted, by his
uncle, William H. Yawkey, a lumber and mining magnate who had
helped Ban Johnson launch the American League. For three years
(1904–1907) Bill Yawkey had been the owner and president of the
Detroit Tigers, and he had maintained a financial interest in the club
throughout the rest of his life. Young Tom led a privileged childhood.
Ty Cobb was brought to the Yawkey estate to play catch with him
(if, given Cobb's less-than-winning personality, you can call that a
privilege). It can hardly be completely irrelevant that Tom's idol became Cobb's greatest rival, Eddie Collins.

On learning that Eddie Collins had been the greatest athlete in the
history of Irving Prep School, a posh academy located in Tarrytown,
New York, Tom insisted on being sent there himself. At Irving he
not only followed in his idol's footsteps by playing second base, but
he also won the Edward Trowbridge Collins Award as the best ath-

lete of his year. That was the high point of his athletic career. The best he could do while at Yale was to play second base for the intramural team at the Sheffield Scientific School. A poor student, he majored in being a rich man's son, a playboy.

Given Yawkey's background, Detroit was his team of choice. But the Tigers were not for sale. He was one of the leading bidders for the New York Giants at a time when Charles Stoneham was toying with the idea of selling the team. He could have bought the Ebbets family's share of the Brooklyn Dodgers, but he wasn't interested in owning half a club.

As far as the Red Sox were concerned, they had always been his for the asking. While Yawkey was shopping around for a ball club, Bob Quinn was shopping around for a buyer — any buyer — who would take the team off his hands. Yawkey could not have been less interested.

In 1932, however, Bob Quinn and the country hit bottom together. The Red Sox lost 111 games and drew a grand total of 182,150 people. That's an average of 2,365 a game. When the Yankees weren't in town, Fenway Park resembled nothing so much as a lonesome prairie. Quinn was ready to turn the club over to anybody who would assume his outstanding debts. And, still, Tom Yawkey wasn't interested.

So what happened to suddenly change his mind? Well, in February 1933 the beloved old headmaster of Irving Prep died. While Tom was attending the funeral in Tarrytown he met Eddie Collins for the first time. He immediately informed Collins that he would be interested in buying the Red Sox, but only if Collins would come and run the club for him.

Eddie did not exactly leap at the opportunity, despite being offered far more money than he had ever made in his life — and a chunk of stock to boot. Having retired four years earlier, Eddie had remained as Connie Mack's "first assistant," waiting to take over the managerial reins of the Athletics as soon as Mr. Mack, who was 70 years old, decided to retire. Collins went to Connie Mack for advice — his polite way of giving the Grand Old Man of Baseball a chance to turn the team over to him. "If you don't take that job," advised the Grand Old Man, "I'll fire you."

When Collins retired after 14 years as the Red Sox general manager, Connie Mack was still managing the Philadelphia Athletics.

.   .   .

On February 25, 1933, less than three weeks after Yawkey had introduced himself to Collins, they were being presented to the Boston press as the new owner and general manager of the Boston Red Sox.

"I do not," Tom Yawkey told the assembled sports writers, "intend to mess around with a loser."

You can laugh at that if you want. Tom Yawkey's 42-year stewardship produced three pennants and no world championships. In his first 33 seasons the Red Sox won exactly one pennant, and, in all honesty, that one came pretty much on the outer cusp of the Second World War years. And yet, under Yawkey the Red Sox were a winning team. He brought respectability back to the franchise. Immediately Red Sox fans could hold their heads up again.

In Tom Yawkey's first year the Sox moved up to seventh place, and if that was only one notch up from the cellar, they had improved their record by 22½ games. They even beat the Yankees eight times, their best showing since the year of Babe Ruth's stomach ache.

In another year they were in the first division. But even that was a disappointment. At the beginning of his reign Yawkey spent so much money buying stars that the Red Sox were always expected to win the pennant. Instead, the Gold Sox would become the Red Flops, and working stiffs who lived from one week's paycheck to the next would somehow be moved to sympathize with poor Tom Yawkey's plight.

Colonel Ruppert had promised to help, and he did. He allowed young Tom to buy his supernumeraries at some not very immodest prices. Shortly after Tom's first season as Sox owner began, the Yankees sold him Billy Werber, George Pipgras, and Dusty Cooke. The following season they sent him Lyn Lary. A very mixed bag. Cooke, who had come to the Bronx three years earlier touted as the next great Yankee, had shown fleeting promises of greatness but had been plagued by a series of injuries. He had, in fact, missed almost the entire previous season with a broken leg.

As if to show how things were going to go for Yawkey, Cooke broke his collarbone in his very first game for the Red Sox while diving for a fly ball. Pipgras was by now 34 years old. After winning his first two games, he suffered an injury of almost supernatural strangeness: he broke his arm while he was snapping off a curve.

Billy Werber was 25, and the Yankees were running out of options on him. Werber could play. He could hit, he could field, and, best of all, he was an exciting base runner and base stealer. If he had possessed just a little more talent, the Yankees might have been willing to overlook his stubborn, crusty personality.

Lyn Lary had been the Yankee shortstop for four years. In 1931 he had played every game, scored 100 runs, and knocked in 107. He wasn't really that kind of hitter, though, and by the first month of the 1934 season, it had become clear that Frank Crosetti, a far superior fielder, had taken his position away.

Yawkey had also been able to buy the Ferrell brothers, Rick, a classy catcher, from the always indigent St. Louis Browns, and Wes from Cleveland. People would look at the Ferrell brothers and think to themselves, "Are you sure . . . ?" Rick was narrow-faced, balding, rigorously silent. Wes was blond, curly-haired, handsome, and, to put it mildly, explosive. He also might have been the best-hitting pitcher since . . . well, since Babe Ruth. He had won 20 or more games in each of his first four seasons in the majors, still a record. He also hit nine home runs in a single season, which is still a record for pitchers.

But it was Connie Mack, in the process of dismantling his great championship teams of 1929, 1930, and 1931, who became Tom Yawkey's Frazee. When Yawkey unpeeled his bankroll to buy Lefty Grove from the Athletics for $125,000, Ruppert announced with ill-concealed anger that he would have been willing to go much higher if he had been given a chance. And when the Red Sox then had the colossal nerve to sweep a series from the Yankees in Boston, the Colonel was on the telephone to Yawkey the next morning demanding payment in full of that $350,000 mortgage which he still held on Fenway Park.

The money was no problem for Yawkey. In fact he laughed about it. But the mean-spiritedness of the man, the willingness of Ruppert, the winner, to expose himself as such a sore loser, was never forgotten.

L'affaire Grove should have let everyone know that nothing was going to be easy. When the best left-handed pitcher in baseball reported to spring training, the best left arm in the game was so sore that he no longer had his fast ball. Which might not have been such a tragedy if not for the fact that his fast ball was all Grove had ever had.

Lefty set to work to learn how to pitch all over again, and became the league's most effective starter. He led the American League in ERA four times, pitching in Fenway Park which was supposed to be death on left-handers.

In 1935 Yawkey bought Joe Cronin, his shortstop and manager from Washington for $250,000, a figure that was to stand as a landmark of wretched excess for decades.

In 1936 he paid $150,000 for Jimmie Foxx, one of the great right-handed hitters of all time, and then put out another $75,000 for Doc Cramer, a nifty center fielder who was coming off a .332 season, and Eric McNair, a good second baseman who would hit .285.

With Foxx had come a pitcher called Footsie Marcum, who had just won 17 games for a last-place club. Footsie (they'd call him Big Foot today) was a character of that age of uneducated and sometimes illiterate southern farm boys.

His career with the Red Sox was most notable for producing one of the great tonsillectomies of the time. Footsie carried his tonsils, pickled, around in a bottle to display to any interested — or uninterested — party, having been assured by the gurus at Harvard that his was the largest set of tonsils they had ever seen.

Between 1934 and 1937 the Red Sox finished fourth, fourth, sixth, and fifth, and not because the high-priced players flopped, either. Four of them are in the Hall of Fame: Foxx, Grove, Cronin, and Rick Ferrell. (And if Rick Ferrell is the player most often cited as proof that the Hall of Fame had become politicized, there would have been neither surprise nor protest if Wes had been the Ferrell who had been named rather than Rick.)

Grove and Ferrell were perhaps the two most temperamental pitchers who ever lived.

The classic Lefty Grove explosion had occurred in Philadelphia, and it could not really be called unprovoked. Grove, in the midst of his greatest season, had won 16 straight games, and he was going for the all-time record set by Walter Johnson and Joe Wood. Up against him was a journeyman pitcher named Dick Coffman, who was about to make his only mark in an undistinguished career. He beat Grove, 1–0, the only time the A's were shut out all year. And that wasn't even the worst of it. The run was scored in the eighth inning when a seldom-used outfielder, Jimmy Moore, misjudged a fly ball.

And that still wasn't the worst of it. Moore was playing only because Connie Mack — for reasons best known to himself — had picked that day to give his regular left fielder, Al Simmons, permission to go home to attend to some business.

Grove charged into the clubhouse. He pulled doors off their hinges, he splintered locker panels, he kicked water buckets and up-ended benches. He pushed over rows of lockers and tore up all the clothing he could get his hands on.

When Moore tried to apologize, Grove savaged him until the poor kid fled in tears, and he was ready to take a swing at his catcher, Mickey Cochrane, a pretty fiery guy himself, when Cochrane tried to commiserate with him.

Then he burst into the manager's office and let Connie Mack have it for allowing Simmons to leave, and even ripped into Simmons in absentia for having left.

According to reports he didn't speak to anybody for a full week — which, all things considered, was probably a blessing.

Wes Ferrell didn't only beat up on lockers and walls. Wes had been known to beat up on himself. And Wes didn't even have the excuse of being left-handed.

The year before Messrs. Ferrell and Foxx came to the Red Sox, Foxx had hit a grand slam home run off him. Now, giving up a homer to the most prolific right-handed home run hitter of all time was not exactly a disgrace, especially since Ferrell was still coasting along with a 10–5 lead in the eighth inning. Never mind. Handsome Wes came back to the dugout and began to chastise himself by banging his head against the wall. Finding that punishment to be insufficient, he knocked himself down with a wicked punch to the jaw and was beating the hell out of himself on the dugout floor before his somewhat bemused teammates decided to break it up . . . if that's what you'd call it.

Jimmie Foxx was a horseman of a different color. Foxx and Lou Gehrig were the powerhouse hitters of baseball. In 1932 Foxx had hit 58 home runs. He had won two Triple Crowns for Connie Mack and had twice been named the MVP of the American League.

In Foxx the Boston fans had their first legitimate superstar — though they were not being called that then — since the departure of Babe Ruth.

In 1938 he hit 50 homers, drove in 175 runs, hit .349, totaled 398 bases, and became the first Red Sox player to be voted MVP in the league. Those 175 RBI have been topped only by Hack Wilson (190), Lou Gehrig (184), and Hank Greenberg (183). He is still the only Boston hitter to reach 50 home runs.

Two times he hit balls clear out of Comiskey Park, a feat matched only by Ruth and Greenberg. When he retired, his 534 home runs put him second only to Babe Ruth.

James Emory Foxx was a good-natured, free-spending farm boy out of Maryland. He ended almost every sentence with a funny little giggle. In those early days Tom Yawkey would invite a few select players to dine with him at a fancy restaurant, and Foxx would wrestle him for the check. When he was with his teammates, he didn't have to wrestle.

During his playing days he carried little bottles of scotch around in his pocket and periodically took a sip. Unhappily, he ended as a drunk. I can remember sitting with Casey Stengel during spring training in 1958 while Casey was holding court, telling how Jimmie's brother Sam was hitting the training camps, trying to cadge five- and ten-dollar bills "for Jimmie."

Casey Stengel was the easiest touch who ever lived when it came to old-time players. But he had decided that it would be the height of irresponsibility to help a great one like Foxx on his slide into the gutter. "Tom Yawkey should take care of him," he said. He had just sent word to Yawkey, in fact, that he should give Foxx a job.

"That's true," Bob Holbrook remembers. "Yawkey arranged for Foxx to become the batting coach for the Red Sox farm club in Minneapolis, and Jimmie never showed up. There was just nothing you could do to help him."

Even his death was messy. He choked on a chicken bone cn July 21, 1967, just as the Red Sox were on their way to a most unexpected pennant.

The Red Sox of the 1930s put some great names on the field, and they were a lot of fun to watch, if you didn't take them too seriously. If you did, of course, they broke your heart.

It was not until the team began to build with young kids from the minors, Ted Williams and Bobby Doerr and Johnny Pesky and Dom DiMaggio, that they became contenders.

But it was Joe Cronin, as player and manager, who epitomized the Red Sox, in both their dreams and their frustrations, for 20 years.

Chapter Eight

Joe Cronin:
1935–1958

*Oh my, yes, Joe Cronin is the best there is in the clutch. With
a man on third and one out, I'd rather have him hitting for
me than anybody I've ever seen — and that includes Cobb
and the rest of them.*

— Connie Mack

Oct. 25, 1934

Clark Griffith
Washington Baseball Club
Washington, D.C.

Dear Mr. Griffith:
    The Boston American League Baseball Club agrees to give
$250,000 and the contract to Lyn Lary for the contract of player man-
ager Joe Cronin, provided Cronin is satisfied by terms submitted by
Boston. Contract to be closed at convenience of parties after Novem-
ber 30th, 1934, by execution of formal contract and the payment of
$100,000 in cash, remainder of cash consideration at convenience of
Boston club, prior to March 1st, 1935, but after Jan. 1, 1935.

Boston American League BB Club
Thomas A. Yawkey, Pres.

These words, written out on a sheet of heavy hotel stationery in
Tom Yawkey's quick, sprawling hand, brought Joe Cronin to the Red
Sox for the largest amount of money ever paid for a ballplayer — by
far. It was a price that weighed Cronin down for more than 20 years.
Since he had cost more than anybody else in history, he was expected, by the sheer logic of mathematics, to produce more than
anybody else. To put it bluntly, he didn't.

In his third game at Fenway Park he made three errors. The next day he made another, and a Ladies' Day crowd started to work him over in the immemorial manner of women who believe the merchandise to be overpriced. The day after that the Sox went into the ninth inning leading, 3–1, behind Wes Ferrell. Cronin booted two balls, the Sox lost, 5–3, and Cronin's brief honeymoon with the fans of Boston was over.

The tale of his miserable beginning in Boston is worth telling here at the top because it is the only time in a baseball career that was to span a full lifetime that Joe Cronin ever lost his nerve.

Joseph Edward Cronin was born on October 12, 1906, in San Francisco, only six months after the earthquake had destroyed all the Cronin family's possessions, save for an old rocking chair. His father drove a team of horses, and his two older brothers were "teamos," too. Joe was the athlete of the family. At the age of 14 he won the junior tennis championship of San Francisco's well-developed playground system.

At Mission High he played in the same infield with Wally Berger, who would go on to set an all-time home run record in the vast pasture of Braves Field by hitting 38 in his rookie year.

The greatest player around San Francisco at the time was a big Italian pitcher and slugger, who had to spend most of his time working his father's grape press. "He'd come to the park around the seventh or eighth inning," Cronin recalled, "and always — always — hit a home run, strike everybody out, and beat us." The big Italian kid was Tony Lazzeri.

Joe's leadership abilities were evident from the beginning. Dolf Camilli was his next-door neighbor. When Joe heard that Dolf had dropped out of school in his senior year, he went to his house, took him by the elbow, and dragged him back.

As a playground instructor himself, Joe worked with half a dozen other kids who made it to the big leagues. Among them was another Italian who was going to become a fixture with the New York Yankees — Frank Crosetti. Once after Phil Rizzuto had pushed Crosetti over to third base, Frankie pulled the hidden-ball trick on Joe. "You blankety-blank dago!" the embarrassed Cronin screamed at him. "This is the thanks I get for teaching you this game?"

There was an even more direct connection with the Yankees. Cronin had signed with the Pittsburgh Pirates just before he turned

19 and was assigned to the New Haven club in the Eastern League. The ex-schoolmaster who was running the New Haven franchise for the Pirates was George Weiss, whom Cronin would lock heads with when Weiss became general manager of the Yankees.

"Weiss did everything," Cronin once told me. "He even drove the team bus himself. He was too cheap to hire a driver." He was also such a martinet that he didn't even allow his young players to talk on the bus.

Joe got to spend the whole 1927 season with the Pittsburgh Pirates — the year they were swept by the Yankees in the World Series — on the bench, admiring the brilliant shortstop play of Glenn Wright.

Then the Pirates sold him to Kansas City in the American Association, where he performed so unimpressively that he was assigned to Wichita in the Western League.

He never got there. Instead of going down to Wichita, Cronin went up to Washington in one of those wondrous stories that show how random chance can come along to determine a man's life.

Joe Cronin became a big league shortstop for the Washington Senators in 1928 because Goose Goslin had hurt his arm in spring training while fooling around with a shotput. As a result, Goslin, who had one of the great throwing arms in baseball, could not lift his arm over his head. Sore arm or not, Goslin was on a hitting tear (he won the batting title that year at .379), so Bucky Harris could hardly bench him. The Senators' shortstop, Bobby Reeves, had to race out to left field whenever a ball was hit to Goslin and practically take the ball out of his hand. In Washington's hot, humid atmosphere Reeves had lost 20 pounds by the time July rolled around. Joe Engle, who was the Senators' entire scouting force, was sent out to find a new shortstop.

Follow this closely. The shortstop who had beaten Joe out at Kansas City was Topper Rigney, who had played for the Red Sox in 1926 and had then been traded to Washington for Buddy Myer.

When Engle inquired about the possibility of getting Topper Rigney back, he discovered that the price had just gone up. He was also tipped off that Kansas City had informed the Pirates that they were going to ship Joe Cronin down to Wichita. Engle had admired the way Cronin had handled himself during fielding practice at the 1927 World Series. The problem was that, since everybody knew how desperate the Senators were, the price on Cronin immediately went up, too. Engle had to pay $7,500 for him, a price so high for a back-up player that he was afraid to tell his parsimonious employer Clark Griffith how much of his money he had spent. Instead, he carried Cronin around with him for a full week while he was completing his scouting expedition.

Before they left Kansas City, Engle wrote a letter to Mildred Robertson, Griffith's niece and adopted daughter, who did all the secretarial work for the club. This was the other letter that was to have such a profound effect on the San Francisco Irishman's life.

Thursday

Dear Mildred:

   Am bring [sic] home to you a real sweetie. Is Joe Cronin so be dolled up about Wednesday or Thursday to meet him. Tall and Handsome. Hold all our mail. Don't show this to anyone.

Yours
"Joe"

It isn't surprising that Mildred Robertson Cronin saved that letter, since it helped to bring her and her future husband together.

Griffith was so unimpressed with Cronin that when the season came to an end, he brought Buddy Myer back to play shortstop. He wanted Myer so badly that he offered the Red Sox two starting pitchers plus Joe Cronin for him. The Red Sox wouldn't close the deal until Grif replaced the unimpressive rookie with the seasoned veteran Bobby Reeves.

A month into the 1929 season Walter Johnson, the new Washington manager, switched Myer to second, a position he had never played before, and put Cronin in at short.

Then in 1930, everything came together for Joe. He hit .346, with 13 home runs and 126 RBIs, and was voted the Most Valuable Player in the league.

And so it was that in 1933 Griffith, who had won a pennant in 1924 with the 27-year-old boy manager Bucky Harris, turned the club over to his 26-year-old shortstop.

In Joe Cronin's first year as manager the Senators not only beat the Yankees to the pennant, they clobbered them, 14–8, in the season series. And they did it through one of the freak plays of all time. With the Yankees behind, 6–3, in the bottom of the ninth, men on first and second, and nobody out, Tony Lazzeri hit a high drive deep into right-center. The ball ricocheted off the wall and came to Goslin on one hop.

Gehrig had tagged up at second. Dixie Walker at first was running all the way. The two of them hit third base so close together that, amidst the screaming of the crowd, it was impossible to hold up one without also holding up the other. Cronin, who had raced out to take the relay, made a perfect throw to the catcher, Luke Sewell, and ball and runners all arrived at the plate together.

Gehrig, old Columbia fullback that he was, drove into Sewell from the first-base side of the plate and knocked him head over teakettle into Walker. Not your conventional bang-bang play, but just maybe the only bang-bang-bang play ever recorded. While Sewell was being bounced back and forth like a pinball, both Gehrig and Walker had in effect tagged themselves out. Instead of two runs in with the tying run on second and nobody out, there were suddenly no runs in and two men out.

"That's where we won it," Cronin once said. "When something like that happens, the players begin to feel they're going to get the breaks and then nothing can beat them. Especially when it happens against the Yankees, and in Yankee Stadium." His greatest disappointment, he added, was the inability of his Red Sox teams to win the clutch games in New York. "We found more ways to lose! A ball would ricochet around in the corner, a fly would be lost in the sun. Always something. When we finally won the pennant in 1946, it was because we finally had a guy who could get us the extra-base hit in Yankee Stadium in the clutch: Rudy York."

Clark Griffith was always castigated for being a man so avaricious that he would sell his son-in-law if the money was right.

Only two things are wrong with that indictment. The first, admittedly technical, is that Cronin wasn't Griffith's son-in-law when the negotiations were begun. The marriage didn't take place until the season was over. The second is that if Cronin had not been his son-in-law, Griffith would never have considered selling him.

The background is this: In 1934 the Senators had undergone a complete collapse. Every player in the starting line-up had suffered a major injury, and Cronin — who had managed to stay healthy until he broke his arm in the final month of the season — was being booed mercilessly.

Last year's genius is this year's bum: nothing very new about that. Except that Griffith could see that, sooner or later, he was going to be placed in a position where he would either have to fire Cronin or be constantly accused — as was already beginning to happen — of nepotism.

During the final phase of the negotiations, the happy groom, arm in a cast, was sailing slowly through the Panama Canal on the last leg of his honeymoon trip. Upon arriving at his hotel in San Francisco, he found a message instructing him to call Mr. Griffith. That was when Joe found out.

Griffith told him that Yawkey had agreed to a five-year contract on whatever terms Joe stipulated and that, in any event, the deal was conditioned entirely on Joe's acceptance.

"Give me a night to sleep on it," Joe said.

But if Griffith had not exactly been engaging in the slave trade, Cronin was not walking into the most ideal possible situation, either.

Tom Yawkey had bought all the golden bric-a-brac from Connie Mack's store, and this exclusive clique of Athletics would sit around and compare Cronin's tactics to Mr. Mack's — never to Cronin's advantage. The old A's pitchers — Lefty Grove, Rube Walberg, Footsie Marcum — were not bashful about letting it be known that they thought Eric McNair, who was shifted to second when he came to Boston, was the better shortstop.

To make matters worse, Yawkey was so diligent about cornering the market in temperamental screwball characters that Cronin could have given the keynote address at the annual convention of New England psychiatrists.

When Wes Ferrell wasn't beating himself up, he was an advanced student of astrology. He could become quite upset whenever Cronin was so insensitive as to start him when the stars forecast disaster.

Wes once walked off the mound in New York because he thought McNair should have fielded a ball that went into center field. When word was brought to him that Cronin had fined him a thousand dollars, Wes said, "I'm going to slug that so-and-so Irishman right on his lantern jaw."

"If he wants to slug me," Cronin sighed, "I'll be passing through the lobby at six o'clock on my way to dinner." Cronin was there. Ferrell was not.

Third baseman Billy Werber felt that the world was against him, so Joe had to treat him with special care. In Chicago one time Billy loafed into second on a force play, and when Cronin asked him why he hadn't hustled, Billy's feelings were so bruised that he snapped back, "If you don't like the way I'm playing, get somebody else." Whereupon he sat down firmly on the bench and motioned to another infielder to take his place. Cronin had to suspend him.

There was no sense in even trying to fine or suspend Lefty Grove. Tom Yawkey was still a hero worshiper, and Old Mose, as Yawkey liked to call him, was his particular pet.

Old Mose had nothing against having his fielders make great plays behind him, but errors he could not abide.

When he was really perturbed, he would stand there on the mound, chewing the thumb of his glove and glaring at the offender. If it were the shortstop-manager whose play that day had been an offense to his sight, Lefty would climb atop the partition separating the clubhouse from the manager's office and scream out his denunciation of Joe's fielding.

Lefty didn't appreciate a lack of hitting support, either. After the Sox had been shut out behind him in Chicago, he drew himself to his full height and screamed, "You think Grove is going to pitch his arm off for you bums?" Whereupon he walked the seven miles back to the hotel rather than mingle with such bums as they. And he continued to walk back and forth to work through the entire series.

It was also said that Grove always retained enough presence of mind to punch a locker or wall with his right hand, never his left — a trade secret he revealed to Billy Werber after Billy had broken a toe kicking a water bucket. In the first place, Lefty advised him, he should have made sure that the bucket was empty, and even then he should have taken care to distribute the weight of the kick over his whole foot.

Ben Chapman came to Boston in 1937 and stole 35 bases. Cronin let him run at will, mostly because Chapman was going to run anyway. Ben Chapman goes down in the annals of baseball as the quintessential clubhouse lawyer — a good ballplayer but a bad guy to have on the club. He second-guessed Cronin endlessly. The joke around the ball field was that Joe had to play him because he was afraid Ben would lead a mutiny if he left him on the bench while Joe was out on the field.

Doc Cramer was a clubhouse agitator of a less virulent stripe. But a clubhouse agitator he was all the same, and he had the material to work with.

And, of course, we haven't even got around to Ted Williams.

All the same, Joe brought fun to the park. Joe Cronin was a showman. His love of the theater went all the way back to his early days in San Francisco. Sometimes he would take a hopelessly lost game and make it memorable by letting Foxx, Williams, or Cramer pitch an inning or two.

His greatest productions, fittingly enough, starred himself. After he had become a pinch-hitter deluxe toward the end of his career, Joe, who dearly loved the clutch, would wait for key spots late in the game. Time would be called. The scheduled batter would trudge back to the dugout. There would follow perhaps 30 seconds of almost total inactivity on the field, and the tension would thicken in the stands. Nobody doubted that Cronin would be coming up, of course, and a great roar would arise as, at last, he came hulking up out of the dugout, swinging half a dozen big bats, which he would strew behind him as he strode to the plate.

His great year was 1943, when he set an American League record with five pinch-hit home runs. He hit four of them with two men on base, the other with one. In a June 17 (Bunker Hill Day) doubleheader, he set another record when he put the Red Sox back into both games, the first time with a three-run pinch homer in the seventh inning, and then with a three-run pinch home run in the eighth.

It was on another peculiarly Boston holiday, Patriots' Day, that the playing career of Joe Cronin came to an end in Yankee Stadium. It was the third game of the 1945 season. Owing to the paucity of players, the 38-year-old Cronin had pressed himself into service as a third baseman. He'd had three hits in eight times at bat and had just made a pair of brilliant plays in the field when he caught his spikes rounding second base and lay there writhing in pain before he was carried off on a stretcher. He had broken his right ankle.

If nobody said that it was the only way anybody could have got Joe Cronin to quit the ball field against the Yankees, it was only because all the poets and philosophers had gone off to war, too.

Chapter Nine

The Fight and the Forfeit: 1939

Joe Cronin hated the Yankees. He hated them when he was a player, he hated them when he was a manager, and he hated them when he was the president of the American League. Maybe that's why he always played so well against them.

— Bill Crowley

CONNIE MACK once said, "Joe Cronin is a .300 hitter who becomes a .400 hitter in the clutch." Nobody played better against the Yankees — or was tougher with the game on the line. Even more than Grove, Foxx, or Williams, it was Joe Cronin who always seemed to find himself at the center of the storm. Talk to any Old Bostonian about the rivalry, and the first thing he will probably talk about is the five-game sweep at Yankee Stadium. If it isn't, it is only because he wanted to lead with The Fight.

In 1938 the Red Sox played at a .591 pace, the same percentage as in their championship year of 1916. For the first time since 1922, they were even able to split a season series with the Yankees.

With Jimmie Foxx having his MVP season, the Red Sox — here in the last of the pre-Williams years — had what was probably their most productive season offensively.

They led the majors in batting at .299, a full 25 points better than the Yankees.

Joe Cronin, having his best year at bat since coming to Boston, hit .325, knocked in 94 runs, and led the league with 51 doubles.

Mike Higgins, the third baseman, hit .303 and knocked in 106 runs.

The Boston outfield was nothing less than spectacular. Ben Chapman hit .340, Joe Vosmik .324, and Doc Cramer .301. Vosmik, who had come to the Red Sox from St. Louis by way of Cleveland, led the league with 201 hits. Cramer was second with 198, and Jimmie Foxx, at 197, was third.

Foxx, as we know, was the batting champion at .349. Chapman's .340 put him third.

With all that, Jimmie Foxx's 50 home runs were more than half of the Boston total. As a team the Red Sox had 98 home runs; the Yankees, led by Joe DiMaggio's 32, had 174.

Foxx knocked in 175 runs. DiMaggio knocked in 140.

Nobody came close to either team in producing runs. But it was the Yankees who topped the list by scoring 966 runs while the Red Sox were scoring 902.

And — oh, yes — the Yankees won the pennant by 9½ games.

May 30, 1938, became a landmark date in the rivalry as the largest crowd in Yankee history, 81,841 paid customers, turned out to watch the Memorial Day double-header — and it will retain that lofty position in the chronicle of crowd control until a new stadium is built in New York or hell freezes over, whichever comes first.

The stadium had been tripled-decked a year earlier. That is the reason why the Yankees were able to outdraw the overflow crowds of the Babe Ruth era. In 1975, when the stadium was rebuilt by the City of New York, the seating capacity was reduced. That is why they will never be able to stuff that many people in again. The actual attendance was 83,533. Another 511 fans demanded their money back because they had been unable to find any standing room from which they could see the field. In other words, 84,044 people had pushed through the turnstiles.

In terms of paid attendance alone it was the largest crowd ever to see a baseball game, breaking the record of the opening of Cleveland Municipal Stadium in 1932, when, curiously enough, Lefty Grove had also been the visiting pitcher. On that day Grove was the winner, 1–0. On this day he wasn't. It was another old adversary, Lou Gehrig, in what was to become his sign-off year, who delivered the blow that knocked Grove out of the box and brought forth the second landmark event of the day: The Fight.

.   .   .

Even with the Great Rivalry, there was no particular reason for such a turnout. That early in the season, the Red Sox were in second place, 2½ games behind Cleveland, and the Yankees were in fourth place, 3½ behind. The pitching match-up for the first game might have had something to do with it: Lefty Grove against Red Ruffing. Grove had run up a record of 8–0, and Ruffing was at 6–1. More probably the big draw was Joe DiMaggio. DiMaggio had held out for the first two weeks of the season, under the misguided notion that having led the prosperous Yankees to three straight pennants, he was entitled to a salary of $25,000. Even more misguided was his belief that he would be supported by the fans. The Yankee front office was not above reminding him that young men of his age were being drafted into the army, and if Joe's patriotism wasn't necessarily being impugned, his sense of loyalty certainly was. For most Yankee fans this was going to be their first chance both to see Joe play and to give ardent voice to their sentiments.

The pitching contest never materialized. Ruffing pitched a three-hit shutout. Grove, having his only really bad outing of the year, was whacked around for eight earned runs in 3⅓ innings.

Archie McKain, a little lefty curve-baller, came in, was touched immediately for two singles, and then sent Jake Powell sprawling with his first pitch. His second pitch caught Powell right in the gut.

Powell picked himself up and headed for the mound with clear malicious intent. McKain advanced with equal firmness and resolve toward Powell. But it was Joe Cronin, racing in from his position at short, who reached Powell first and caught him with a booming right hand to the jaw. Jake Powell worked as a sheriff's deputy in South Carolina during the off season. He knew how to handle himself, too. Before they were finally pried apart and banished, they had put on one of the best toe-to-toe slugfests ever seen on a ball field.

But that was only the beginning. In order to get to the visiting team's locker room, Cronin had to pass through the Yankee dugout. Powell was waiting for him in the runway, along with half a dozen of his intrepid teammates.

Cal Hubbard, who was umpiring the game, had been an All-Star football tackle at both the college and professional levels. As big Cal liked to tell the story, he happened to glance over at the Yankee dugout and found it to be strangely devoid of uniforms. *Mmmmmm, Cal Hubbard mused to himself, I do believe that young Irish lad may be in need of some assistance.* Calling time, Cal went trotting into the runway and found a somewhat bloodied Cronin in the center of a wild melee. Cal proceeded to even up the odds considerably by reaching in with a huge paw and bouncing half a dozen Yankee uniforms — complete with occupying players — off the adjoining walls.

Along with Powell, Cronin was fined and suspended for ten days. He also won himself considerable respect from his players.

The Red Sox lost the second game on a wild throw by Mike Higgins, after frittering away a 4–0 lead. The Yankees had jumped into second place, the Red Sox had fallen to fourth, and from there on it was just a matter of time.

The Memorial Day double-header stands as a footnote of sorts to the career of Joe DiMaggio, following the hostility that had been engendered by his holdout.

The first time Joe came to bat in the double-header, the record crowd stood up in a roaring, dissonant mass, and although there was no consensus in the press box on whether the cheers outweighed the boos, there was total agreement that it was the loudest reception ever accorded a player in Yankee Stadium just for coming to the plate. Even louder than the reception given to Babe Ruth upon his return from his suspension in 1922.

Immediately, Joe began to win the opposition back by lashing a typical DiMaggio double into the gap, the first of his three doubles in the first game.

In the second game, the Yankees were able to draw within a run of Boston when DiMaggio's fifth hit of the day was followed by Lou Gehrig's home run. By then, Joe had become the Great DiMadge again, with every dissenting voice having been stilled.

The next year, 1939, was Ted Williams's first season, and, in all probability, Joe DiMaggio's greatest. The Yankees finished at 106–45 (.702), which ranked them with the 1927 team as the only American League team to finish above .700.

The Red Sox came in second again, a distant 17 games behind. And yet, it was the Red Sox who took the season series, 11–8. And did it in the most dramatic of fashions by winning seven straight games over the second half of the season. And, if it's a Cracker Jack prize we're looking for here, they swept a five-game series in Yankee

Stadium to give Tom Yawkey and Boston fandom their greatest moment of ecstasy in the prewar era.

Best of all, the streak began at a time when the season appeared to be going down the drain.

When the Yankees came to Boston at the beginning of July, they were leading the league by 13½ games, and were being compared, with absolutely no apologies, to the 1927 team. Worse yet, if you were a Red Sox rooter, they had done it for the most part without Joe DiMaggio and Lou Gehrig. DiMag had missed five weeks with torn ligaments when his spikes caught on a muddy field during the seventh game of the season.

If you want to find the date, it should be easy. A day after DiMaggio was carried off the field, Lou Gehrig played his 2,130th game, one of the holiest numbers in the theology of baseball. What that means, for the benefit of recent converts, is that he was never going to play another.

The next time the Yankees appeared in Fenway Park, the scene of so many of Gehrig's finest days, he was just barely able to fulfill the purely ceremonial role of walking up to home plate to hand the line-up card to the umpire. By July he wasn't even able to do that.

The Red Sox took the first two games of the three-game series in Boston with their two left-handers, Fritz Ostermueller and Lefty Grove. The key victory came behind Grove when Joe Cronin hit a two-run homer to tie the game and Williams hit a three-run homer to win it.

When the competition moved to New York the next weekend, the Yankees were 11½ ahead. In between those two series there had occurred that most emotional of tributes, Lou Gehrig Appreciation Day, the day when Gehrig gave his "I'm the luckiest man in the world" speech.

The Red Sox won five straight. The two heaviest-hitting teams of the time played five games over three days, and they were all closely contested, tightly played games. Emerson Dickman, a handsome young right-hander who was just coming into his own, won two games in relief, both by scores of 4–3. Fritz Ostermueller and Denny Galehouse needed no help in the Saturday double-header, as they stopped the Yankees, 3–1 and 3–2.

The Red Sox won the first game when the Yankees failed to complete a double play. The Yankees lost the final game when their

pitcher made two awful throws to the bases. For once it was the Red
Sox who hit the long ball when they needed one and made the great
play when they needed it. In a complete break with tradition, it was
the Red Sox who had the relief pitching.

Jimmie Foxx hit two crucial home runs, plus a gigantic triple and a
double. Bobby Doerr saved the Galehouse game in the ninth inning
with a dazzling play on the Yankees' awesome rookie Charlie Keller.

But when it was all over, it was Joe Cronin (who was still being
referred to in the New York press as the Boy Manager) who beat
the series over the head and took it home with him to be framed and
mounted and placed in his trophy case. In the three games in Boston,
Cronin had knocked in six runs, two in each game. In New York he
did even better.

The first game was the key. The Yankees had Red Ruffing (11–2)
ready to pitch. He was on his way to his second straight 21–7 season. Against him Cronin sent out Jake Wade as his sacrificial lamb, a
wild lefty who had won one game early in the season, would never
win another, and was gone before the summer was over. Not unexpectedly, the Yankees had Wade on the ropes in each of the first five
innings. Most unexpectedly, they were not able to put him away until
Joe Gordon's double in the sixth inning tied the score. Emerson Dickman came in with the bases loaded, struck out Babe Dahlgren and
Ruffing, and shut the Yankees down the rest of the way.

The tone of the series, by unanimous agreement, was set in the
third inning of the first game, when Cronin went charging around the
field from one umpire to another after they had reversed the original
decision and awarded the Yankees a double play on what was clearly
a trapped ball. In the next inning "a still irate Cronin" stepped up to
the plate and hit a home run into the right-field stands to give his
team a 2–0 lead. It was at that moment, in the view of almost every
writer in the press box, that the atmosphere in the whole ball park
changed.

The winning run came across in the eighth, when Cronin, who had
opened the inning with a walk, scored from third while Jim Tabor was
just barely beating out the double-play throw to first.

If Friday had been Joe Cronin's day to shine, then Saturday turned
out to be Joe McCarthy's day to suffer. It was a day of oppressive
heat, a day fit only for mad dogs, Englishmen, and beetles. Beetles?
Yup. An infestation of Japanese beetles invaded the park, homed

right in on the Yankee dugout, and remained there — green-bodied, vicious-looking insects — swooping back and forth in tight formation directly in front of Joe McCarthy's corner.

They were like a "moving curtain," wrote one New York writer, cutting off McCarthy's view of the field. Not a pretty sight, perhaps, but what was going on out there on the other side of the curtain wasn't so pretty, either.

The Red Sox scored early off Oral Hildebrand, with the eventual winning runs driven in by Williams and Cronin. They would have scored at least twice as many if it hadn't been for the brilliant fielding and throwing of Joe DiMaggio.

In the second game Denny Galehouse and Marius Russo both pitched hitless ball into the sixth inning. Joe Cronin drove in the first run in the seventh. The Yankees came right back to tie the score on singles by DiMaggio and Keller.

And then it was Bobby Doerr's turn. He broke the tie in the eighth by dropping a double down the left-field line and then saved the game, after Jimmie Foxx had hit a home run, with a spectacular force-out on a drive by Charlie Keller.

It was a highly partisan crowd of 47,652 that showed up for the Sunday double-header. But they were not partisans of the Yankees. For the first time in memory the New York fans were rooting for the Boston Red Sox to pull off the sweep and keep the pennant race alive.

They saw the Yankees outhit the Red Sox and the Red Sox outplay the Yankees.

Cronin was sitting pretty. For the opener he had Lefty Grove, who was 8–2 and on his way to leading the league in both winning record (15–4) and ERA (2.54). Grove was pitching better than ever — except, it seemed, when he pitched in Yankee Stadium. The Yankees roughed him up for 10 hits and three runs in six innings, before Emerson Dickman came in again to stop them cold.

Lefty Gomez, who was hooking up with Grove for perhaps the twentieth time in his career, left at the end of the sixth with a blistered finger, but not before Foxx had narrowed the lead to 3–2 with a 460-foot triple that carried beyond the flagpole in center field.

That was still the score when Joe Cronin stepped to the plate with two out in the eighth inning and hit a two-run homer to win it.

Suddenly the Red Sox had a chance to sweep the Yankees in Yankee Stadium, and nobody had to tell them that it would be a long, long while before any Red Sox team came this way again.

The Red Sox were pitching Eldon Auker, who threw the ball from down and under in the manner of Carl Mays. Auker was the pitcher who had opposed Dizzy Dean — though not for long — in that tumultuous seventh game of the 1934 World Series. He was also the pitcher who had lost the final game against the Yankees in the Boston series.

In that game the Yankees had hammered him for eight hits in three innings and scored six runs. In New York they reached him for four hits and two walks in 1⅔ innings and scored a grand total of one run. He was replaced by Jack Wilson, a big right-handed fast-ball pitcher for whom the word "potential" had apparently been invented. When he was good, which was every now and then, he was very, very good. And this was one of those times.

The pitcher for the Yankees was Irving ("Bump") Hadley, a Massachusetts native inevitably referred to in the Boston press as "Lynn's Irving ('Bump') Hadley." The Sox couldn't do a thing with him, but it didn't matter because Hadley did it to himself; first with a wild throw to second that let in one run, and then with a wild throw to second that let in two more.

In the end McCarthy sent in his lucky charm, a rookie named Atley Donald. "Winning Pitcher" Donald, he was being called; the kid didn't seem to know how to lose. He had come up to the Yankees from the Newark Bears, who were unquestionably the best minor league team ever fielded, with a record of 19–2, and he was 9–0 for the Yankees so far in 1939.

Not today for him, either. Jimmie Foxx very quickly made it 5–1 with a two-run homer. DiMaggio's single, knocking in two runs, was too little and too late. The Yankee lead had been cut to 6½ games.

The question in the press box was this: When was the last time the Yankees had lost two double-headers on successive days? The answer was 1913, when they had finished not first but seventh.

You couldn't blame Joe DiMaggio. The Yankee Clipper had four hits in the opener and two in the nightcap, and had driven in three of the Yankees' six runs. For the series he had gone 10 for 20 and lifted his average to .435.

                    .   .   .

Joe McCarthy, having seen his team beaten in every possible way, was livid. "Who the hell are the world champions here," he raged in the clubhouse. "Us or the Red Sox?"

The Red Sox, playing like champs, ran their winning streak to 12 games, all of them on the road. Unfortunately for them, the Yankees went off on a winning streak, too, and when the Boston tear was over, only another half-game had been knocked off the Yankee lead.

It didn't matter to Tom Yawkey. The Red Sox had beaten the Yankees five straight in Yankee Stadium, and as far as he was concerned, the season was already a success. On their return to Boston, Tom Yawkey hired the main ballroom of the Parker House, ordered a piano sent up, and threw a party for his players that was talked about for years.

The party wasn't over for Yawkey. It wasn't over for Cronin, either. They just had to wait until the Yankees returned to Fenway Park in September. And if the Yankee lead was back up to 13½ games by then, so what? That didn't have anything to do with the Red Sox.

As usual, a weekend series was scheduled — a single game on Saturday and a Sunday double-header. The Sox won the first two to run their streak against the Yankees to seven straight wins. They lost the second game of the double-header on a forfeit. And you know there has to be a story to go with that.

The focus turns once again on Cronin and DiMaggio, with a cursory glance in the direction of Fritz Ostermueller.

In the Saturday game Cronin had three doubles off Ruffing and knocked in three runs. In the opening game on Sunday, he came up twice with the bases loaded and drove home five runs with a double and a single. Over the course of the seven-game winning streak, Cronin had knocked in 14 runs. Over the full 10 games, he knocked in 20 runs. And that's not counting the forfeit game, in which he hit his fifteenth home run.

But let's go back to Saturday. A bad day at Fenway Park for Red Ruffing. He had been whipping along at a 20–4 clip and leading the league in all categories. But on this day he had nothing — possibly because the train had arrived late and the players had been rushed right to the ball park. Whatever the reason, he allowed the first five batters to reach base. Joe McCarthy, who could do some bizarre things under certain circumstances, left him in to take a 10-hit, 12–7 shellacking that almost ruined him for the rest of the season and, without question, cost him the won-lost and ERA titles.

If Joe Cronin was still doing his thing against the Yankees, Joe DiMaggio was still doing his against everybody. DiMaggio had gone into a slump after the New York series and fallen to .399, but he was coming into Boston with a 17-game hitting streak alive and his average back up to .408. With only 30 games left in the season, he seemed to have every chance of becoming the first .400 hitter in nine years.

Off Ostermueller, who was defeating the Yankees for the third time, he hit a home run and a double and ran his hitting streak to 18 straight, the longest in the American League that season.

The streak came to an abrupt — and unnatural — end the next day, when he had to leave the game in the first inning. The ligament in his right knee popped as he was crossing first base after slapping into a force play. Fortunately the injury wasn't as serious as it had seemed, and he was back in the line-up for the second game. All he got were four hits. He was officially credited with three.

Take my hand and we will return again to Fenway Park in the days of the 6:30 P.M. Sunday curfew.

As the second game was getting under way, the Red Sox were not only trying to make it eight straight, they were slavering over the prospect of sweeping the Yankees in Fenway Park after sweeping them at Yankee Stadium. With the Red Sox taking an early lead on home runs by Williams and Cronin, it looked as if they might succeed.

Even after Joe DiMaggio hit a two-run homer (his twenty-fifth) in the sixth to give the Yankees their first lead of the day, Ted Williams hammered his second home run of the day (his twenty-fourth) to take it right back.

Joe Gordon exploded his twenty-fourth in the seventh to tie the game, 5–5, and when the Yankees loaded the bases with nobody out in the eighth, Red Sox fans began to watch the clock.

Keller and DiMaggio had opened with singles, and a walk to Bill Dickey filled the bases. George Selkirk slapped into a force play at the plate, but when Jimmie Foxx dropped the double-play throw to first, Joe DiMaggio, always the superb base runner, came wheeling all the way around to put the Yankees ahead. Joe Gordon — a murderous hitter against the Red Sox always — followed with a double, and the score was 7–5 with runners on second and third, one out, and nine minutes to curfew. Not to worry. In order for the Yankee runs to count, the Sox would have to finish their turn at bat. Otherwise the game would revert to the seventh inning. What were the odds of squeezing in five outs, not to mention the time lost in changing sides, when the home team was going to be taking a most casual, not to say uncooperative, attitude toward bringing the inning to a close?

Cronin ordered that Babe Dahlgren be given an intentional base on balls, a conventional enough strategy — hohoho — with men on second and third and one out. It never happened. Dahlgren swung at the first two pitches and suddenly the inning was over. So, as it developed, was the ball game.

Here's how it happened. On the first pitch, Selkirk came trotting in from third so that he could be tagged out at the plate. On the second pitch, Joe Gordon did the same thing. Johnny Peacock, a man of severely limited imagination, obliged them both by making the putouts.

Cronin came in to lodge what he hoped would be a time-consuming protest on the grounds that the Yankees were engaging in tactics that were probably illegal and certainly unfair in having their batter swing during a perfectly legitimate intentional base on balls, and then compounding their offense — and possibly even desecrating the Sabbath — by deliberately running into the putouts at the plate.

The umpire, once again, was Cal Hubbard, and when Hubbard ruled that the Yankees had played within the rules so let's get on with it, the angry crowd, rising in righteous wrath, pelted the field with a barrage of pop bottles and assorted items of garbage.

It was the worst thing they could have done. Cal Hubbard ruled that the actions of the Boston crowd had made it impossible to resume the game before the curfew set in and awarded the game to the Yankees.

Let's tote up the damage. Momentarily the game went into the record book as a 9–0 forfeit, and the Red Sox registered a loss instead of a tie. A week later, league president Will Harridge reversed Hubbard and ruled that the game had ended in a tie.

As far as player statistics were concerned, it made no difference. All records still reverted to the seventh inning. Joe Gordon lost his double and his fourth RBI of the day. But the real victim was Joe DiMaggio. Joe lost his eighth-inning single. The hit had raised his average for the season to .412, with 27 games to play. When it was taken away from him, his average went back to .410. One hit wouldn't seem to mean that much in the vast scheme of things, except that the laws that govern the way-it-is tell us that in the same vast scheme of things, it's exactly this kind of aberration that comes back to haunt you.

Joe slumped briefly after leaving Boston, then had another big day with 21 games left, and was still hitting .408 with only two weeks to go. Over those final two weeks, the Clipper was plagued by an inflammation that — shades of Babe Ruth — made his eyes water so badly that he slumped to his final mark of .381.

He still finished with 30 homers and 126 RBIs, and was the runaway choice for MVP.

Ted Williams became the first rookie to lead the league in runs batted in. Ted had 145 to beat out DiMaggio, whose 126 had come in 103 fewer times at bat. Joe Gordon finished fifth with 111.

This was the highest batting average the Great DiMadge would ever have. It fell to Ted Williams — as we all know — to become the majors' next .400 hitter two years later.

But, then, 1941 wasn't a bad season for Joe DiMaggio, either. It was, in fact, the season by which they would both be measured — Ted and Joe — in memory, literature, and song.

Chapter Ten

1941

Joe DiMaggio is the best all-around ballplayer I have ever seen.

— Ted Williams

Ted Williams is the best left-handed hitter in the game.

— Joe DiMaggio

I N the summer of 1941, a 26-year-old Joe DiMaggio and a 22-year-old Ted Williams, both at the very top of their game, put together seasons that will last for as long as there are plaques in Cooperstown and men to read of their deeds.

Joe DiMaggio reeled off his 56-game hitting streak, the greatest of all time. And Ted became the last man to hit .400. And if no one was aware at the time that what baseball was seeing was the last of the .400 hitters, neither was anyone aware that an era was coming to a close, and that Joe and Ted — Ted and Joe — were bringing it to a close not with a period but with an exclamation point.

They traveled on different wires, moved to different rhythms. Then, as now, it was the consecutive-game record that captured the attention of the nation, because we all love a cliff-hanger.

By its very nature a consecutive-game streak has no latitude for failure. With DiMaggio it was a life-or-death story every day. The Williams quest for a .400 season, by contrast, didn't turn into a do-or-die proposition until the last day of the season.

Looked at one way, DiMaggio's 56-game streak is a freak record, and Williams's .406 average is a solid accomplishment. Baseball is, after all, a game of the long season. What is so important about hitting in 56 out of 56 games, instead of 55 out of 56? You could almost say, "So what?"

There are statistics that define accomplishment, and there are statistics that exist only because there are statisticians with mouths to feed.

Except for this:

The publicity builds both ways. Once you make it mean something, it means something. The combination of the New York–centered press and the DiMaggio persona made it mean everything.

"In the whole streak," as Joe was to remember it, "I had only one lucky hit, a blooper that I hit off my ear against Thornton Lee in Chicago." Well . . . not exactly. What Joe undoubtedly meant was that he could remember only one lucky hit once he had become aware that he was on a streak that was of a different scope and magnitude from, say, his 18-game and 23-game streaks of the previous two seasons.

There were opposing pitchers who wanted to give him the best possible chance, and opposing pitchers who wanted to be the one to stop him out of professional pride or personal ambition or, in one notable case, sheer malice.

And, as in all affairs of man, great and small, there was some luck and some unluck:

• A couple of pop flies on balls hit off the handle.
• A couple of bad bounces.
• A couple of topped balls.
• A fly lost in the wind and sun.
• A helpful official scorer or two.
• A little help from his manager and a lot of help from his teammates.

It's all in retrospect, anyway. It's just a little game we play. On the day a streak begins, nobody knows anything has happened. Nobody has ever asked, "Where were you on May 15, the day the DiMaggio streak started?" But if you happened to be in Yankee Stadium, you were watching the Yanks take a 13–1 drubbing from Chicago. Although Joe had knocked in the team's only run with a first-inning double, he had also gone 1 for 4 on the day to fall to .304, his lowest

average of the whole season. The real story of the game was that
the Yankees were in disrepair. Tommy Henrich was in the worst
slump of his career. The rookie second-base combination of Phil Rizzuto and Gerry Priddy, of which so much had been expected, had
flopped. The Yankees had lost their fifth straight game — their tenth
loss in 14 games — and dropped below .500 for the only time all
year, a losing streak that was in no way unconnected to the terrible
slump that had descended on Joe DiMaggio himself.

The odd thing about it was that DiMaggio, who had made Opening
Day for only the second time in six years, had come out of the blocks
with a blazing eight-game streak, during which he had hit .528, including four home runs, four doubles, and a triple, and had 14 runs
batted in. He had then gone into a nosedive, batting only .190 in 20
games.

While a healthy Joe DiMaggio was starting a season for one of the
rare times in his career, Ted Williams had come out of spring training
limping. Ted had chipped a bone in his ankle that spring and been
restricted to little more than pinch-hitting duty over the first 11
games.

Sixteen years later, when Ted was flirting with .400 again, I put a
question to him: "In view of the change in travel conditions, in night
baseball, in improved pitching, and the fact that at the age of 38 you
are hardly getting any leg hits, might not a valid case be made that
you are having an even greater season now than you had in 1941?"
His answer was no. "Nobody wants to remember it now, but I played
that whole year with my ankle taped up. I didn't get any leg hits at all
in 1941. None."

Nor did anybody seem to remember that Ted had a hitting streak
of his own that year which ran parallel to DiMaggio's for the first 23
games.

If both streaks started on May 15, then obviously each player had
gone hitless the previous day. Joe had actually been shut out on two
consecutive days by Bob Feller and Mel Harder, while Ted had been
collared by an almost excessively mediocre White Sox pitcher named
Bill Dietrich and had seen his average drop from .373 to .339.

On May 15 Ted went 1 for 3 against Cleveland, but the next day
he had only one hit in four times at bat and dropped from .339 to
.333, the lowest *he* was going to go all season. That one hit, how-

ever, had knocked in two runs. The following day he got three hits off Bob Feller, and in another week he went over the .400 mark in Yankee Stadium.

The Red Sox and Yankees played three series during the Di-Maggio streak, beginning with a home-and-home series in late May and ending with three games in Yankee Stadium during the first week of July. Nobody was following either streak in May, but by July the whole country was tuned in to Joe DiMaggio.

In those May games DiMag's streak was preserved as the result of a bewildering decision by Joe Cronin, and then almost wrecked by the inexplicable action of his own manager, Joe McCarthy.

DiMaggio had a modest eight-game streak going when he faced the Red Sox in a weekend series in New York, and in four of those games the hit hadn't come until his last time at bat. After the first two meetings with Boston, it was six games out of 10 on his last swing of the bat — and both of those last-gasp hits had contributed to what may well have been the two most interesting games of the year.

On Friday, May 23, the Yankees were leading, 9–7, in the ninth inning, and it had been Joe's eighth inning single that had given the Yankees their lead.

With two out in the ninth and the tying runs in scoring position, Cronin sent up the only left-handed hitter still on the bench who could even be thought of as a pinch-hitter, a veteran minor-league pitcher named Oscar ("Tom") Judd. And what did Judd do but single through the gathering darkness to tie the game, 9–9.

Because of Judd's hit, the game was going to have to be replayed in full as part of a double-header the next time the Sox came to town. Not only did both of those games count in the DiMaggio streak, but it was in the replay of that 9–9 tie that Joe was going to challenge Wee Willie Keeler's ancient, doddering, and wholly irrelevant record.

Just like the Babe, right? Of all the similarities that run between Ruth's 60 home runs and Joe DiMaggio's 56 games, none is more remarkable than the tie game that gave each of them the benefit of two games for the price of one. Equally remarkable — bring up the *Twilight Zone* music, professor — is the coincidence that the score in both of the tie games was 9–9. And as a final coincidence — give us a rim shot here, drummer — the score became 9–9 in the ninth inning of game nine of DiMaggio's streak.

If we go back to Babe's first home run chase, we also find the complication of a record suddenly unearthed from the olden days of baseball — a little nineteenth-century music, maestro — that provided an opportunity to break the record twice, with the second time being by far the more satisfactory. Moreover, the Babe broke that record against the Yankees, and Joe was going to do the same against the Red Sox.

It is a wonderment.

The significance of Joe's last-ditch hit in that Saturday game, May 24, was that he never should have been allowed to swing at the ball. Last of the seventh, the Red Sox were leading, 6–3, on two hits by Joe Cronin. All the Yankee runs off lefty Earl Johnson had been allowed on errors. Then in the seventh, four straight hits, highlighted by a line shot off Johnson's left leg by pinch-hitter Red Ruffing, brought Joe DiMaggio to the plate with runners on second and third, two out, and the Red Sox leading, 6–5.

First base open? Two men out? Every percentage said to walk him. Rule number one in playing the Yankees was: "Don't let DiMaggio beat you." Instead, Cronin came to the mound to tell Johnson, in those time-honored words of managers, "Don't give him anything to hit." What that meant, and still means, is, "If he wants to swing at something not so good, let him."

The trouble was that DiMaggio knew exactly what Cronin was saying, and with the winning runs on base, Joe DiMaggio was not there to be walked. He guessed that Johnson would be trying to throw him a hard curve, low and away, off the plate. Earl Johnson put the ball exactly where he wanted it, and Joe not only went down to get it but was able to line it into left field for a game-winning single.

Sunday's game featured Lefty Grove, who was on his way to winning 300 games. He had already won number 295 against the Yankees in Boston. None of them was easier than number 296. Old Mose would have had a shutout if it hadn't been for a couple of errors by Jimmie Foxx, who was playing third base in place of an injured Jim Tabor.

DiMaggio had a hit on his first time at bat, and that was it. Ted Williams had three singles and a double. All four hits, including the line double, were hard shots that went through the infield between second baseman Joe Gordon and first baseman Johnny Sturm. "The least you could have done," McCarthy yelled at Sturm after the fourth hit, "was wave at it."

But Ted was the one who was waving. He was waving goodbye to the rest of the hitters in the league. The four hits brought his average up to .404 and put him at the top of the American League to stay.

His average was up to .421 when he took the field at Fenway Park to face the Yankees in their traditional Memorial Day double-header.

DiMaggio shouldn't have taken the field at all. The Yankees had just arrived from Washington, where they had participated in the first night game ever played in Griffith Stadium, followed by an afternoon game that had been called because of rain in the sixth inning.

In the night game, which had been played in cold and blustery weather, Joe had gotten his hit in his last time at bat, a triple, to set off a game-winning rally. In the rained-out game he had been both lucky and unlucky — unlucky because the rain had washed out his sixth-inning single, lucky because he had just barely managed to beat out a high hopper off the plate in his first time at bat. Otherwise the streak would have ended after 12 games, unsung and indeed unnoticed, on a washed-out single in Washington.

But it was alive at 13, and because of the unusual circumstances that had kept it going, the New York writers began to mention it in their columns for the first time.

Joe himself was scarcely aware of it. All he knew was that the weather had settled into his bones and his neck was killing him. To show how badly he was hurting, he made four errors during the double-header — including a muffed fly ball — and only the compassion of the official scorer saved him from being charged with two more.

Still, he managed to help his team win the first game before the usual packed house. The Red Sox had carried a 3–1 lead into the ninth, with the third run coming in on the dropped fly ball. Earl Johnson was breezing along on a two-hitter.

Red Ruffing started Johnson on his demise when he pinch-hit for Tommy Henrich (which shows you how Henrich was hitting) and singled off the wall. Then DiMaggio got to Johnson on his last chance again with a line shot to left, and the Yankees went on to score three runs and bring their winning streak to six games.

The second game on Memorial Day 1941 is beyond argument THE WORST game Joseph Paul DiMaggio ever played. It was bad enough that he had struggled through the first game, but between games he had stiffened up so completely that he could barely move his neck and right shoulder (the first indication of a condition that was to become chronic).

McCarthy didn't ask DiMaggio how he felt, whether he could play, or what round it was, and in the code of the day — a code that said, "It isn't my place to go to the manager" — Joe contented himself with asking Crosetti and Gordon to come out as far as they could to take the throw whenever a ball was hit to him.

The Yankees were humiliated, 13–0, and no one more than DiMaggio, who made three errors. In the first inning Ted Williams hit a ground single through the middle and Joe couldn't move his head enough to field it cleanly. In subsequent innings his throws to the plate were so far off the mark that they went rattling against the railing in front of the box seats along the third-base line.

That his streak remained intact proves that there are forces within the universe that smile on the brave and reward the intrepid.

The question as to why Joe McCarthy didn't take him out of the game after the Yankees had fallen behind, 10–0, by the fourth inning — as Joe Cronin did with Ted Williams — is typical of the many questions that are inspired by the actions of Joe McCarthy.

In the fifth inning DiMaggio hit a cramped little fly to right, an easy out, except that Pete Fox, the right fielder, lost the ball in the sun and the buffeting wind, and by the time he was able to straighten himself out, the ball had been blown away from him.

When the green light signifying a base hit flashed on in the newly constructed Fenway Park scoreboard, the crowd booed lustily. Because up to then, you see, Mickey Harris had been pitching a no-hitter.

McCarthy pulled Charlie Keller and Red Rolfe out of the game the next inning. Cronin, being no fool, sent in a substitute for himself.

Joe DiMaggio played the full nine innings.

In those two series in May, Ted was 7 for 11 in New York and 3 for 5 in Boston. Joe, with a hit in each game, was 5 for 18, for a not very impressive average of .277.

Overall, Ted's streak was at 17 games, and his batting average was .429. Joe's figures were 16 and .331.

The two teams caught the same train out of Boston. At Buffalo their cars were uncoupled and they went their separate ways. Through the entire month of June they would continue to go their separate ways. They would not be meeting again until July 1. The schedule makers couldn't put all their games on weekends and holidays. No, they would only be meeting in a Tuesday double-header at Yankee Stadium. And they would draw a record weekday crowd of

52,832 to witness the Great DiMadge make his final assault on the major league record.

Ted's streak had ended at 23, two days after he had reached his high mark of .439. It came to an end on a warm Sunday afternoon in Chicago, when he was shut down in both ends of a Sunday double-header by Ted Lyons and Thornton Lee.

The end of the streak didn't mean much to Ted. The first game had presented a pitching duel between two crafty veterans, Lefty Grove and Ted Lyons, and Williams had spent the better part of his postgame commentary gushing about what a pleasure it had been to watch the old masters at work. (Grove and Lyons were to become linked together in a more consequential way later that season, for they turned out to be the only pitchers to figure in both Babe Ruth's 60 home runs and Joe DiMaggio's 56-game streak.)

During Ted's 23 games, he had hit .487 (43 for 88). DiMaggio with his streak intact was 32 for 87 (.368). On the season Williams was far ahead in batting, at .433 to Joe's .333.

The next two months, however, were going to be golden ones for DiMaggio, and as Joe caught fire, so did the Yankees. Phil Rizzuto came back into the line-up, this time to stay. Charlie Keller was a powerhouse. But it was "Joe, Joe DiMaggio, we want you on our side" who was The Man, and with all eyes turned toward him, he wasn't waiting until his final time at bat anymore. As often as not, the hit was coming on his first trip to the plate.

Not that the month of June started out especially well for the Yankees. Quite the contrary. On June 2, after they had been beaten by Feller, the news came over that Henry Louis Gehrig had died. He was 37. Joe McCarthy and Bill Dickey immediately caught a train back to New York. The players, clearly shaken, were beaten twice in a row in Detroit. But after that, for the rest of the month, and indeed the rest of the season, the Yankees' fortunes soared on the wings of the DiMaggio streak.

• During the remainder of the month of June they won 17 out of 21 games.

• In the month of July they took 25 out of 29, a single-month record that still stands. Add them together, tack on the first two days of August, and you get 44 out of 52, another record. Not until the 1977 Yankees of Reggie Jackson, Thurman Munson, and Mickey Rivers won 40 of their last 50 games to beat the Jim Rice–Fred Lynn–Carlton Fisk Red Sox did any other team come close. (All right, the Kansas City Royals won 43 out of 53 that same season, but we're not talking about *them.*)

While Ted was taking the collar against Lyons and Lee, DiMaggio came out of his double-header with a streak of 24 games and a rising tide of excitement around New York about his run at the Yankee record of 29, which had been set by Roger Peckinpaugh in 1919 and matched by Earle Combs in 1931. Both were still very much on the scene, Combs as the first-base coach for the Yankees and Peckin-paugh as the manager of the Cleveland Indians. Combs was going to be on the field whatever happened; and while the god of dramatic confrontations had been unable to arrange for DiMaggio to break the record against Peckinpaugh's team, he had done the next best thing. The Yankees were on their way back to New York to face the Cleveland Indians in the three games that would end with his tying the record.

For game 27 Babe Ruth was in the stands and Bob Feller was on the mound. Feller liked to pitch DiMag high and tight, with plenty of heat, even though he was aware that if he missed just a little toward the plate, he would be right in Joe's wheelhouse. When the count ran to 3–0, McCarthy gave DiMaggio the hit sign, and with Feller moving the ball in enough to be sure of a strike, DiMag ripped the ball to the fence in right-center for a double.

That early on, McCarthy was demonstrating that he was going to help Joe all he could. His help turned out to be a mixed blessing. There would be at least four other times when Joe got the green light to swing on 3–0. Only once more would he be successful. But that success produced what was certainly the most soul-satisfying of all his hits.

Ruth wasn't present the next day, but in what we can call a tribute if we want to, Joe sent one into the upper tier in right field where the Babe used to hit them.

In another echo of Babe Ruth, a fan grabbed Joe's bat after the game and tried to escape across the field. DiMaggio caught him and retrieved it.

The hit that tied the Yankee record became almost anticlimactic. The spectators had to wait through a rain delay of an hour and a half, and then groan through two unsuccessful turns at bat before Joe lined a double off lefty Al Milnar.

He had tied Peckinpaugh, against Peckinpaugh's team. He was going to have to break the mark against Jimmy Dykes's Chicago White Sox.

Luck was with him. Luck and Luke Appling. He got just one hit, a routine ground ball on his third time at bat that took a wicked hop and ricocheted off shortstop Appling's shoulder.

Curiously enough, the one "lucky hit" DiMaggio remembers, the "blooper" off Thornton Lee, came the next day. And it wasn't really that lucky. It was a pop fly to short center that was just barely out of Appling's reach. Makes you wonder if he fixed on the wrong Appling play.

The real blooper, the hit he seemed to be describing, came two days after that. Facing Dizzy Trout, who was always tough on him, he blooped a handle hit over the head of Rudy York at first base. It came in the first inning and it was, again, his only hit.

But in chronicling the bloop hits, one must never forget that no man ever hit more balls on the nose, walloped more long drives that were caught in the no man's land of Yankee Stadium, than Joe DiMaggio.

DiMaggio was an amazingly appealing figure. He was a hero for the times. There was no showboat in him, no wasted motion. Perfection was the only word that could be found to describe him. Even Yankee haters could not help but root for him to go all the way.

It was a long, long way, though, from the Yankee record of 30 games to the ultimate goal of 41, and the press set up its own targets to keep the tension high. Three years earlier George McQuinn had set a modern record, if you wanted to see it that way, by hitting in 34 straight games. And then, on the final approach to George Sisler's 41 was Ty Cobb's 40.

The games were filled with incident and flourishes and personalities. Take game 36. The first two times up DiMaggio did nothing, and then he hit a Bob Muncrief pitch that was caught against the wall 457 feet away.

Muncrief was a fast-ball pitcher. He was a rookie. And he was that rarest of all specimens, a winning St. Louis Browns pitcher. Muncrief was losing, 4–0, when Joe came up for one last try in the eighth. He had nothing to lose by making Joe chase bad balls. He had everything to gain by becoming the Man Who Stopped Joe DiMaggio. Instead, he went right at him again. Fast ball, high and tight, fouled off; another fast ball even farther inside; and then a curve inside that Joe lined into left field for a single.

Asked why he hadn't simply thrown four pitches out of the strike zone, Muncrief said, "That wouldn't have been fair — to him or me. Hell, he's the greatest player I *ever* saw."

Luke Sewell, the Browns manager, was even more direct: "He means too much to baseball to be cheated out of his chance of the record through a technicality."

Johnny Babich of the Athletics had no such compunctions and no such awe. Before game 40, with Joe right on the lip of Sisler's record, Babich announced that he was going to stop him by not pitching to him. Don't laugh. Babich had announced a year earlier that he was going to keep the Yankees from winning the pennant, and he had done exactly that. He beat them five times, ending with the game that virtually eliminated them with four games left in the season.

Babich almost didn't get his chance to become the spoiler, though, because Joe almost didn't get past the Brownies. For seven innings Marius Russo had been pitching a no-hitter, but as he said afterwards, the focus on DiMaggio was so absolute by then that nobody had even noticed.

For although the Browns were hitless for seven innings, DiMaggio was hitless too.

Joe had started the day against Eldon Auker by fouling out on a 3–0 pitch. The second time he reached on an error, and the third time he grounded out. The Yankees were leading. There would be only two more innings, and the considerable possibility existed that DiMaggio's streak was coming to an end. In the last of the eighth inning, Joe was the fourth batter due up. The Yankees were ahead, 3–1. Unless somebody got on base — or the Browns committed the miracle of scoring some runs — the streak was over.

When Red Rolfe, the second batter of the inning, drew a walk, Tommy Henrich ran back to the bench to ask McCarthy for permission to bunt in order to guard against the possibility of grounding into a double play. In quick succession the following things happened.

1. Henrich bunted Rolfe to second.
2. The crowd grew silent.

3. The Great DiMadge lined the first pitch down the left-field line for two bases.

4. Everybody went crazy.

"I'll get him out the first time," Babich had said, "and walk him the next three." He didn't even do that. On Joe's first time at bat, Babich walked him on four straight balls.

Here is how Joe DiMaggio described what happened after that.

"Well, when I came up the second time that day in Philadelphia, it looked as if Babich was out to stop me by deliberately walking me. Not only was he pitching outside, but he was throwing curves out there.

"Our bench must have felt the same way, because the guys were giving Babich hell. Then, after he'd thrown me three wide ones, I looked over and saw McCarthy giving me the 'hit' signal. That was all I wanted. Babich came in with another bad pitch, about chin high. I belted it through his legs and made second base on it.

"After I pulled up, I looked at Johnny. He was white as a sheet. That drive had come mighty near to bowling him over."

Put yourself out there in Babich's place. A line shot between your legs that keeps rising until it goes over the outfielders' heads. Mighty near to bowling him over? Mighty near to deballing him would be more like it.

That put Joe in Washington for a double-header and a chance first to tie and then to break Sisler's record.

To make the occasion even more memorable, his bat was stolen between games, and he had to go for the record — right down to his last turn again — with a new one.

But, then, it turned out to be a shaky day all around. The Washington pitcher in the first game was Emil ("Dutch") Leonard, who only had the best knuckleball in baseball. Maybe the best knuckleball in the history of baseball. First time up, Joe turned a questioning look at the umpire following a strike call, something he *never* did. In the end, however, the decisive pitches were the only two pitches Leonard threw that weren't knucklers. Given the hit sign on the 3–0 count, Joe swung at a pitch that had him jammed and sent a weak fly to center. In the sixth inning Leonard tried to catch him off balance on the 1–1 pitch with another fast ball — a fast ball, after all, is a knuckleballer's change of pace — and DiMaggio rifled it toward the gap in left-center. George Washington Case, in center field, was the fastest player in the league, and there was that moment of held breath . . . before the ball eluded his final lunge.

The record-breaker in the second game came in the seventh inning against a nondescript relief pitcher, Arnold ("Red") Anderson. Joe lined his second pitch to left and for the second time that day the Washington crowd went bonkers, and — assuming that it was possible to go ballistic in 1941 — the Yankee bench went ballistic.

Now all kidding aside, that was the record. But what happened next was a rerun of the business with the original Babe Ruth home run record. This time Ned Williamson came back to life disguised as Wee Willie Keeler. At least Wee Willie Keeler was a name to reckon with — and a name that reached back to the dawn of Yankee history.

The *San Francisco Examiner* had been keeping a daily box on the progress of their local hero, and one of the writers had dug up a dusty old record book to show that Wee Willie had hit safely in 44 consecutive games in 1897. Now, the relevance of Keeler's era to the game as it was being played in 1941 was about the same as that of Lindbergh's flight to Paris to John Glenn's flight into space. For one thing, in 1897 foul balls weren't counted as strikes, and for another — of overriding importance where Willie Keeler was concerned — he could bunt forever on two strikes without having to worry about being called out.

So it was let's-pretend time again. And why not? Especially since Joe would be going after Wee Willie's record at Yankee Stadium. And against the Boston Red Sox.

With an off day on Monday to build the suspense.

And thus the record Tuesday crowd.

To make the day perfect, the Boston pitcher was Mickey Harris, the kid from the Bronx — the kid who had really stopped Joe on Memorial Day, notwithstanding the fact that Joe had lucked out on the windswept fly ball.

Harris was still handling DiMag with ease. Fortunately, Joe's teammates weren't having much trouble with him, and by the fifth inning, Joe found himself facing Mike Ryba, a jack-of-all-trades kind of pitcher.

And now came the most distasteful moment in the entire streak. Jim Tabor fumbled a routine ground ball, had trouble finding the handle and threw badly to first. The official scorer was Dan Daniel of the *New York World-Telegram*, a man not exactly famous for his ability to separate his own mind, heart, and soul from the fortunes of the New York Yankees.

Dan Daniel presented Joe with a base hit. The call was so raw that half his colleagues in the press box howled in disgust.

Unlike Fenway Park, Yankee Stadium did not have a hit and error designation on the scoreboard. And so when Joe came up again and belted a patented DiMaggio line drive to left, a cheer went up for five minutes. There may have been some cheering in the press box, too. Who wanted a make-believe hit to go with a make-believe record?

His next step was to tie the record. The second game of the double-header was the replay of the 9–9 tie. That one was easy. The Boston pitcher was Jack Wilson. Good fast ball, mediocre curve — DiMaggio's meat. First inning, another line shot to left, and Joe was tied with the wraith of Willie the Wisp.

He drove the final stake into Willie's heart the next day. Lefty Grove had been scheduled to pitch, a matchup that had clearly been made in Cooperstown. Unhappily, the day was so hot that Joe Cronin had to replace the aging Lefty with Heber ("Dick") Newsome. Not that Cronin was doing DiMag any favors. Heber ("Dick") Newsome — he was always referred to as Heber ("Dick") — had come out of the deep bullpen earlier in the season as a rainy-day replacement for Grove and gone on to become the ace of the Red Sox staff.

The record-breaker worked out just about right. DiMaggio began the day with one of those 400-foot outs that he lived with in his years at Yankee Stadium. On his second time at bat he hit a line drive that went over Ted Williams's head like a cannon shot and into the bleachers. "He broke Wee Willie's record," Lefty Gomez said, "by doing what Willie said to do. He hit it where they ain't."

It was, for the record, the only home run he hit against the Red Sox all season.

For Joe there would be a dozen more games before he was stopped. And then another 16 on top of that.

Ted Williams had been able to manage only one meaningless single in each of the three games, and had dropped to .401, his lowest average since he had first achieved the .400 level in New York, five weeks earlier.

Ted had not been swinging the bat well. He looked tired and drawn. Skinny as he was, he had a history of wilting in the heat of late June and early July. Still, Williams had batted .412 during the 45 games to Keeler's record, against .375 for DiMag.

One more historic event was going to inscribe itself indelibly in the Book of 1941. The All-Star Game was just around the corner, and when the two of them got there, both streaks were still alive. Ted had brought his batting average up to .406. Joe was up to game 48 and counting.

The All-Star Game belonged to Ted Williams, as no All-Star Game before or since has belonged to any other player. Ted always did love to hit in Detroit's Briggs Stadium.

Not that Joe didn't help out.

In the bottom of the ninth inning DiMaggio comes to the plate with the bases loaded and one out and hits what looks like a double-play ball to short. Running hard, though, he is able to beat the throw to first, bringing Ted Williams to the plate. Two on, two out, and the American League trailing, 5–4.

You've seen it a hundred times. The count goes to 2–1 and Ted hits the ball over everything. Over the fence, over the roof, over Mount Rushmore. And how many times have you seen the picture of a hand-clapping Ted Williams bounding toward first, in unconcealed, childish delight.

It was the biggest thrill, Ted has always said, of his career.

You can't argue with Ted about what gave him a thrill. But the shot did nothing to help his ball club, and it did not exactly inspire him to greater deeds. After the thrill came the dampener.

The Red Sox were staying on in Detroit, and before Ted left town, his season almost turned to disaster in the midwestern rains.

The weather was terrible. Then, when they were finally able to play, Ted got collared by Buck Newsom. The next day Ted walked three times before popping out. It was after the second walk that he twisted his ankle while scrambling back in the rain-soaked dirt around first base to avoid an attempted pickoff.

He had to sit out the second game with an aggravation of that injury to his ankle and his average down to .399. He would spend another nine days recovering on the bench.

During those nine games he pinch-hit four times: sacrifice fly, out, walk, and three-run homer.

The sacrifice fly is worth looking at, because there had been a change in the scoring rules a year earlier. Although it was still being called a sacrifice and the hitter credited with a run batted in, he was now being charged with a time at bat.

Take away that time at bat, and Ted would have been hitting an even .400 going into the final game of the season and the siren song of the .3996 would never have been heard.

An argument could be made that the enforced rest, coming when it did, was exactly what he needed. The three-run pinch homer was hit on the last day of the road trip and sent Ted back to Fenway Park ready and eager to return to the line-up. So ready, in fact, that he took off on a run of 19 hits in 35 times at bat that brought his average up to .412. Five of those hits were home runs, including one grand slammer.

And when Lefty Grove won his 300th game along the way, Ted contributed with a home run, a single, and two walks. (It is always written that Grove stumbled and slouched toward that 300th. Not so. In the two preceding games, Old Mose had first been beaten, 2–0, by Buck Newsom, and lost the other in the tenth inning on a dropped fly ball. It was *after* he won his 300th game, at age 41, that he began to stumble.)

While Ted was sitting on the bench, Joe DiMaggio's bat was smoking. From the time he broke Keeler's record, he had gone 24 for 44 to raise his average for the 56-game streak to .408. He was leading the league in RBIs with 76 and was tied for the home run lead with 20, and, as he told the New York sports writers with uncharacteristic swagger, he was far from giving up on catching Williams for the batting title. And why should he? He had brought his average up to .375, the highest it was going to be all season, and Ted had fallen back to .395, the lowest he was going to be.

In Ted's two years with the Red Sox, Joe had outhit him, .381 to .327 and .352 to .344, and had won the batting title both times.

Unhappily for Joe, he could not have chosen a worse time to open his mouth. How was he to know that his streak was about to end?

Until then it had been humming along almost too easily for Joe. When he lashed a single to center in game 56 for the first of his three hits off Cleveland pitching, it was the seventh time in nine days that the hit had come on his first time at bat.

For game 57, the Number That Never Was, the Indians were moving from little League Park to huge County Memorial Stadium to accommodate a Friday night invasion of 67,468 fans.

Few people can recall what Joe did in any other game during that entire 56-game streak. Did you really know that he had broken Sisler's record off Red Anderson and Keeler's off Heber ("Dick") Newsome? But everybody knows that he was stopped by the dazzling infield play of Ken Keltner, and by a couple of pitchers, one of whom was named Smith.

Al Smith and Jim Bagby, to be precise. Not to mention the rains of the Midwest — the same midwestern rains that had caused Williams to catch his spikes turning back to first base on Birdie Tebbetts's attempted pickoff.

It looked as if Joe was going to make things easy on his rooters again when he whacked a drive down the third-base line. Keltner backhanded it on the line, slid across the grass in foul territory, and gunned Joe down. There was no other third baseman who could make that play like Keltner — nobody who could go behind third like he could, and nobody who had the gun to complete the play. One other thing: Keltner always played deep for Joe, but on this day he was playing even deeper. To begin with, Al Smith had no speed. Also, his best pitch was a screwball, and Keltner fully expected that Joe would be pulling the ball hard.

But don't forget the weather. Hank Greenberg always said that the difference between the great hitter and the good hitter is one bounce. A great hitter's ground ball shoots through the infield on two bounces, whereas with other hitters there is an extra bounce that allows the infielder to make the play.

Because of the sponginess of the wet field, the ball took an extra bounce this time, and even then it seemed to be behind Keltner when he reached back to flag it down.

The dampness around the batter's box played a part, too. Joe didn't get away as quickly as he normally did. He came out of the box so slowly, in fact, that he was able to see the ball go past Keltner, and then see Keltner make the play, backhanded, behind his body.

The second time up, Smith walked him and was booed by the crowd. When Joe came up again in the seventh, he hit another rocket down the line. By this time the field had dried out somewhat, and Keltner had moved a bit closer to the line. He backhanded this one, too, and gunned him out.

Joe was up again in the next inning with one out and the bases full. The Yankees had scored two runs to increase their lead to 4–1, and with runners on second and third, Smith had put Tommy Henrich on first to set the stage for DiMaggio.

Jim Bagby was brought in from the bullpen — not a bad pitcher. A starting pitcher, really, he had come up with the Red Sox, and his only prior claim to fame was that Joe Cronin, in a fit of showmanship, had tapped him as an unknown rookie to pitch the opening game of the 1938 season.

His real claim to fame was going to be that he did the job on Di-Maggio. And did it easily, on a ground ball to the left of shortstop Lou Boudreau. Like DiMaggio, Boudreau wore the number 5. It was no coincidence. Joe was Lou's idol. Lou had asked for DiMaggio's number in college and again when he came to Cleveland. The ball took an erratic hop, but Boudreau, whose greatest asset was the quickness of his reflexes, fielded it easily and, since he was moving toward second, turned an easy double play.

So there it was. Robbed twice, a walk and almost a break. What else could be left? But it ain't over, as somebody from the neighborhood was going to say, until it's over. It wasn't over yet.

All things considered, the Yankees could have done without those last two runs — without one of them, anyway. Because here's the drill: If Cleveland ties the game in the ninth, the game goes into extra innings, and there is every possibility that Joe will be given another chance.

It almost happened. Lefty Gomez, who rarely pitched a complete game anymore, gave up a couple of quick singles in the bottom of the ninth and was relieved by Johnny Murphy. (Is it possible that good old Lefty had been looking to help the Indians do what he may so passionately have wanted them to do?)

Pinch-hitter Larry Rosenthal tripled to the right-center-field wall. The score was 4–3, with the tying run on third base and nobody out.

Perfect.

Peckinpaugh sends up Hal Trosky, his slugging first baseman, to pinch-hit. For a couple of years, Hal Trosky had been just a shade below Gehrig and Foxx and Greenberg in the pantheon of slugging first basemen. For six straight years Trosky had knocked in over 100 runs; and in 1936, Joe DiMaggio's first year, Hal Trosky's 162 RBIs had led all the rest.

Who better to hit the long fly ball that would clear the bases and tie the score? Trosky grounds to Johnny Sturm at first base, and Rosenthal holds at third.

Question: Would Johnny Sturm have thrown home in an attempt to cut off the run that would have tied the game and brought Di-Maggio to bat again, or would he have settled for the out at first? We'll never know.

Now Clarence Campbell (whose nickname was, of course, Soup) becomes the key batter. He hits the ball right back to Murphy, and *now* Rosenthal breaks for the plate and is an easy out. That's by the book. You don't take a chance with nobody out, and you're running as soon as the ball is hit on the ground when there is one out. Still, this wasn't a game to be played by the book. It was a game that was for The Book.

All right. Man on first and two out. Roy Weatherly (whose nick-name was, of course, Stormy) hits the first pitch to Phil Rizzuto and it is routine all the way.

The scene in the Indians' locker room was strange. Keltner, un-aware that he had just bitten himself off a great big chunk of the DiMaggio legend, couldn't understand why all those reporters wanted to talk to him. All he was concerned about was that the Yan-kees had come in and knocked the Indians out of the pennant race.

Because, what the hell, he made that play all the time.

Very quickly he would discover that he had achieved his historic identity. "There were fans waiting outside the Cleveland Stadium," he told author Maurie Allen years later. "But they were waiting for DiMaggio. They booed me." And then he said, "It's funny. I played 13 years in the game and I bet more people ask me about the night that DiMaggio was stopped than about anything else."

In New York they remember Ken Keltner as the man who stopped Joe DiMaggio.

In Boston they would remember him as the man who wrecked the Red Sox in the play-off game of 1948.

The Yankee locker room was positively funereal. Joe, still in his sweat shirt, lit up a cigarette and sat down wearily on his stool. Dis-appointed as he was, he understood that his teammates were waiting for him to say something. "Well," he said, in a voice that carried throughout the room, *"that's* over."

And then, nodding to clubhouse man Pete Sheehy to open the door, he prepared to take on the writers.

He went out and hit in the next 16 games, and everybody likes to point out that if it had not been for Kenny Keltner and his magic glove, Joe's streak would have gone to 73 games. You couldn't get Joe to say so, though. "The pressure was off, after Cleveland," he'd shrug. "It was altogether different."

Whatever you want to call it, the mini-streak came to an end most unexpectedly, in a double-header against the St. Louis Browns. The Yankees had taken the Browns 15 out of 17. They had won seven straight double-headers. The pennant race was well over, and 37,829 bloodthirsty New Yorkers gathered in Yankee Stadium to watch Joe DiMaggio add another couple of games to his new let's-see-how-far-he-can-take-this-one streak.

Two St. Louis pitchers stopped him cold — Johnny Niggeling and Bob Harris.

The only record that fell was the record for the number of streaks that came to a screeching halt in a single game.

• For DiMaggio, it was the first time in 84 games that he didn't reach first base.

• For Red Ruffing, it was the end of a 12-game winning streak.

• Having failed to reach base for the first time since May 3, Joe failed to reach base again in the second game.

While the DiMaggio express was streaking across the landscape of the nation's consciousness, Ted Williams had been tooling along behind with the kind of consistent hitting that could hardly be ignored.

• As Joe was making his final assault on the Yankee record, Williams was going 7 for 11 and lifting his average to .425.

• On the day Henrich bunted to make sure that Joe would get another chance to bat, Ted went 3 for 5 and was hitting .412 for the season.

• On August 3, the day Joe's skein of 72 out of 73 games unraveled, Williams was extending his own hitting streak to 12 games.

From that point on it was Joe DiMaggio who receded into the background and Ted Williams who was riding the 1941 express toward the Triple Crown.

Joe's season began to dribble away on August 19, when he went down for three weeks with a sprained ankle. By the time he came back, Ted had rapped out 11 homers and knocked in 26 runs to take over the home run lead from Charlie Keller and leap onto the leader board in RBIs for the first time all year.

Not that the Yankees were doing anything to help him while Di-Maggio was away. When the Yankees clinched the pennant in Boston on September 4, the earliest ever, they had a lead of almost 20 games. Despite that, Atley Donald, a control pitcher, walked Ted four straight times, to a rising chorus of boos, before Ted managed to single in his final at bat. The four walks to Williams were the only walks Donald issued all day.

The same thing had happened earlier in New York — four straight walks, to the booing of New York fans, after Ted had doubled his first time at bat.

By the time Ted finally found himself on the same field with Di-Maggio again, with one week left in the season, he had locked up two-thirds of the Triple Crown, and was tied with Joe, for all practical purposes, for the third. I say "for all practical purposes" because Ted and Joe each had 118 RBIs and Charlie Keller, who had broken his ankle a week earlier, was still leading with 122.

Ted had caught Joe by hitting his thirty-sixth home run, a tremendous drive into the bleachers which came on his last swing of the bat at Fenway Park in the 1941 season.

Curiously enough, Ted's prospects for winning the Triple Crown were being given minimal attention, even in Boston. The paramount concern was that Ted was leaving Fenway Park, batting .406, with six games left to play — a single game followed by a double-header in both Washington and Philadelphia. That was the good news — Washington and Philly. No sweat there.

And then, as if to demonstrate how difficult it is to hit .400, Ted ran into nothing but trouble.

In the opening game in Washington, he had one cheap hit and dropped a point to .405. The hit was a gift double on a fly ball that Doc Cramer, finishing his career in Washington, had butchered.

From there it became hairy. Dutch Leonard, the knuckleballer, shut him out in three times at bat, and one Dick Mulligan, a rookie pitcher who had just been called up from the minors, held him to one single in four times at bat.

And now he was down to .401.

DiMaggio, meanwhile, had knocked in three runs against Philadelphia to take the RBI lead away from the disabled Charlie Keller.

There were three days left in the season.

On Saturday at Shibe Park, against a rookie knuckleballer named

Roger Wolff, Ted walked the first time, doubled the next time, and then made out three times in a row. When he returned to the dugout after that last out, he was batting .3996.

According to the mythology, Joe Cronin asks Ted if he wants to sit out the Sunday double-header to protect what is technically a .400 average. But numbers aren't "technically" anything. Numbers are constants. It is one thing to round a number off during the season for the sake of convenience, space, and clarity. It's quite another to say that .3996 equals .400. You cannot turn less than .400 into .400 by official fiat. And you certainly cannot do it by journalistic convention.

Mythology aside, nobody tried to, either. The Associated Press report of the game declared that Ted's average had been "trimmed from .4009 to .3996, with only two games left in which to re-enter the select class."

The *Boston Globe* reported that he had fallen below .400 for the first time since he had reached an even .400 on July 25, the day Grove won his 300th game.

In the list of leading major league hitters, published daily, Ted was posted at .3996.

Nobody said that .3996 equaled .400.

All to the good. All to make what Ted did in that final Sunday double-header in Philadelphia an accomplishment to be rolled around on the tongue and savored.

On the first pitch thrown to him, he lined a single to right. The next time up, he hit the second pitch over the right-field fence. Two more singles followed in the first game, and then hits in his first two at bats in the nightcap. The second of those, which many Boston writers called the hardest ball they had ever seen Ted hit, was a line drive that streaked into right field, rising as it went, and was still on the rise when it ricocheted off the loudspeaker horns on the top of the right-field wall. The ball came back onto the field, and Ted had to settle for a double.

He went 6 for 8 on the day to finish with an average of .406, thereby writing one of the classic stories in baseball history.

I give myself a part in the story. In April 1955 I was sent to Boston by *Sport* magazine to do an article about Ted Williams. By one of those strokes of fortune that can befall you when you don't know what you're doing, it just so happened that some of the great players of the Red Sox past had been brought in to honor Tom Yawkey. Among them was Bobby Doerr, who was, is, and always will be a sweetheart. When we got around to talking about that last day in 1941, Bobby pointed to the box seats behind the Red Sox dugout. "That's Bill McGowan sitting there," he said. "He was the umpire behind the plate. Maybe you ought to talk to him."

McGowan told me that as Ted came to the plate for the first time, Frankie Hayes, the A's catcher, had said, "I wish you all the luck in the world, Ted, but Mr. Mack told us he'd run us all out of baseball if we let up on you. You're going to have to earn it."

McGowan himself had then said, "Well, Kid, you gotta be loose to hit."

The quotes from Hayes and McGowan that I put into my article have become part of the day's legend. I've heard Ted tell it somewhat differently. What Frankie Hayes said to him, according to Ted, was: "Mr. Mack said we're not to make it easy for you, Ted. But we're going to pitch to you." That makes sense. In four separate games during the second half of the season, the Athletics had walked Ted four times. They had even been walking him intentionally with runners on first and third.

Never mind what Ted says. He was only the hitter. I'm the writer. I got there first with my version, and it's my version that has come down the corridors of time in the name of research and repetition and received wisdom.

That's my piece of the legend, and it's enough for me.

Chapter Eleven

Ted and Joe

Sometimes I ask myself why I played baseball as hard as I did. I didn't have to play when I was banged up and I had eye infections and bone spurs and sore arms and crippled knees. I can't explain it, even to myself. Something inside just kept saying, "Play ball all the time as hard as you can — and win."

— Joe DiMaggio

I want to walk down the street after I'm through and have people say, "There goes the greatest hitter who ever lived."

— Ted Williams

FOR 13 seasons, including a three-year hiatus to fight a war, the Red Sox–Yankee rivalry was illuminated and made resplendent by the presence of Joe DiMaggio and Ted Williams, the two most magnetic players of their time. When they were on the ball field, nobody else mattered; and when they were on the ball field together, you felt privileged to be there.

The only other thing they had in common was an unhappy childhood. Joseph Paul DiMaggio was born in Martinez, California, in 1914, the eighth in a family of nine children born to Giuseppe Di-Maggio, a fisherman who had left the old country in 1898. Joe hated working on his father's crabbing boat — hated the roil and smell of it. Once he was able to get a job playing baseball in a San Francisco industrial league, he never set foot on the docks again.

Only Italian was spoken in the DiMaggio house. Joe never spoke at all. Not in the house and not in the streets. He was more than inordinately shy; he was pathologically silent.

He had never left his neighborhood or mixed with middle-class kids until he attended high school, and the experience proved to be so traumatizing that he was either expelled for truancy or just stopped going. Either way, he was left with a feeling of inadequacy that never completely left him.

Theodore Samuel Williams was born in San Diego in 1918. His mother was a fanatical Salvation Army worker who was known as "Salvation May, the Angel of Tijuana." His father was a footloose, hard-drinking former army sergeant who departed the scene early in Ted's life. Ted's earliest memory was of standing on a street corner alongside his mother while she harangued a hostile and hooting crowd. There was also an older brother, a small-time hoodlum whom Ted apparently hated and feared.

Like Joe, he found his escape on the baseball field. By the age of 14, Teddy Williams was a tall, gangling, and incredibly skinny hitting machine. He was 19 years old when he left San Diego to report to his first Red Sox training camp. He never went back.

As happened so frequently with the great figures of the rivalry, each of them could very easily have been playing for the other team. With Joe, it was a freak knee injury that sent him east to New York instead of Boston. A couple of months into his second season in San Francisco, Joe's left foot fell asleep one day as he was riding in a taxicab, and when he stepped out, the whole leg gave way. "There were four sharp cracks in the knee," he recalled. "The pain was terrible, like a whole set of aching teeth in my knee."

What happened then tells you who Joe DiMaggio is. He reported to the ball park the next day and informed his manager that he had suffered a minor injury but was available to play. Sent up as a pinch-hitter, he hit the ball out of the park and went walking around the bases. That finished him for the next three months.

The injury scared everybody off, most notably the Boston Red Sox. Roy Mumpton, who covered the Red Sox for the *Worcester Telegram,* can recall how Eddie Collins would tell some of the old timers that because of his friendship with the San Francisco owner, Charlie Graham, the Red Sox had been given first refusal rights to DiMaggio for $75,000.

When the time came to put up the money, however, Tom Yawkey, who had disgorged great gobs of cash on stars like Foxx and Grove, was not in the mood to pay that much for a minor leaguer with a bum knee.

"I could have had the three of them," Collins would groan, "Williams, Doerr, *and* DiMaggio."

In fairness to Yawkey, he was not alone. Only the Yankees, with their professional organization, were willing to bid at all. Acting on the recommendation of their western scout, Bill Essick, the Yankees had their own doctor conduct a thorough examination, and when the report came back favorable, Ed Barrow was able to pick him up at a bargain-basement price of $25,000.

As if to prove that there can be a rough justice in the universe, it was the same Bill Essick who came to Ted Williams's house two years later to offer Ted a contract — and lost him for want of a $1,000 payment that Ted's mother was demanding for herself.

Instead, Ted signed on with the San Diego Padres just before Eddie Collins, on the only trip he ever made to the West Coast, dropped in to exercise his option on Bobby Doerr and decide whether he also wanted to pick up his option on the Padres shortstop, Bobby Myatt. He didn't like what he saw in Myatt, but he loved the swing of the gangling 17-year-old Ted Williams. The Padres owner, Bill Lane, wouldn't take his money for an option. Instead, he gave Collins his word that if the time ever came when he put Ted up for sale, the Red Sox would be the first to know.

This time Collins did not permit Yawkey to let the Kid get away.

And right there any connection that might be said to exist between Ted and Joe comes to an end. Temperamentally, no two men were ever further apart, as the manner of their reporting to their first spring training camp attests.

Joe drove down to camp with his fellow San Franciscans Tony Lazzeri and Frank Crosetti. The story goes that they were three days out of San Francisco before Joe spoke the only words he would speak during the entire trip.

"You wanna drive for a while, kid?" Crosetti asked him.

"I don't know how," said Joe.

When they arrived at Huggins Field in St. Petersburg, Red Ruffing looked him over and said, "So, you're the great Joe DiMaggio." Joe could only gulp. But he became the Great DiMadge almost from the beginning, and the Great DiMadge he remained.

Ted Williams was brought to his first training camp by Bobby Doerr after the worst flood of the century had hit California, washing out the roads, knocking down telephone lines, and leaving Ted and Bobby cut off from the world. Doerr, ever resourceful, had been able to contact Ted through a ham radio operator and arranged to meet him in El Paso.

He found Ted waiting with another Californian, Babe Herman. The three of them boarded a train for Florida, and for two days and two nights Doerr listened to the 19-year-old rookie swap lies with the great Babe Herman about their mighty slugging feats.

Ted hit camp bellowing about when he was going to do to big league pitching and left, after he had been sent back to the minors for another year's seasoning, bellowing about what he was going to do when he returned.

In hitting they were opposites in every way. Joe always stood back in the box, spraddle-legged, his bat held high. He had a sweeping follow-through that made his swing look far less compact than it actually was.

Ted, all twist and fidget, would jiggle up and down in the box, pump the bat forward a couple of times, and give the neck a good twist, as if he were wringing the neck of a chicken.

Batting form is a matter of style and comfort. It was in their basic philosophy of hitting that they differed so completely, and it was in this difference that the debate about their value to their respective teams was always joined.

Joe believed in going after the first pitch that looked good to him. With men on base, he widened his strike zone. He wasn't paid to get a base on balls, he would say. He was paid to knock in runs.

Ted always wanted to work the count down. The more pitches he saw, Ted believed, the greater his advantage. It was almost a religion with him not to swing at a pitch outside the official strike zone, regardless of the situation.

As a result, he always led the major leagues in bases on balls, on-base percentage, and runs scored, with figures that not only rivaled Babe Ruth's but in certain categories exceeded them.

He led the league in hitting six times and lost out on two other occasions only because, through injuries or walks, he did not have the requisite number of at bats. In lifetime batting average, at .344, he is surpassed only by Ty Cobb and Rogers Hornsby.

Within the Red Sox inner circle, players and club officials alike — no doubt frustrated by years of losing — would say that Joe was primarily concerned with winning and Ted was primarily concerned with his batting average. Unfair, perhaps, to Ted, considering the strength of their respective supporting casts, but impossible to refute.

DiMaggio was the nonpareil. In the years before he went into the army, the Yankees won six out of seven pennants and five World Series. In 1940, the only one of those seasons they didn't win the pennant, Joe still led the league in hitting. In his 13 seasons the Yankees won 10 pennants and nine World Series.

After DiMag had been in the league for a couple of years, Connie Mack was asked to compare him to Ty Cobb. DiMaggio, said the old man, "is the greatest team player who ever lived."

It was said that the nonchalance with which DiMaggio appeared to play, the ease with which he made seemingly impossible catches, tended to obscure his true worth. Don't believe it. It was the ease and the grace that told you how great he was.

When he ran the bases, he seemed to stretch out in long, ground-eating strides. Going from first to third on a single, with his neck arched and running low to the ground, he had the look of a thoroughbred turning into the stretch with mane flying.

Ted, by contrast, came out of the batter's box in a tangle of legs and a flapping of arms that reminded you of a fledgling bird trying to leave the nest. He wasn't fast. He was not a good base runner. Although he learned to play the tricky left-field wall at Fenway to perfection, his overall fielding tended to be spotty.

By his own admission, Joe wasn't that fast a runner after the knee injury. In his freshman year in San Francisco, Joe was able to hit safely in 61 straight games by beating out a lot of infield hits. "In his first year," an old scout who had been a coach in the Pacific League once told me, "he was the fastest thing I've ever seen. He would beat out an ordinary ground ball to the shortstop. And he could steal at will."

He had a slide that fooled umpires. He would hook slide with his left toe pointed toward the base, pull the foot away, then slip in from behind the fielder, touching the base with his hand. In his first year he had to explain what he was doing to at least one umpire who called him out when he knew he had pulled off his feint perfectly.

Joe was a clotheshorse. His friends, never numerous, were upper-echelon Broadway saloon types who were able to throw around him the protective cordon that he desired.

Ted had to be bound and gagged before you could get a necktie on him. His friendships covered a wide spectrum, and he had a keen, inquisitive mind and a broad range of interests. He was eminently approachable.

Ted Williams was loud, voluble, and profane. He dominated any room he was in by the force of his personality, by the decibel count of his voice, and, in time, by his overpowering personal presence.

Joe DiMaggio spoke with care. He had a curiously stilted way of speaking, as if he were listening closely to what he was saying. He was not a team leader in any obvious sense. He was not a man to engage in locker room repartee. He would come into the clubhouse, drink half a cup of coffee, and quietly smoke a cigarette. His team-mates idolized him. They did not approach him unless he made the first move.

Their last at bat was as revealing as their first trip to training camp.

For Joe, it came in the final game of the 1951 World Series, against the New York Giants. He came up to the plate in the eighth inning carrying the secret knowledge that he would never be standing there again.

Years later, shortly after he had married Marilyn Monroe, he talked about that day wistfully to sports writer Jack Orr, an old friend who was down on his luck and in need of an interview for a magazine article.

"I still remember how I felt. Just one more hit, boy. Just get that one more hit. The pitcher was Larry Jansen. I caught a good one, a double to right-center. I slid into second and got up feeling awfully proud of myself. I knew it was my last time up after 20 years' playing. I wanted to go out with a hit, and I'd done it. Then I went to center field for the ninth, my last inning. I had mixed-up feelings about it. I was glad because the injuries wouldn't be piling up the way they had for the last couple of years. But I wondered how I'd get along, because I really had no idea what I would do for a living. I wondered if I'd be one of those baseball hangers-on who tell about how it used to be back in their day. I wondered if somebody would hit one to me and I could make a good catch. I wondered how it would be the next spring, if I would begin wanting to play ball. All of that stuff was running through my head.

"We were ahead, 4–1, you remember, but they started to rally. They had the tying run on base. I began thinking to myself, *Oh, oh, they're going to tie it up and I'll be back tomorrow afternoon, going through the same thing, trying to make my last hit a good one.* I wanted to go out with that last hit. I don't know why, but it seemed very important.

"They put up that pinch-hitter, the catcher, his name began with a *Y* [Sal Yvars]. He hit that liner to Bauer, and Bauer caught it on his knees, and the Series was over. I took one look back at the flagpole for the last time and then I ran into the dressing room."

The next day he told the Yankees, privately, that he was going to retire. Dan Topping offered him $100,000 to play one more year, with the promise that he would be expected to play only 70 or 80 games — exactly the wrong thing to say to Joe DiMaggio. "When you can't play every day," he said, "it's time to hang up the spikes."

A couple of weeks later, he turned down an equally fat offer to go on the stage, like Babe Ruth, and tell a few baseball stories. "What am I?" he asked. "Some kind of freak?"

Joe's last game capped off his ninth world championship. Ted's last game was played for a team that was finishing in seventh place, 32 games behind the Yankees.

The year was 1960. Ted was 42 years old. The Red Sox weren't going anywhere, and Yawkey wanted him to retire. Actually, Yawkey had wanted him to retire a year earlier, after Ted had hit .254 in an injury-plagued season. Fat chance. Ted began his final year by hitting a 500-foot home run, the longest of his career (a home run that tied him with Lou Gehrig), and he ended by hitting the most dramatic.

It came in the top of the eighth on a cold and dreary afternoon in Boston. A blustery wind was blowing in. Jack Fisher was pitching for Baltimore. Fisher, who was born on the day that Ted reported to spring training his first year with the Sox, did not want to go down in baseball history as the fresh young kid who had walked Ted Williams his last time at bat. He got his wish. From the moment Ted swung, there was not the slightest doubt. The ball cut through the heavy air, a high line drive heading to straightaway center field, toward the corner of the bullpen.

Ted raced around the bases at a pretty good clip, ran back into the dugout, and ducked through the runway door to get himself a drink of water.

The fans were on their feet, deafening the air with their cheers for a good four or five minutes. They began to chant: "We want Ted . . . We want Ted." The first-base umpire motioned for him to come out. The Red Sox manager, Mike Higgins, urged him to go out. The players crowded around him, urging him to acknowledge the cheers.

Ted sat there with a happy smile on his face. But he could not bring himself to do it.

Ted Williams wanted those cheers badly — so badly he would not admit to himself how much he wanted them.

Chapter Twelve

Page and Pellagrini

Does anybody believe that if we'd had Joe Page instead of the Yankees we wouldn't have won three more pennants and they would have won three less?

— Joe Cronin

EDDIE Pellagrini and Joe Page are linked together by one of those random coincidences that owes more to the short and transient life of ballplayers than to anything resembling comparative skills.

Joe Page was such a significant figure in the creation of the Yankees' Third Dynasty that everybody — *everybody* — agrees that if he had been pitching for the Red Sox instead of for New York, the Sox would have won at least two more pennants.

The name Eddie Pellagrini attaches itself to the saga of Joe Page as the most minor of footnotes — not so much a footnote as an afterthought.

Pelly was in the batter's box when it all began for Page in Yankee Stadium, and he was standing at third base when it came to an end for him in the Polo Grounds.

Let's open by throwing the bio of Eddie Pellagrini up on the screen. Pelly was a little guy (5 feet 8 inches, 140 pounds) who played one helluva shortstop and could hit the ball out of sight. He was a local Boston kid out of Roxbury Memorial High, a tailor's son. He cost the Red Sox exactly nothing. Today he'd be a high draft choice. In those days he was merely invited to the Red Sox tryout school at Fenway Park, run by Hughie (.438) Duffy. You wanted a tryout, all you had to do was ask. If you showed anything, you were invited back. I don't know of anyone who was signed out of those tryouts except for Pellagrini. He was certainly the only one who made it to the big leagues.

He had not been a great baseball fan growing up, and he had never been a Red Sox fan. "When I was in fourth grade, a teacher made me stand up at the blackboard and figure out what Babe Ruth was making, week by week. After that I began to look at the Yankee box scores to see what Ruth and, pretty soon, Gehrig were doing." When Ruth and Gehrig departed, Pelly's interest in the Yankees departed with them.

The first time he took the field in Yankee Stadium, nevertheless, was a mind-bending experience for him.

"The first thing that hit me was the enormity of the stadium. I was overawed. There were all those people. There was so much space, I wondered how you could judge a fly ball. I wondered about the throwing errors. When there's a lot of open space behind first base, a lot of guys will throw the ball away because you can't pick out the first baseman."

He had come out of the navy in the spring of 1946 touted as the guy who was going to push Pesky over to third base. It didn't quite work out that way. The first game he ever started was against the Yankees, back at Fenway Park. It was not his first time at bat. His first at bat had come two days earlier against Washington after Pesky had been beaned. He came up for the first time in the seventh inning with the score tied and took two quick strikes without being able to move his bat. And then Sid Hudson threw him a knuckler that could have been called either way.

"How can you take a pitch like that?" Al Evans, the catcher, growled.

"Good eye," said Pelly, coming back to his feisty self. And that loosened him up so much that he hit the next pitch completely over the net in the deepest part of left-center. His first swing in the majors, and he hit the longest ball he would ever hit in his life and, while he was about it, won the ball game.

Two days later, against the Yankees he hit a triple, a double, and a home run, and on his last time at bat he hit a ground shot toward right field that Snuffy Stirnweiss made a good play on to throw him out.

A home run on his first time at bat and just misses hitting for the cycle in his first game. Never mind what he hit for the rest of the year. Never mind how many home runs he got in the rest of his career. The beginning was the stuff of dreams.

Joe Page was a big, handsome black-haired guy, one of seven children of a coal miner from Cherry Valley, Pennsylvania. Even more so than Pellagrini, he was a walk-on. Joe was 6 foot 3, weighed 210 pounds, and he could throw the hell out of the ball. He walked into a minor league training camp in Pennsylvania and, when he couldn't make the team, was picked up by the Yankee farm club in the same league. He was brought up to the Yankees during the bottom-of-the-barrel war years, and even against such uninspiring competition became far better known as a ladies' man and bon vivant than as a pitcher.

Although his postwar career was relatively short, he played a central role in the careers of three Yankee managers, Joe McCarthy, Bucky Harris, and Casey Stengel.

By 1946 Marse Joe was an unhappy man. Larry MacPhail had bought the Yankees (along with Dan Topping and Del Webb), and MacPhail — who, under the best of circumstances, was a man who meddled in everything — wanted a manager of his own choosing.

The blowup occurred on a plane ride between Cleveland and Detroit. MacPhail had made the Yankees the first team to travel exclusively by air, and that took McCarthy out of his private sitting room and placed him in close proximity to his players.

To complete the scenario, Joe was brooding over the sloppy play of his team in Cleveland, and when Joe brooded, Joe drank. Altogether a highly combustible combination.

His baleful eye fell upon Joe Page, who was pitching dreadfully and — far more worrisome to Joe McCarthy — had latched onto the Yankees' returning superstar, Joe DiMaggio. Against the remonstrances of his wife, who was seated with him, McCarthy went over, sat down beside Page, and proceeded to chew him out about his casual, carefree attitude toward life, his baseball career, and the New York Yankees.

Shape up, Joe warned him, or he would find himself back in Newark. Just the wrong thing to say to Joe Page. "O.K. by me," he told his manager. "Maybe I'd be happier there."

Whereupon Joe McCarthy exploded in a drunken rage, within full view of his own players and a planeful of passengers.

When the plane landed in Detroit, McCarthy's wife took him home to Buffalo. Three days later Joe McCarthy, the most successful manager in all of baseball, resigned.

Now let's flash forward to May 26, 1947, a date written in indelible ink upon the tablet of the Yankee–Red Sox rivalry. As with so many of the other unforgettable games in their long history, this one was played before a record crowd. It was a Monday night, and 74,747 people turned out, the largest major league attendance ever for a single game. (Actually, the number was greater than that. Why Yankee Stadium couldn't handle as many people as in 1938 has never been explained, but here again the ball park was so packed that 1,140 customers who had bought standing room demanded their money back.)

Why such a crowd on a Monday night in May? Well, the Yankees had beaten Boston, the defending American League champions, three straight times over the weekend to knock them out of first place; Spec Shea, the Yankees' undefeated rookie sensation, was going for the sweep; and finally — as if to prove that Larry MacPhail was indeed in town — there was going to be a home run contest before the game between the Yankee and Red Sox sluggers, featuring Joe DiMaggio and Ted Williams.

By the third inning the Red Sox were leading, 3–1. There were runners on first and second with nobody out, and the next three batters were Ted Williams, Rudy York, and Bobby Doerr.

Into the game came Joe Page.

Bucky Harris was MacPhail's new manager, and for Joe Page this was a last chance. With the coming of Spec Shea and the addition of Allie Reynolds, Page was no longer even a part-time starter, and he had shown himself to be too wild and inconsistent to pitch in relief.

Frankly, he would already have been gone if it hadn't been for a hitless three innings he had pitched at Fenway Park a couple of weeks earlier. And even there, he had celebrated so far into the night that on his return to the hotel room he shared with Joe DiMaggio, the normally reticent Clipper had bawled him out, pretty much in the same manner that Joe McCarthy had a year earlier, and had then instructed the Yankees' traveling secretary to get Page a room of his own.

Now we return to Joe Page, jumping over the bullpen railing, with the stands packed, Williams, York, and Doerr coming to bat, and his own career hanging in the balance.

Ted Williams hit a routine ground ball down to first base, but when the first baseman fumbled it, the bases were loaded. And everybody knew that you couldn't give a team like the Red Sox four outs.

Immediately, Page threw three straight balls to Rudy York, all far outside, and Bucky Harris was ready to come and get him. "One more ball," Bucky would say after the game, "and Joe Page was on his way to Newark." Rudy York swung at the 3–0 pitch and missed, swung at the 3–1 pitch and missed, swung at the 3–2 pitch and missed.

The count on Bobby Doerr went to 3–1. Once again Joe Page was one pitch away from Newark, and once again he struck the batter out.

And that brought up Eddie Pellagrini, who had won the shortstop position from Johnny Pesky. Pellagrini sent a weak fly ball to right field. "I knew I didn't hit it good, but because it wasn't hit good I thought it had a chance to fall in." The ball carried farther than he thought it would, and Joe Page was out of the inning.

In seven innings Smoky Joe Page allowed only two singles (one on a topped ball), struck out eight batters, and issued only two passes.

His buddy, the Great DiMaggio, broke the game open with a three-run home run. The Yankees moved into second place and went on to not only win one of the true upset pennants in Yankee history, but to win it with ease.

For Page, this game marked the beginning of a whole new career. That season he won 14 games and saved 17 others. After every one of those games, Bucky Harris would lift his glass in a toast and say, "Gentlemen, to Joe Page."

The next year Page fell off just enough to allow the Indians and Red Sox to sneak in ahead of the Yankees, but in 1949 he came back to break the Red Sox's heart.

The paths of Page and Pellagrini crossed again in 1954. No longer young, either of them, no longer hopeful. Pellagrini, having kicked around, was finishing up his career with Branch Rickey's dreadful Pittsburgh Pirates. Joe Page, having been released by the Yankees when his arm went bad, had been laboring in the minors for two years when Rickey decided he might be able to get one more year out of him.

Page drove all night to the Pittsburgh camp in Fort Myers. He spotted one familiar face in the clubhouse — Eddie Pellagrini. "He came over and asked if he could room with me."

By the time the schedule brought the Pirates to New York to play the Giants, Page had pitched a few times in relief, with very indifferent results. That didn't bother Joe Page. He told Pelly that they were going out to have a little fun, and on the promise that they'd be back by ten o'clock, Pelly, who wasn't exactly setting the world afire himself, agreed to go with him.

"He knew where to go in New York," Pelly recalls. "I've got to give him that. Everybody knew him."

At the appointed hour Pelly got him into a cab. "We went back to the Commodore Hotel and he kissed me off there. I tried to grab him and pull him out. But I'm just a little guy and, holy mackerel, he was strong. He kept the cab, and I didn't see him again until he came to the park the next day."

Instead of fining Page, the Pirates made him pitch. "He's nervous as a kitten, and he gets in a little jam. I walked in. 'Come on, we get these guys out and we'll go to a good restaurant and get something to eat.'"

He couldn't do it. "I remember them taking him out, and he's taking that long walk to the Polo Grounds clubhouse in center field, and it was like it took him half an hour to get there. I thought, *I'm watching Joe Page make his last walk. My God, there goes a great career.* It was so sad.

"And I remembered how he'd hop over the railing during his great years with the Yankees and come strutting in with his jacket hooked over his shoulder. He was a cocky bastard. He'd come to the mound, and it was like, *Give me the ball and get the hell out of here.*"

They handed Page his release before the game was over, and Pelly never saw him again. "And, you know, we never once talked about that inning in Yankee Stadium when it all began for him. I don't know if he even remembered that it was me he got for the last out."

Chapter Thirteen

Joe McCarthy and the
Play-Off Season of 1948

It's just folklore that the Red Sox have never been able to beat the Yankees when they had to. In 1948, when we finished in a tie with Cleveland, we beat the Yankees seven out of eight games down the stretch. We had to beat them the last two games of the season to reach the play-offs. Over a two-year period we won more games than New York or Cleveland and we finished in a play-off and one game behind.

— Birdie Tebbetts

THAT Joe McCarthy would come out of retirement to manage the Boston Red Sox was mind-boggling but not really surprising. He was hired to put some iron into the Red Sox, to do for them what he had done for the Yankees — turn them into a team instead of a collection of prima donnas.

What he gave to the Boston fans was the most exciting and, in the end, most galling two seasons since Babe Ruth had been spirited away.

An unfailing pattern unfolded for the McCarthy Red Sox. They would start miserably, come storming back to push into the lead, and then blow it.

In 1948, the first year of McCarthy's reign, the Sox managed to fall 11½ games behind by the end of May, yet with 21 games left to play, they charged into first place, 4½ ahead of Cleveland, the eventual winner.

In 1949 they were 12 games behind on July 4, went a game ahead with five left to play, and carried that lead into Yankee Stadium for the final two games.

In 1950 the Sox were 8½ games behind the Yankees in June when

McCarthy quit, but under Steve O'Neill they got within half a game of the leaders with 12 games to go.

To up the stakes even further, McCarthy came to Boston in what turned out to be a watershed year in the popularity of major league baseball. With Cleveland coming out of the starting gate fast to declare itself in on the festivities, there ensued a fierce three-team pennant race that established new attendance records in New York and Boston and an all-time record in Cleveland, a race so fierce that the three teams were in a flat-footed tie with seven games left.

For two consecutive years McCarthy's teams went down to the final game of the season. In his first year he did what the Red Sox had not been able to do since 1904: beat the Yankees, head to head, at the end of the season, with everything on the line. And yet, even there, they didn't win the pennant by defeating the Yankees. They went into a play-off with the Cleveland Indians and lost when Joe McCarthy came up with a pitching selection that defied belief.

Joe McCarthy was a teacher, a disciplinarian, a stickler for detail. "Attitude and aptitude" were his watchwords. Good habits and proper preparation, he preached, were the ingredients that paved the road to perfection.

The first thing he had done upon joining the New York Yankees prior to the 1931 season was to have the clubhouse card table smashed with an ax. "Do your card playing at home," he snapped. "Think baseball when you come here." No more shaving equipment in the clubhouse, either. "This isn't your bathroom, it's a baseball stadium."

His players were ordered to wear a shirt, tie, and jacket in public. The sight of an unbuttoned shirt could drive him into a frenzy. "You don't walk into a bank and see people behind the windows with unbuttoned shirts and hairy chests," he would rail. To play for the Yankees called for the same kind of professional appearance.

He was a mass of quirky prejudices. He hated pipe smokers: "Smoking a pipe breeds complacency." Southerners were too hot tempered: "They defeat themselves." The worst breed of southerner was a hillbilly: "They're all moonshiners back there, and they're just naturally against the law. They resent any kind of rules or discipline."

Nonetheless, he had been looked on as an icon by Yankee players.

He protected them from the front office, they'd say. He never criti-
cized them to the press, and he never embarrassed them in front of
their teammates. And so if Joe occasionally embarrassed himself by
turning up on the bench drunk, they were happy to band together to
protect him.

"Joe was the boss," DiMaggio said. "If you put out for him, he
never let you down." And besides, Joe would add, the players all
knew that McCarthy knew more baseball than any of them.

The great question when he came to Boston was whether he
would be able to get along with Ted Williams — most particularly
whether he would try to impose his dress code on the mercurial Kid.
Joe answered that one by showing up on the first day of spring training wearing a garish sport shirt and no tie. "If I can't get along with a
.400 hitter," he said, "then there's something wrong with me."

Ted Williams came to swear by him, too. "The best manager I
ever played for," Ted would say. McCarthy didn't run up and down
the dugout. He didn't rage at the umpires. "He just sits there and
works the game. And he runs a perfect game. He's thinking. He
remembers."

Johnny Pesky felt the same way. Still does. "On the long train trips
he would sometimes sit with the players, talk baseball, and you would
always learn something new. During the game he would sit on the
bench and move an infielder over two feet, and that would be the
difference between a hit and an out."

Well, it's clear that the big stars loved him. Nobody ever cares
what the lesser players think. Jimmy Dykes, who had somehow managed to keep an inferior White Sox team competitive over the years,
called Joe McCarthy "a push-button manager," by which he meant
that he wrote out the same line-up every day and almost never used
his substitutes. That worked out all right in New York, where he was
winning every year. It did not make for a happy squad in Boston.

Mickey Harris was a wise-ass left-handed pitcher off the streets of
the Bronx. Joe Cronin had always liked him for his brashness. When
Mickey was good, he was very, very good. When he wasn't so good,
Cronin would go a long way with him. "He's a lucky pitcher," Joe
would say. "I've got a hunch on him." And Mickey Harris won 17
games for Joe in 1946 to help the Red Sox win the pennant.

Having grown up in the Bronx, in the shadow of Yankee Stadium,

Mickey was in such awe of McCarthy that he became petrified when he was in his presence. Tongue-tied. Stuttered and stumbled all over himself. Joe McCarthy decided that Mickey Harris didn't have any guts. Mickey Harris spent more and more time between assignments while pitchers of far less ability were losing ball games. Hours after everybody else had left the clubhouse, Mickey would be sitting in front of his locker with his head in his hands. "Why won't he pitch me?" he'd cry out to the clubhouse kids. "What have I done wrong? Why doesn't he like me?"

And if some of the Boston sports writers were asking the same question, that had no effect on McCarthy. He never challenged any Boston writer about anything that was written about him. But, then, he never gave the slightest indication that he bothered to read the Boston papers, either.

McCarthy was 61 years old when he came to Boston. He had never really left New York. He was an aloof and solitary figure by nature, a man who kept his own counsel. The surest way to get him talking and bring a sudden smile to his face, the Boston writers discovered, was to drop the name of one of his old Yankee players.

When Joe himself initiated a conversation, it would usually be to wax nostalgic about the Broadway theater. He would become more animated talking about Ezio Pinza's performance in *South Pacific* than about anything that had happened in yesterday's ball game. He even dressed like a Broadway sport: natty dark suit and sport shoes, wide-brimmed hat, always a well-groomed, manicured look, with hair neatly trimmed and parted carefully down the middle.

Say what you want about him, you also have to say this: in his two full seasons with Boston, Joe McCarthy had the best record in terms of wins and losses of any Red Sox manager since Bill Carrigan. Having said that, you have to add very quickly that he was given a far better team to work with than Joe Cronin ever had.

Chief among the additions were three players from the St. Louis Browns — their two best pitchers, Jack Kramer and Ellis Kinder, and their power-hitting shortstop, Vern ("Junior") Stephens.

The vagaries of baseball. The Red Sox were able to make the deal with St. Louis because the Cleveland owner, Bill Veeck, thought that Lou Boudreau was the worst manager who ever lived. Since Boudreau wasn't willing to continue playing shortstop for the Indians if he was replaced as manager, Veeck arranged to send him to St. Louis for Stephens, Kramer, and Kinder, along with the stack of money that the always struggling Brownies needed to stay in business.

The deal collapsed at the last second for a variety of reasons, not the least of which was that Veeck had reason to believe that the Browns were planning to shuffle Boudreau right over to Boston.

If the Red Sox were losing Boudreau in the fallout, they had only to double back and pick up the original St. Louis package — Stephens, Kramer, and Kinder, plus Billy Hitchcock, a valuable utility infielder. In return the Red Sox gave the Browns six undistinguished and eminently expendable players — including Eddie Pellagrini — and yawkeys of cold hard cash, amounting to something in excess of $300,000.

To go with the St. Louis righties, McCarthy was inheriting a fine left-handed rookie pitcher, Mel Parnell. And to handle them he had Birdie Tebbetts, the best Red Sox catcher since Bill Carrigan. Tebbets had come over to Boston midway through the previous season.

Like most great managers, McCarthy was a great judge of talent. In spring training he fell in love with Billy Goodman, a skinny little rookie from Atlanta. Billy stood 5 foot 10, weighed 146 pounds, and seemed to rattle around in his uniform like a bag of bones. He couldn't run much, but he slid ferociously. He fielded without grace and had a stiff and ungainly way of throwing, but he made all the plays. He was a left-handed hitter who slapped singles to the opposite field. In Atlanta he had played every position, including catcher.

Given all their talent, the Red Sox were the overwhelming favorites to win the pennant. They crashed on takeoff. The McCarthy era in Boston began with the Red Sox being swept at Fenway Park by the Philadelphia Athletics. As the month of May came to an end, they were nine full games under .500, and an insuperable 11½ games out of first place.

At that low point of the season, McCarthy told Tom Dowd, the traveling secretary, that the time had come to turn to the Bible. "We've been going no place," he said. " 'But a little child shall lead them.' Goodman is playing first base tonight."

With Goodman in the line-up, the Red Sox went out and won 17 of the next 22 games. The Yankees slowed them down momentarily by taking two out of three in New York, but that was only a breathing spell. Facing the Yankees again a week later, the Sox broke through the .500 barrier by sweeping a three-game series in Boston to launch themselves on a 22-out-of-26 romp that carried them through to the end of July.

Not solely because of Goodman, of course. Ted Williams had been going at a .400 clip all along, and Junior Stephens, who hadn't been hitting a lick, not only began to hit but to hit game-winning home runs. In personality Stephens was the opposite of Goodman. Goodman was extremely quiet and dressed as if his suit had come off the wrong rack in a bargain basement. Stephens always had a smile on his face and a laugh on his lips. His locker was in the middle of the clubhouse, and players and writers alike would automatically make it their first stop. As a bon vivant, he was a Red Sox version of Joe Page, a heavy drinker and a dedicated ladies' man. (At the age of 48, Stephens dropped dead on a golf course, and the operative phrase at his funeral service was, "Well, Junior certainly didn't cheat himself.")

There were two late-season series between New York and Boston on which their fortunes swung, a three-game series in Boston in early September and the final two games in October. The Sox won four of the five. And yet, if you could pick out one game that symbolizes the McCarthy era in Boston, it would be the one they lost.

Let's go back a little. Two weeks before the September series, the Red Sox had gone into first place by half a game after beating Cleveland on a three-run homer by Bobby Doerr.

The Yankees, stalking the leaders as they had all year, had been winning, too, and they were sitting in third place another half-game behind the Indians. Their big surge had begun when Bucky Harris moved Yogi Berra — who was little more than a hitter trying to be a catcher in those days — out to right field and brought Tommy Henrich in to play first base. The move kept Yogi's bat in the line-up and gave Tommy Henrich, who was 37 years old by the book and 40 according to his birth certificate, a new lease on life.

The red-hot Yankees proceeded to win 14 of their next 18 games before the meeting in Fenway Park but only managed to lose ground to the even hotter Red Sox, who were winning 12 out of 14.

On September 8 the Red Sox were 1½ games ahead of the Yankees and 2½ ahead of Cleveland, and a World Series atmosphere pervaded the city. So much so that American League president Will Harridge, a man who never showed up in a ball park if he could help it, came in from Chicago to grace the event with his presence.

All kinds of streaks were on the line. The Yankees had won nine straight games. The Red Sox had won seven straight and — even more important, perhaps — were coming in with a five-game winning streak over the Yankees. To make their success even sweeter, the Red Sox had been doing it to the Yankees the way the Yankees had traditionally done it to the Sox: by spotting them a big early lead and coming from behind.

In the first two games of the series they did it again. In the opener the Yankees scored four runs in the first inning, and the Red Sox came right back with five runs of their own.

A day later they overcame the Yankees' early three-run lead with an eight-run explosion in the third inning.

Everybody was contributing. The pivotal hit in the opener had been a booming triple to the top of the center-field fence by Birdie Tebbetts, who had been exhibiting the kind of power in his old age that he had never shown before.

In the second game it was Ted Williams who opened the door to the big inning when he came up with the bases loaded and scorched a ground ball through the teeth of the exaggerated shift that had been set up against him.

The Red Sox were suddenly 3½ games ahead of New York and 4½ ahead of Cleveland. And there were only 21 games left to play.

"What could well be the beginning of the end, so far as the continued reign of the Yankees as champions is concerned," read John Drebinger's lead in the *New York Times*, "we believe to have been written across the rolling green of the fens today."

The next day's lead could well have been, "Joe DiMaggio strikes again."

It almost was. "With an effort born of desire," wrote Drebinger, "Joe DiMaggio swung from the heels today and as a consequence the Yankees are not ready to be counted out."

For Joe this had been in many respects his most remarkable season. His brother Dom certainly thought so. Throughout his career, going all the way back to a malfunctioning diathermy machine in his first spring training — going all the way back to San Francisco — Joe DiMaggio had been beset by injuries and illnesses. Wherever possible they had been hidden from the New York press. Throughout the 1948 season, however, he had been limping so perceptibly that shortly after the All-Star break the Yankees announced that Joe was going to be rested as much as possible for the remainder of the year because of a bad charley horse that had developed as a result of "accumulated sliding injuries." In a complete departure from Yankee tradition, the reporters who covered the team were even invited into the clubhouse so they could examine the huge "strawberries" on both hips where Joe's skin had been rubbed away, leaving raw, ugly bruises.

The whole thing was a charade. The way Joe slid, his hips were always rubbed raw. The true story, as Joe told columnist Jimmy Cannon in confidence, was that a bone spur was developing on his left heel, just like the one that had been surgically removed from his right heel a year earlier. "We're still in the pennant race," he told Cannon, "and we don't want to tip off the other clubs. I can take it for the rest of the season."

He had missed exactly one game.

He was not only leading the league in home runs and runs batted in, but he had spreadeagled the league in both categories. The more noticeable the limp, it sometimes seemed, the farther he would hit the ball.

In other words, Joe DiMaggio had been carrying the Yankees on his back even before, as Drebinger wrote, he "swung from his heels" in the third game of the series in Boston to keep his team alive.

Once again the Red Sox had fought back from an early 6–2 Yankee lead to draw even in the eighth inning on doubles by Dom DiMaggio and Johnny Pesky.

And it was right here, with the momentum running so powerfully in his direction, that Joe McCarthy sent in Earl Caldwell, a 43-year-old relief pitcher who had been picked up a couple of weeks earlier after he had been released by the Chicago White Sox. Caldwell was a fussy old guy, which isn't too surprising when you consider that even as a young man he had been known as "Grandmother" because of his practice of coming into the clubhouse, rain or shine, carrying an umbrella and a pair of rubbers.

Will McDonough had been taken to that game by his sister, and although he has covered countless games since, this is the one game that he most clearly remembers.

"I had to be about 12 years old," McDonough says. "They had Yogi Berra playing right field, and we're sitting in the bleachers, watching outfield practice, and a ball that was hit over Berra's head in front of the bullpen bounced off the railing and came back and hit him in the face, decking him. They had to help him off the field, but he came back out with a big shiner and played the entire game. What I remember is the Yankees had a lead, and the Red Sox tied it, and DiMaggio came up in the tenth with the bases loaded. McCarthy had put in Earl Caldwell, a sidearming righty, an inning earlier, and when DiMaggio came to the plate, everybody around us was screaming for McCarthy to take him out. He got the count to 3–2 and had to throw it over the plate, and DiMag ripped it to left field, foul by a foot off that little bit of screen outside the foul line. Everybody goes, *Wheeeww,* like we've escaped the bullet. Then he pitches again, and Joe hits a line drive to center field that carries all the way into the bleachers for a grand slam.

"Now, about 35 years later and I'm at the fishing tournament that [John] Havlicek has every year on the Cape, and Joe DiMag is one of the guys invited to play golf, and I started telling him about that day. He says, Yup. He knew the whole time at bat, who was on and all that: 'On 3–2, I knew he wouldn't throw me a fast ball. He threw me something off-speed. That's what I fouled to left field.' And he went back through the whole thing, pitch by pitch, and remembered every-thing about it, down to the final adjustment he made after pulling the ball foul."

The Red Sox were still 2½ games ahead of the Yankees and 3½ ahead of Cleveland. But they had been given the chance to put the season away and they had blown it.

What the hell was McCarthy doing, everybody was asking, turning the ball over to an Earl Caldwell and completely ignoring a proven winner and Yankee beater like Mickey Harris? Mickey hadn't pitched in three weeks.

Five days later McCarthy put Caldwell into the same situation in Chicago. Caldwell gave up another grand slam home run, and Mickey Harris finally went back to work.

With nine games left in the season, the schedule called for the Red Sox to play a day game in Cleveland that the Cleveland papers were calling the most important single game of the entire season. In the sprints and spurts that had become characteristic of this three-way pennant race, Cleveland had just won six straight (13 out of 15), to ease past the Yankees by half a game and pull to within a game of the Red Sox.

There are Boston writers who will always believe that Bill Veeck played upon the finer sensibilities of Tom Yawkey that day to finesse the Red Sox out of the pennant.

Admittedly there was a tragic story involved. A couple of weeks earlier Don Black, a rehabilitated alcoholic in the midst of a spectacular comeback, had collapsed in the batter's box after fouling off a pitch. A blood vessel had broken in his brain. He was in a deep coma.

Since all the proceeds of the game were being turned over to Black's wife, Veeck requested that the game be played at night, and Yawkey, being Yawkey, readily agreed.

Don Black Night turned out to be a great success for everybody except the Boston Red Sox. A record crowd of 76,772 turned out; Mrs. Black was handed a huge check; and the Indians got to pitch Bob Feller under the lights. Feller stopped the Red Sox cold with a three-hitter, his best performance of the year.

When the Sox boarded the train for New York, they were in a dead heat with the Indians. After the first game against the Yankees, they were in a three-way tie. Another lost chance for the Red Sox. The Yankees, cashing in all their opportunities, had left only three men on base. The Red Sox left 14.

It was the first time since Opening Day that the Yankees had a share of the lead. It was also going to be the last.

"We're in the driver's seat," Lou Boudreau had said, "because Boston and New York are going to be knocking each other off over five of the eight games remaining." He left it for the writers to add that his own team would be playing against second-division ball clubs.

Happiness for the Cleveland Indians was watching the Red Sox and the Yankees fulfill Boudreau's prediction. The Red Sox won the second game behind Jack Kramer to knock the Yankees off the top. The Yankees returned the favor the next day.

With five games left in the season, the Red Sox and the Yankees were tied for second place, a game behind Cleveland.

They were still a game behind when the time came to lock horns again, at Fenway Park, over the last two days of the season.

Their fate was in Cleveland's hands. If the Indians won both of their games against Detroit, it didn't matter what happened in Boston.

If the Indians split, either the Yankees or the Red Sox could pull out a tie by winning both games.

If the Indians lost both games, it was possible for either of the other two teams to win.

If the Indians lost two and Boston and New York split, the season would wind up in a three-way tie.

For the opening game it was Jack Kramer against Allie Reynolds.

If Jack Kramer ever makes a movie of his 1948 season he can call it *The Year of Living Lucky*. In the final stats he had the best winning record (18–5) of any starting pitcher in the American League — and the worst ERA (4.35). All he had to do was walk out onto the mound and the Red Sox bats began to throb. In the games Kramer started for them, the Red Sox averaged more than eight runs per game. In the games he won, they had better than 8½.

Kramer was said to be the strongest man in baseball, a reputation he had earned in St. Louis by pinning big Jeff Heath to the clubhouse floor in a matter of seconds. And still, Joe McCarthy babied him all season. Only three times did he pitch Kramer on three days' rest. On 16 occasions he gave him four days' rest, three times five days, four times six days, and once seven days. Alone among the rotation pitchers Kramer was never used in relief.

One of the reasons for the irregular starting assignments was that McCarthy always saved Kramer for the Yankees, and since nothing succeeds like success, it was hard to argue with that. Going into the final week of the season, Kramer's record against New York was three wins and no losses. On closer examination, however, those figures became far less impressive. The scores were 8–6, 7–3, and 9–6. In two other starts he had been knocked out of the box. He had left trailing, 6–5, in a game the Red Sox later pulled out, and he had been knocked out early in the Caldwell game at a time when a strong performance might have nailed down the pennant.

Never mind. Shift the focus again, and over the last week of the season McCarthy's handling of Kramer paid off handsomely. In Yankee Stadium he had pitched one of his best games of the year to beat the Yankees, 7–2, and keep the Red Sox tied for the lead.

And here, in his last and most important assignment, he justified McCarthy's faith in him completely by pitching his very best game of the year.

Give Ted Williams some credit. It was the Kid's first-inning home run after Pesky's walk that staked Handsome Jack to a 2–0 lead. It was his double, after another walk to Pesky, that set up two more runs in the third. By the fourth inning the score was 5–0, and Kramer breezed to a 5–1 victory. The Yankees didn't so much as threaten until Joe DiMag doubled high off the wall in the seventh inning, limped into third on a ground out, and limped home on a fly ball to Dom.

Back in Cleveland, the rookie knuckleballer Gene Bearden was stopping the Tigers, 8–0, to clinch at least a tie for the Indians.

The Yankees were out of it. The Red Sox were still breathing. On Sunday, the final day of the season, two things had to happen for the Sox to stay alive: the Indians had to lose, and the Red Sox had to win.

The Boston writers were sure that the starter was going to be either Ellis Kinder or Mickey Harris. Kinder had won his last five decisions after recovering from a sore arm. Harris, rediscovered after a month of wandering in the wilderness, had hurled a four-hitter against Detroit and had pitched 8⅓ innings of one-hit relief against Washington to give the Red Sox a win that was sorely needed.

McCarthy jumped over both of them to tap Joe Dobson. Dobson had been the leading Red Sox pitcher until he was hit on the wrist by Bob Feller at the end of July. He had missed three weeks recovering, and over the steamy six weeks since his return he had been able to win only three games.

Bucky Harris's selection was almost as surprising — or at least it would have been if the Yankees hadn't already been eliminated. To the dismay of most of his veteran players, Harris started rookie Bob Porterfield (5–2) instead of Vic Raschi (19–8), his leading pitcher. A case could be made. Raschi had lost all four of his starts against the Red Sox, accounting for one half of his total losses.

Although nobody wanted to say so, Harris was pitching Porterfield as a personal message — as in "Up yours, George" — to his general manager, George Weiss. For the second time in three years, the New York front office had undergone a complete power transplant. Larry MacPhail was gone. He had sold out his share of the ownership after he had gone more berserk than usual during the celebration of the 1947 World Series triumph and tried to punch out a couple of his employees — Weiss for one.

George Weiss was in complete charge, George Weiss wanted his own manager, and George Weiss did not want MacPhail's man, Bucky Harris. The constant squabbling between the two had found

its nastiest expression in Bucky's demands that Porterfield be
brought up from the minors. Weiss didn't believe Porterfield was
ready. But Harris had prevailed. And although Porterfield had actually pitched quite well, Bucky Harris was under no illusions that he
was going to be back as manager.

Neither of the starting pitchers was around long enough to make a
difference.

The entire DiMaggio clan was gathered in Boston for Dominic's upcoming wedding.

Big brother Joe, the prospective best man, was staggering to the
finish line. Literally. In the intervening series in Philadelphia, he had
been unable to reach balls he normally would have gobbled up. One
game had been lost when his leg buckled under him on a drive that
went for a double. In the final game before coming to Boston he had
dropped a fly ball to allow the Athletics to get back in the game.

As dinner was breaking up at Dom's home, Joe had told him, "You
gave us hell today, but tomorrow I'll hit my fortieth."

"I don't think you will," said Dom. "But I'm going to hit my ninth."

Between them they were going to have seven hits. Only one of
them was going to be right about the home run.

The Yankees were leading, 2–0, before the Red Sox disposed of
Porterfield in the third inning with a five-hit attack that piled up five
runs.

Dom DiMaggio started it with a single, and Williams knocked him
in with a double down the left-field line. Billy Goodman was at bat
with men on first and second and three runs already in, when a great
cheer went rippling around the ball park. The news had come over
the portable radios the fans had carried into the park that out in
Cleveland the Tigers were on a rampage. The crowd was still cheering as Billy stepped back in and lined a single to center to knock in
another run.

With the ending of the round a deafening roar went up as the post-
ing of Boston's big 5 on the left-field scoreboard was followed almost
immediately by the appearance of a lovely 4 for Detroit.

Dobson was knocked out in the fifth, two outs short of qualifying
for the win. Joe DiMaggio again. Joe had already knocked in the first
Yankee run. He brought home two more, and narrowed the score to
5–4, when he rattled his second two-bagger off the left-field wall.

Earl Johnson came in to pitch to Johnny Lindell and became the winning pitcher on one pitch, courtesy of Joe DiMaggio, when Lindell hit a ground ball to Pesky, who tagged DiMaggio coming up the line and threw across the diamond for the double play.

Joe DiMaggio, the man who never made a mistake on the base-paths, had made a high school error to kill the rally. What does that tell us? It tells us that Joe was so bone tired that his concentration had deserted him.

Tired or not, Joe wasn't done for the day. Neither was Dom. True to his prediction, Dom hit his ninth home run of the season. The best Joe could manage as the year was winding down for him was two measly singles. As he left the field for a pinch-runner, after touching off his fourth hit in the ninth, the crowd stood up and gave him the most thunderous ovation ever accorded an opposing player in Boston.

He stayed around long enough to serve as Dominic's best man and then went directly to Johns Hopkins in Baltimore for an operation on his heel. Although he was told that the operation was successful, it wasn't. And because it wasn't, the greatest drama of Joe DiMaggio's life was going to take place on his return at — where else? — Fenway Park.

For the Red Sox, the entire season had come down to one play-off game.

The subhead in the *Boston Globe* on the morning of October 4 read:

McCarthy uncertain, could be Kinder, Parnell

But that was only because Joe McCarthy almost never announced his pitching selection ahead of time. Something about not wanting him to lose sleep, worrying. The pitchers for the play-off game were going to be Mel Parnell and Bob Lemon. Everybody knew that.

Everybody was wrong.

A story began to circulate — though not until the following spring — that McCarthy had asked Birdie Tebbetts to sound out the starting pitchers, and that Tebbetts came back and told him, "You won't believe this, but none of these guys wants to pitch. The only one who really wants the ball is Denny Galehouse."

In one of the several variations and refinements — all of which, according to the Boston writers, came from Tebbetts — McCarthy thereupon reached into his drawer and handed Birdie a piece of paper which had been folded over, once. On it was written the single name *Galehouse*. There is an alternate version that says two names were written down, Galehouse and Kinder.

Lou Boudreau had a surprise pitching selection up his sleeve, too — a surprise, that is, to everybody except his own players. Immediately after the loss to Detroit he held a closed-door meeting in which he told his players that he wanted to send Gene Bearden back on one day's rest. Bearden was on a roll. He had pitched two straight shutouts. He was a knuckleball pitcher, which meant that he hadn't thrown his arm out. In fact, knuckleball pitchers are supposed to be more effective if their arm isn't too strong.

"Johnny Berardino and Joe Gordon were the only ones who objected," Boudreau recalls. "They went back and forth, and then Gordon got up and said, 'You've picked the pitchers for 154 games, Lou. You can pick them for 155.'"

Several Boston writers had been sent to Cleveland to cover the final series there, just in case, and they accompanied a very glum and depressed group of players on the long overnight train ride to Boston.

Clif Keane of the *Globe* was startled to find Bob Lemon, the putative starting pitcher, sitting in the club car, drinking heavily. "Gordon and Keltner were drinking heavily, too. And so was Bob Feller."

Ken Keltner came over to Keane and sat down. "I'm going to hit that wall 147 times," he kept telling him between drinks, over and over. "I'm going to hit that wall 147 times."

Keane: "Boudreau is peeking in. Lemon's drunk. Keltner's drunk. Gordon's drunk. Feller's drunk. Everybody in there is drunk because we had the whole club car."

Boudreau: "I peeked in the club car and decided the best thing was not to look in anymore. That was a hard-drinking, hard-living club. I never had bed checks during the season because I was afraid that half of them wouldn't be there."

Keane remained in the club car with the *Post*'s Gerry Moore until four in the morning. "We were not," he says, "the last ones to leave."

Johnny Donovan, who is currently the Red Sox attorney, was a bat boy in 1948: "The Cleveland club came right to the ball park after riding on the train all night. And all our people were wondering who

McCarthy was going to pitch. When he came out of his cubicle and put the ball in Galehouse's locker, there were only two people in the clubhouse. That was Johnny Orlando and myself. Both of us were shocked. What Joe's rationale was I never did know.

"The ball game was over, boom, boom, when they went out there. It was like batting practice."

Don Fitzpatrick, at the age of 19, was the visitors' bat boy for that play-off, just as he was going to be in the visitors' clubhouse for the 1978 play-off game 30 years later. Both clubhouses were off the Boston dugout behind first base. The way it was set up, the door to the visitors' clubhouse was just off the runway, only a step or two inside. Fitzie was inside the clubhouse when he heard his name being called.

"One of the coaches came down — I don't remember which one — and told me to go out and tell Galehouse that Mr. McCarthy wanted to see him. He was out there shagging. I told him, and he went in. I don't know whether I knew why he was being called in, but I'm sure he did."

Keane: "We came in just before the game by train. Boudreau thought Parnell was going to pitch, and when he saw that a brisk wind was blowing out, he put in his whole right-handed line-up. Eight right-handed hitters, even though it meant putting Allie Clark, a substitute outfielder, on first base. I was standing behind the batting cage talking to Lou when [senior coach] Bill McKechnie came over to tell him that Parnell isn't pitching, it's going to be Galehouse. Boudreau says, 'I don't care. Same line-up. I'm playing the right-handed hitters.'"

Boudreau didn't necessarily believe it. Prior to the start of the game, he sent McKechnie down to Tarpaulin Alley behind the bullpen to find out whether McCarthy had Parnell warming up under the stands.

Mel Parnell: "Everybody thought I'd be pitching. My parents had come up from New Orleans to watch me. I was in bed the night before at nine o'clock, expecting to be pitching this ball game. I think any pitcher on our staff would have welcomed that opportunity. Because if you pitch that big a game and win it, it means at least an extra $5,000 to you the following year. That was a lot of money then. I was home with my wife and kids, and they were constantly on me during the night to get to bed early because tomorrow was the biggest game of the year, and just to get away from them I went to bed. Because they kept reminding me, and I didn't want to be reminded."

It didn't particularly register on him when he picked up his cap and found no baseball under it. Last game of the season, what was the difference? If there was no baseball in his locker, there was no baseball in anybody else's locker, either.

"I was sitting in the clubhouse taking my time getting dressed, as the pitcher pitching that day usually does. McCarthy came up from the back of me and put his hand on my shoulder and said, 'Son, I've changed my mind. I'm going with the right-handed pitcher today. The elements are against a left-hander.' I thought he meant it was going to be Kramer.

"With that, I got dressed and ran out on the field during the batting practice, and when I went out on the field all the guys asked me, 'What are you doing out here?'

"I said, 'I'm not pitching. The Old Man changed his selection. He's going with Denny Galehouse.' Because in the meantime, he'd sent Fitzie to run out on the field and call Galehouse in. I think it had some kind of effect on the team, because I think they expected it would be me, Kinder, or Kramer."

Jim Hegan, the Indians' catcher, was a local kid from Lynn. (There are knowledgeable baseball men who will tell you that Jim Hegan was the greatest defensive catcher who ever lived.) "A funny thing about the play-off game," Hegan said when he came home after the World Series. "We were really low that night on the train, we couldn't help but feel we'd muffed our chance. We were discouraged until we stepped onto the field, then everything changed. The pressure was off. We were relaxed and confident."

Parnell: "I was in the bullpen, but I wasn't used. We were kind of stunned out there. In all fairness to Galehouse, he was a great pitcher in his day, but his day had passed. It was the tail end of his career. We kind of felt it was a bad choice, simply because Denny was getting on in age. The old saying is that in a game like that you go with your best, and if you lose with your best, you have no complaints. I felt at that time I was the man for that game, because I was the leading pitcher on the staff and it was my turn."

It was young Don Fitzpatrick sitting on the Cleveland bench through it all, who had the best fix on what was happening. And, as Fitzie saw it, Bearden was luckier than Galehouse.

"With a pro like Galehouse, if he got by the first inning he might have done it. There was electricity in the ballpark, believe me. It was a very high tension game. Bearden was tight, but he got away with it. Galehouse didn't."

He had to get by the first inning, and he almost succeeded. He got two outs, and then Lou Boudreau hit a home run. But Bearden didn't get by the first inning, either. And he barely squeaked through the second.

I can add something to that. Bill Veeck and Hank Greenberg, the president and the general manager of the Indians, both told me that Lefty Weisman, the long-time Cleveland trainer, was slipping Bearden one of those miniature bottles of brandy during the early innings to keep him going.

"I don't know about that," Don Fitzpatrick says. "Veeck and Greenberg were sitting in a box alongside the dugout, that's true enough. All I can remember, looking back, is that Bearden would come back to the dugout at the end of the inning, and Lefty would meet him at the water fountain to find out how he was feeling. If he was slipping him a drink, I wouldn't have been able to see it. All you could see from where I was was Lefty's back."

Bearden had a shaky start all right. The Sox came right back in the bottom of the first on a double by Pesky and a single by Stephens to put a quick end to Bearden's scoreless streak, and also put a little doubt in the minds of the Cleveland players about the wisdom of sending Bearden back out on one day's rest.

In the second inning Lemon and Feller were up and throwing in the bullpen after two walks and a single around a very fortunate strikeout–throw-out double play had put runners on first and third with two away. A hit by Dom DiMaggio here would have given Boston the lead, and quite probably knocked Bearden out of the game. Instead, Dom bounced to Keltner, who fumbled the ball briefly but recovered in time to nip him.

Galehouse never got a man out in the fourth. After singles by Boudreau and Gordon and a home run by Ken Keltner, the game was as good as over. Between them Boudreau and Keltner did all the damage. Keltner didn't hit the wall 147 times as he had promised. He did hit it two times and cleared it once, and that was plenty good enough. For Boudreau the tally was two singles, two home runs, and a significant role in six of the runs that were scored in his team's 8–3 victory.

After the second inning, the Red Sox got only two more hits. Bobby Doerr hit the only fast ball Bearden threw all day over the left-field wall, and Ted Williams had a meaningless single with two out in the eighth.

If Boudreau's gamble on Bearden paid off, you will note that Lou had been careful not only to consult his players about it but also to get their permission.

But what about McCarthy's decision to pitch Denny Galehouse instead of Mel Parnell?

Parnell: "I don't know where that story about Tebbetts going around the night before came from. Tebbetts didn't talk to me. I don't know any pitcher he did talk to. McCarthy would never ask anybody if they wanted to pitch a ball game. He told you. He was the manager. That was our job, to do what he told you."

Birdie Tebbetts, normally the most cooperative of men, is no help at all. "There are only two people who know what happened," Birdie says. "One of them is Joe McCarthy and he's dead, and I'm not going to say anything." It's all on an old reel-to-reel tape in his closet, Birdie says. "I dictated the whole story into it at the time. When I die, you can go and look for it."

Birdie will not concede that it was he who spread the story around, off the record, to his favorite Boston writers. But putting that aside, if the story is true, why not say so?

Denny Galehouse says it is. "I remember that Tebbetts went around and asked various pitchers about how they felt about pitching in the play-off game, and I was among the ones he asked. I said to Tebbetts, 'Hey, if he wants me to pitch, I'll pitch.' That's almost word for word. Birdie came out of McCarthy's office afterwards and came over to me and said he thought it was probably going to be me but to go along as though it wasn't.

"When it came down to the decision time, the morning of the play-off game, I was out there and the ball was in my locker."

So how come nobody else saw it?

It's very possible, Galehouse says, that he got in early and took the ball before anybody saw him. "I might have folded the ball in my glove or put it in my pocket or something. I don't recall."

Sure. But if he knew he was going to pitch, why did Fitzie have to be sent out to get him?

"I know I was out shagging in the outfield with all the other pitchers during batting practice. It was something they didn't want to let be known early. But I knew it the night before, after the Sunday game."

Listen, it was a long time ago. Denny scouted for years for the Red Sox, and he is now a scout for San Diego. He says himself that when the Red Sox let him go early in the next season, both Joe Cronin and Joe McCarthy assured him that he would always be taken care of.

"I had pretty good stuff warming up. In fact, Bill McGowan was behind the plate, and he told a few people afterwards I had real good stuff. And I felt like I did. He said my fast ball was good, everything was good. Just one of those things where they hit it."

Boris ("Babe") Martin was the bullpen catcher. He had come over from St. Louis toward the end of 1947. Although he was on the active roster, he almost never got into a game. Obviously he served other purposes. Babe was a teetotaler. Quite religious. He was the kind of veteran who was kept around to serve as a good influence on those for whom a good influence was sorely needed. Joe McCarthy clearly liked him and found him very useful to have around. And Babe was friendly with Joe McCarthy's wife, who was also known as Babe.

Babe Martin knows what happened: "The guy who was scheduled to pitch was Mel Parnell. Joe McCarthy, who was the greatest manager I ever played for, decided that Mel, who had pitched very well against Cleveland all year, would be the starting pitcher. The night before the game, Joe had a premonition that Mel was maybe a little bit too young to start such an important game, and this premonition brought on Denny Galehouse. Denny was a great competitor. He just wasn't able to go ahead and muster enough for that particular day."

Premonition? PREMONITION?

"Joe was a very religious man. He'd turn his lights out . . . he was staying at one of the downtown hotels with his lovely wife, Babe. The ballplayers who used to play for Marse Joe told me that he did this for many years. If he wanted to turn to somebody, he would turn those lights out and he would discuss his problem with the Lord.

"Somehow or other it just came to him that he should go ahead and switch. Of course, it was the wrong move. He had been an awfully successful manager. Who am I to say that my good manager would be wrong?

"He'd sit in the dark with the lights out. This is what people who had been with him over at the Yankees said when I talked to them about it. They just said, 'Babe, Joe has done this for 40 years.' He did it, I suppose, during the early part of the 1948 season as well as the play-off game against Cleveland. Who am I to say whether he was drinking while he was thinking? I'm not going to go into any-body's lifestyle.

"I think the reason he may have gone with Denny instead of Mel was the left-handed situation at Fenway Park, with that short fence. Mel had been very successful in that ball park all year. Again, who am I to go ahead and question the manager? He was the best I ever seen."

He sat in the dark, talking to the Lord. So that's the answer to the great Galehouse mystery. The Lord told him to do it.

Mrs. McCarthy, the other Babe, later told Mel Parnell pretty much the same thing. "We all knew that he would indulge quite a bit at nighttime," Mel says. "His wife told me that at one time he would lock himself in a room by himself with a bottle and he'd be drinking and thinking baseball. Whether he did that the night before the play-off, or whether that was what she was trying to tell me, I can't say."

Babe Martin warmed Galehouse up before the game. "Denny had good stuff. In a ball game it's a completely different situation. That Cleveland club was one of the finest ball clubs I had ever seen, and everything just went right for them that day. Nothing went right for us."

Boudreau agrees. "It was one of those days. The second home run I hit, I was fooled so badly by a Kinder change-up that my hand came off the bat. I actually hit the ball over the fence one-handed. That only happened to me one other time in my life."

If McCarthy sat in the dark and discussed his problem with the Lord, how did the answer come out Galehouse? In the immediate post mortems, everybody was inclined to focus on a game a month and a half earlier in Cleveland in which Galehouse had relieved Parnell in the first inning and gone on to pitch two-hit ball over 8⅔ innings. Pitching great ball after the game has been lost, of course, doesn't mean much. Going back to a game in August means even less. A couple of weeks later Galehouse had started against Cleveland and been chased in the second inning of a 9–0 rout.

In his last start during the regular season, he had been knocked out of the box by the St. Louis Browns in a four-run fourth inning — an unhappy harbinger.

The last time he had pitched in relief he had given up seven hits in three innings in New York.

.   .   .

Except for that one bad outing in Cleveland when Galehouse had come in to relieve him, Parnell had faced the Indians three times and been effective. Parnell and Bearden had met twice during the season. Both games are noteworthy. In early June, right in the middle of the Red Sox's first winning streak, Bearden had stopped them, 2–0, on a Boudreau drive into the right-field bleachers which everybody in the ball park, except the umpire, Charlie Berry, could see was at least two feet foul.

That was a call that loomed larger and larger in the minds of Boston fans as the season was coming to a close. And long after. The current Boston manager, Joe Morgan, grew up in the Boston suburb of Walpole as a Red Sox fan. Before a recent Old Timers' game in Fenway Park, Morgan came over to Boudreau, who was seated in the Red Sox dugout, and pointed to the right-field foul pole. "I was here that day," he said. "But," he said, swinging his finger toward the left-field stands, "I was seated over there."

Nothing more had to be said. "Charlie Berry said it was a fair ball," Boudreau grinned, "so it must have been."

In their second meeting, in August, it was Parnell who had defeated Bearden in the game that put the Red Sox into first place for the first time.

The fallout was so harsh that there was some question about whether McCarthy would be brought back to fulfill the second year of his contract.

When Harold Kaese of the *Globe*, an early admirer who had become increasingly disaffected, wrote that the Red Sox had the pennant won "until the manager folded under the pressure in the final western swing," he was delivering a coded message. The message to his readers was that the pressure had driven the manager to the bottle. The message to Tom Yawkey was that the sports pages could not be counted on to continue to protect a manager who could make a public spectacle of himself by staggering all over the field — as McCarthy had in St. Louis — or could select a Galehouse over a Parnell with the pennant on the line.

Once the decision had been made to bring him back for another year, a cover story had to be devised. And if it was first articulated by Tebbetts, as the writers of that era remember, it was promoted relentlessly by the brilliantly controversial columnist of the *Record-American*, Dave Egan, a figure of moment in the journalistic wars that raged in the badly overcrowded newspaper market of Boston. Egan's stock in trade was heroes and villains. Heroes to be defended at all costs and villains to be upbraided mercilessly.

Joe McCarthy was one of the heroes, and since Joe was coming back, the villains became, perforce, the pitchers who had been bypassed for Galehouse, most notably Parnell and Kinder.

Mel ("the Pleader") Parnell, Egan labeled him. Or "Mellifluous Mel."

"Egan was a force for education within the community," says Bill Crowley, the former Red Sox publicity man. "He had guys on every street corner in Boston running to the dictionary to find out what *mellifluous* meant."

For as long as Joe McCarthy remained in Boston, the column about the pitchers who had betrayed their great and noble manager was rewritten almost monthly.

You have to say this about Egan: he was not a man to be dissuaded by anything that was happening in the real world. All the while he was battering Parnell and Kinder for their faintness of heart, they were setting the kind of pitching records that hadn't been seen in Boston, or anywhere else, since the days of Lefty Grove and Wes Ferrell.

Chapter Fourteen

The Season of 1949

Shit in the neck again.
— Ellis Kinder

THE 1949 team may have been the best the Red Sox ever had. After another slow start, they reached down to their ever-helpful friends in St. Louis and bought Al Zarilla, a strong left-handed hitter who had finished fourth in batting behind Williams, Boudreau, and Cleveland's Dale Mitchell. Even more important, in Parnell and Kinder they had the best lefty-righty combo in baseball.

"Next year I'm going to win 20 games," Kinder had shouted in the clubhouse after the play-off loss. He did even better. He won 23. Parnell won 25 and demonstrated that he knew how a left-hander was supposed to pitch in Fenway Park by also leading the league in ERA.

Ted Williams led in everything except, of all things, batting average, and he didn't lose that until his last time at bat. Vern Stephens, batting behind Ted, tied him for the leadership in RBIs by knocking in a robust 159.

For the Yankees, Joe DiMaggio missed the first 65 games, and then had the greatest return since General MacArthur came sloshing ashore in Bataan. The Yankees had two rookie outfielders to invigorate their line-up — Gene Woodling, who had led the Pacific Coast League in hitting, and Hank Bauer. In the infield they had the Rookie of the Year in Jerry Coleman, a slim, fancy-fielding shortstop who was converted into a slim, fancy-fielding second baseman. (It should be noted here that the rookies in the years immediately after the war were not necessarily the fresh-faced kids of more innocent times. Woodling and Bauer were both about to turn 27, and Coleman was

25.) Best of all, they had in place the three-man pitching staff that was to take them to five straight pennants: Allie Reynolds, Vic Raschi, and Eddie Lopat.

But more than anything else, the Yankees had a new manager in Casey Stengel who, at the age of 59, was no kid himself.

Joe DiMaggio had come to camp with every assurance that the operation on his right heel had been successful. Instead, he found the pain so excruciating that it became necessary for him to return to Johns Hopkins, once shortly after spring training began, and again just before it was to end.

On Opening Day he sat on the bench in an overcoat to observe the unveiling of the Babe Ruth plaque in center field. He was also able to watch the Yankees pull out a win on a two-out homer by Tommy Henrich in the ninth inning. With Henrich continuing to perform his heroics, the Yankees sprinted off to an early lead. By the time of DiMaggio's return, Henrich had 16 home runs. Twelve of them had been instrumental in winning games.

For two full months Joe DiMaggio sat in his hotel room with his leg in a cast — a recluse, available to nobody except a few close friends, soured on the world, and terrified that his career was over.

And then, just as the doctors at Johns Hopkins had told him, he woke up one day and the pain was gone.

From there he faced the slow process of working himself back into condition. He took batting practice until his hands bled. He experimented with various types of shoes to cushion the impact on his still-tender ankle. The appointment at Fenway Park on June 28 was wholly fortuitous, conditioned in great part by the circumstance that had the Yankees playing an exhibition game against the New York Giants on the day before they were scheduled to open a road trip in Boston.

Joe went to bat five times in the exhibition game, popped up four times, walked in his last at bat, and was taken out for a pinch-runner. His performance left him so far from satisfied that he allowed the team to leave for Boston without him.

The next morning he went to the stadium again to take some batting practice, found that he was getting good wood on the ball, and almost at the last moment decided to catch the 3 o'clock flight to Boston.

The Boston papers, having jumped the gun, were trumpeting that he was going to play. When Joe arrived at the ball park, the lines were already forming for what was going to be the largest crowd ever to see a night game in Fenway Park.

The record crowd hadn't turned out just on the chance of seeing Joe DiMaggio. After a spluttering start, the Red Sox had won 10 out of 11 and lifted themselves up to within five games of New York. In Boston, where hope sprang eternal, that was all that was needed. Faith, of course, was something else again.

Johnny Donovan: "They had a specially constructed protective shoe there for DiMaggio. It had been designed by George Owen, who had been a great football and hockey player at Harvard, and had played hockey briefly for the Bruins. The shoe was higher and was heavily padded, inside and out. Even the heel was padded where you would normally have expected to see one of the spikes. He didn't run the way he normally did. He didn't even walk like Joe DiMaggio."

When the Clipper came out to the bench, Casey Stengel was being asked about his starting line-up. "I don't know," Stengel said. "I'm waiting for DiMaggio to tell me whether he can play."

DiMaggio had taken a seat on the far end of the bench alongside Phil Pepe of the *New York Daily News*. He bent down and tightened his shoelaces. Everybody on the bench was looking toward him. "What about it, Joe?" Pepe asked.

"Yeah," DiMaggio said, as he straightened himself up. "I'm going to play." He didn't tell Stengel he was going to play, you will notice. He allowed Stengel to overhear him telling Pepe.

Johnny Pesky: "I'll never forget it. He had that spur on his heel, and everybody was trying to write him off. The thing of it was that coming off an injury, they felt he wouldn't be able to plant himself at the plate. He didn't have to. Everybody always talked about his style and grace. Don't forget that he was a big, strong guy. He buried us that weekend."

Right-o. Joe's power came from his upper body. All you have to do is recall the home run he had hit in San Francisco with the fractured knee. Joe didn't stride into the ball. He had that wide stance at the plate, and he'd just kind of tap his front foot an inch or two forward before he swung.

Babe Martin: "He flew in, and the way he was walking we didn't think he was going to play. And our ball club felt real good about the fact that the Big Guy wouldn't be there. As soon as his name was announced, it seemed like our ball club lost a little bit of its zest.

"We had just brought Mickey McDermott up from Louisville, and

Mickey was just a fantastic strikeout pitcher, threw the fast ball through a brick wall, and had a great, great curveball." In Louisville, Mickey McDermott had struck out 117 batters in 77 innings. In one game he had fanned 20.

Babe Martin knew Joe a little on a personal basis, because he and Jack Kramer "bummed around" with Dom DiMaggio, and they had been invited to have dinner with Joe and Dom a couple of times when the Red Sox were in New York. "The guys were telling Joe, 'Watch this guy, he's a little wild. Watch this guy. Throws hard, got a great curve ball. Maybe this shouldn't be a good time for you to come back.'"

Babe knew that was a big mistake. "That just gave Joe much more determination. Anybody who told Joe that this was going to be tough for him, it just infuriated him to the point where he would show this guy that he was up against the master. And he hit line drives off Mickey up against the wall and over the wall that you wouldn't believe. I'll never forget that as long as I live. I just marvel."

First time up, he fouled off half a dozen pitches, mostly off to right field. And then he lined a single to left to start a two-out rally, as Johnny Lindell walked and Hank Bauer, the right-handed hitter whom Stengel was platooning with his other rookie outfielder, Gene Woodling, hit a three-run home run.

In the third inning Joe DiMaggio came up with Rizzuto on first base and drove the ball into the net above the left-field wall.

The Yankees were ahead, 5–0, but the game was far from over. The Red Sox fought back, closing the gap to 5–4 in the ninth, and had the tying run on first with nobody out and the top of the order coming to bat. Into the game came Joe Page, who was merely having the season of his life. Page didn't exactly blind the Red Sox this time. You could say, if you wanted to stretch it a little, that he dazzled them with his footwork.

After Dom DiMaggio had sacrificed the runner to second, Johnny Pesky smashed a sizzler through the box that looked as if it were going into center field. Luckily for Page, the ball hit his trailing foot and caromed right to Jerry Coleman, who was able to throw Pesky out. That brought up Ted Williams, who had two scratch singles on the day. The tying run was now on third. Ted himself represented the winning run. With a chance to take the game away from Joe DiMaggio — and write another chapter in the great rivalry within the

Great Rivalry — Ted hit a Page fast ball to the wall in the deepest part of left-center, where DiMaggio swallowed it up.

Johnny Pesky remembers something else about that game. Pesky remembers taking Rizzuto out so hard on a double play that he knocked him woozy. "Christ, I got hell for it from their bench. I was a little guy and he was a little guy. I wasn't trying to hurt him. The Yankees played hard against everybody; against the Yankees we bore down a little harder. Every time we got together it was like a war. DiMaggio once got me on a double play that almost killed me. They could do it to you, and you weren't supposed to say anything."

In the eighth inning DiMaggio walked, and Berra hit a routine double-play ball to Doerr. Fortunately for John, he had been moved over to third base on the arrival of Vern Stephens, because, bad foot and all, DiMaggio knocked Stephens head over teakettle.

On Friday, Williams had fallen just short of taking the game away from DiMaggio. On Saturday, DiMaggio took the game away from Williams, after the Red Sox had gone out to a 7–1 lead.

In the first inning the Red Sox batted around and scored four runs. And the Yankees had been lucky to get away that cheap. Four runs in, bases loaded, one out, and Ellis Kinder hit a hard hopper off the glove of the relief pitcher, Clarence ("Cuddles") Marshall. A day earlier Pesky's hard smash had caromed off Page's leg and gone directly to Jerry Coleman. Kinder's smash bounced around like a pinball. It went off Marshall's glove, hit second base, bounced up off Coleman's glove, and fell dead at the feet of Phil Rizzuto. All Rizzuto had to do was step on second and throw to first base to double up the far-from-speedy Kinder.

Ted Williams had contributed a double to the first-inning rally. In the second inning he beat out a bunt against the Williams shift and scored ahead of Stephens' home run.

Under normal circumstances, believe me, WILLIAMS BUNTS would have been a front-page story in Boston. But this was the DiMaggio Series. Anything that anybody else did, every Red Sox lead or rally, was only going to be setting the table for Joltin' Joe.

Ellis Kinder was control and changes of speed. The best change-up in baseball. And so, leading, 7–1, with two men out in the fifth inning, Kinder did the last thing in the world he wanted to do: he walked the two hitters in front of DiMaggio, and Joe drove them both in ahead of himself with a gargantuan blast into the net in the deepest part of left-center.

Gene Woodling doubled in the seventh inning with the bases loaded to tie it up. Hank Bauer knocks in three runs one day against the left-hander; Woodling knocks in three the next day against the right-hander. Casey Stengel's platoon system was already beginning to make itself felt.

So now it's Joe DiMag in the top of the eighth with two out and nobody on — exactly where you want him. The only way he can put his team ahead now is to hit a home run. Earl Johnson's first pitch comes in knee high, catching the inside corner. A perfect pitch. Just like in 1941. Remember?

DiMaggio hits it out of the ball park, and Casey Stengel comes out of the dugout, salaaming ostentatiously as the Great Man crosses the plate.

With that home run it had become so clear that a transcendent chapter in the legend of Joe DiMaggio was being written that even the Boston fans could not help but root for him.

As Sunday's game was about to get under way, a small biplane flew over Fenway Park pulling a banner that read: THE GREAT DIMAGGIO.

Mel Parnell had started the season with two shutouts. His record was 10–3. Going against him on Sunday was Vic Raschi, who had finally beaten the Sox for the first time in April.

Lefty Mel Parnell, like Lefty Grove before him, had broken the code for pitching at Fenway Park. Simply put, you didn't worry about that looming left-field wall; you left that up to the hitter. Parnell had a natural screwball. "The screwball would go down and away from a right-handed hitter," Mel says. A dead fish. His best pitch, however, was a slider. "My theory on pitching at Fenway Park was to throw the slider in. Keep it inside on the right-handed hitter. If you try to hit the outside corner and miss toward the plate, that's when the hitter gets his arms extended and hits with power. If I pitch to the inside corner of the plate, left to right, and miss, I'm more likely going to miss inside. This crowds the hitter, keeps his elbows close to his body, makes him swing. A lot of times they'll go for that pitch because they have the left-field wall on their minds. Even if they hit the ball good, they'll be helping me because it's going to go foul."

What really made pitching in Fenway Park so difficult, Mel says, was the limited amount of foul territory along both base lines. "Pop fouls that would have been outs in any other park went into the stands at Fenway."

So, it's game three and the Yankees are leading, 3–2, in the seventh. Two men on. DiMaggio hits a high foul off behind first base, near the stands but eminently playable. Sure-handed Billy Goodman is waiting there to put it away. Sure-handed Billy Goodman drops it. Given a second chance, DiMaggio hits the ball high off the light tower that rises above the left-field wall.

In the three-game sweep, DiMaggio had hit four home runs and a single, and batted in nine runs.

For the Yankees, the Dage was back and all was right in the world.

For the Red Sox, the Dage had come to town and they were now eight games out of first place. It was not about to get any better.

Still shell-shocked, they were swept again in Philadelphia, and came staggering into New York for the annual Fourth of July double-header carrying six straight losses.

In the first game of that double-header, they suffered the most demoralizing kind of loss it is possible to inflict upon an already demoralized ball club. The fireworks were provided, in a manner of speaking, by Mother Nature and Johnny Pesky.

Johnny Pesky grew up in Portland, Oregon, and was bat boy for the Portland ball club in the Pacific Coast League. Of the original core of Boston position players, Pesky was the only one who had actually been signed by the Red Sox. Williams and Doerr had been bought from San Diego and Dom DiMaggio from San Francisco.

Johnny Pesky moved rapidly through the minors, piling up base hits wherever he went. The year before he came up to Boston, he was MVP of the American Association. With the Red Sox, he became the first major league player ever to have 200 hits in each of his first three seasons. And in all three of those seasons he led the league in base hits.

In one respect, and one respect only, he was very much like Lou Gehrig. He was totally without ego. Little fellow with a big nose. Ted Williams tagged him with the name "Needlenose," which soon enough became shortened to "Needle." To opposing players he was "Pinocchio."

His first look at Yankee Stadium was memorable, although not necessarily for the usual reason. Pesky had broken in with a splash, and was already leading the league in base hits. "First time I step into the batting cage, Charlie Keller and Joe D. are watching, because Williams is going to hit next, and everybody stops when he gets in." Anxious as he is to look good, Pesky hits nothing but little dribblers past the mound.

"How can this guy be getting all those base hits?" Keller asks Williams loudly. "He can't even get the ball to the infield."

"You may not know it, but you're looking at the base hits." Ted answers. "He beats 'em out."

Pesky: "They always made fun of me, but I didn't mind. I hit a few balls real good, too."

Casey Stengel always had fun with him. "I played against him for 10 years," says Pesky, "and he'd never admit he knew who I was. I'd see him at the World Series in the fall. He'd be holding court. I'd go by and shake his hand and say, 'Hi.' He'd look up and say, 'Hi.' I'd say, 'Johnny Pesky,' and he'd say, 'Oh yeah, the little shortstop in Boston.'" It didn't matter what position Pesky was playing or who he was playing for. To Casey Stengel he was always "Oh yeah, the little shortstop in Boston."

Pesky was a good shortstop who was always underrated. For some reason he was constantly being compared to Phil Rizzuto — still is — even though he had been moved to third base during the great years of the rivalry. The dominant feeling among the Yankees, in fact, was that the Red Sox were doing them a favor by playing Junior Stephens at short instead of Pesky.

Roy Mumpton of the *Worcester Telegram* covered the Red Sox through Pesky's entire career. "Pesky was a very smart player," Mumpton says, "who made two dumb plays in highly visible situations."

The first one took place in that showcase of showcases, the seventh game of the 1946 World Series, when he held the ball for a split second as Enos Slaughter came roaring around third with the winning run.

Pesky had one bad habit for a shortstop. He'd bring his arms up in a little pumplike motion before he threw. And that is what he did this time on the relay from the outfield.

Joe Cronin never forgave him. In 1947 Pesky played every inning of every game and had over 200 hits for the third straight season. His total batting average for the three years was .330. And still, Joe

Cronin, in one of his first acts as general manager, cut his salary by $500. "Because," Cronin told him, "you're a horseshit shortstop."

Ted Williams understood better than anybody else what a good hitter Pesky was. Whenever possible, Ted would huddle with him before he went to bat so that Pesky could fill him in on what the pitcher was throwing. "He hits .300 and he's always swinging with two strikes," Ted would say. What Ted meant was that because Pesky was batting directly in front of him, Pesky's job was to get on base by hook, crook, or base on balls.

Pesky's second highly visible misplay brings us back to Yankee Stadium on July 4, 1949. It was a day that started as the hottest Fourth of July in the recorded history of New York City (a distinction it still holds) and ended in a torrential rainstorm.

We're looking at the ninth inning of the first game. The temperature is still scorching. The Red Sox are trailing, 3–2. The bases are loaded with one out on singles by Pesky and Williams and a walk to Stephens. The batter is Al Zarilla, who is in the throes of an 0-for-14 slump. As Zarilla steps into the box, the sky suddenly turns dark and a rising wind comes sweeping across the park, blowing down the screen in center field and whipping up a sandstorm across the infield.

When the game was resumed, after no more than five or six minutes, it was still dark overhead, and particles of sand were hanging in the air over the infield. Zarilla hit a line drive, a legitimate single to right field, and just as the ball was passing over Jerry Coleman's head, a small twister came swirling up behind him, completely blocking Pesky's view.

Cliff Mapes, thinking fast, came running in as if he were going to make the catch. His intention, clearly, was to freeze Williams long enough to prevent him from scoring from second. In his wildest dreams, he could not possibly have thought that he had any chance of keeping Pesky from scoring.

But, having lost sight of the ball, Pesky had retreated back to third base. Suddenly, all was confusion. Kiki Cuyler, the third-base coach, was trying to get him to turn around. Ted Williams was bearing down on him from second base, screaming. Pesky, getting the message, took off for the plate again, stumbling just enough as he turned to make the difference.

Cliff Mapes had one of the best arms in baseball. He threw a strike to the plate, and as Pesky came sliding in, Yogi Berra stretched for the ball like a first baseman. Art Paparella, the umpire, called Pesky safe, and Berra started jumping up and down. "You never tagged him," the bewildered umpire said. Berra, pointing excitedly to the runner on third, had to explain that he didn't have to.

If Paparella hadn't grasped the situation immediately, he had plenty of company. Half the people in the ball park hadn't understood what was happening either, including Al Zarilla, who was laboring under the impression that he had picked the perfect time to break out of his slump.

"Zarilla was standing on first base," Ed Lopat says, laughing at the memory. "And we were all up on the top step of the dugout shouting, '0 for 15, Zeke! 0 for 15!' "

But the inning wasn't over. There were now two out, and the bases were still loaded. Bobby Doerr hit a high fly to right field, long enough to reach the short right-field porch, it seemed, until the winds, swirling around the three-tiered stadium, caught hold of the ball and pulled it back just enough for Mapes to make the catch leaning into the first row of seats.

The winds — the cursed Yankee winds — had taken two straight hits away from the Red Sox and run their losing streak to seven games.

The Red Sox lost the second game, too, after taking a 4–2 lead on a triple by the repentant Johnny Pesky. Joe DiMaggio tied it with his fifth home run against the Red Sox in a week.

The winds of the first game had been the leading edge of a torrential storm which hit the Stadium a few minutes later and brought on a 48-minute delay. When play resumed this time, the Yankees scored another couple of runs before the descending darkness brought the game to an end.

The Red Sox losing streak had reached eight games, and they had dropped to fifth place, 12 games behind the Yankees.

"That finishes the Boston Red Sox," Casey Stengel chortled.

"We were that far behind in 1948," Joe McCarthy reminded everybody. "We came back then, and we can come back again."

Yeah, sure. What else was he going to say? May 31 was not July 4, Joe. There were 34 completed games lying between those two dates, and those games could never be called back.

But come back the Red Sox did. And so strongly that when they returned to Yankee Stadium in late September to play a makeup game, they were tied for the lead. In that game, the game of Pesky's revenge, they moved into first place.

The turnaround had begun on July 5, all credit due to Mickey McDermott. Nobody had expected that it would be McDermott who would stop the bleeding. But when you think about it, why not? Except for the home runs by DiMaggio and Bauer, Mickey had done a more-than-credible job against the Yankees in Fenway Park.

In Yankee Stadium he stopped them with four hits, and although he also walked eight men, that only gave him a chance to show the doubters how tough he could be when he had to.

Joe DiMadge had two of the four hits. He came up again in the eighth, with the Yankees trailing, 4–2, a man on base, and a chance to put the crown on his golden week. He hit the ball out of the park, foul by no more than a foot.

Little brother Dom was the hitting star this time. He knocked in the winning run with a homer. He had also knocked in the first run with a triple.

After McDermott's game, the Red Sox kept winning and Dom DiMaggio kept hitting.

When the Yankees and Red Sox met again a month later, Dom was on a 34-game hitting streak, a Red Sox record that still stands. He was stopped by Vic Raschi. On Dom's last at bat he hit a scorching line drive that looked like a sure base hit coming off the bat. As so frequently happens, though, he had hit it too well, and the ball carried all the way out to brother Joe.

"If I hadn't caught it," said Joe, when the writers tried to make something special of it, "it would have hit me right between the eyes."

But if Raschi had stopped Dom, he had not stopped the Red Sox. Ellis Kinder, in the midst of a winning streak of his own, defeated Raschi, 6–3. Two days later Mel Parnell beat Allie Reynolds, and the Red Sox had cut the lead to 5½ games.

It was down to two games in late September when the Yankees came back to Fenway for the last time. Kinder and Parnell, who had become a two-man pitching staff, were waiting for them again.

The Red Sox were on a seven-game winning streak. There were eight games left to play, and five of those games were going to be played against the Yankees.

In the first game Kinder shut out the Yankees, 3–0, for his twenty-

third victory of the season. It was also his twentieth successive starting assignment without a defeat (he had lost a game in relief along
the way), and his thirteenth straight win. In the second game Parnell
won his twenty-fifth. Ted Williams hit a home run in each game to
bring his season total to 43. Johnny Pesky had three hits in each
game for a total of 14 since the disastrous occurrence of July 4.

The Yankees were not exactly in top shape. Joe DiMaggio was out
again. After struggling with nagging injuries and a persistent cold, he
had been knocked out of the line-up two weeks earlier with a debili-
tating case of viral pneumonia. Yogi Berra was sidelined with a broken thumb. Tommy Henrich had fractured the second and third lum-
bar vertebra processes in his back running into a fence in Chicago.
By all rights he should have been out for the season. But with Di-
Maggio down, Tommy was playing first base in a corrective corset.

Both games were, of course, sellouts. Sunday's game, the last
home game of the season, set an all-time Boston attendance record
for the second straight season and in the process brought the Yankees an all-time major league record for road attendance.

The fans saw a game to remember.

Dom DiMaggio, Old Reliable for the Red Sox, led off with a single.
With the Yankees looking for a bunt, Pesky, who could handle the
bat as deftly as Rizzuto, chopped the ball over the third baseman's
head and down into the left-field corner for a double. Williams was
purposely passed. Bases loaded, nobody out, and Allie Reynolds was
able to escape without a run being scored on him.

You could feel the apprehension in the air. The last time the Yankees had visited Fenway Park, the same thing had happened. Reynolds had walked the first three batters, and all the Red Sox had been
able to get out of it was two runs on a Bobby Doerr single. They had
not scored again all day. In the eighth inning, with the Red Sox behind, 3–2, Doerr had tripled with one out. Stengel sent for Page, and
Page had not only struck out four of the five men he faced, but had
struck out the side in the ninth on 10 pitches.

Joe DiMaggio had laid it out bluntly after the game: "When you
have a chance like Boston had in the first and don't make the most of
it, you don't win." That was the main difference between the two
clubs, Joe was saying. "When the Yankees have that kind of a chance,
we cash in big."

Now the Red Sox had let Reynolds off the hook again, and when
Henrich opened the second inning with a double and went to third on

a groundout, you could all but see the momentum swinging over to the Yankees.

But not for long. In one of those plays that goes almost unnoticed, Birdie Tebbetts pulled it right back to the Red Sox. Here's what happened: Johnny Lindell sent a line drive to right field, plenty deep enough to bring in the run. Al Zarilla took the ball knee high and cut loose with a magnificent throw, on the line all the way to the plate. Birdie gave it the Wooden Indian treatment, whereby the catcher stands there with his hands on his hips looking as if he has no play. You know how often that works? One time in a thousand, maybe.

We are now going to turn the lectern over to George Sullivan, the new Red Sox bat boy. George would grow up to become a sports writer and columnist for both the *Post* and the *Globe,* and for a couple of years he was also the Red Sox publicity man.

But in September 1949 he was still a 15-year-old schoolboy who had been taken on as visiting-team bat boy through school connections.

"I almost blew the play. I was 15 years old and a red-hot Red Sox rooter. The hardest thing for me all along was not to root from the dugout. I had just pulled the bat out of the way and I was standing only a few feet from the plate. Birdie was standing there with his hands on his hips. I didn't think he saw the ball, and it was heading right for his forehead. I was just about to scream, "Look out, Birdie," when at the last second he just snapped into action, took the throw, and put the ball on Henrich, who was going into a belated slide. Charlie Silvera, who was only playing because of Berra's injury, was the next batter, and that meant he was supposed to be the coach at the plate. It was the only time I ever saw Stengel blow his top in the dugout. He was screaming at Silvera, and Silvera was saying that he had gone down to his knee, which is the way you are supposed to do it when the crowd is making that much noise."

It didn't seem possible, but for poor Silvera the day was about to get worse.

Silvera put on his equipment, went back out to catch, and took a foul flush in the groin. "His cup worked against him instead of for him," Sullivan recalls. "We formed a circle around him, and Gus Mauch, the Yankee trainer, actually undressed him at home plate. He was in tremendous pain, and in fact I went running out to get the stretcher and held one corner as we were carrying him through the Red Sox dugout and into the clubhouse. At that time both teams used the same runway at Fenway Park, and once we got out of sight of the fans and up the runway he just started screaming, he was in such pain. My heart went out to the guy."

Ralph Houk, who had just been called up from the minors, was the only catcher left. He got behind the plate just in time to watch Johnny Pesky single in two runs. The score remained 2–0 until Pesky singled again with two out and Williams uncorked a colossal drive that landed 15 rows up in the right-field bleachers for his forty-third home run.

The Red Sox had won nine straight. They had won their last 22 games of the season at Fenway Park. They were tied for first place. As originally drawn up, the schedule had called for the Red Sox to finish with three games in Washington and two in New York. But the amended schedule had them stopping off at Yankee Stadium on the way to Washington to make up a game that had been rained out earlier in the month and then returning to New York to bring the season to an end.

Who could have planned it better? Head to head for the tie breaker with six games left. The Yankees had the home-field advantage, sure. But DiMaggio was still out, Berra was still out, and Silvera had suffered his unfortunate mishap.

And that was why Ralph Houk was behind the plate again for the most famous play he would ever be involved in. Houk wasn't really a rookie — he had been brought up over the last half of the two previous seasons for defensive purposes — but for 1949 this was his first start as a Yankee.

For a makeup game being played on a Monday, there were 66,156 people in the stands.

The Red Sox started fast and finished fast. The Yankees had it, and the Yankees threw it away. They gave the game away in a harrowing eighth inning during which they missed a chance for a triple play, made two errors, walked two men, and saw Joe Page fail to cover first base. All of it leading up to an umpire's decision at home plate on — wouldn't you know it — Johnny Pesky.

The Red Sox had taken a 3–0 lead off Allie Reynolds in the first inning, after another of those bases-loaded-and-nobody-out situations which had become so familiar. By the eighth inning, however, they were losing, 6–3, and Joe Page was mowing them down.

Birdie Tebbetts opened the inning with a legitimate single, and pinch-hitter Lou Stringer walked. With a 3–2 count on him and both runners going, Dom DiMaggio rifled a drive that appeared to be headed for left-center. Phil Rizzuto leaped high in the air, felt the thwack of the ball in the webbing of his glove, and — as he was to tell Arthur Daley after the game — was so sure that he had a triple play staring him in the face that for just that one split second he could not understand why the runners were still going. Until he looked into his glove. The ball had broken through the webbing and rolled out to short left field. A run was in, and there were still two men on and nobody out.

Then things got sloppy. George Stirnweiss, who had taken over at second base after Coleman had gone out for a pinch-hitter, fumbled a ground ball hit by Johnny Pesky.

That was how Johnny Pesky got to first base.

Ted Williams, hitless on the game though passed twice, smashed a ground ball toward right field which Tommy Henrich dove for and missed. Stirnweiss fielded the ball nicely but had nobody to throw it to. Joe Page had neglected to cover first. Another run was in. The score was 6–5. The bases were still loaded.

Johnny Pesky was on second base.

Vern Stephens flied deep to Gene Woodling in right field, and Dom DiMaggio came in with the tying run. The score was 6–6, and, equally important, Johnny Pesky had dashed over to third with the go-ahead run.

Now that everything was set up so nicely for Johnny Pesky's revenge, all that was needed was a play at the plate.

Ready on the right? Ready on the left? O.K. Roll 'em.

Bobby Doerr dropped down a squeeze bunt. Pesky came flying in from third. Henrich, anticipating the bunt, had come swooping in and, bad back and all, made the play perfectly. The throw had Pesky beat. Of that there was never the slightest question.

"Safe," ruled umpire Bill Grieve.

"No, no, no!" screamed Ralph Houk, as the Yankee bench, led by Casey Stengel, erupted onto the field.

A furious argument ensued during which Ralph Houk broke the major-league high jump record, which had been set on that same spot by Yogi Berra on July 4. Before it was over, Stengel had been thrown out for making physical contact with Grieve, and the only reason Houk didn't go with him was that Grieve was aware that the Yankees didn't have another catcher.

Ellis Kinder, who had shut the Yankees out two days earlier, came in and mowed them down again over the final two innings.

Cliff Mapes, one of the heroes of the earlier Pesky imbroglio, was one of the few Yankee players who had not been inserted into the line-up. If he had been in right field instead of Woodling, Pesky would never have tried to go to third. Now that the game was over, though, Mapes was going to get a piece of it. Big Cliff had been nursing a raging anger over the call, and as the players and officials left the field and headed toward their respective dressing quarters, he was waiting to accost Grieve in the runway. "How much did you bet on the game, you sonofabitch?" he screamed at him.

Grieve shouted back that no umpire had ever been indicted for throwing a game, and that was more than could be said for the players. If the other two umpires on Grieve's crew hadn't stepped in to pull them apart, we might well have been treated to the first slugfest between an umpire and a player. (It may have been fortuitous that one of the umpires was Cal Hubbard. It also may not have been. Big Cal, the very personification of law and order, always seemed to be on the field when the Red Sox and Yankees were mixing it up.)

Stengel and Houk were fined $150. Mapes was fined $200 and ordered to apologize.

Six years later, when Ralph Houk became manager of the Yankees Triple-A farm club at Denver, he brought Pesky along to coach for him. They continued to argue the play vehemently from their adjoining lockers until one day there appeared on Ralph's locker a photographic sequence of the play that had been printed in *Life* magazine. Underneath the sequence, one of the youthful Denver players had written, with obvious delight, "Is he safe, Ralph?"

They still can't see each other without rearguing the play. And they saw each other every day during the 1981–1984 seasons, when Ralph Houk was the manager of the Red Sox and Johnny Pesky was, once again, one of his coaches. "The ball beat me there," Pesky always tells Houk. "But I got under you. I just got a piece of the plate on the side."

Houk's response never changes, either. "I sat down on home plate, you sonofabitch," he says. "You'd have had to be a mole to get in there."

Privately Pesky will tell you that when he looks at that strip of photographs he has to admit that there was no way he could have been safe. "Only don't tell that to Ralph Houk."

.   .   .

Safe was what Bill Grieve had called him, though, and for the first time in the season the Red Sox went into first place.

They were still in first place by that single game when they returned to New York, three days later, to meet the Yankees in the final two games of the season.

They were going to be the worst two days in the history of Boston baseball. The dregs. The flood that wiped out Johnstown. The earthquake that destroyed San Francisco. The Beast that ate Detroit.

This is the series that would forevermore scar the memories of Boston fans. The defining series. It told Boston what it was, told Bostonians who they were, established a philosophy by which they would have to live, and converted all subsequent disasters into one more failure within a philosophical unity.

One other thing had happened during the day of Pesky's revenge. Back at the Hotel Edison, Joe DiMaggio's temperature had dropped to normal for the first time in two weeks. The bulletin released that afternoon by his doctor read: "He will be permitted to get out of bed tomorrow and should be able to work out by Thursday. He should be ready to play in the final series of the year with the Red Sox this week-end."

On Thursday and Friday he went out to Yankee Stadium with his older brother, Tom, for a light workout. Tom DiMaggio was in town because the Yankees had designated Saturday as Joe DiMaggio Day, and the whole family had come in from San Francisco to take part in the festivities (just as they had gathered in Boston at the end of the 1948 season for Dominic's wedding).

At Joe's request, Dom came onto the field to stand alongside him during the presentations. He found Joe so drawn and emaciated and incredibly weary that, as the gifts piled up and the speeches droned on, it became increasingly necessary for Joe to lean on him for physical support.

Upon his return to the Red Sox dugout, Dom told his teammates that he didn't see how Joe could possibly play. Over in the Yankee dugout, Joe was telling Casey Stengel that he would try to go five innings.

The Red Sox were going to pitch Parnell and Kinder again. Joe McCarthy, the manager who had always treated his starting pitchers with kid gloves, had thrown the whole season onto the shoulders of

Kinder and Parnell, the two pitchers he had by-passed in the play-off game against Cleveland. Between them they had started seven straight games down the stretch (spread out over a period of 10 days). And in those games whichever one wasn't pitching was in the bullpen.

In the preceding series at Washington, McCarthy had felt free to go to his other pitchers because the Red Sox had beaten Washington 16 out of 19 times over the season. But still, Kinder and Parnell had both been in the bullpen, and they had been used in two of the three games. Parnell had come in, pitched out of trouble, and then let in the winning run on a wild pitch.

Parnell had already gone 291 innings, which was more innings than McCarthy had ever asked from a pitcher in his 20 years of managing. Parnell had started 32 games and, because he was always so effective, completed 27 of them. He had relieved five times down the stretch. His weight was down, and he had a sore elbow.

Not to overstate this. All pitchers lose weight toward the end of a tough pennant race. Not every pitcher has a sore arm, but almost every pitcher will have an arm that is sore.

Against him was Allie Reynolds. The best you can say for Reynolds was that he did not start the game by loading the bases. He waited until the third inning to do that. Not that Allie didn't have a rocky first inning. Dom had opened the game, once again, with a base hit, then moved to second on a hit by Williams and scored on Stephens' long fly after a wild pitch had allowed him to go to third.

In the third inning Reynolds got Dom but walked Pesky, Williams, and Stephens. Doerr blooped a pop fly to short right field that fell just beyond Coleman's glove to score Pesky, and right then Casey Stengel stopped the game and sent for Joe Page.

Page was in the bullpen that early because everybody was in the bullpen. Before the start of the game, Stengel had asked Page how far he thought he could go. "I can go a long way," Page had said.

"Then go down there," Stengel told him. "I won't wait today."

Page walked Zarilla to score Williams. Then he walked Billy Goodman on four pitches, and the score was 4–0. Five walks and a bloop hit. The bases were still loaded and Birdie Tebbetts was at bat.

Clif Keane: "Birdie swung at three pitches over his head, and that could well have been the turning point of the ballgame. Another base on balls, and who knows?"

How could a smart player like Tebbetts, who had been through the toughest of pennant races, swing at three bad pitches in that situation? Let's put it this way: In every opposing dugout, whenever a Nolan Ryan or a Sandy Koufax pitches, the manager and the coaches walk up and down chanting, "Make him bring the ball down . . . Make him bring it down." And while they're saying it, 10 batters go up and strike out on rising fast balls. The answer is that the ball looks as if it's right down the pipe when they start their swing. It's only after they have begun their swing that the ball explodes upward.

Joe Page's fast ball was exploding. Parnell, a good hitter, struck out, too. For the rest of the game Page was untouchable, allowing only one single.

Phil Rizzuto has always said that when he came up at the bottom of the third, Tebbetts, always the needler, told him, "Well, we'll pitch Quinn tomorrow." Frank Quinn was a bonus pitcher from Yale whom the Red Sox had signed in midseason. Rizzuto went back to the bench and passed on that message ("Do you know what that Tebbetts said to me?") with an almost spluttering indignation.

Tebbetts says that's nothing more than a banquet story that Rizzuto has told so often that he has probably come to believe it. And anyway, he says, do you really think that professionals would become so indignant over a slighting remark that they would become inspired to go out and play harder than they would normally play?

But Jerry Coleman says: "I don't know about that. Rizzuto did tell us that when he came back to the bench. And I have a memory of Tebbetts saying the same thing to me. Not directly to me, but just kind of saying it softly to the air."

He couldn't have said it for long, because the Yankees put themselves right back into the game. And it was Joe DiMaggio who got things started. The first time at bat he had struck out, but in the fourth inning he sliced a drive down the right-field line that bounced into the stands for a ground-rule double. ("You didn't want to run," Page kidded him after the game. "I didn't have the strength to go around," Joe said.) Hank Bauer, always productive in a showdown series, singled him home.

Then Johnny Lindell singled, and Jerry Coleman — little Jerry Coleman, the nervous rookie — brought Bauer in with a long fly. The Yankees were back within striking distance, and Page was as fast as anybody had ever seen him.

Mel Parnell was neither as fast nor as sharp as he had been for the past two months. In the fifth inning Rizzuto, Henrich, and Berra rapped out successive singles. The score was 4–3, and with Joe DiMaggio coming to bat again, McCarthy brought in Joe Dobson.

For Birdie Tebbetts, the whole season turned on the next pitch. DiMaggio lined the ball back to the box for what should have been, Tebbetts felt, an inning-ending double play. Instead, the ball bounced off Dobson, dropped onto the mound directly behind him, and the score was tied.

Tebbetts: "The one thing I learned about in the three years that I was with the Red Sox is that a pitcher will throw a ball up to the hitter and then throw their body to first base or turn their back or their feet will be tangled. They will not be ready for a ball hit back through the box. There were many balls I can remember, including balls in both of the final games in New York and the game we lost in Washington — and they are indelibly marked in my mind — that would have been double plays. And we lost those last two games."

They were marked so indelibly in his mind that when Birdie became manager of the Cincinnati Reds, his pitchers became known as the best fielders in the league — possibly because he imposed a fine on any pitcher who failed to field a ball that was hit back through the box.

In the bottom of the eighth, there were three right-handed batters due up for the Yankees. Stengel sent in two left-handed pinch-hitters, Bobby Brown and Cliff Mapes, and Dobson got them both. That brought up Johnny Lindell. Why did Stengel let Lindell bat? He had Woodling on the bench. He had Keller on the bench. The presumptive answer is that with two out and nobody on, the percentage was to save them. Or maybe it was because Lindell had been swinging the bat well all day. In three times up, he had two singles and had sent Ted Williams back to the fence for a long fly ball. The one other possible answer is that no one has ever really been able to figure out what went on in the deepest recesses of Casey Stengel's mind.

Johnny Lindell whacked a high inside fast ball into the left-field stands for a home run. It was the first home run he had hit since July 1, and only his sixth home run of the year. It brought his batting average for the year up to .232.

Tebbetts: "Lindell was a curve-ball hitter. We threw him a high fast ball. That's the pitch we had been getting him out with all year. It was the right pitch to throw him. Which doesn't mean that he had no right to hit it."

.   .   .

If the Red Sox were not overly discouraged, it was because they had developed an unlimited faith in Ellis Kinder. His record was 23–5. He hadn't lost a game since July 24. He hadn't lost as a starting pitcher since June 9.

Ellis Kinder was one of the more astonishing figures in the annals of the rivalry. Ellie was out of the little town of Jackson, Tennessee. He started pitching late in life. If there had not been a welfare, shantytown team like the St. Louis Browns, there would never have been an Ellis Kinder. If there hadn't been a war, we would never have heard of him, either. Ellie was 30 years old when the Browns drafted him — *drafted* him — from the Memphis Chicks of the Southern Association. Then he went into the service. So 1946 was his first year in the bigs. Never mind what the record books say. He was 34 years old when he came to the majors, an age at which the average player is being phased out, and spent two years with the Browns before he was traded to the Red Sox. Ellie had control and smarts, constant changes of speed, all thrown off the same arm motion. What Ellie had developed — if baseball were gymnastics, it would be called a Kinder — was a straight change off his fast ball. Not a change-up curve like everybody else had, but a straight change. Off his motion, it looked like a fast ball. The ball came in with nothing on it, and at the last split second the batter's eyes lit up and he took a big swing, only to find that the ball hadn't got there yet.

He was a textbook illustration of McCarthy's misgivings about hillbillies. Ellie had been around, and he was sufficient unto himself. Ellie didn't give a damn. The best way to get him not to do something was to have somebody in authority tell him to do it.

He had a wife back home, and he also had a "wife" in Boston.

But most of all, Ellie drank. Even in an age when alcohol was such an accepted vice that it wasn't looked on as one, Ellie's reputation had scared off baseball people for years.

One time during his first season with the Red Sox, Roy Mumpton of the *Worcester Telegram* and Bob Holbrook of the *Boston Globe* were coming back to the South Side of Chicago by train after a night on the town when they sighted a drunk lying on the steps in front of the railroad station.

"Jeez," Holbrook said, "I think that's our new pitcher."

"We were only a block from the hotel," Mumpton recalls, "so we tried to get him up to walk him back. Oh, was he drunk. We had to get a cab to turn around and take us to the hotel." With the help of the cabbie and a couple of bellhops they were able to carry him into the elevator, and from there Mumpton and Holbrook got him to his room and put him to bed.

Mumpton: "I never saw a guy so drunk. The next day is a double-header, hot as hell. Now, they announce the battery for the second game, and the pitcher for the Red Sox is Ellis Kinder. I look at Holbrook, and we say, 'This is going to be great.' "

Kinder went the distance and won.

When Arthur Richman of the *New York Mirror* came to the Boston dressing room for the post game interviews, following the loss of the Parnell game, he found himself surrounded by the old St. Louis contingent — Stephens, Kramer, and Zarilla. "Now, look," they said, "take Ellie out tonight, and if he doesn't get to bed, O.K. Let him drink to his heart's content."

Artie was the kid brother of Milton Richman of United Press. In his younger days Milton had been a Brownie farm hand, and the Richman brothers were still very close to the Browns of that period, and to Ellis Kinder in particular. Ellie had taken Artie under his wing, and become his "daddy," even to the point of taking him home to Tennessee at the end of the season to show him how they did it in the boondocks. Ellie had a thing about teaching kids the facts of life, and in Artie he had found a willing student.

Johnny Donovan will never believe that Kinder was out drinking that night. Johnny Donovan, you will recall, was a 16-year-old bat boy then but is presently the attorney for the Red Sox. He makes a great story. A poor kid out of Chelsea, he became a bat boy at the age of 14, the first year he could legally work, graduated to every other task around the clubhouse, was promoted to the ticket department, attended Holy Cross on the money he had been able to save, earned his spending money as a stringer for the *Boston Post,* and was able to attend law school on his earnings as night watchman at Fenway Park. (In other words, Tom Yawkey provided him with a perfect environment for reading his law books while paying him a salary to make sure the pigeons didn't steal the ball park.) Johnny Donovan had gone on to become a representative in the state legislature, and when the Red Sox found themselves in all kinds of trouble after Yawkey's death, John Donovan, Esquire, was asked to return as vice president and chief counsel.

But let's go back to Johnny Donovan, bat boy. Joe McCarthy took good care of the clubhouse kids. In 1949 he instituted the practice, which is now general in baseball, of taking them along on an occasional road trip, and with the great series coming up in New York, he had put all the clubhouse kids on the travel list.

In Boston, McCarthy had given Johnny a special task — to make certain that Kinder was in the park on the days he was supposed to be pitching. If Ellie wasn't in the clubhouse by the appointed time, Donovan would go down to the Buckminster Hotel and get him.

Before that final game in New York, McCarthy had another special assignment for him: it was the 16-year-old bat boy's job to make sure that Kinder spent the night in the hotel.

You will never convince Johnny Donovan that Kinder wasn't in his room that night. "I was in the lobby when he came down at 9 or 9:30, and I thought, *Oh, oh!* But half an hour later he came back through the lobby carrying a stack of newspapers and heading for the elevator."

At 11 o'clock Johnny Donovan went up and knocked on the door of the room that Kinder was sharing with Joe Dobson. "He answered the door in his shorts. Half asleep. He was fine. I saw him again in the morning, and he was as clear-eyed as he had ever been."

Wrong. Ellie had thrown a feint at him. He had a date to meet Artie Richman at midnight.

The *Mirror* building was on 45th Street, practically around the corner from the Commodore, and needless to say, Artie was well acquainted with the bars in the neighborhood. "We went to a bar on Lexington Avenue, not far from the hotel. Ellie loved to have a toddy. Of all the baseball men I've met in my life, Ellis Kinder probably could hold his toddies better than any man I ever knew. We were out to 4 or 4:30 that morning, and he was as loose as a goose. He was confident. My God, he hadn't lost a game in 20 starts. He felt like he was unbeatable. There was no way he was going to lose.

"I left him at 4:00 or 4:30 with a dolly he was taking back to the Commodore, even though he was rooming with Dobson. But that didn't stop Ellie.

"The next day he came to the ballpark. His eyes were a little bloodshot, of course. He hadn't had much sleep, and he still had a lot of alcohol in him." Just the way his teammates wanted him. "Rizzuto hit the ball down the left-field line, leading off, and it got into the gully. I can still see it . . ."

Roland Hemond is the president of the Baltimore Orioles. He grew up in Central Falls, Rhode Island, and was a dedicated Red Sox fan. The only two times he ever skipped school, it was to run into Boston, with his mother's permission, to see the Red Sox play. He got his first job in baseball with the Boston Braves, and still rooted for the Red Sox. He even kind of rooted for them in the nine years he was general manager of the Chicago White Sox.

Roland Hemond: "In 1949 I was in the Coast Guard, stationed at Mitchell Field in New York, and I was able to get passes every time the Red Sox came in. The only game I missed was on July 5. For the one time in my life I gave up on my Red Sox after that heartbreaking loss when Johnny Pesky lost sight of the ball during the July 4 double-header.

"On that Sunday afternoon, I'm in my Coast Guard uniform sitting down the left-field line, right by the pole. Rizzuto was the best right-handed bunter I ever saw at dropping the bunt toward third, and a lot of times he'd start to move his hands to make it look as if he was going to bunt, and he'd flick his wrist and rap the ball over the third baseman. And that's what he did on the first pitch of the game. He hit the ball over the third baseman's head down the line, and the ball is right under me. I was about to reach down and field it, and there was a policeman next to me and he yelled, 'Get your hands off!' Automatically I pulled my hands back. Ted Williams had come over to field it. There was that little kind of gully there, and Ted tried to block the ball off by pressing his body into the corner, but somehow the ball got through him and Rizzuto was able to go to third. Joe McCarthy plays the infield back, it's the first inning, and Henrich steers a ground ball to Doerr at second and the run scored. And that's how the game remained, 1–0, into the eighth inning when McCarthy pinch-hit for Kinder.

"If I had touched that ball, it would have been a ground-rule double and everything would have been different. And I've always wondered whether in pulling my hands back, I might have cost the Red Sox the pennant, and perhaps even changed the course of both those franchises.

"I talked about this story for years, and one of the Cleveland writers looked it up and he said, 'You can sleep well, Roland. DiMaggio tripled with two out in that first inning.' And he had. I had forgotten about that. Except that you don't know if they would have pitched different to DiMaggio if Rizzuto had been on base. This is something we all do, although we know that every time that something else happens, everything changes. Especially when you have a pitcher like Kinder who allowed only two more hits for the rest of the time he was in the game."

Oddly enough, Bill Crowley remembers the triple that Hemond forgot more vividly than anything else that happened in that game. Crowley was a Boston kid who had come out of the army and somehow landed a job, on no experience, announcing the Yankee games with Mel Allen. There you had DiMaggio, dead tired. He had played nine innings the day before. He had told Stengel, once again, that he would try to go five. "In the first inning, with two out and nobody on, he drilled the ball into the gap in right-center. The difference between being on second and being on third in that situation is almost negligible, and yet there he was, going all out to turn the drive into a triple. You could see the pain in his eyes from the press box. You could see him straining. And before the day was over, if you remember that game, he paid for it."

Vic Raschi was pitching the game of his life, too. Raschi was out of Springfield, Massachusetts, one of those cities that was divided equally between Red Sox and Yankee rooters. The Springfield Rifle, they called him, a bulldog of a competitor. He had led the league for half a season, battled through an autumn slump, and had come back to the top of his form during the last week or two of the season.

Against the Red Sox he was 4–1 on the season, reversing the previous season's dismal 0–4.

Raschi versus Kinder, the two pitchers who had been by-passed in the previous year's finale. Kinder had allowed three hits; Raschi had allowed two.

When, with Kinder due to lead off the eighth inning, McCarthy sent up a pinch-hitter, he set in motion one of the all-time second-guessing situations. Kinder fancied himself a pretty good hitter. He hated to be pinch-hit for. At least, he would say, he could hit better than anybody the Red Sox could send up for him, and when you consider that the Red Sox' pinch-hitter, Billy Hitchcock, had not had a hit in 16 opportunities that year, it is hard to argue with him.

But the Red Sox had brought up a left-handed–hitting outfielder, Tom Wright, who had led the American Association in batting. Wright had been sent up twice to pinch-hit, and he already had a hit to show for it.

Taken by itself, the move was successful in the sense that Tom Wright worked Raschi for a base on balls. If Dom DiMaggio had been able to do anything, McCarthy would have been hailed for making a gutty decision. But Dom DiMaggio didn't knock him in. Dom Di-Maggio hit into a double play.

Look. When you're a run behind in the eighth inning and your pitcher is leading off, you pinch-hit for him. That's all there is to it. McCarthy had Parnell in the bullpen, along with everybody else, and although Parnell had been hit hard the previous day, how often have we seen it happen that a good pitcher who has been battered one day will come back and be unhittable the next?

Parnell wasn't merely a good pitcher, he was a great pitcher, and he would be facing two left-handed hitters, Henrich and Berra. There was this about Tommy Henrich, though. The better the pitcher, the better Tommy hit him. Bob Feller always said that Henrich was the toughest hitter for him to get out. So did Parnell. Henrich hit Mel's first pitch into the right-field stands. Berra followed with a single, and to the amazement of everybody on the club, most particularly Tex Hughson, McCarthy called for Hughson to face Joe DiMaggio.

"They're really scraping the bottom of the barrel," Hughson said as he was handed the ball. He hadn't pitched in three weeks.

To put it mildly, Tex Hughson hated McCarthy. Hughson had come back from a dangerous operation that spring, and McCarthy had used him so capriciously — bringing him in from the bullpen every day for a week or so and then forgetting him completely for weeks at a time — that it had been impossible for him to work himself back into any kind of shape. (When Hughson sent word that he just could not work that way, McCarthy decided that he was gutless. He later decided that Earl Johnson, who had come out of the war a decorated hero, was so gutless that he released him.)

Joe DiMaggio, who had *not* hit into the double play on Saturday, hit into a double play on Sunday.

Ninety-nine percent of the time, a double play in that situation will pretty much signal the end of the inning. But Johnny Lindell, who was carving a whole season out of these two days, singled. Bill Johnson, the right-handed–hitting third baseman in another of Stengel's platoon positions, also singled, and when Williams fumbled the ball in left field, Hank Bauer (running for Lindell) went to third. Very important. With second base open, Cliff Mapes was walked to bring up Jerry Coleman, the number-eight hitter.

The count went to 3–2, all three runners started moving, and Hughson reached back for something extra on his fast ball.

Johnny Donovan, sitting in the Red Sox dugout, had the impression that Coleman had either ducked away from the ball or tried to check his swing.

To Roland Hemond, looking in from his front-row seat in left field, it looked like a choked swing that resulted in a little pop fly to right field. "A real tough hit to field. The ball stayed in the air quite a bit, but out of reach of everybody. Zarilla made a gallant effort, dove for it, and came down hard on his shoulder, but it was just one of those balls that was impossible to get to."

Jerry Coleman: "It wasn't a checked swing. It was up and in. Not a good pitch to swing at. I was a little overanxious, shall we say. The ball was at the letters, probably a marginal strike inside. Hughson threw it as hard as he could throw it, and I didn't get out in front of it. I hit it on the trademark, and, of course, it found the right hole. I thought something on the order of, *Oh, damn* . . . I didn't expect much out of it, I'll say that, and when I realized what was happening, I started picking up some speed."

To Al Zarilla, the ball was coming down too fast. To Jerry Coleman, it was drifting to earth like a parachute. "A dying quail was what it was called in those days. Today it would be called a flare. Actually it was a double. I've read where some say it was a triple. I was thrown out at third base." What happened was that another run was coming in, the fifth run. In that spot it was Coleman's job to protect the runner trying to score by drawing the throw to himself.

Coleman: "I drew the throw. It was cut off, I believe, by Billy Goodman, and they had me at third base. At that point we had five runs, with Raschi pitching. What did we care? And then we had to care."

Tebbetts: "He didn't duck. It was a swing. The ball was a good pitch, it was in on him, and it just sawed the bat off in his hands, and he just hit a lazy bloop hit into right field, which as time goes on, like he always says to me, 'I don't care what you say, it was a line drive.' "

Eddie Lopat had the bullpen view, the view from behind. "All the pitchers were in the bullpen. Zarilla dove for the ball, and the ball hit the edge of his glove and trickled right up his arm and fell behind him. He's sprawled out and guys are running around the bases."

Tebbetts: "It was not a very solidly hit ball, but we see the same kind of hit in every ball game that we go to, and they count. So it doesn't make any difference what kind of a hit it was. It hurt."

With everybody running the bases, or moving into defensive assignments, all eyes had swung away from right field and followed the relay that had started toward home plate and ended with Pesky tagging Coleman out at third.

The inning was over; the Boston players began their disconsolate trek off the ball field. Roland Hemond's eyes had remained glued to Al Zarilla, because it had struck him that only Ted Williams, who had come all the way over to right field, was showing any interest in helping his fallen teammate.

Top of the ninth inning, and the Red Sox rallied. Pesky, hitless against the Yankees in both games, went out on a foul fly. But Williams walked, and Stephens singled to center. Bobby Doerr hit a long fly to right-center field, and as Joe DiMaggio raced back after it, his legs gave out and the ball went over his head for a triple. DiMaggio took himself out of the game and was replaced by Cliff Mapes. Al Zarilla, the other fallen fielder, then flied out to Mapes. But Billy Goodman kept the game alive with a single to center that scored Bobby Doerr and brought the tying run to the plate. At this point Henrich walked over to Raschi to utter the usual words of encouragement.

Raschi did not like to be disturbed while he was working, and he was not happy that he had lost his shutout. "Give me the goddam ball," he barked, "and get the hell out of here."

Tebbetts hit a pop fly off first base. Henrich waved Coleman off. This one Henrich wanted for himself.

Lopat: "Tebbetts was running down the base line and we were all yelling, "Hey, Birdie! Where's Quinn?"

Let's go back to Doerr's triple. It is always written that Joe DiMaggio unselfishly took himself out of the game because he knew that he was hurting the team out there.

Or, as it was described to me several times, he made such a magnificent effort that his knee gave out.

The question that should have been asked was what the hell was he doing out there with the Yankees leading, 5–0. He had told Stengel, once again, that he would try to go five innings.

Look at that for a moment, too. When Joe had decided to play back in June, he didn't tell Stengel; he told Phil Pepe. In those final two games he told Stengel how far he'd try to go, and merely signaled him at the end of five innings that he was going to stay in there.

And now it was Joe, not Stengel, who took himself off the field in the final game. The other side of that transaction is that Casey Stengel, who was only the manager, couldn't have removed him without bringing on a firestorm.

Question: Why didn't Stengel send in some strong legs for the top of the ninth, with his team ahead, 5–0? DiMaggio had just hit into a double play. He wasn't going to bat again. The answer is that Casey had wanted to do exactly that. And Joe DiMaggio had overruled him.

Lopat: "After the All-Star Game, Joe couldn't put any pressure on his ankle. He had those special rubber pads in his shoe, and in those last games he was dragging that leg, but he wouldn't come out. That's when Casey wanted to take him out. Joe said, 'No, I'm not coming out. This game is too important.' That's when the ball went to right-center and he was halfway over there. Usually he'd suck it up, but his leg collapsed — boom — and he was sitting down."

Casey Stengel had never before had a player who played only when he wanted to and who sucked up all the glory. Stengel hated him, and all the Yankee players knew that. They also knew that the feeling was mutual. DiMaggio and Rizzuto would talk about Stengel on the bench, and they didn't care if Stengel overheard.

DiMaggio would say, "He doesn't have to go through all these moves. He's just trying to make himself look smart."

They hated each other.

For Ted, it was an awful series. He had started the season slowly, blazed in the summer months, and taken over the league lead in everything. He held the batting title to the last day (going into the Yankee series he was leading George Kell of the Tigers .344 to .340).

His only hit was a drive that had bounced off the umpire Cal Hubbard in the first inning of the first game. He lost the batting title on his last at bat to Kell, who had gone 2 for 3, .3429 to .34275. He would have been the only American Leaguer except for Ty Cobb to win the batting title five times. It also cost him what would have been his third Triple Crown.

He did win the MVP, but even so there were some snide remarks from New York that he had snuck in only because the Yankee vote was split between Phil Rizzuto and Joe Page. That's not true. Between them the Red Sox and Yankees dominated the voting: Williams got 272 votes, Rizzuto 175, Page 166, Parnell 151, Kinder 122, Hen-

rich 121, and Stephens 100. Where was Joe DiMaggio in this season
of his star-spangled return in Boston, the year of the three-day hitting feat that springs to mind immediately after the 56-game hitting
streak? DiMaggio was in twelfth place with 18 points, one point behind Vic Raschi.

Just before the game was over, Artie Richman went down to the
Boston clubhouse to see Ellie Kinder, who was already packing his
stuff. Clutching his throat in the time-honored sign of the choke,
Kinder told him, "Shit in the neck again." In Boston they'd have
agreed with him. All over Boston they were saying that if the Yankees hadn't scored those runs after Kinder left the game, the final
score would have been 1–0.

Birdie Tebbetts was about to be married to Mary Hartnett, the
secretary to the governor of New Hampshire. Before the game was
over, he had gone across to the box seat where she was sitting and
told her that win, lose, or draw, they'd stay in New York for the first
few games of the World Series.

"When I got back to the hotel after the game was over, I met her
in the lobby of the hotel. I said, 'Mary, let's pack and go home.' She
said, 'I'm already packed. The bags are already down here.' I guess
she knew I wasn't staying."

John Donovan: "I'll always remember the drive back, and going
through Spanish Harlem, and the streets were wet from the kids
playing with the hydrants, and the sound of the tires running through
that, and getting to the train in Grand Central to come to Boston,
and it wasn't until you were in mid-Connecticut that there was any
chatter. By then it was the beer talking."

They had just about reached New Haven when Ellie Kinder went
storming into Joe McCarthy's sitting room to bawl the hell out of him
for taking him out of the game, and to get a few other things off his
chest about the way McCarthy had humiliated his lesser pitchers all
season long.

A handshake that transcends rivalry, between a Red Sox and an ex-Red Sox: Ted Williams and Babe Ruth in 1944. The rivalry was always more intense among the fans than among the players. *(The Sports Museum, Boston, Mass.)*

The indomitable Babe: the best left-handed pitcher in the days of "inside" defensive baseball, on the mound for the Red Sox in 1916. *(The Sports Museum, Boston, Mass.)*

The Red Sox "Royal Rooters" storm Fenway for Game 7 of the 1912 World Series. *(The Sports Museum, Boston, Mass.)*

"My main purpose in buying the Red Sox is beating the Yankees." — Tom Yawkey, Red Sox owner, February 23, 1933 *(The Sports Museum, Boston, Mass.)*

Bought by Yawkey in 1935 for a whopping $250,000, Joe Cronin, as player and manager, epitomized the Red Sox, in both their dreams and their frustrations, for twenty years. *(The Sports Museum, Boston, Mass.)*

In hitting, Lou Gehrig spread himself across the batter's box and attacked the ball like a woodsman chopping down a tree. A typical Gehrig home run shot out of the park on a line, and it could just as easily have left the park in left field as in right field— or anywhere in between. *(The Sports Museum, Boston, Mass.)*

Yankee Babe Ruth up at bat at Fenway. *(The Sports Museum, Boston, Mass.)*

Casey Stengel, the "Greatest Living Manager." He knew things that nobody else knew. Or maybe he was just crazy. *(The Sports Museum, Boston, Mass.)*

"Sometimes I ask myself why I played baseball as hard as I did. I didn't have to play when I was banged up and I had eye infections and bone spurs and sore arms and crippled knees. I can't explain it, even to myself. Something inside just kept saying, 'Play ball all the time as hard as you can—and win.'" —Joe DiMaggio *(The Sports Museum, Boston, Mass.)*

A baby-faced Mickey Mantle comes to camp. *(National Baseball Library, Cooperstown, N.Y.)*

Mickey right-handed, and Mickey left-handed. In the beginning, he struck terror in the hearts of opposing pitchers from either side of the plate. In the end, he was two different batters. *(AP/Wide World Photos; National Baseball Library, Cooperstown, N.Y.)*

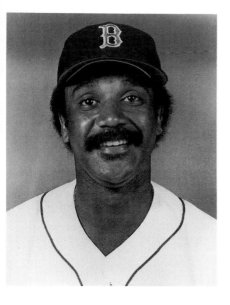

Entering the 1978 World Series only four short of Joe DiMaggio's greatest season in total bases, Jim Rice was the major-league leader in hits, triples, home runs, runs batted in, and total bases, and was second in runs scored. But in the play-off game of 1978 maybe you had to be lucky, too. *(The Sports Museum, Boston, Mass.)*

Yaz and Ted, 1978. *(The Sports Museum, Boston, Mass.)*

Joe and Dom DiMaggio. Little Dom, probably the
most underrated ballplayer of the era, was always overshadowed by the accomplishments of his big brother and
the overpowering presence of teammate Ted Williams.
(Courtesy of the Boston Red Sox)

Joe Page. Okay, this is a posed picture. The
real thing, with Joe Page hopping over the
bullpen fence with his jacket flung over his
shoulder, was a sight that terrified opposing
batters from 1947 to 1950. *(UPI)*

Chapter Fifteen

Stengel and Mantle

*I don't say I have any better judgment than anybody else.
But when I'm getting beat, I know why I'm getting beat.*
— Casey Stengel

WHOMEVER George Weiss selected as the new Yankee manager
in 1949 was going to be faced with a rebuilding program. Of
that there was no doubt. As Harold Kaese had written at the end of
the 1948 season, "The Yankees are a team in disrepair. Joe Di-
Maggio is on his last legs. Keller's back has given out on him. Henrich is hurting."

When George Weiss's manager turned out to be that aging clown
Casey Stengel, the resident reaction ran the full gamut from shock
to disbelief. Still, Stengel was nothing if not his own entertaining self.
When he was informed that nobody was picking the Yankees to finish
better than third, Casey's reaction was: "Third? That's pretty good.
I've never finished that high before."

The preseason poll of baseball writers showed 118 votes for Boston, 79 for Cleveland, and six big votes for Stengel's poor little
Yanks. It was not until his fifth year that the Yankees were the preseason choice. In his first seven years they were picked only twice.
When Stengel went after his third straight pennant, the writers were
still favoring the Red Sox 149 to 32 over New York.

Instead of finishing third in his opening season, he was on his way
to establishing the Third Yankee Dynasty, known to baseball historians as the greatest dynasty of them all.

Under Stengel the Yankees won nine times in his first 10 years,
and the one year they lost, they still won 103 games — more than in

any of their pennant years. In 12 years under Stengel they won 10 pennants and nine world championships, and when he was forced to retire after the loss of the 1960 World Series, the Yankees went on to win four more straight pennants under his successors, Ralph Houk and Yogi Berra. The Red Sox were not the principal competition. After the failures of 1949 and 1950, and a complete collapse over the final two weeks in 1951, Boston baseball slipped into a slough. For 15 years the Red Sox became known as baseball's foremost country club: a team with some talent, and the always exciting Ted Williams, but never really in contention.

The only time the Red Sox took the season series (13–9) was in 1959, as the Yankees finished in third place, only four games above .500, and the Red Sox finished in fifth place, four games under.

The rest of the time the Red Sox were dormant and the Yankees dominant.

Each of the Yankee dynasties was driven by a star of the first magnitude. Miller Huggins had Babe Ruth. Joe McCarthy had Joe DiMaggio. And Casey Stengel had Mickey Mantle, who may just have been the greatest natural talent of them all. Huggins had to tame the Babe. McCarthy wrote DiMaggio's name in the line-up and left him alone. But Stengel almost seemed to resent Mickey Mantle.

The most remarkable thing about Casey Stengel was that he was a minor league manager at the age of 58. Under normal conditions, a man who hasn't made it by then can go sit on a rock, study the tides, and wait for Social Security to come and get him. It wasn't that he had lacked for opportunity, either. For 21 years he had been managing ball clubs, high and low. In his nine years in the majors he had never taken a team out of the second division. His only claim to fame was that he was the first manager ever paid not to manage, and to make his humiliation complete, it was the Brooklyn Dodgers, in their most dreadful period, who were willing to pay him to get out of town.

After 21 years of working with inferior talent the old man finally had the players who could — to use his favorite word — execute.

The game of baseball was about to change.

With a full squad to work with, Stengel showed that the bench and the bullpen were just as important as the starting line-up. He demonstrated, almost daily, how games could be won by protecting even a good hitter from his one weakness, and contrariwise, by selecting the best possible spot to utilize a weaker hitter's strength.

It was Old Casey Stengel who showed them that your top pinch-hitter should be wheeled in at the first opportunity to break the game open instead of being saved until the late innings. And it was Stengel who showed everybody that, in the age of the lively ball, the relief pitcher could be the most valuable man on the squad.

A game in Fenway Park, in July 1949, perhaps best demonstrates the Stengel method. Stengel started Ed Lopat, a left-hander, and replaced Hank Bauer, who had hit two home runs the previous day, with Gene Woodling. According to conventional wisdom, (a) you did not pitch left-handers in Fenway Park; (b) you packed the line-up with right-handed power hitters, for reasons that Bauer had amply demonstrated; and (c) in any park, at any time, you always stayed with a hot hitter.

After seven innings Lopat was leading, 3–2, and the winning runs had been knocked in by Woodling. With everything coming up roses for Old Case, he hit yet another of those unconventional buttons and called Joe Page out of the bullpen to start the eighth inning.

Back then it was taken for granted not only that the starting pitcher had a right to stay in the game until he got into trouble, but that it was courting disaster to take him out. That wasn't how Casey saw it. After seven innings of Lopat's assortment of slow stuff, he figured that Page's fast ball would overwhelm the Red Sox. Smoky Joe overwhelmed six straight batters, and the Yankees won, 3–2.

In making out his starting line-up, Stengel would keep every conceivable variation in mind: the park, the weather, the wind, the starting pitchers (both his and theirs), and, perhaps most important of all, whether he wanted an offensive or defensive line-up on the field for that particular game.

Not only did he change the players in his line-up almost daily, but he also would change their positions in the batting order. Hank Bauer would find himself on the bench in games he felt he should be playing, and he even began to find himself, to his total bewilderment, being used as the lead-off man. "Why am I leading off?" he would mutter. "I'm not a base-on-balls hitter." Right or wrong, Stengel had his reasons. Hank Bauer could start the game with a home run (as he would do 18 times in his career). He could score from first base on a double, and he could break up a double play to keep the inning alive. "Give me a run in the first inning," Casey explained, "and it changes the whole complexion of that ball game."

He platooned within the platoon. He knew what his players could do better than they did; he knew their strengths, and he knew their weaknesses. He would use Woodling against a sidearming curve-baller, but he would sit Woodling down and play Irv Noren, another left-handed hitter, when the Yankees were up against an overhand curve-baller.

There were times, true enough, when his thinking was inexplicable. A classic instance came when he pinch-hit Joe Collins for Hank Bauer in the third inning against Early Wynn. Collins had hit zero home runs on the season, Bauer had hit 16. Collins hit a three-run homer, and the Yankees won, 3–0.

His use of Johnny Mize over a couple of years amounted to something very close to sheer artistry. Baseball, when it is watched day in and day out, develops into a pattern of waiting for the wheel to come around to the big man. Casey not only had his two big men in Mantle and Berra, but he gave himself an extra turn of the wheel with Mize. You get enough free spins and you can even beat a roulette wheel. The beauty of it was that Casey had the guts not to hold onto Mize until the end. If he had a chance to break the game open in an early inning, in came Big Jawn.

Casey's system called not so much for platoons as for interchangeable parts. In his first year with the Yankees, he played eight different first basemen. In Phil Rizzuto's declining years, he had four good-field, no-hit shortstops in Rizzuto, Jerry Coleman, Billy Hunter, and Willie Miranda, and yet he was able to turn the shortstop position into an offensive threat by shuttling a pinch-hitter into any key spot. In many games he was able to use two pinch-hitters in that spot and still maintain his quality in the field. There were games in which none of the shortstops came to bat.

I once suggested to Stengel that he had been around for so long that he could remember other occasions when, in the particular set of circumstances that confronted him, the percentage had been to do the exact opposite of what the percentage was supposed to be. Casey did not exactly go along with me. Not by a long shot. "There are a lot of people," he snorted, "who think they know percentage and don't. There are a lot of people who don't think percentage has changed in 100 years. Percentage isn't just strategy, it's execution. If the situation calls for a bunt, and you have a batter who can't bunt, what's the percentage of bunting? The idea isn't to protect yourself from the second-guessers, it's to win the ball game." And with a sort of involuntary glance toward the press box, Casey growled, "After something hasn't worked, the percentage is zero. Even I can see that."

For all his platooning, Stengel was never afraid to jettison the lefty-righty business. "If there's a right-handed hitter who can't hit an overhanded curve ball, and you've got a right-handed pitcher in there who hasn't got an overhand curve, don't you think you might be better off with a left-hander who has?"

The prime example, though, is probably his use of Bob Kuzava in the seventh game of the 1952 World Series. The left-handed Kuzava, low man in the bullpen, was brought in to face Duke Snider — the sole left-handed hitter in the Brooklyn line-up — in the seventh inning with the bases loaded and one out. He got Duke on a pop fly and, to the surprise of everyone, was left in to pitch to Jackie Robinson. Kuzava not only got Jackie — on that famous windswept pop-up that Billy Martin just reached — but he breezed past the Dodgers for two more innings, something lefties were not supposed to be able to do at Ebbets Field. But Casey had a pretty good figure. Kuzava had shown good stuff to Snider; Lopat (another left-hander) had done well during the Series, and Casey had always felt that the Dodgers saw so few left-handers during the season that there was always a good chance of catching them off balance for one swing around the line-up.

Casey's own players sometimes had a much simpler explanation. "How would I know," they would say. "He's crazy."

Joe DiMaggio and Phil Rizzuto thought he was an old fraud who won because he had the best team at the beginning of every season and made all those moves just to dazzle the sports writers.

There were two very distinct sides to Old Case. There was the face the public had come to know and smile at — the gimpy, dog-eared old man, winking, grimacing, and babbling on in what was taken on faith to be profound — if not always decipherable — wisdom. The public Stengel was no myth. He was a wonderfully funny and engaging man, a wit and a comic both. "The first job of a manager," he said, in a line that was first quoted and then appropriated by Billy Martin, "is to keep the two guys who hate you away from the four guys who are still trying to make up their mind."

There was the other Casey Stengel, though, the old curmudgeon who derided his players. Those years of failure had apparently gnawed at his liver. He called his players "road apples." He couldn't or wouldn't remember their names, and when he did, he'd mispronounce them. The most persistent criticism was that he would rip his players apart to the newspapermen for an item or a laugh.

Clete Boyer never made any secret of his distaste for the Old Bastard. "Open the papers in the morning," Boyer once told me, "and you can read how lousy you are."

Joe Page hated him. "He wins because he's got the players. But he's nothing but a clown. He was a clown when he came and he'll be a clown when he goes," Page told me. He was back home in Pennsylvania by then tending bar. "He overworked me," Page said bitterly. "He used me 60 times in 1949, and then he shipped me off with a dead arm, without a word of thanks."

It wasn't only the players he shipped away who hated him. The New York Yankees, taken as a whole, hated their manager worse than they hated the Red Sox.

Hank Bauer would stand around the bat rack, burning while Casey was putting on his act for the writers. Off the record he told a few of them, "He's still got all of you guys fooled with that crap, hasn't he?"

He had the players, all right, and he liked to switch them around. Mantle was originally signed as a shortstop. Stengel made an outfielder out of him. Bill Skowron was a third baseman who had trouble going back on the ball. Stengel converted him into a first baseman. Tony Kubek was a great shortstop whom Casey did his damnedest to convert into an all-purpose utility man.

Casey would talk to the players he admired, and he loved the guys who got the most out of their abilities. And if they were also happy-go-lucky, so much the better. Billy Martin, whom he had discovered in Oakland, was his particular pet. He would refer to Billy as "my boy" and would quote him during clubhouse meetings; he would begin to chuckle as soon as Billy Martin opened his mouth, just like everybody else did with Stengel himself.

Tony Kubek fascinated Stengel. Tony was big and rangy, even as the 17-year-old kid Stengel first saw in instructional camp and immediately spotted as a potential outfielder.

George Weiss wanted Kubek at shortstop. Stengel saw him as someone who could fill a multitude of purposes, not the least of which was to give Mantle a periodic rest.

In Kubek's first year with the Yankees he started in left field 30 times, center field 14 times, at third base 37 times, and shortstop 35 times. In 12 of those games he played more than one position, once moving to yet a fifth position, second base. In four games he played both the infield and the outfield.

The trading of Billy Martin during Kubek's freshman year was not totally coincidental. By trading Martin for Harry Simpson, George Weiss was not only getting rid of a player he had no fondness for, he was also taking away one of Stengel's infielders and giving him another left-handed–hitting outfielder. Kubek was immediately brought in from the outfield and placed at third base. By the following year he was the regular shortstop.

Kubek was one of the great Yankee shortstops, in the tradition of Crosetti and Rizzuto. Luis Aparicio, recognized as the best of his day, once spent a whole afternoon raving to me about Kubek's ability to cover ground. Tony never seemed to get the credit, though. Somehow that early reputation as a utility man always seemed to hang over him. Great shortstops are not customarily sent to play the outfield.

With Martin gone, Casey tried to talk to Tony, but Tony would turn his back on him, much as Casey himself turned his back on Mantle. Once during the unhappy 1959 season, Tony cornered the old man against the dugout wall and told him off. Casey loved it. Next day Casey was chuckling. "Did you ever hear Koo-beck swear before? Did you hear what he said to me?"

If Casey had to bow down to DiMaggio, he went to heroic lengths to avoid paying any similar homage to Mickey Mantle. Stengel handled Mantle by ignoring him. When he spoke about him to the press, it was to criticize him for refusing to follow instructions. The most puzzling moment emerged during the luncheon that was held to announce what turned out to be Casey's final two-year contract with the Yankees. To Casey it was a fitting occasion to list the great players of his 10-year tenure. He had to make the obligatory bow to DiMaggio, of course, by naming him the greatest of them all. But from there Stengel went on to name almost every Yankee who had ever made an All-Star team — except, most conspicuously, Mickey Mantle.

"I wonder if Stengel was that smart in the way he treated Mantle," Jerry Coleman can still say. "Especially when he was young and would get his head down."

There is a story about Mantle's signing that comes right out of the pulp magazines. Tom Greenwade, the Yankee scout, is driving down a dirt road just outside Commerce, Oklahoma, stops to watch some kids playing ball, and sees Mickey hit a couple of towering drives completely out of the cow pasture and into the adjacent river. A sudden rain squall comes up, and during the delay, Greenwade signs Mantle on the fender of his old beat-up Chevrolet.

An alternate story is that Greenwade was at the game to scout another player on Mickey's team, and signed Mickey instead.

There is still another story, however, that is passed around the table when old scouts get together. According to this one, Mickey and his father had already attended a Yankee tryout camp in Banson, Oklahoma. After Mickey had been put through his paces, they waited around for a day to find out whether the Yankees were interested, and when nobody said so much as a word to them, they hopped back into the car and drove up to a St. Louis Browns camp in Joplin, Missouri. And here is where the story becomes tantalizing. During the whole three days of the scheduled tryout it rained, and with the Joplin ball club about to come off the road, the tryout camp had to be called off. Given the Browns' all-pervasive lack of talent, can anybody doubt that if it had not been for the rain, Mickey Mantle would never have left Joplin unsigned?

Meanwhile, back in Banson, the tryout camp had ended without anybody being signed. Very embarrassing. These regional tryouts were opened with great fanfare and publicity, almost as copromotions with the local press. Hastily the Yankee scouts and officials got together and agreed that the best-looking kid they had seen was that switch-hitter from Commerce. The blond kid with the crew cut.

And that was why Tom Greenwade had driven up to the ball field in Baxter Springs, just outside Commerce. Not because he had happened to be driving by. Not because he was there to scout another player. He was there by appointment. He had been sent to sign Mickey Mantle.

According to this same old scouts' story, Greenwade had seen Mickey play before, presumably when he had scouted Mickey's teammate, and he hadn't been impressed. He offered Mickey $500 to finish out the season at their Independence farm club and, when Mickey's father balked, tacked on an $800 bonus. The Yankees couldn't have given him any more. The way the rules read, a combined total of $1,500 would have made him a bonus boy and would have forced the Yankees to put him on their major league roster.

They were starting him in Class D, the lowest of the seven classifications in organized baseball.

The passing of the torch from Babe Ruth to Joe DiMaggio to Mickey Mantle is celestial material, and if you look hard enough, there is, once again, a connective tissue. Joe DiMaggio had played his first game in baseball on the same day that Babe Ruth called his shot in the 1932 World Series. Mickey Mantle reported to the Yankees' Class D team in Independence, Kansas, on June 14, 1949. He was hitting in the number 7 spot and batting .311 the day Joe DiMaggio returned to the line-up in Fenway Park to bury the Red Sox.

The Yankees began to realize what they had in the kid from Commerce when a bigger and stronger Mickey Mantle, playing his first full season at Joplin in the Class C Kansas-Oklahoma-Missouri League, hit .383 with 26 home runs, 14 left-handed and 12 right-handed.

Casey Stengel, who was not called the Old Professor for nothing, was instituting a pre–training camp instructional school for the Yankees' best minor league prospects the following spring, and Mantle was invited.

Bill Dickey was pitching batting practice the first time Mantle came to bat. Even if you want to allow for a little hyperbole, it was a scene right out of *The Natural,* minus the silly mysticism. "The boy hit the first six pitches nearly 500 feet, over the lights and out of sight. He hit them over the fences right-handed and left-handed, *and he hit them over the right-field fence right-handed and the left-field fence left-handed."*

When they held the sprints, Mantle didn't merely beat everybody — he ran away from them. "I always thought that Ben Chapman was the fastest man I've ever seen in a baseball uniform," Dickey said. "I couldn't see how anybody could be faster than Ben. But I think this kid could have outrun him."

Casey Stengel awarded him center field as Joe DiMaggio's replacement, hoping — it can be said with some certainty — that DiMag would take the hint. The playing careers of the Clipper and the Switcher overlapped for just one year, and in the final day of the overlap, they became tied together by a coincidence so otherworldly as to qualify for something out of the occult. It happened in the second game of the 1951 World Series. Mickey was playing right field and leading off. "Take everything you can over in center," Stengel had told him. "The Dage's heel is hurting pretty bad."

In the fifth inning Willie Mays (there are omens all over the place here) lifted a routine fly to short right-center. Mantle went tearing over for the ball, heard DiMaggio call for it, and pulled up short. As he put on the brakes hard, his knee collapsed, and he toppled to the ground. The official explanation was that his spikes had caught in the rubber cover of a drainage hole embedded in the grass.

Joe DiMag quickly reached across Mickey's body and caught the ball. Then he bent down to help Mantle, "I was afraid he was dead," DiMaggio said later. "I shouted, 'Mick, Mick!' and he never moved a muscle or batted an eye. Then I waved to our bench to send out a stretcher."

Mantle suddenly opened his eyes and burst into tears. He had plenty to cry about. He had torn two ligaments in his right knee.

It was not to be the only time he cried. After the seventh game of the inexplicable loss to Pittsburgh in the 1960 World Series, Mantle came into the clubhouse, sat in front of his locker, and cried his eyes out. "It was so moving," publicity man Bob Fishel said, "I thought I might burst out crying myself."

Joe DiMaggio would have understood. Something similar had happened to him after the Yankees had been upset by the St. Louis Cardinals in 1942. "Charlie Keller and I just sat and looked at each other for what seemed like hours. I don't think I ever felt so low in my life. We didn't cry, but we weren't far from it. After all, we were the Yankees, we weren't supposed to be beaten. It was hard to take."

The injury to the right knee that early in his career was something that Mickey had to live with. He had come to the Yankees with chronic osteomyelitis, a bone marrow inflammation that ate away at the bone of his left foot, next to the ankle, a condition that dated back to an accidental kick he had received while playing football at Commerce High.

Throughout his entire career, he played each game with the knowledge that every slide could be his last.

Playing with both legs taped, he was still the fastest man in baseball. Before every game his right leg was taped from ankle to thigh, and a protective shield was taped around the area that had been weakened by the bone infection. Halfway through his career his right leg became visibly thinner than his left and took on such a pale, sickly cast that his teammates tried to stay out of the training room while he was taping himself.

At first the taping was considered more of a precautionary measure. By the second year he tried to do without it in spring training and immediately pulled a muscle. "If I left it off during the game," he says, "I could play all right, and it would be easier to run without all that weight on it. But it would begin to ache toward the end of the game, so I'd end up wearing it anyway."

Even with the wrapping, though, the leg would begin to hurt. The longer the game, the worse the pain would become. A four-hour game could become pure torture. Mickey was always going to have trouble. Everybody knew it. Stengel's attitude was that if the legs got so bad that Mickey couldn't play, it was going to be up to Mickey to tell him. But Mickey wasn't going to beg off as long as he could stand on his feet. Despite his show of innocence, Casey was perfectly aware of Mantle's condition because the trainer kept him informed before every game.

And yet, to be perfectly fair about it, Mickey wanted to play every game. He always feared that his career was going to be cut short. When he was taking a shot at the home run record in 1956, his answer to the inevitable question was that he always tried to hit home runs, and if he were able to play 154 games, they would come.

The Yankees lost the 1955 World Series in all probability because Casey had insisted on playing an obviously crippled Mantle over the last month of the season. By the time the Series came around, Mickey could hardly run at all. After limping through the first two games, he had to give up. Hank Bauer had pulled a thigh muscle in the first inning of that second game, and with Mantle out, Stengel had to make do with a crippled Bauer.

History repeated itself two years later when Stengel kept putting Bill Skowron back into the line-up before Bill's wrenched back had healed. By the time the World Series opened, Skowron was wearing a corset. He was also sitting on the bench. Mantle was playing on the bad leg again. In the third game he also injured his shoulder so badly that he could hardly throw.

By sheer accident, Mantle's first and last times at bat came against the Boston Red Sox. Although Mickey had been taken to spring training after his Ruthian explosions in the instructional school, his contract was still assigned to the Kansas City farm club.

In spring training he led the team in hitting at .402, and Stengel wanted to bring him up to the Yankees. But George Weiss was reluctant to rush him. In the final exhibition game against Brooklyn at Ebbets Field, Mickey had three singles and a long home run. Casey Stengel had won. That night the 19-year-old Mickey Mantle was signed to a Yankee contract on the train to Washington. Although he would become permanently identified as Number 7, he was initially assigned uniform number 6. Probably at the suggestion of the Yankees' publicity man Red Patterson. "The Law of Natural Progression," announced Patterson. "Babe Ruth wore number 3; he was succeeded by Lou Gehrig, who wore number 4 and was succeeded by DiMaggio, who wore number 5. Do you notice that Mantle wears number 6?"

The Washington game was rained out, and Number 6 took the field for the first time back in Yankee Stadium against the Red Sox.

He began by singling in his second at bat to knock in a run.

But when the Yankees played in Boston a week later, Mantle was held out of the line-up. Joe DiMaggio was in center field, remember, and Stengel was not about to throw as inexperienced an outfielder as Mantle into the huge sun field at Fenway Park.

Mantle had jumped five classifications at once, Stengel reminded everybody, and was trying to learn how to play a strange position. When spring training opened, he didn't even know how to throw from the outfield. As a shortstop, he had always thrown flatfooted. Playing the outfield, he had to be taught how to lift his left leg for leverage on his throw. When a fly ball was hit behind him, he would put his head down and begin to run. Stengel had to show him how to look over his shoulder as he ran back. "This is the big leagues," Casey told him. "We don't have no ploughed fields for you to run through. You're not going to be stepping into any pile of cow manure."

"He never wore sunglasses until a couple of weeks ago," Stengel told the Boston writers, "and he can forget how to flip them down."

Better if he hadn't played the next time the Yankees came to Fenway Park. Mickey had gone into a terrible slump, and during the Memorial Day double-header it didn't get any better. Mickey struck out three times in the first game and twice more in his first two times at bat in the second. "Get in there for Mantle," Stengel snapped to Jackie Jensen. "We need somebody who can hit the ball."

The five straight strikeouts in Boston cost him his starting position, and before long he was sent back to Kansas City, where he became so discouraged that he called his father and said he was coming home. After his father came to Kansas City and bawled the hell out of him, Mickey started to hit again, and he was brought back to New York at the end of August — just in time to wreck his knee in the World Series.

Mickey always denigrated his fielding. He had never been able to get a good jump on the ball like a DiMaggio, a Mays, or a Snider, he would say. He had to depend on outrunning the ball. But that was a lively ball he was outrunning, not the dead ball that Tris Speaker had been able to outrun in the old days.

He never did field well at Fenway Park, though. He was always leery about racing back into that triangular cutout in center field, with its sharp corners, points, and angles.

On top of that, the fence itself wasn't padded, a holdover from the regime of Joe Cronin. To Joe's way of thinking, any Boston center fielder would have the fence well gauged, and if the other team's center fielder cracked himself up, who cared? (It wasn't until Fred Lynn crashed into the fence during the 1975 World Series, and lay there in a crumpled heap for a scary few minutes, that the new regime decided that padding wasn't such a bad idea after all.)

Hitting was something else again. Until 1956, when he hit 52 home runs, his favorite park was Fenway. In 1956, his breakthrough year, he hit only one in Boston — but that one happened at exactly the right time.

By the All-Star break that year Mickey had 29 home runs and 97 RBIs, and was not only heading for a Triple Crown but threatening almost every hitting record in existence. Over the second half of the season the pitchers stopped giving him anything to hit. Mickey kept going after bad balls and ended up with 52 homers and 130 runs batted in.

Everybody was still asking him about going after Babe Ruth's record, and Mantle would always answer that he would be happy with 59. What he really wanted, he would say, was to win the Triple Crown. Then, as Mantle slumped, Ted Williams came after him for the batting title, and by the time of Mantle's last visit to Fenway Park, Ted had caught him.

"I admired Ted so much and I wanted it so bad," Mickey says, "that I put down a couple of drag bunts early in the series just to make sure I got off to a good start. When I beat both of them out I knew I was going to win. That's the one thing I remember most in all the years I played in Fenway Park."

Well, yes and no. Yes, he did beat out a couple of drag bunts early in the series, but the bunts were not what got him off to a good start. On his first time at bat he hit a tremendous home run off the Red Sox ace right-hander, Frank Sullivan. The ball traveled an estimated 480 feet and just failed to clear the cement wall that runs up the side of the center-field bleachers. Only two men had ever hit a ball completely over that wall — Jimmie Foxx and Hank Greenberg.

From that beginning, Mickey went on to go 6 for 9 in the series and become the fourth hitter in modern baseball to win the Triple Crown. The first since Ted Williams himself. (The others, for the record, were Lou Gehrig and Rogers Hornsby.)

In 1957 he hit .365, the best batting average he would ever have, and lost out to Ted's midlife .388. He was admittedly embarrassed when he beat Ted in the voting for the MVP award, his second MVP in a row.

Mickey Mantle idolized Ted Williams. "I was like everybody else. When he took batting practice, I got up and watched. He was the best hitter I ever saw."

Even when they were in the clubhouse together at All-Star games he found it difficult to speak to Ted at all, let alone address him as an equal. After Mickey had retired and was vacationing in the Florida Keys, he drove down to Islamorada in the Everglades, where he knew Ted had his home. He found the house but couldn't bring himself to go in. Every morning he would drive to Islamorada and cruise slowly around the house, hoping Ted would come out. He was never quite able to work up the nerve to ring the doorbell. He knew that Ted prized his privacy, and he was afraid Ted would think he was imposing.

From the pure p.r. angle, Mickey always had a rough time. A new breed of New York sports writers tended to look on him as either a dumb country boy or a surly young man who would sometimes turn aside their questions with a sneer and a shrug. The fact was that Mickey was a bewildered, suspicious young fellow who had been stung often enough to have reason for both the bewilderment and the suspicion. He could also warn approaching sports writers off with

The Stare, just like DiMaggio. The difference was that with Di-Maggio they backed away, and with Mantle they wrote scathing columns.

Joe DiMaggio had run away from being the immigrant fisherman's son from San Francisco. Mickey Mantle never wanted to be anything other than the country kid from Commerce, Oklahoma. If he was gullible to the end . . . well, he seemed to be saying, that's the way we country boys are.

With friends and fellow ballplayers he was always good-natured, relaxed, and quite funny. He was the star, greater than any other star, but he was content to serve as an appreciative audience for his buddies and fellow night riders, Whitey Ford and Billy Martin. "There are leaders and followers," Billy Martin would say. "I'm a leader."

There were leaders and followers, Mickey Mantle would say. "I'm a follower."

In 1961, when Mantle was engaged in a home run battle with Roger Maris through most of the season, the New York press tried to build up a rivalry between them. Pure fantasy. Roger and Mickey roomed together in New York. Neither man had a jealous bone in his body.

"I don't think we ever had an argument," Mickey says. "He was like a brother to me. I loved him." Maris, who was an early riser, would whack Mickey across the head with the morning newspaper to wake him up. "Hey, roomie," he'd say. "You've got to read this. We're having another fight."

To Mickey's surprise, his career extended over 18 years. In the first 12 years he played in 10 pennant winners and won five world championships. The last two World Series he played in were lost, foreshadowing the end of the long years of Yankee dominance. The great scouts on whom the empire had been built — Paul Krichell, Bill Essick, and Joe Devine — had died. The farm system was drying up. Bob Topping and Del Webb, seeing the future clearly, sold the club to CBS and got out just as the drought was descending.

Mickey's own decline had already begun, too. He had always been a much better hitter right-handed than left-handed, and as his legs continued to deteriorate, the difference became even more marked. Right-handed he was a very good low-ball and curve-ball hitter, but the high fast ball was becoming increasingly difficult for him to handle.

Jam him and his knee would buckle to the point where it was impossible for him to make the necessary adjustment with his hips. Left-handed he could still murder a high fast ball, but he couldn't handle anything else. Change speeds and make him reach for the ball, and the front knee would begin to buckle halfway through his swing.

The book on him was open to everybody: Keep the ball up and in on him right-handed, and down and out left-handed. Never, never throw a change-up curve, low and away, when he is batting right-handed. Set him up for the change-up curve, low and away, left-handed.

Still, he stayed around long enough to be wearing a Yankee uniform in 1967 when the Red Sox came from ninth place to first in the year of the Impossible Dream.

He ended with 536 home runs, plus a record 18 homers in the World Series. The one that broke Babe Ruth's Series record was hit in 1964 off Barney Schultz, a knuckleballing relief pitcher for the St. Louis Cardinals. Mickey was leading off the bottom of the ninth inning in a 1–1 game. Schultz was just coming in.

"You might as well go home," Mickey told Joe Pepitone, the next hitter. Mickey had been told by a Yankee scout that Schultz always tried to get a quick strike on the hitter by throwing something less than his best knuckleball on the first pitch.

Schultz threw one pitch, and Mickey hit it almost up on the roof.

His longest home run came off Bill Fischer, who is currently the pitching coach for the Boston Red Sox. "My one claim to fame," Fish says. "After 25 years, I'm still asked about it."

"It was the hardest ball I ever hit," Mickey says. "The one off Chuck Stobbs in Washington was supposed to have gone over 500 feet, but that one was a long fly that was helped by the wind." The ball he hit off Fischer was still rising when it hit the top of the facade in right-center field, missing going out of Yankee Stadium by no more than a foot. If it hadn't hit the facade, according to the ever-present physicists with their ever-ready calipers and slide rules, it would have carried 600 feet, easy.

It was not only the hardest ball Mickey ever hit, it was also the only time he ever stopped and watched the ball. That wasn't done in those days. George Weiss was always after him to play up to the fans, like Babe Ruth, by tipping his cap as he rounded the bases. To Mantle that would have been showing up the pitcher. Mickey always kept his eyes lowered decorously as he came around the bases. Professionals didn't showboat, and what was to be gained except being knocked on your ass?

His final home run came on September 20, 1968. A week later Ralph Houk wrote his name in the starting line-up for the last game of the season at Fenway Park. Mickey flied out, limped back to the bench, and was replaced in the field by Andy Kosco. The season was over, and Mickey's baseball career had ended, too.

Chapter Sixteen

The Impossible Dream: 1967

*I had been thinking of 1949. I had a feeling in the last two
days that we would do to them what the Yankees did to us.*

— Bobby Doerr

I T was the Year of the Impossible Dream, the year the Red Sox
came from ninth place to first to pull off a 100–1 shot, certified Las
Vegas odds, and win a pennant that New England has never forgotten.

It was the Year of the Yaz, the greatest single season in terms of
winning ball games that any ballplayer has ever had. It was the year
of Gentleman Jim Lonborg, their one-man pitching staff. And it was
the year of the all-but-unbearable tragedy that befell Tony Conigliaro.

It was also the year of a new manager, Dick Williams. A stern
disciplinarian. A tough guy. A real sonofabitch. "There was fine and
dandy in his eyes," wrote Bill McSweeney of the *Boston American*,
"and a bit of ice water in his heart."

But, most of all, it was a watershed year in the fortunes of the
Boston Red Sox. Before 1967, the Red Sox had not been out of the
second division in nine years. After 1967, they were a team that was
always going to have to be reckoned with.

The change in the fortunes of the Boston franchise began with the
advent of Dick O'Connell. An accident of timing. The mystic law of
random chance. A living example of the casual, offhand way in which
the Red Sox were operated. Unlike Ed Barrow and George Weiss,
O'Connell was not an old baseball bucko. Dick O'Connell had little
interest in baseball. He didn't even like the game. Or, at least, it
served his purpose to make a show of not liking it.

In the Second World War, O'Connell had been assigned to the super-secret Naval Intelligence headquarters in the Pacific, where he had worked with Jim Britt, who announced the Red Sox games over radio, and Eddie Doherty, their assistant general manager.

Upon returning to Boston early in 1946, he had immediately landed a job in Texas as a bridge construction consultant for the navy. He had promised that if he got home before Britt did, he would get in touch with Jim's wife and tell her where Jim was. But he had lost the address and phone number, so before he left for Texas, he dropped in at Fenway Park to see whether Doherty knew how to find her.

He found Doherty closeted with Specs Torpocer, the farm director. The Red Sox had bought the Lynn franchise in the Eastern League that morning, Doherty told him, and he was going to have to find somebody to run the team.

O'Connell instantly decided that he didn't really want to go to Texas after all. "That sounds good to me," he said.

It sounded even better to Torpocer. "He didn't know where I came from. He didn't care. He had come in from his home on Long Island for one day, and he was only interested in seeing how fast he could get back."

O'Connell's climb up the executive ladder coincided with two of the great dates in Red Sox history. When the Red Sox sold the Lynn franchise at the end of the 1948 season, Joe Cronin brought him to Boston as assistant general manager. The appointment was announced on the same day the Red Sox defeated the Yankees to force the play-off with the Indians.

The news of his appointment as business manager was announced on the day that Ted Williams hit a home run in his last time at bat.

O'Connell was smart. He saw that baseball was going to be run by the financial people. And he had had a revelation. He showed Tom Yawkey that he didn't have to lose money, and that he didn't have to lose ball games either.

Everybody always wrote, with varying intonations of amusement or impatience, that baseball was only a hobby with Tom Yawkey, no more than an expensive toy, not unlike the racing stables and breeding farms owned by other rich men.

The income tax laws allowed a rich man to pursue a hobby as a business, with the sole proviso that he showed a profit in one year out of five. O'Connell was able to explain to Yawkey how he could pick a year to cut back on everything, spend as little as possible, and make sure that the bottom line was writ in black. Then for the next four years he could spend and spend, and as the spending translated into a winning ball club, he would be able to plough the tax savings back into player personnel.

At the end of the 1965 season, just as the league was about to expand to 10 teams, O'Connell was placed in charge of the baseball operation as well as the business side. Everything.

He cleared out all the old Yawkey retainers. He beefed up the scouting department. He professionalized the organization. The first thing he did, however, was to send Dick Williams, a utility infielder, to Toronto to become the manager of the Red Sox Triple-A farm club.

Dick Williams had just completed an undistinguished, much traveled, 13-year playing career in Boston. After working his way up through the highly disciplined, talent-laden Dodger chain, he had been brought up to Brooklyn at the age of 25, and almost immediately broken his shoulder bone making a diving catch on a fly ball. Still, he had managed to hang on as a marginal, almost anonymous member of five championship Dodger teams.

He hung on because he was known — in the parlance of the game — as a good guy to have on the bench. A great bench jockey, an accomplished sign stealer, and an all-purpose utility player. In other words, a guy with a quick, cutting tongue and a sharp intelligence.

By the time he brought his talents, such as they were, to Boston, he was 35 years old and moving into his seventh clubhouse in six years. And whether that meant there was always a market for his special talents, or just that he was a better guy to have on the bench than in the clubhouse, is open to a wide range of speculation.

Suffice it to say that in his two years as a player with the Red Sox, he had done nothing to disturb the prevailing country club atmosphere. On the contrary, in the words of one of his teammates, "He took advantage. He was one of the guys who would be playing poker in the clubhouse before the game, and even while the game was going on." The only thing that distinguished him was that he would almost always win. And if he might sometimes say, "This place is a disgrace," as he was pocketing his winnings, the losers could be excused if they took that to be his way of rubbing it in.

"He was a malleable guy here as a player," Frank Malzone says.

Nothing special. Always trying to talk somebody into taking a day off so that he could get into the line-up.

But he was also letting Dick O'Connell know that he wanted to manage. They had spent hours talking about the changes that were going to have to be made before the Red Sox could even think of becoming a winning team.

On the first day of spring training in 1967 he made a speech such as they had never heard before. He had been there in the country club himself, he told them, and he knew what was going on. "I saw guys lose every bit of pride they had playing on this club," he said. "Well, I'm here on a one-year deal. I can put you in the first division. I can put some pride back into you, and if you don't want to be proud of yourself as a baseball player, I can find some distant places to send you." And if he couldn't do that, he warned them, he knew how to embarrass them.

Well, if all the managerial speeches built around the motif of pride were laid end to end and cemented over, they would pave the road to the nether depths of the second division. But then he dropped the hammer. Missing curfew wasn't going to bring a $50 fine anymore; it was going to cost $500. "And don't come to me, because there are no second chances. The $500 will come out of your next paycheck, and you can explain it to your wife."

And one other thing. There would be no more climbing the backstairs to cry on Mr. Yawkey's shoulder. "Those days are over." Not only wouldn't it do them any good, but very bad things were going to happen to anyone who tried.

Did he really have that kind of commitment from Tom Yawkey? Not likely. What he did have was a commitment from Dick O'Connell that O'Connell himself would intercept any player who showed his face in the office, for any reason, and tell him, "You have no business up here."

As a natural leader, he understood how to flaunt the symbols of leadership. Ted Williams always came to camp to serve as a batting instructor. Ted is a dominating figure. He is loud and expansive and domineering. The rookies always gathered around him to hear him expound and pontificate. He was a natural magnet for the visiting press.

As long as Ted Williams was in camp, Dick Williams was never going to be the King Elephant. Ted did not remain in camp.

One of the things Dick had done was set up a volleyball court at the far end of the field to keep his pitchers busy. Ted thought the idea was ridiculous — and Ted has never allowed an opinion to go unexpressed. That was all D. Williams needed to demand that T. Williams be sent away. The next thing you knew, T. Williams was on his way to the minor league camps at Deland and Ocala.

That still wasn't enough. The real reason he didn't want him around, he stated for the record, was that T. Williams had played on too many losing teams down through the years, and he did not want Ted's losing ways to rub off on his young players.

There was absolutely no give in him, no bend at all.

Every manager likes to say he has no doghouse. Dick Williams told his players, most emphatically, that he did have a doghouse and that anybody who messed up on him would find himself in it. The fines started in training camp and never stopped. The doghouse was never without a tenant.

In the fifth game of the season (the third game played in Yankee Stadium), a rookie relief pitcher named Bill Landis walked the first two batters he faced. Out came Williams to warn him that if he didn't throw strikes, he was going to be put so deep in the doghouse that he would never get out.

The next batter came up. Landis walked him. Dick Williams returned to the mound and without saying a word handed Landis a can of dog food and signaled for another pitcher. Landis didn't pitch again for 28 days.

In that same game Don McMahon, a veteran relief pitcher, dropped a double-play ball at first base to allow the Yankees to tie the score. The game went 18 innings, and the Yankees finally won on a hit by Joe Pepitone.

"From there on," McMahon said, "he got a rancid expression on his face like I smelled bad or something, and he had it on his face all the time I was there." Which wasn't for long. He was traded for a utility infielder, Jerry Adair.

A week later Williams told another of his relief pitchers, Hank Fischer, to knock down the opposing pitcher. When Fischer didn't follow orders, he was briefly in the doghouse and then was permanently gone.

"He had a cutting tongue," says Tim Horgan, then of the *Boston American*, "and he liked to hurt people. There wasn't a player who wasn't tear-ass at him at some point in the season. There were some who hated him. And he wanted it that way." Tony Conigliaro, benched for not hitting, went to Williams during the game and pleaded to be allowed to pinch-hit.

"Sit down," Williams snarled. "You couldn't hit when you were playing every day. How the hell are you going to hit now?"

"I came to hate him so much," Conigliaro told his biographer, Jack Zanger, "that if they hadn't held me back a couple of times I would have killed him."

Normally the writers sat in the back of the bus and interviewed the players. Williams ordered the writers to sit up front with him to eliminate any chance of their getting a story from a griping or disaffected player.

And yet, recalls Horgan, "I always said to myself, *I'd like to work for a guy like that*, because there was no reputation, no politics, no bullshit. He didn't care who you were. If you produced, you played."

Jerry Adair, for instance, was picked up as a fill-in player. "And he had just a hell of a year. Another manager would have taken Adair out when his starting people got healthy. Williams didn't. He left him right there. He did the job at short and at second and at third, and when the regulars bellyached, he said, 'Hey, you weren't doing the job. When this man stops doing the job, you'll be back.' How the hell could you argue with him?"

He sat everybody on the team down at one time or other. And the amazing thing was how often the man who replaced a benched player would produce, and how often the regular player would go off on a hitting tear as soon as he was put back in the line-up.

He had one starting pitcher, Jim Lonborg. Early in the season he took Lonborg out of a game in Baltimore while he was holding a 4–3 lead, and Lonborg went storming back to the locker room and ripped up his uniform.

Williams bided his time. Then two months later to the day, Lonborg was getting shellacked in Minnesota — the only time all season, really, that he came up absolutely empty.

Williams let him get battered for three homers and seven runs all told in less than four innings before he came out to get him. "If this doesn't meet with your approval," Williams said as Lonborg was leaving, "don't take it out on your uniform."

Yaz didn't escape, either. During his Opening Day address to the troops, Williams had looked directly at Yaz and announced that there would be no captain on this baseball team. "There is one chief here — me — and everybody else is an Indian." And, he added, directing another shaft at Yastrzemski, there would be no closed-door meetings of players from which the manager and coaches were barred.

When Yaz was in an early season batting slump, Williams benched him for a game. There was a shouting match in Anaheim later in the year after Williams had accused Yaz of loafing on a fly ball. "I think they both were beginning to sense by then that something was happening," is the way former trainer Buddy LeRoux remembers it. "Although I can't believe they thought we were actually going to win it. They both decided to make accommodations."

Carl Yastrzemski could very easily have been a Yankee. He had grown up in Bridgehampton, Long Island, and dreamed of playing shortstop for the Yankees. He had even worked out with them at Yankee Stadium and talked to Lee MacPhail, the general manager. Just as with Ted Williams, the Yankees were the first club to send a scout to his house with a contract.

Ray Garland was the Yankee scout who came to talk to the Yastrzemskis. "He did what Yankee scouts always do," Yastrzemski's father, Carl Sr., says. "He tried to sell the pinstripes."

Carl Yastrzemski, Sr., was a natural athlete himself, a Long Island potato farmer, shrewd and self-possessed. He knew exactly what he wanted for his son: six figures plus tuition for college to replace the athletic scholarship to Notre Dame which he would be giving up. "My wife was alive then," Carl Sr. says. "He gives paper and pencil to both of us. He was going to write down a figure, and we were going to write down a figure." Garland's figure was $45,000, the largest sum the Yankees had ever offered to a high school player. "My figure was $100,000. Garland looked at it and threw the contract and the pencil up in the air."

That was the end of the Yankees. Mr. Yastrzemski didn't exactly tell Garland that when the pencil came down he was gone, but he might as well have. In the tradition in which the Yastrzemskis had been brought up, you did not come into a man's kitchen and bounce things off his ceiling.

The truth of the matter was that the senior Yastrzemski had favored the Red Sox all along because of the friendship he had developed with Bots Nekola, the area scout. Bots Nekola had played ball against Carl Sr., he was also Polish, and — as Carl Jr. always liked to say — he was taking Mr. and Mrs. Yastrzemski out to dinner on a social basis.

Carl signed with the Red Sox in the end for $108,000, plus a four-year education at Notre Dame. The Red Sox were not the high bidder. The Cincinnati Reds were outbidding the Red Sox all the way, and the cagey old potato farmer had been able to use their offers to put the squeeze on the Red Sox until he decided that enough was enough.

For Carl Yastrzemski, 1967 was the Year of Redemption.

Even the most casual fan had become aware that after six years of squandering his talents, he had taken himself in hand, hied himself to a gym four or five times a week to work himself into the best possible physical condition, and finally, after years of resistance, heeded the advice of one of his elders, a wise old high priest named Ted Williams, to make certain adjustments in both his batting stance and his philosophy of hitting. Yaz went into the season with the reputation that he was lousy in the clutch (he had knocked in more than 80 runs only once and was always right up there in grounding into double plays), sulked when things weren't going right for him, couldn't hit left-handed pitching with a paddle, threw too high for the cutoff man, and was such a ridiculously overoptimistic base runner that he was sometimes thrown out by distances that had to be seen to be disbelieved.

Although he had hit .321 one year to win the batting title, his lifetime average was only .272. He was a left-handed hitter who hit to left and piled up a lot of doubles at Fenway Park by bouncing the ball off the wall.

In 1963, the year he won the batting title, there had been serious talk about trading him to the Yankees, straight up, for Tom Tresh, who had just been named Rookie of the Year.

During the 1966 season one of his teammates told Larry Claflin of the *Boston American*, "We have a player here who would be the best player in the world if he wasn't so damn selfish." And Claflin, who happened to be Yaz's best friend among the writers, didn't even have to ask whom he meant.

Frank Malzone, the Red Sox superscout, was a teammate of Carl's through those early years. Despite the batting championship, Malzone says, Carl had never been anything more than a mediocre hitter. "In 1967 he learned that he could pull the ball and hit with power. And that made all the difference."

But there was more to it, something that went back to the terms of his original contract. After leaving Notre Dame at the end of his freshman year, Yaz had been persuaded to do what few players ever do: he had actually continued his education during the off season, first at Notre Dame and then at Merrimack College in Massachusetts. "The big thing," Yaz told me the following spring, "was that it was the first time I didn't have any tension on me during the off season." For six years he had been on a treadmill between the ball field and the classroom. "Always I'd start school a month behind with the midterms staring me in the face. I'd end up cramming through the Christmas holidays and always catching up by studying at night."

It was the first relaxed winter he had ever had, the first time he had been able to afford himself the luxury of sleeping late in the morning. "For the first time I could remember I didn't always have to be on a schedule. You have to do that once the season starts in April every single day. You don't have Sunday off. It's every . . . single . . . day. And then it had been attending classes or playing catch-up, every . . . single . . . day."

And so with time on his hands, he had finally been able to turn his attention to his real career.

He did not step up to the plate on Opening Day and reveal to the world that this was the new Carl Yastrzemski. The magic date was May 14. The Red Sox were tied for eighth place (11–14), the worst position they would be all year. Yaz had two home runs and was hitting only .260, the worst he was going to be, too.

Ted Williams had given him the philosophy and the rules. It was Bobby Doerr who applied the final fine-tuning. Bobby had returned to Boston that year as batting coach, and he kept a diary. His entry for May 14 reads:

> After last night's game, Yaz asked me if I could come out to the park with him this morning to throw him some batting practice. We went to the park about 10 A.M. before the day's double-header. Yaz tried many different things to get out of his slump. During the batting session this morning I thought Carl's hands were a little low. We discussed it a bit and Carl felt we were on to something. When he got back in, he held his hands higher, about to the level of his left ear. After the adjustment he started to hit almost everything really good

by raising his bat. He leveled his swing and the ball carried with a good backspin.

Up to now, with his hands dropped, he'd been hitting with an uppercut causing an overspin on the ball. A lot of potential home runs were sinking and dying in the outfield. I think this will help Yaz a lot with his production. That seems to be what happened today. He hit a home run into the center-field bleachers his first time up in game one, and also homered in the second game.

With the league expanded to 10 teams, the Red Sox and Yankees were now playing 18 games against each other instead of 22, broken down into three home-and-home series — three games in each city in April, two each in June, and a final four-and-four series extending from late August into early September.

In each of the three series in Yankee Stadium, there was one game that turned out to be vital to the unfolding of the Red Sox's season.

1. A near no-hitter by rookie Billy Rohr in April.
2. A beanball battle in June.
3. A dramatic, not quite off-the-bench home run by Carl Yastrzemski at the tail end of August that kept the Red Sox in first place.

The Yankees also made a contribution to the Sox's pursuit of the pennant — singular in the history of the rivalry — when they volunteered to lend them catcher Elston Howard for the stretch drive.

Everybody agrees that it was Billy Rohr's near no-hitter at the beginning of the season that gave everybody a sense that something special was happening.

Billy Rohr was a 21-year-old, part-Cherokee left-hander from Texas, who came within one strike of becoming the first pitcher ever to pitch a no-hitter in his first appearance in the major leagues.

Rohr's catcher, Russ Gibson, was also playing in his first major league game. He almost didn't make it. Gibson was nearly 28 years old, and he had just about given up a year earlier when Dick Williams talked him into hanging on for another year in Toronto by making him a player-coach.

Gibson was from Fall River, 50 miles outside Boston — wall-to-wall Red Sox territory. "I lived for the Red Sox. Tried to get to every game I could. The toughest part was always trying to get in to see a Yankee–Red Sox game. It's unbelievable what a rivalry it is around here. As thrilling as it was to finally step onto the field at Fenway Park, the biggest thrill for me was the first game I ever played in the majors, and that was in Yankee Stadium. That was the game where Billy Rohr had a no-hitter going into the ninth. What a way to break in."

For reasons never explained, the team took a chartered bus to New York rather than a plane. "I've been riding buses for ten years in the minors," Gibson announced, standing alongside the driver. "I figure I finally made it to the big leagues, and my first trip, what happens? I'm back on the bus." What happened in New York was that he caught a no-hitter for 8⅔ innings.

Against Rohr was Whitey Ford, making the 432nd start of his career. Whitey, who was trying to come back after two operations, was pitching his eleventh Opening Day game at Yankee Stadium.

Ford pitched well. After a lead-off home run by Reggie Smith, he allowed only two singles into the eighth, and one of them was a bunt.

In the sixth, with the score still 1–0, the Yankees' highly touted rookie outfielder Bill Robinson ripped a one-hop smash off Rohr's left shin that caromed right to third baseman Joe Foy, who threw him out. Rohr limped around the mound for five minutes pleading with Williams to allow him to stay in the game.

Gibson was instructed to keep a close eye on the young pitcher to make sure he wasn't favoring the leg. After the inning was over Gibson told Williams, "The kid has better stuff now than before he got hit."

Gibson then led off the eighth with a single, and with two out, Foy, a Harlem product who was hell on Yankee pitching all year, gave his wounded pitcher a little breathing room by hitting a two-run home run.

After the Sox went down in the top of the ninth, everybody in the ball park stood as Rohr walked to the mound. Rohr himself turned slowly around as if he were checking his defense. "I wanted to remember this," he said later.

The lead-off man, Tom Tresh, lashed a drive to deep left, and everybody could see it was over. But was it? Yaz, playing shallow to cut off a single, went racing back with his back to the plate, dove flat out in full stride, threw out his glove, did a complete somersault, and bounced up, holding the ball aloft in his glove.

The reaction of the New York crowd left no doubt about whom they were rooting for. Joe Pepitone popped to right field. And that left it up to Yankee catcher Elston Howard. Dick Williams came trotting out of the dugout to remind Rohr that Howard liked to go after the first pitch. Rohr's first pitch was outside and in the dirt, and Howard swung and missed.

"The ironic thing," says Russ Gibson, "was that he struck Howard out. On the 1–2 count, he threw a fast ball right down the middle. Cut the plate in half. I couldn't believe the umpire called it a ball."

On the 3–2 pitch, Rohr threw the first curve ball he had thrown to Howard all day. "I didn't think he'd be ready for it," he said.

For years Elston Howard had made a living taking the outside pitch to right. He lined the pitch over the second baseman's head for a clean single. "It was the first time I ever got a base hit and got booed in New York," said Howard.

Tim Horgan covered the game for the *Boston American.* "That was a big turning point for the entire season. You can look back and say it was just another game, but it wasn't. The Red Sox had been really awful. Nowhere. It gave everybody the confidence that they could beat the Yankees. It didn't matter that the Yankees were phasing out. There was always something special about beating the Yankees in Yankee Stadium."

Will McDonough, who also covered the game, goes even further. "When I think of the Yankee–Red Sox rivalry, I don't think of Williams or DiMaggio. I think of the catch Yaz made in the Stadium to save the no-hitter for Billy Rohr."

Rohr wasn't done. Neither was Howard. Remember, no one had ever pitched a no-hitter in his first major league appearance. (Save your letters. Bobo Holloman pitched a no-hitter on his first start, not his first appearance.) Seven days later Rohr faced the Yankees again in Boston and went into the eighth inning with a 6–0 lead. Only three other pitchers had ever started out with two straight shutouts. This time there were two out in the eighth when Elston Howard knocked in the Yankees' only run with a long single to left-center.

All New England was hailing the arrival of the new Mel Parnell. By the end of the season, Elston Howard was in Boston, and the new Parnell was back in the minors. The two shutouts in his first two starts were the only games Billy Rohr ever won.

"Too much too soon," Russ Gibson says. "He couldn't handle it."

In his next three starts Rohr gave up 12 runs and 15 hits over a total of 7⅔ innings.

Echo of the past: In 1907 Tex Neuer came to the Yankees in the last month of the season and shut out the Red Sox, 1–0, in his first start. He went on to win three more games, two of them shutouts, finished with a record of 4–2, and disappeared from sight.

When the Red Sox came back to Yankee Stadium in June, the best thing they had going for them was Jim Lonborg, who had already won eight games for a team that had more losses than wins. He was also leading the league in strikeouts and — not at all coincidentally — he had already hit eight batters.

The hot batter for the Red Sox was Joe Foy, the third baseman. Benched briefly for nonhitting, he had come back into the line-up when an injury to shortstop Rico Petrocelli brought on a shifting-around of infielders. When the Red Sox arrived at Grand Central, a message was waiting for Foy that his home in Harlem had just been destroyed by fire. He grabbed a taxi, raced to Harlem to satisfy himself that his family was all right, and came back to hit a grand slam home run — his third homer against the Yankees of the season.

Retribution came in the second inning of the next day's game. In the first inning Foy had singled and ridden in on Tony Conigliaro's three-run home run. When he came to bat in the second, the Yankee pitcher, Thad Tillotson, drove him back with his first two pitches and hit him on the top of his batting helmet with his third.

In the next inning Ralph Houk let Tillotson come to bat, and Lonborg drilled him. Tillotson yelled something at Lonborg, Lonborg yelled something back. Foy came in toward the mound to lend his voice to the chorus, and what followed was a wild melee featuring that well-known tag team of Reggie Smith and Rico Petrocelli. Smith picked Tillotson up, lifted him over his head, and slammed him to the mat before he himself was buried under half a dozen members of the onrushing Yankee bullpen crew.

Meanwhile, Petrocelli and Joe Pepitone, the boys from Brooklyn, were engaged in a private encounter which had started as a jawing match — a game of let's pretend — and ended in a real fight.

To add to the festivities, a flying squadron of special cops came running onto the field to institute a little law and order. One of the special cops, however, happened to be Rico Petrocelli's big brother, and he did what big brothers instinctively do: protect the kid.

It was Pepitone who could have used a big brother. Rico had already flattened his buddy Joe, and by the time the bodies were pulled apart and sorted out, Peppy was lying there, on the bottom of the pile, holding a badly sprained wrist.

The next day a new rule went into effect at Yankee Stadium barring special cops from the field while a fight was in progress.

Today, Lonborg is a dentist practicing in Scituate, Massachusetts. "Nobody had to tell me anything," he recalls. "I knew what I had to do. It was probably the only time in my career that I intentionally threw at anybody. Tillotson came up, knowing he was going to go down. As far ahead as we were, I was surprised that Ralph Houk let him come to bat."

Why was it surprising? Houk had been Casey Stengel's fight starter in happier times, and as badly as the Yankees were going, the Major was out to shake his team up. In case there is any doubt about that, Lonborg was hit the next time he came to bat, and Reggie Smith was also sent flying.

The target practice came to an end when Dick Howser, who hadn't been bothering anybody, was struck squarely on the batting helmet and had to leave the game.

A fight always brings a team together. The Red Sox had won the ball game and put two Yankees out of commission. "It was crucial to the season," says Russ Gibson, who was behind the plate. "We already knew that in Lon we had the best pitcher in the league, and now we knew that he would stand up for us."

Unlike Carl Yastrzemski, Jim Lonborg had been sought after by nobody out of high school. A small, skinny kid, he had barely made his school team and rarely got into a game. The son of a doctor in San Luis Obispo, a straight-A student, he went to Stanford University on an academic scholarship as a premed major.

In the spring of his freshman year, he sauntered down to the baseball field and asked for a tryout. Over the winter he had grown a little and added some weight, and suddenly he was throwing a fast ball that exploded. At that moment his life changed.

For two years he pitched in one of those high-class summer leagues which major league baseball subsidizes for the most promising college players. Lonborg was pitching at Winner, South Dakota, when Bobby Doerr, who was then a roving scout for the Red Sox, came to town with an offer of $40,000.

He had to choose between a medical career and baseball. "I am a physical person," Lonnie explains. "The things that move me are physical things."

In the spring of 1967 his life changed again, courtesy of pitching coach Sal Maglie.

In his first two seasons with the Red Sox, Lonborg had been called Gentleman Jim by the Boston press because he was always so polite and articulate. That wasn't exactly what Sal Maglie had called him. To Maglie, Jim and his California buddy Jerry Stephenson — who complemented his own gentlemanly demeanor by sporting two-toned hair — were each "half a fag."

"One of the things that Maglie taught me that spring was the importance of pitching inside. Not so much to be throwing at guys but to establish that you were going to pitch inside." Widening the plate, it was called. "I happen to have a baseball that moved more than most people's. When the ball was inside to a right-hander, I ended up hitting a lot of guys. Once I started to throw there, the ball was going to take off even more, and the guys weren't going to be able to get out of the way."

There were 19 guys who weren't able to get out of the way in 1967.

The other thing about that spring training for Lonborg was that he enjoyed the well-organized, highly disciplined system of Dick Williams, with its emphasis on fundamentals. Jim understood what Williams was doing better than most. "If somebody made a bonehead play, he made sure they knew about it right there. First because he had his own anger to vent, and second because he wanted to impress the fact upon us that bonehead plays were going to be followed by humiliation."

Lonborg got a taste of Williams's method in Anaheim early in the season, although he had already struck out 12 batters in his second start to establish himself as the unchallenged ace of the staff. Against California he had a no-hitter going for six innings and was leading, 1–0, in the bottom of the ninth. Then the Angels tied the score on two singles around a walk, and had the winning run on third with two outs. Jim was ahead of the hitter, 1–2, when he bounced a curve ball which ricocheted off the shinguards of Russ Gibson and back out onto the field as the winning run crossed the plate.

Lonborg: "I came into the dugout. Rico Petrocelli was in there, and I just sat there on the bench. Rico slapped me on the leg and said, 'Hell of a game, Jim,' and Dick Williams was standing there at the railing, looking out at the ball still sitting on the field."

Williams turned to them and said, "Hell of a game, my ass."

"Jeez," Rico said, "the kid just pitched his heart out."

"Look at the scoreboard!" Williams barked.

Jim Lonborg got the message. "What Dick was saying was that it was a bad pitch at the wrong time. I know for a fact that I never bounced another curve ball when I was ahead on the count with a runner on third base. Because it was imprinted on my mind what a horrible thing it was to happen at that time."

After the beanball battle in New York, the Red Sox moved into a tie for second place, and then lost six straight to fall seven games behind the White Sox with only one game left before the All-Star break. It was positively crucial to win this one. To go into the mid-season break on a seven-game losing streak would be close to fatal. A win was needed to give the team something to carry over.

It was such an oppressively hot and humid day in Detroit that by the fifth inning Lonborg was reeling. In the sixth he was leading, 3–0, when he bent over to take a deep breath and blacked out. He was taken off the field babbling. Out of his head. He had lost 12 pounds.

"The most important game of the year," Dick Williams called it, in his postseason summation.

No argument there from Lonborg. "I felt more pressure than any game I pitched all year," he said. "I'm supposed to be the stopper, and I knew how much the guys were counting on me."

Stopper he was. With the gutsy victory over Detroit he had brought his record to 11–3 for a team that was only two games over .500.

After the All Star game, the Red Sox reeled off 10 straight wins to move into contention. And then they hung.

In August, the Yankees handed them the final piece of the puzzle: Elston Howard, the wise old head behind the plate.

Dick O'Connell says: "We figured that if we lost a couple more, we were out of it. The conspicuous weakness was in catching." Russ Gibson was a freshman, and Mike Ryan, a Boston boy out of Holy Cross, was only in his second full year.

O'Connell met with Lee MacPhail in Chicago, and the Yankee general manager told him that he thought Elston Howard was exactly what the Red Sox needed.

Now, why would Lee MacPhail want to do that?

The answer is twofold.

In the first place, nobody wanted the White Sox to win. Or, to put it more pointedly, none of the other owners in the American League wanted Art Allyn, Jr., the owner of the White Sox, to win.

This was an untold story dating back three years earlier to Allyn's objections to the sale of the Yankees to CBS. Art Allyn was a quiet, retiring man. But the Allyn family had bought the team from Bill Veeck, and Veeck had gotten Allyn all worked up about the antitrust implications of having CBS as both an owner and a bidder for radio and television rights. And, even more destructive, of announcing the sale one week after a bill had been reported out of the Senate Judiciary Committee giving baseball the legislative exemption from antitrust that it had been seeking for nine years.

As it happened, Allyn was right. The sale of the Yankees to CBS killed the Senate bill then and there. But that wasn't how the Lords of Baseball saw it. The way they saw it, the bill would have sailed through with only a minimum of trouble if Allyn had just kept his mouth shut.

And that wasn't all. In addition to the matter of CBS per se, there was the problem of an obvious conflict of interest involving Joe Iglehart, who was chairman of the board and chief stockholder of the Baltimore Orioles and also the investment banker for CBS and one of the corporation's major stockholders. In order to approve the sale to CBS, eight votes in favor were needed from the owners of the other American League clubs. With Charlie Finley of Kansas City joining Allyn in opposition, Baltimore could not get away with an abstention. Prodded by Veeck, Allyn demanded that a vote be taken according to the rules, so that Baltimore would be forced to go on record one way or the other.

A secret meeting was subsequently held in Tampa, wherein Joe Cronin, as president of the American League, Commissioner Ford Frick, John Fetzer of Detroit, who was a power in league councils, Tom Yawkey, and Dick O'Connell met with the league attorney, Paul Porter, of the politically potent Washington firm of Arnold and Porter, to devise a strategy for saving the Baltimore club for Iglehart.

The upshot was that Allyn's motion calling for full disclosure of Iglehart's relationship with CBS was ruled out of order. The league voted to allow Iglehart to put his CBS stock in trust (whatever that was supposed to do). The Justice Department gave the sale a qualified, and obviously politically inspired, approval.

Bill Veeck later came out with *The Hustler's Handbook*, in which he described in minute detail the methods that had been used to push through the sale and exposing the two hats worn by Iglehart. That chapter was printed prepublication by *Sports Illustrated*, and a few days after the magazine hit the stands, Joe Iglehart withdrew as the operating head of the Orioles.

No, the New York Yankees did not want Art Allyn's White Sox to win the pennant, and neither did anybody else in the American League. Not even Finley, because Finley's only friend in the league was Dick O'Connell.

And, oh yes, the general manager of the Baltimore Orioles while all this had been going on was Lee MacPhail, now general manager of the New York Yankees.

But handing Elston Howard over to the Red Sox wasn't going to be easy. Howard balked at going. What, after all, was in it for him? He had played his entire career in New York. He wanted to manage. The Yankees owed him something; the Red Sox owed him nothing. Aging players who begin to move around lose some of their luster and most of their identity.

The deal wasn't clinched until Tom Yawkey called Howard and told him how much both he and the Red Sox wanted him. In truth, Yawkey was only confirming to Elston the deal that had already been made between Dick O'Connell and Elston's wife.

"Mrs. Howard was a very bright woman," O'Connell says. "In a way, she was the first agent I ever dealt with. She made the decisions, and she signed the contract."

She had agreed to the transfer only on the condition, which both teams obviously had signed on to, that Elston could return to the Yankees at the end of the year.

"Let's be open about it," O'Connell chuckles. "We borrowed Elston Howard for a month and a half."

What it comes down to, O'Connell concedes, is that there used to be — and maybe still is — an old boys' network in baseball. "I had friends in the league who were willing to help us, because they knew they'd get a payback when they were in need."

Just as the Red Sox were getting a payback for their effort on behalf of CBS and Iglehart.

Addendum: In the spring of 1972, Lee MacPhail paid a call on Dick O'Connell in Winter Haven. He was looking for a left-handed relief pitcher. He walked away with Sparky Lyle.

Payback time?

Three weeks after Elston Howard joined the Red Sox, they knocked off the White Sox in Chicago to move into first place for the first time in 18 years.

Feelings between the two teams ran high, mostly because Chicago manager Eddie Stanky had turned almost every game into a beanball battle, with special attention being paid to Yaz. Earlier in the season Stanky had sneered, "Yastrzemski is an All-Star from the neck on down." And Yaz had responded with four hits, including a home run.

August 27 — the first game of a double-header. The Red Sox were leading, 4–3, in the bottom of the ninth on Yaz's thirty-third and thirty-fourth home runs.

Ken Berry, the speedy White Sox center fielder, was on third base with one out. Good casting. Stanky, the great prognosticator, had predicted that now that the Red Sox were in first place, they were going to choke, and following his manager's lead, Berry had been wrapping a towel around his neck on the bench and pulling it tight to let the Red Sox know what was in store from them.

Duane Josephson came to bat for Chicago and sent a relatively weak fly ball to right. Playing right field for the Red Sox was Jose Tartabull, the weakest throwing arm in the league. Barry tagged up. Tartabull came running in to make the catch. He had to reach twice to dig the ball out of the webbing of his glove. He wanted to throw on a line, one bounce, to the plate. Instead, the ball squirted out of his hand and came lofting in on the fly, rather high and off to the right side of the plate.

Howard leaped to make the catch with his glove hand and came down on his left foot even while he was sweeping his glove across the plate like an infielder.

Elston Howard: "When I had to jump for the ball, I wasn't thinking of blocking the plate. I was just trying to get the ball down quick. But his foot came into the tip of my shoe and it kept it from getting in, and that was it."

Almost, but not quite. Blocked from the plate, Berry had come diving in from behind to touch the plate with his hand. Howard's sweeping glove got to him first.

When umpire Marty Springstead's hand shot up, Eddie Stanky went crazy. A fan came running out and threw beer in Springstead's face.

The replay showed that the call had been correct. Al Lopez, the recently retired White Sox manager, was in the ball park. "I never saw a play like that before," said Lopez, one of the great all-time catchers, "in 50 years."

Bill Crowley, the Red Sox publicity man, had been watching their rise to the top with disbelief. It wasn't until the last week in August that he felt the Red Sox might really pull it off.

"The guy who made the biggest play of the year was Elston Howard, on that tag on Berry at the plate in Chicago on Sunday. We came out of Chicago roaring, and that's where Yaz hit the pinch home run in Yankee Stadium to keep us from losing two straight games in extra innings."

It wasn't really a pinch home run. It wasn't even his first time at bat. And it was his only base hit of the entire series.

Monday was Carl Yastrzemski Night at Yankee Stadium. More than 100 friends and neighbors from Bridgehampton were on hand to honor him. If he didn't do much of anything, neither was he given much of a chance. He had to settle for three walks and a sacrifice fly.

On Tuesday the Red Sox were scheduled to play their fifth double-header in nine days. Before the night was over they had played the equivalent of a triple-header — 29 innings — and come out with a split. Jim Lonborg won the opener, 2–1, striking out 11, walking nobody, and knocking in the winning run himself.

The second game went 20 innings before the Yankees won, and although Yaz had kept the game alive in the fifteenth inning with a great sliding catch, that was his sole contribution for the entire day. He had swung for a home run every time at bat and gone hitless.

The game ended at 1:57 A.M. "I have never felt so tired in my life," was all Yaz could manage to say.

On Wednesday afternoon he went directly into Buddy LeRoux's training room for a rubdown. In addition to a pervasive weariness, he had a slight muscle pull in his thigh.

He was still on the training table when Dick Williams came in to ask him how he felt. "I can play a little defense and pinch-hit," Yaz told him.

"Better sit down and rest," Williams said.

Yaz had never been any good at sitting out games. By the fifth inning he was up and pacing. Another inning and he could feel his strength returning. In the eighth inning, with the score tied, 1–1, he asked Williams to put him in.

In the ninth he came to bat against Al Downing, and popped out to run his hitless streak to 0 for 18.

Downing had obviously decided that with a tired Yaz coming off the bench cold, he could throw the fast ball by him. But even though he had swung under the ball, Yaz had snapped his wrists around fast. As he took his position in the outfield, he told himself that if he had another chance to hit, he would continue to go for the long ball.

While he was picking up his bat to leave the dugout in the eleventh inning, he told Fitzie, "He's going to try to throw the fast ball by me again, and I'm going to hit it out of here."

It wasn't the first time he had called a home run during the season, and it wasn't going to be the last. But he never hit a ball better. It went deep into the bleachers in right-center field for his thirty-fifth home run and sent the Red Sox back to Boston in first place.

Competitively, if not necessarily artistically, it was a pennant race to keep pulses pounding in four reasonably healthy American cities. If you wanted to be dramatic and upbeat, you could compare it to a horse race in which four thoroughbreds come stampeding down the stretch, eyeball to eyeball, with each horse sticking his nose out in front, falling back and coming on again, right down to the finish line.

If you wanted to be a grouch, you could describe it as the year of the Great Groundhog Race, in that every one of the teams poked its head up into first place, squinted at the sun, blinked, had trouble breathing in such rarefied air, and went burrowing back into the more congenial subsurface where it knew it belonged.

To put it bluntly, the American League was in its Reconstruction Era, with everybody milling around trying to find out what they were supposed to do now that the New York Yankees weren't there to maintain law and order.

The Red Sox had gone into first place for the first time on the 128th game of the season. From there to the finish, they were never more than a game ahead and never more than a game behind.

• They were tied for first place nine times.

• They were half a game behind 10 times (on two of those occasions they were in third place).

• They were one game behind four times (twice in second place and twice in third).

For 19 consecutive days after that final series in Yankee Stadium, they were either tied for first or within a half-game either way.

And then, with 12 games left, they lost three games to Baltimore at Fenway Park to fall into third place. Only a game behind, to be sure, but headed out for an eight-game road trip, beginning with a two-game series against the surging Detroit Tigers.

In both games against Detroit, the Red Sox went into the ninth inning trailing the Tigers and rallied to pull out a win.

As they left the field after the first game, they found themselves in a four-way tie for first place. Chicago was still playing a night game out on the Coast, though, which meant the White Sox were either going to take a half-game lead or fall into fourth place, half a game behind everybody.

Emulating Detroit, the White Sox blew it in the ninth inning.

With the Red Sox back home and four games left to play, the standings read like this:

> Minnesota —
> Boston   1
> Chicago   1
> Detroit   1½

They were going to be playing two games against Cleveland, a team they had been beating up on all season, and two against a Minnesota team that had been trouncing them with regularity for three years.

Do I have to tell you that they lost both games to Cleveland?

All summer, the players had been retreating to the sanctuary of Buddy LeRoux's training room to let the music blare forth from the radio and talk things over among themselves. "There were a lot of times we thought it was over," LeRoux says. "And the players would be saying, 'Jeez, we had a super year. Better than anyone expected.' Next thing you knew, we were back tied for first place again. When we lost to Cleveland, though, it was sickening."

They were now half a game behind Chicago, whose pitching had made them the universally acknowledged favorite. Chicago was playing a twinight double-header against last-place Kansas City. They had their two best pitchers going, Joel Horlen and Gary Peters. If they won both games, as expected, they would move a game and a half ahead of the Red Sox, and the Red Sox could kiss their pennant hopes goodbye.

Haywood Sullivan was in his second year as Dick O'Connell's assistant. "After the two losses to Cleveland, I went home and went to bed and I cried. In the early morning hours, I suddenly woke up, turned on the radio, and heard that Chicago had lost twice to Kansas City. It was unbelievable. We were alive." Sullivan leaped out of bed, put on his clothes, and because he felt the need to do something, drove to Fenway Park and sat there in the darkness.

Instead of finding themselves in first place, riding high, the White Sox had dropped to fourth place, one and a half games off the lead, and to all practical purposes had eliminated themselves.

Detroit, by not playing, had gained on everybody. They were tied with the Red Sox, a game behind Minnesota, with two straight double-headers coming up against California.

For the Red Sox to win the pennant, they had to beat Minnesota twice while Detroit was losing two of their games in California.

The last two games against Minnesota were 1949 in reverse. Bobby Doerr, the only living link on the field, had felt it coming on. The Boston fans hadn't. Neither had the sports writers. If the losses to Cleveland hadn't been enough to dampen their spirits, there were two off days before the final weekend series, and it rained heavily both days. The rain continued right into Saturday morning. And then — could it be a sign? — the sun came out.

And there was this, too: Despite the miracle of the 1967 season, the Minnesota Twins were not the New York Yankees.

There were two ways you could prove it.

1. The first game was slightly less than a sellout.
2. The Red Sox got every conceivable break.

Jim Kaat, the Twins' best pitcher, was coasting along with a 1–0 lead in the third inning when he suddenly grabbed his arm and had to leave the game. He had blown out his elbow. The freakiest of accidents, at the worst possible time, to the one Minnesota pitcher the Red Sox most feared. "It was," Buddy LeRoux says, "as if God had decided to even the slate."

Zoilo Versalles, the Twins' shortstop, had been the MVP of the American League in 1965. But Versalles was a man of moods. Before the game the Red Sox had been told to go into second base hard whenever possible, the clear implication being that Versalles had been showing no great desire to play. In both games Versalles set up the winning Red Sox rallies by doing the strangest things on what should have been routine double plays.

With Kaat gone, the Sox scored two runs in the fifth on two legitimate hits, a bad-bounce single, and a Minnesota lapse. Reggie Smith led off the inning with a double. Dalton Jones, pinch-hitting for Russ Gibson, hit a soft ground ball to Rod Carew, and as Carew was about to make the play, the ball took an erratic hop and ran up his arm. Jerry Adair singled in the first run, and the second run came in when the new pitcher, Jim Perry, neglected to cover first base on Carl Yastrzemski's ground ball to the right side of the infield.

In the seventh Mike Andrews tried to check his swing, but the ball hit the bat and dribbled down the line for a base hit. Jerry Adair then hit the ball right back to Minnesota's star relief pitcher Ron Kline for an easy inning-ending double play, except that Versalles dropped the throw at second. Two men were on base on "hits" that had gone a total distance of about 60 feet, and Yaz was coming to bat. Any time Yaz came to bat with two men on base during the last weeks of the season, he seemed to hit a home run. This time he hit his forty-fourth, breaking Ted Williams' single-season Boston record for a left-handed batter.

When Boston woke up on Sunday, it was to the news that Detroit had lost its second game. If the Red Sox beat the Twins again, the worst they could come out with was a tie.

The Red Sox had Jim Lonborg (22–9) pitching against Dean Chance (20–13). Lonborg had never beaten Minnesota. He was 0–3 on the year, and 0–6 lifetime. Dean Chance, meanwhile, had won three straight over the Red Sox, including a five-inning no-hitter against Lonborg. As the game got under way, the scoreboard showed the Tigers leading, 2–1, in the second inning.

Minnesota scored in the first and third innings to take a 2–0 lead, and Yaz the Savior was responsible for both runs.

With two out in the first, Lonborg had walked Harmon Killebrew on four pitches. Nothing to worry about there. The strategy in both games was to pitch around him. But then Tony Oliva hit a high fly to left field. Yaz went back against the wall, looking as if he had a chance, and leaped as high as he could. The ball hit a good foot or two above his glove and bounced back to Reggie Smith.

The heavy-footed Killebrew was just rounding third. He hesitated for a moment, which seemed the prudent thing to do, but Billy Martin was waving him on. Smith's strong throw seemed to be coming in perfectly, and a roar went up through the crowd. But then the wind caught hold of the ball, and you could see it begin to die. George Scott, positioned perfectly, decided to cut it off and make the throw directly. Standing only a few yards from the plate, he made an atrociously wild throw that sailed high over Gibson's head.

Dean Chance took the mound with a 1–0 lead, and, as the Red Sox could attest, Chance had been known to pitch shutouts.

The Twins' second run came in the third inning, and once again, the key players were Killebrew and Yastrzemski. After Cesar Tovar had singled with two out, Harmon got his bat out in front of a fast ball and jerked a line-drive single into left field. With two out, and the field still soft and lumpy from Saturday morning's heavy rain, Yaz decided to let the ball come to him and, if necessary, block it with his body. But the ball went through Yaz, hit the wall behind him, and bounced back through his legs. Two cheap runs for the Twins to match the cheap runs the Red Sox had scored on Saturday. The scoreboard showed that Detroit had gone ahead, 5–1, and who would have thought it would be Carl Yastrzemski who would be kicking the pennant away?

But there was something else going on. On the surface Dean Chance was outpitching Lonborg. But if you were charting the pitches, you weren't so sure. For the first five innings Lonborg had thrown 73 pitches, even though he had allowed only three hits. Nothing unusual there. Pitchers with a lot of stuff have to throw a lot of pitches because so many of them are going to be missed or fouled off. Lonborg, though, was simply falling behind the batters and resorting to his breaking pitch far more than his fast ball to get them out.

Dean Chance seemed to be working very easily. In the same five innings he had thrown only 38 pitches while allowing four hits. But there was something odd there. When Chance had his best stuff, he — like Lonborg — had to throw far more pitches than that. There had been only three swinging strikes and only four foul balls, which could only suggest that his fast ball wasn't doing a thing.

Lonborg had a strong sixth inning. My own notes, jotted down at the time, read: "Is beginning to throw fastballs more than curves. Has found his groove."

Lonborg led off the sixth. As he reached for the batting helmet, he thought, *Bunt.* On his first time up he had singled off Chance's first pitch, a fast ball down the middle. He was guessing that Chance would start him off the same way.

Since Chance always fell off the mound toward first base after delivering the ball, Lonborg's plan was to bunt it hard enough down third base to push the ball past him. He did. A hard-bouncing bunt between the mound and the line. Chance got off the mound very quickly, and that — ironically enough — was what hurt him. For just a moment it seemed as if he were going to be able to make the play himself. And then he looked to the onrushing third baseman, Cesar Tovar. Tovar looked to him, and they both stopped. In that fraction of a second, the ball was past him. Tovar, coming on again, bobbled the high bounce, and whatever chance he had of getting Lonborg was gone.

To Cal Ermer, the Twins' manager, that was the turning point of the game. When the pitcher starts off an inning by getting on base that way, you can all but smell the coming rally. But that wasn't the turning point. Jerry Adair, swinging at the first pitch, hit a ground ball slightly to the right of second base and past the diving Rod Carew. The ball was hit well enough, although a better-fielding second baseman might very well have turned it into a double play. Dalton Jones, a surprise starter at third base, was coming up with men on first and second and nobody out. My notes read: "Place in bedlam. Will he have Jones bunt and give up Yaz's time at bat?"

Yaz was hot. He had 21 hits in his last 42 at bats, was 5 for 6 in the Minnesota series and 2 for 2 on the day. Although Jones was 0 for 2, he had gone out on two hard line shots. On the first pitch Jones squared away to bunt while Chance was still in his wind-up, but fouled a tailing fastball down toward third.

And now comes the real turning point of the game. Williams took the bunt sign off, something he had been doing all year with great success, and Jones slapped the ball past the charging Tovar and on into left field.

Dean Chance had thrown only four pitches, but the bases were loaded and nobody was out. Standing on third, his hands on his knees as he got back his breath, Lonborg grinned up at the third base coach, Ed Popowski, and asked, "Can you think of a better guy to have up there?"

My notes again: "Ermer is out to talk to Chance. How can he hear him with all that screaming?"

Yaz assumed, logically enough, that Ermer had gone out to tell Chance not to give him anything he could pull, and so he decided to just try to hit the ball where it was pitched. Instead, Chance's second pitch caught a good hunk of the plate, the kind of pitch Yaz had been taking all the way all year. Mentally committed as he was to go with the pitch, he lined it into center field for a two-run single. The score was tied, and Ken Harrelson was coming to bat.

Harrelson ran the count down, another vital detail of the game. With a 3–2 count, Williams had Yaz running. Harrelson chopped down a sinker, and the ball hit a hard spot on the soft turf and took a high, high bounce, which Versalles fielded about a step away from second base. If Yaz had not been running, Versalles, with the double play laid out so nicely in front of him, would quite probably have let the run score and got his team out of the inning.

Double play or no, you could hardly believe your eyes when you saw that the throw was going to the plate. Dalton Jones wasn't fast to begin with, and he was playing with a pulled hamstring, but he was still a couple of steps beyond the plate when Versalles' throw reached the catcher.

Two wild pitches and a base on balls scored another run. Reggie Smith then hit a hard shot toward first that bounced off Killebrew's leg and kicked into foul territory, allowing another run to score.

Five runs had come in on only two real hits.

Nobody on the Red Sox would say it for publication, but they all concurred, off the record, "Versalles choked."

In the eighth inning Minnesota had its final chance. With two on and two out, Bob Allison, representing the tying run, lined a hit down the left-field line. Allison was going for two bases all the way. Yaz backhanded the ball in the left-field corner, whirled, and fired to second, without looking. The throw was perfect. It was the seventeenth base runner Yaz had thrown out that season. In my notes I wrote: "Doesn't Allison know that this is Yaz's year?"

The Red Sox hadn't won the pennant yet; they had only assured themselves of a tie. Detroit had taken the first game in California. The second game was just getting under way. Beer was the drink of choice while they were waiting. The champagne was still on ice. Three hours and 14 minutes after the Sox had defeated the Twins, Dick McAuliffe, who had hit into only one double play all year, hit into another, and the Red Sox had become the first certified 100–1 shot ever to win a pennant.

Chapter Seventeen

1977 and Free Agents

Sometimes you think it's going to be easy. Sometimes it looks like it's going to be easy. But winning a pennant is never as easy as we were making it.

— Don Zimmer

WITH the advent of free agency in 1977, the Red Sox and the Yankees experienced the greatest two years in the rivalry since the pennant races of 1948 and 1949 went down to the last day.

The Red Sox fired the opening shot in the new era — an accomplishment which may someday rank alongside the firing upon Fort Sumter — by signing Bill Campbell for a breathtaking $1,050,000 over three years. Campbell had been the leading relief pitcher in the American League for two seasons.

The Yankees then signed Don Gullett and Reggie Jackson. Gullett had defeated the Yankees in the opening game of the 1976 World Series. He was a left-hander, a commodity always in short supply, and although he had never been able to get through a season without some kind of injury, he had the best won-lost percentage in baseball.

But it was Reggie Jackson, as a practitioner of high visibility, who had been the player with the most glamour and sizzle. Although the deal with the Yankees called for $3,050,000 over five years, Reggie wanted everybody to know that he had turned down better deals from both Montreal and San Diego in order to come to New York. "I wanted the sociology and all that," he explained upon being introduced to the New York press. "I wanted the place that was best for me."

More than anything else, he emphasized, it was the enlightened attitude of George Steinbrenner that had convinced him. "There were certain things he expressed to me, and certain ideologies and philosophies that we reached an accord on."

Sociology, ideologies, and philosophies. Reggie talked like that.

The man who was about to add his legend to those of Babe Ruth, Lou Gehrig, Joe DiMaggio, and Mickey Mantle had established his true lineage years earlier by telling a group of New York writers, "If I were playing in New York, they'd name a candy bar after me."

He had a line ready for the press conference, too. "I didn't come to New York to be a star," he said. "I brought my star with me."

For all Reggie's misconceptions and Steinbrenner's pettifogging, the Yankees signed Reggie only because their first choice, Bobby Grich, had decided to sign with California, and Reggie Jackson was the only free agent left on the Yankee list. And still, Yankee general manager Gabe Paul had counseled against it. As Gabe saw it, they would be imposing a mercurial, ego-driven, wildly articulate player on a pennant-winning team, and they would be paying him far more than they were paying any of the players who had won it for them.

There was no way Jackson could be brought into that particular situation, Paul felt, without becoming a destructive force. Darold Knowles, a teammate at Oakland, had pinned him forever with the immortal line, "There isn't enough mustard in the whole world to cover this hot dog."

Billy Martin didn't want him either. "Don't I have anything to say about it, as the manager?" he asked. No, he didn't.

On the first day of spring training, Reggie walked into camp and took over the press coverage. "You've never met anybody like me," he told the writers, as if he were congratulating them on their good luck. "I'm not just a ballplayer. I'm a multifaceted person, a myriad of personalities. There's a lot of stories you could write about me. I'm a businessman who happens to be a ballplayer."

The myriad of personalities was also a maze of contradictions. A living kaleidoscope. Shake him and he'd come out different every time. "Part of the reason they pay me," he said, "is that I like living in this environment. They're looking for me here. I'm the hunted on the team of the hunted."

Reggie was Autobiography in a roomful of Biography. Reggie wrote his own script. Reggie went for high drama. *Sturm und Drang.*

Lots of agony and torment. An abundance of emotional crises. Reggie sparkled, Reggie bubbled, Reggie was going to be getting himself in a whole lot of trouble.

By the All-Star break, he was wailing, "I don't want to play in New York. I don't want to be here anymore."

Something else had happened before the beginning of the 1977 season in addition to the beginning of the free agent draft. Two expansion teams had been taken on — Toronto and Seattle. With the addition of the two new teams, the number of games between the Yankees and Red Sox was reduced from 18 to 15.

Within that framework, the schedule makers had done their job well. Ten of the 15 games were packed into a 34-day period beginning in late May: a pair of two-game series a week apart, to be followed by a pair of three-game series two weeks later. And then it was going to be 80 grinding games — half the entire season — before they would meet again for the five games that were going to decide the pennant.

In those first two games the turbulence brought on by the free agent era came to a head for both teams.

The first meeting was on the thirty-ninth game of the season during what had become a time of torment for Reggie Jackson. He had been benched by his manager in his home town of Oakland against Vida Blue, and benched again the previous Saturday in a televised Game of the Week. His manager was also refusing to bat him in what was to Reggie the highly symbolic cleanup position. He was being pulled off the field in the late innings for defensive purposes. All in all, he had fallen into such an emotional funk that he was striking out every other time at bat.

It was on May 23, the day of their first meeting, that everything hit the fan. In Reggie's first days of euphoria back in spring training camp, he had given a truly astonishing interview to Robert Ward of *Sport Magazine,* an interview in which Reggie had pitted himself against Thurman Munson by attacking Munson's credentials as a leader and describing how he was going to take over the team.

A couple of advance copies of that issue had hit the Yankee locker room and were being handed around the clubhouse from player to player.

"You know this team," they read. "It all flows from me. I've got to keep it all going. I'm the straw that stirs the drink. It all comes back to me. Maybe I should say me and Munson . . . but really, he doesn't enter into it. He's being so damned insecure about the whole thing."

Reggie, dressing in the corner of the locker room, could hear his teammates cursing him. A couple of them veered toward his locker as they headed out the door and kicked his shoes or whatever else was lying around.

When he took batting practice, the other players left the area around the batting cage. Drive after drive went soaring into the bleachers, while out in the field and along the sidelines, his teammates turned their backs to him.

The Red Sox had a one-man sideshow of their own to present on their visit to New York. Bill Lee, who had last been seen on that ball field holding onto his left arm as he was being helped from the scene, was making his second start of the season. Although his recovery from the shoulder separation had been very slow, he was the only left-hander on the Red Sox staff — the *only* one — and that meant that he was always going to be penciled in to open against the Yanks.

With Reggie not talking, the reporters gathered around Lee for whatever words of wisdom he wished to impart about the fracas that had almost cost him his career.

"I had a dream the other night," Bill Lee began. "A vision of the Ghost of Christmas Past. It came into my room, and it had Steinbrenner's face and Billy Martin's body. I don't like Steinbrenner's politics . . . I don't like him personally. He tries to use his economics to gain superiority. I dislike Billy Martin and his archaic baseball. There's a part of him that functions perfectly, and a part of him that's not screwed on. It's Martin's system. His win-at-all-costs type of ball. You have to have limits, that's what civilization is founded on. I don't like the way he tried to master his players through fear and intimidation. They were all robotized for the fight. They were other people, they weren't themselves."

The next day the *New York Times* headline read:

Red Sox Top Yankees, 4–3
Game Quiet

It was, on the contrary, a game that went into the great book of unquiet Yankee–Red Sox contests. Let's hope that the Paper of Record does better when war breaks out.

The early going featured consecutive home runs by Boston's Dwight Evans and rookie third baseman Butch Hobson, and the catch of the year by Paul Blair on Fred Lynn's long drive to the concrete wall in right center. At first it didn't seem possible that Blair could reach it, and then it seemed as if he would get there just in time to splatter himself against the wall. And then he caught the ball over his head, right where the sign read *417 feet,* and by some miracle of footwork brought himself to an instant halt.

Reggie got one of the runs back in the second inning on a line-drive double and an error. On his next time at bat his scorching ground ball down the first-base line was turned into a double play. In the seventh he teed off on one of Lee's sinkers and hit a tremendous home run to tie the score, a ball hit so powerfully that he stood at the plate and watched it disappear into the stands. And maybe did a little thinking about brotherhood, the meaning of life, and the Nielsen ratings. Reggie never loitered in his home run trot; he ran with a purposeful forward thrust, as if he were being swept along by a wind at his back. As he headed toward the plate, his teammates gathered in the well of the dugout for the ritual handshakes and backslapping. Reggie came toward them and then, ignoring the outstretched hands, veered off sharply toward the far end of the dugout.

What you have to understand is that there was nothing insincere about the congratulations that were being tendered. Once the bell rings, personalities are forgotten. Without a productive Reggie Jackson, the Yankees were not going to win. Everybody on the team knew that, and nobody knew it better than Reggie himself.

Bill Lee: "I could see that something was going on over there, but I had a different view of it. I felt bad because I knew when I was healthy I could get Jackson out at the drop of a hat. See, 1977 was a rehabilitation year for me. I felt I was letting my teammates down just because I hated the Yankees so much."

It was a shaken Yankee ball club that took the field when the inning was over. Reggie himself immediately played Hobson's legitimate single into a double by completely overrunning the ball. Denny Doyle, the little second baseman, laid down a bunt, and a distracted Willie Randolph, who never made that kind of mistake, failed to cover first base. Before the inning was over both runners had scored, and it was Doyle's run that proved to be the winner.

The Yankees got one back in the last half of the inning when George Scott (who was probably Reggie's closest friend in baseball) dropped the throw to first on Munson's two-out ground ball, where-upon Bill Campbell picked Munson off first base. This was *Thurman Munson,* the smartest base runner on the ball club.

The game came to an end, with Reggie up and two men out. One swing of the bat and Reggie could have tied the game and given himself another chance to either shake his teammates' hands or treat them to a rerun of his "Screw you" routine. Instead, he ended the game by flying out.

"Maybe Reggie was mad at me because I didn't play him a couple of games against left-handers," an infuriated Martin said. "Go ask him. I'm sure he'll have some answers for you. Ask him about the ball that got away from him at the start of the eighth. He probably forgets about those things."

Munson fended off the reporters at first. "I'm just glad to be here," he kept saying, putting on a goofy smile. But he couldn't contain himself forever. Told that Reggie had said he had a bad hand, Munson exploded. "He's a fuckin' liar. How's that for a quote?"

Thurman Munson had done his best to accede to front office pressure to remain quiet about the article, but once he was talking, he let his feelings be known. "I'll kiss your butt if the New York fans think anybody likes to play baseball more than I do. For a man to think Thurman Munson is jealous of anybody else in the world, he has to be ignorant or an imbecile."

In fact, Munson said, not without truth, he had tried to make his new teammate feel at home. "I've probably talked to him more than anybody else."

And, he said, he was not interested in an apology.

When Munson walked out of the clubhouse, the magazine was sticking out of his hip pocket. "I'm going to go home," he said pointedly, "and read it again."

That was the first game of the Yankee–Red Sox series. There were still 14 to go.

When Thurman came to the plate against the Red Sox the next day, he received the greatest ovation of his career. Jackson was greeted by a mixture of boos and cheers, with the boos easily predominating.

The first game had come around to Reggie Jackson in the seventh inning. This one came around to Thurman Munson. Or, to look at it from the other side of the field, to Luis Tiant. Going into the seventh inning, with the Red Sox leading, 5–2, Graig Nettles and Carlos May, the first two batters, hit home runs on consecutive pitches, and suddenly the score was 5–4. Under normal circumstances this is where you bring in your relief pitcher. Especially when you have Bill Campbell, who had been practically unhittable for three weeks.

But for Don Zimmer, the Red Sox manager, there was something else to be considered. The Yankees weren't the only team whose season was being buffeted by the fallout from the reentry draft. After the Red Sox had ushered in the new era by signing Campbell, Luis Tiant, who had been both the sail and the anchor of the Sox pitching staff for five years, had refused to report to training camp until the Red Sox sweetened the pot for him, too. It took so long for the Red Sox to appreciate the force and brilliance of his logic that Luis, who was 36 going on forever, was still trying to pitch himself into shape. Without a Luis Tiant who could be counted on to go the distance, the Red Sox had the same chance of winning that the Yankees had without a productive Reggie Jackson. Zimmer, hoping that Luis' time had come, stayed with him. Bucky Dent immediately singled, and now the tying run was on base. And still Zimmer stayed with him. Willie Randolph laid down a perfect sacrifice bunt. Zimmer came to the top of the dugout steps — and hung there. He was going to let Tiant pitch to Mickey Rivers. ("I can still remember it," Zimmer says. "It has always been a rule of mine that when I start out for a pitcher, nothing is going to change my mind. That was the one time in my life I hesitated. I butchered it up and cost us the ball game.")

Rivers slashed a line drive down the left-field line. The game was tied, and Mickey was obviously going to try to carry the go-ahead run into scoring position. This is what the game of baseball is all about. Nobody was better than Yaz on this play, at racing over, scooping up the ball, and making a strong, accurate throw to second base. Nobody was faster than Mickey Rivers between home plate and second base — an eight-second filmstrip. Yaz made the play to perfection, Rivers went diving in — baseball, the game of inches — and Rivers was on second base with the winning run.

The batter was Thurman Munson. Having blown the chance to get Tiant out of there while he still had a lead, Zimmer decided he might as well give Tiant a chance to pitch out of the inning and perhaps still win the ball game.

Munson hit a soft liner into center field for a single, and the Yankees had pulled it out.

For Reggie Jackson there were five more depressing days in New York before the Yankees went to Boston. A repentant Reggie wanted to call a team meeting the next day to apologize, and when Martin refused, Reggie went around and apologized to everybody personally — including the pitchers who had been in the bullpen.

Munson listened to his apology and said nothing. A lot of his teammates listened and said nothing.

On the plane to Boston, a couple of the New York writers asked Munson whether he would shake Reggie's hand if Reggie hit a home run. Initially Munson's response was that there wasn't a chance, but as the writers began to argue that it was his job as team captain to bring the team together, not to widen the breach further, he grew increasingly pensive, and finally conceded that they had given him something to think about.

For the second straight week, it was going to be the Yankees and the Red Sox on "Monday Night Baseball." The last time America had seen Reggie Jackson swing a bat, he had hit a home run off Bill Lee and gone off to a corner to sulk about it. In Boston it was national TV again, it was Bill Lee out there again . . . and yes, America, it was a home run again.

When Jax got to the dugout, Munson was there to shake his hand.

In the end, however, it was Munson's game rather than Jackson's, starting in the fifth inning, when Thurman drove in what proved to be the winning run on a fielder's choice. Reggie gave a run back in the last of the inning by bobbling a ground ball, and as the Red Sox came to bat in the bottom of the ninth, the score was 5–4.

Butch Hobson was on second with two out when Denny Doyle hit a line single to short center field. Mickey Rivers was the only center fielder in the major leagues you'd have sent the runner home on in that situation. Mickey had no arm. He threw like a girl — before girls became athletes. Damn if his throw wasn't perfect. Hobson, a former quarterback and safety for the 1972 University of Alabama Orange Bowl team, came barreling in. Munson tucked himself in like a turtle to absorb the force of the crash, flipped Hobson over his shoulder, and reached back to tag him out.

Jackson, who had been taken out of the game at the beginning of the inning for defensive purposes, was the first player out on the field to grab his hand.

After those three tense games, the fourth one looks easy on the scoreboard, as the Red Sox won, 5–1, behind Reggie Cleveland, who had been making a career as a Yankee killer. He had beaten the Yankees three straight times in 1976, and had a 6–1 lifetime record against them. This time it wasn't so easy. He won the game by getting Reggie Jackson out with men on base — more than once. Seven runners Reggie left stranded.

The month of May had come to an end. The Yankees were a game and a half behind the surprising Baltimore Orioles, but they were a game ahead of the Red Sox. And everybody knew that Baltimore wasn't going to stay on top forever.

If you think the May games were packed with interpersonal tension and overwrought dramatics, you ought to stick around for June.

The scores tell why the June series came to be known as the Boston Massacre: 9–4, 10–4, 11–1. The Red Sox hit 16 home runs, an all-time record for three consecutive games. They weren't Fenway Park home runs, either. They were monster shots which disappeared over the left-field net and into the right-field stands and center-field bleachers.

Catfish Hunter started the first game, and Rick Burleson hit his second pitch into the screen, the first of only three home runs Rick would hit all year. Fred Lynn hit a 3–2 pitch into the bleachers in right-center. Carlton Fisk and George Scott both hit homers that cleared the wall and the screen. Before the day was over, Dick Tidrow gave up monster home runs to Yastrzemski and Fisk.

Six home runs. A humiliation.

Saturday, June 18, was another Game of the Week, and Reggie was in a happy mood. In five games in which he had been on national television, he had hit .363, with four home runs. He was on a 13-game hitting streak. By the time the game was over, Reggie's average would be up to .410, and he would be on the slippery edge of a nervous breakdown.

It was a hot, sunny day, and a crowd of 34,603 was gathered, the largest afternoon crowd in Boston — here we go again — in 20 years. The Red Sox hit five more home runs — two by Yastrzemski, two by Bernie Carbo, and one by George Scott — bringing the total to 11 home runs in two games. But the home runs weren't the story.

In the sixth inning the Red Sox were leading, 7–4. Fred Lynn was on first base. Jim Rice, trying to check his swing, hit a pop fly out to short right field, and suddenly all hell broke loose. At first Reggie seemed to be under the impression that Willie Randolph was going to be able to make the play. Be that as it may, he started slowly, showed no great enthusiasm about going after the ball once it had fallen, and made a weak throw in the general direction of the pitcher's mound as Rice went wheeling into second.

Everybody knows that Mike Torrez was the Red Sox pitcher who threw the ball to Bucky Dent. Almost nobody remembers that Mike Torrez was also the Yankee pitcher who threw the ball that led to the Martin-Jackson explosion.

Torrez: "It was like Reggie didn't see it, first of all. He could say the sun got in his eyes. But when he didn't run after the ball, that's when the hair on the back of my neck went up. I could have been out of the inning, and now it looks like I'm going to be out of the game."

Thurman Munson came out to the mound. "What the *bleep* is that spook doing?" he said. "Mike, do you believe that *bleep!* The *bleeping* nigger didn't run after the ball."

"He didn't," Torrez said. He could see Billy Martin coming in from the side. "What the *bleep* is going on out there?" demanded Billy. "This *bleeping* guy doesn't want to play today?"

Munson: "Billy, did you see the *bleeping* nigger? He didn't even run after the ball, the *bleep-bleeper.*"

The more they talked, communicating their outrage to one another, the angrier they all became.

"Sonofabitch," Martin said. "He's trying to show us all up. I should take his *bleeping* ass out of the game and put someone in there to show him up."

Torrez: "What's he trying to do, show up everybody here by not hustling after the ball?"

Martin: "I'm going to take the sonofabitch out. I don't give a *bleep.* I'm going to get that sonofabitch."

Munson: "Take that sonofabitching spook out. The sonofabitch doesn't want to play ball today. Something must be bothering him. Maybe he's got a hangnail or something."

When Reggie saw Paul Blair come running out, he took one step toward him and then kind of rocked back in confusion and disbelief.

Blair waved him in, and when Reggie got to him, he asked, foolishly, "You coming after me? Why?"

"You got to ask Billy that."

As Reggie came running in with that purposeful stride of his, the center-field camera — that other scorekeeper — followed him every step of the way. Martin had been leaning forward on the edge of his dugout seat, waiting. Jackson spread his hands out in an expression of total bewilderment. "What did I do?" he asked. "What did I do?" Martin came off the bench at him, his chin jutting out combatively. "What do you mean, what did you do? You know what you did!"

Reggie continued on down the steps as if he hadn't heard him. "Why did you take me out? You have to be crazy to embarrass me in front of 50 million people." (That's all he was concerned about, the players on the bench would tell the others afterwards, that he had been embarrassed on national television.)

"I don't give a *bleep!*" Martin barked. "When you decide to play, then you play right field. And not until."

Elston Howard, now a Yankee coach, had moved to interpose his body between them. Reggie spat a curse. Billy spat one back. "You don't know what you're doing, old man," Reggie said. "You showed me up in front of 50 million people." He turned his back and began to walk away.

"What? What! *Old man?*" Elston Howard tried to pin Billy against the dugout pole, but when he saw the look in his eyes, he let go. "You called me an old man?" Billy screamed. "I'll show you who's an old man!" Dick Howser, another coach, blocked Billy's charge just long enough to give Yogi Berra a chance to wrestle the manager to the bench. Reggie had already whipped off his glasses, and he was goading him on. "Let's go, old man. Come on, old man! Let's get it over with, *old man!*"

Through it all Billy was screaming, "Let me go! I'm gonna break his *bleeping* ass!"

It was over, though. Jimmy Wynn had wrapped his arms around Reggie, and Yogi was holding Martin tight. "You never did like me," Reggie shouted as a final thrust. "You never did want me on this ball club. Well, I'm here to stay, so you better start liking me."

He had set it out for him, the final taunt. If one of them went, he was telling Billy, it wasn't going to be the $3 million player. It was going to be the manager who couldn't get along with him.

The team, however, was solidly behind Billy Martin. "I would have liked to take a swing at him myself," Thurman Munson said, off the record.

When the unanimity of the feeling against him was relayed to Reggie, he went beyond a defense of the particular play into what he believed to be the real issue. "I can't win here," he said. "I am alone."

Sometime around eight o'clock that night Reggie called Mike Torrez to tell him he had a couple of writers in his room. He wanted Mike there for a very specific reason. "If I go too far," he told Torrez, "stop me." The writers were Phil Pepe of the *Daily News* and Paul Montgomery of the *Times*. (Montgomery wasn't really a sports writer. The regular beat man, Murray Chass, was on vacation, and Montgomery, a foreign correspondent just back from Nicaragua, had been given the assignment as a form of rest and recuperation.)

It was some interview. Reggie was sitting on the floor, bare-chested except for a gold cross and two gold medallions. A blonde (a Boston girlfriend) was in the shower. Mike Torrez was sitting next to Reggie with a bottle of white wine. Reggie seemed to have only the most fragmentary memory of the play in question. He had no recollection of having said anything when he came back to the dugout. He had merely held out his arms, he said, in a "What did I do wrong?" gesture.

He revealed for the first time that he had been taking cortisone shots for a sore arm since spring training. "With my bad arm I'm not going to take a chance throwing to second, so I fired home. I didn't want the run to score."

That wasn't how it had happened. His story made no sense. At one point Reggie sat on the bed and read the Bible. He had been a born-again Christian for three years, he told the reporters, and frequently turned to the Bible for solace.

Then suddenly he was exclaiming: "I'm just a black man to them who doesn't know how to be subservient. I'm a black buck with an IQ of 160 making $700,000 a year. They've never had anybody like me on their team before." Only George Steinbrenner treated him like he was somebody, he said, as his voice began to break. "The rest of them treat me like I'm dirt." The tears were running down his cheeks. "I'm a Christian," he wailed, "and they're fucking with me because I'm a nigger and they don't like niggers on this team."

The Yankee pinstripes were supposed to be Ruth and Gehrig, Di-Maggio and Mantle. "I've got an IQ of 160. They can't mess with me." He was a man in torment, a man so clearly on the slippery edge that Mike Torrez, who had been watching him with concern, stood up and told the writers, "I think you'd better leave."

Reggie himself soon left, after making a phone call. In this time of his greatest anguish he was looking for succor not from one of his own teammates but from a member of the Boston Red Sox, George Scott.

The visit with Scott did little to restore his equilibrium. Around 11 o'clock he came back to the hotel driving Scott's green Cadillac. He called his room to tell whoever was still there that he'd be up in a few minutes, and then startled the tourists and salesmen sitting around the lobby by delivering a long, 'rambling speech about all the terrible things that had been done to him. He was so far out of it that it was impossible to tell whether he was on the edge of a breakdown or just blitzed. "The Yankees have never *bleeped* anybody like I've been *bleeped*," he kept repeating. But in the end Reggie was always Reggie, and before he left he was going to remind everybody who he was. "It's you people I feel sorry for," were his departing words. "You're the ones who are going to miss out when I'm gone next year."

On Sunday the Red Sox completed the Boston Massacre by belting five more home runs, as they overwhelmed a demoralized Yankee team, 11–1. To rub it in, it was little Denny Doyle, the weak-hitting second baseman, who broke the game open with a three-run home run, the first homer he had hit in 204 games.

One of the casualties was Reggie Jackson's 14-game hitting streak. Not that the pressure had gotten to him. Against Ferguson Jenkins, a top pitcher who had his good stuff, Reggie had smoked three line drives. Unfortunately, they all went right at somebody. Where the pressure buckled him, as always, was in the field. He stumbled around badly under a couple of fly balls and made a miserable throw to the cut-off man for an error.

The other home runs came late, against a shell-shocked Dick Tidrow. Bernie Carbo, the first batter he faced, hit one. Jim Rice hit one in the eighth, and two pitches later Yaz hit another over the bullpen and into the bleachers. Yaz was now 9 for 14 on the series, with four home runs and 10 RBIs, and the message was flashing on the scoreboard that the Red Sox had just tied the all-time record for

home runs in three consecutive games. George Scott, who was leading the league in homers, boomed one final blast into the center-field
bleachers, the most distant part of the field.

Billy Martin was being his optimistic self. Undiscouraged, he said:
"If this was September, I'd be worried. This is June. We'll be in first
place next Sunday."

It had never occurred to him that he might be in imminent danger
of losing his job because of the dugout battle with Jackson. After the
game he was sitting in the Boston press room with Gabe Paul and
Don Zimmer. "The way you're drinking," Gabe told him drily, "you'd
think we won."

On the plane to Detroit, the main topic of conversation was whether
Billy had wanted to be held back. Billy's reputation as a brawler
meant not a thing to the players of a new generation. To them he
was just another old-timer, and a skinny little one at that. "Would you
want to take on Reggie?" they asked one another. Noooo. Reggie
was one solid block of muscle.

By the time they woke up in the morning they had something else
to talk about. Milton Richman, sports editor of UPI, had a story on
the wire that Billy Martin was going to be fired within a couple of
days "as a result of the Jackson episode, coupled with the three
losses in Boston," and replaced by Yogi Berra. There was only one
man who could have been the source for that story. And George
Steinbrenner was there in Detroit waiting for them.

The players were in an uproar. Thurman Munson and Graig Nettles, among others, let it be known that if Martin was fired over
Jackson, they would walk out with him. The word from New York
was that the Yankee Stadium switchboard was being flooded with
calls demanding that Billy Martin be retained.

Gabe Paul laid it on the line for George during a meeting in Steinbrenner's motel suite. Fire Martin and he'd be making Jackson the
manager of the ball club and placing the new manager in a wholly
untenable position.

George Steinbrenner had not marched into Detroit with his ban-
ners flying in order to fold his tent and steal quietly away. Not when
there was still discipline to be imposed and headlines to be harvested.
He began by calling Billy to the suite and exacting some concessions
from him. Subdued but hardly contrite, Billy kept insisting that nobody was going to tell him how to manage the team. Once he had

been assured that it was not his ability as a manager that was being questioned but his willingness to assume his responsibilities, he said, "All right. What do I have to do to keep my job?"

From there, George turned his visit into a two-day circus with himself as the ringmaster, cracking the whip.

He ordered Billy and Reggie to go to the ball park together and put on a display of unity. So they came to the park together in separate taxis and walked into the clubhouse with their arm around each other's shoulder, smiling dutifully and fooling nobody.

George himself took over the manager's office and had all the key players line up outside the door so that they could be chastised, in turn, like naughty schoolboys.

And then he went into the clubhouse and harangued the troops. "You guys are a finger snap away from firing your manager," he began. "If you love him so much, you guys had better get on the ball."

For two days he had been saying that Billy's future was in Gabe Paul's hands. He had told Billy Martin the same thing in their hotel room meeting. It had been restated in the official announcement of Billy's retention.

Asked that question the next day at the park, he turned his story completely around. "It was my decision entirely," he said. "We were headed for a complete collapse. Dissension on the team was terrible. We are getting no leadership and no fire. Something had to be done quickly."

He had told Billy, he said, "The next time you drive me to the wall, I'll throw you over it."

He had told Reggie Jackson, "If you get into the race thing again, I'll beat your head off."

He had also taken Munson to task, he said, for failing to carry out his duties as team captain.

He said that several players had come up to him and told him what a lift his pep talk had given them. Others had stopped him in the lobby to urge him to take a greater part in the running of the club. "We want you around," he quoted them as saying, "watching things, pulling for us."

Actually, he had been doing that all along. Publicly, everything was Gabe's decision. Privately and off the record, he let it be known that the tension on the team was beyond anything Gabe seemed to be aware of, and that he, Steinbrenner, was getting annoyed at being called in to clean up every minor problem.

George and Gabe had been through it before.

The curse of George's life in those first winning years was that he knew he needed Gabe Paul and he wished that he didn't, and so from time to time it made him feel better to make believe that he didn't.

It wasn't a matter of who was making the decision. It was, as George reminded his players so frequently, his ball club. Every decision in the end had to be approved by him.

But in constantly stating that it had been Gabe's decision, and then announcing that he had been forced to step in and save poor old bumbling Gabe, George was making it look as if Gabe Paul's reputation was his to punch around as he wished.

Gabe Paul walked out of the hotel and caught a plane home to Tampa. George was on a plane the same night. The next morning he was at Gabe's door, hat in hand, to promise that if he would come back, it would never happen again.

At least Gabe got a three-day vacation out of it. He remained in Tampa while the Yankees were salvaging the final game in Detroit, stayed on for another day while the Yankees were playing the Mayor's Trophy game, and returned to Yankee Stadium for the opening game of the Boston series just in time to be confronted with yet another chapter in the Billy & Reggie story.

The Red Sox came into New York flexing their muscles. They had followed the massacre of the Yankees by going to Baltimore and taking four straight from the Orioles. They had seven straight victories, and 16 out of 18. Bill Campbell was unhittable. In his last 10 appearances he had two wins and eight saves, and an infinitesimal earned run average of 0.94. The Red Sox were five games ahead of both New York and Baltimore. They had knocked Baltimore out of the race — everybody seemed to agree about that — and by winning two out of three games in New York, they could just about dispose of the Yankees.

Billy Martin's job was on the line, and everyone knew it. The New York fans gave him a standing ovation when he brought the starting line-up to home plate. He came back to the dugout, grinning. "When George heard that I'll bet he shit."

Bill Lee was opening for the fourth straight time, and if this was going to be Billy Martin's last chance to get at him, he wasn't going to let it pass. Billy, you'll recall, liked to call Lee "the Lady." Never a man to let an ongoing feud get away from him, Billy had arranged to have a dead mackerel dropped into the crotch of Lee's pants in the visitors' locker room together with a note that read: "Stuff this up your pussy. It might help you throw harder."

"Really romantic, huh?" Lee sniffed.

Martin pulled a surprise starter out of the hat — Catfish Hunter. After the bombardment in Boston, Hunter had been written off. For publication, Catfish maintained stoutly that there was nothing wrong with his arm. No matter how hard he got hit, he would always say that he wasn't discouraged because his arm felt good. In truth, it hurt like hell. That's why he couldn't get the ball down.

But Hunter had a special position on that ball club. He was the guy who had always won the big game in the past. As a leader himself, Billy understood the importance of symbols.

And while Billy was settling scores, who else might he have been thinking of? After Reggie had lost a fly ball in the lights in Detroit, Billy had not been able to resist the temptation to offer him some advice. "Maybe," Billy suggested, "he ought to get his eyes examined."

Good idea, Reggie decided. The Yankees were playing the pain-in-the-ass Mayor's Trophy game on their return to New York, and the eye examination gave Reggie a perfect excuse for ducking it.

Reggie arrived at the park the next day only an hour before game time, which meant that he had missed batting practice. Big deal.

Just before Reggie came out of the clubhouse, Billy erased his name from the line-up and replaced him with Roy White. Martin's story, which was not exactly corroborated, was that the trainer had told him that Jackson's eyes were still dilated. "I've been worried about his eyes," Billy said nastily. "Both at bat and in the field."

When Jackson saw the altered line-up, he slammed his bat down and walked out to the outfield without bothering to take along his glove.

Whenever Billy benched Jackson, there was a left-hander pitching against them. But in this case the percentages didn't apply. In the nine times Reggie had faced Lee during the season, he had five hits, including two home runs. And besides, Reggie was swinging the bat good, and when Reggie was swinging the bat, he hit everybody.

Gabe Paul, having accepted Steinbrenner's apology, arrived at the park in the second inning. He sent the club physician to the locker room to examine Reggie's eyes and then called the dugout to tell Martin that Jackson was available.

Catfish Hunter was more than available. He went to two outs in the ninth inning before he was replaced. The third out was a big one, another of those plays that go practically unnoticed yet influence a game and perhaps an entire season.

For Hunter it was a spotty performance. Although he allowed only five hits, three of them were home runs: a solo shot by Yastrzemski, picking up right where he left off in Boston, and two-run shots by Butch Hobson (also in the second inning) and George Scott. Going into the ninth inning, Scott's home run was the difference.

The Yankees had taken a temporary lead on Munson's first-inning single. In the second, Paul Blair had hit a two-run homer that retied the score.

Yaz, who always fielded marvelously at Yankee Stadium, went up over the wall to make the catch and came down empty-handed. A fan in the left-field bleachers had stripped the glove right off his hand. The glove came back. The ball didn't.

Hunter actually retired the last two batters he faced. But he had walked Bernie Carbo to start off the inning, and with the top of the batting order coming up, Martin brought in Sparky Lyle.

Rick Burleson hit Lyle's first pitch into the gap in right-center and all the way to the fence. Now, Carbo was slow and Mickey Rivers was fast, but with two outs, Carbo was running at the crack of the bat. Rivers picked the ball up at the fence and made a casual, almost underhanded flip to the cut-off man. But where was Carbo with the insurance run? He may have stumbled a little rounding second, but still . . . Remember the Rivers throw that had cut off the tying run in the first trip to Boston? Eddie Yost, the third-base coach, had said at the time that under the same circumstances, he'd send the runner home against Rivers's arm every time. But maybe the memory was sitting there somewhere in the back of his head. Because here, with Rivers conceding the run, he held Carbo up at third.

Carbo's buddy, Bill Lee, remembers that play very well. "Carbo had a hard time running from first to home unless he hit it out. He tends to get piano legs about 20 feet from home plate. Yost knew that. But you play for the win on the road, you take your chances, and that's got to go into your coaching theory too."

Ah, the little things that come back to haunt you. Instead of trailing 6–3, the Yankees went into the bottom of the ninth trailing 5–3. Bill Campbell had come into the game in the sixth inning, very early for him, with runners on second and third and nobody out and, as was his habit, pitched out of the inning without a run being scored. In his three innings the Yankees had only one hit off him. He was breezing to his fifteenth save of the season, the eleventh straight appearance in which he had saved the game or won it. After Rivers had opened the Yankee half of the ninth by grounding out, Martin sent Available Jackson to the plate to pinch-hit for Bucky Dent. Jackson, greeted by boos, grounded out, too.

Two out, nobody on, and it was beginning to look as if the Yankees were never going to beat the Red Sox again.

And now Willie Randolph hit a fly ball into left-center, something between a line drive and a fly. Up in the press box, Bob Ryan, on his way down, said, "The Cap'n's got it." But wait, Yastrzemski had been playing Randolph in too shallow, and he had apparently misjudged the distance. The ball sailed over his frantic leap and rolled to the fence, and Willie Randolph went wheeling around to third base. The Yankees were still two runs behind, but they were alive, and the tying run was at the plate in the person of Roy White. White, a switch-hitter, had originally been inserted for Jackson to bat right-handed against Lee. Against Campbell, he was batting left-handed.

Carlton Fisk called for a screwball, a pitch that Campbell used sparingly, generally when he was going for the third strike. The pitch stayed high, and . . . *boom* — it was into the upper deck in right field like a cannon shot. Two pitches and the Yankees had climbed back from the dead.

Another not-at-all inconsiderable factor was that Bill Campbell had to keep pitching. Even that early in the season, the question for the Red Sox was how often they were going to be able to go to Campbell before his arm fell off.

Don Zimmer allowed him to pitch the tenth inning, and that was it. With three left-handers due up for the Yankees in the eleventh, Zim brought in Ramon Hernandez, a left-handed reliever of indeterminate age whom Boston had just picked up from the Cubs to fill an obvious need.

Hernandez did not get a batter out.

He walked Graig Nettles and, with Rivers at the plate, immediately committed a balk to send Nettles to second. Disastrous. Now he had to walk Rivers and pitch to Reggie Jackson. If Nettles had still been on first and Rivers had sacrificed him to second, Jackson would have been walked. Given this second chance to swing the bat, Reggie slashed the first pitch down the right-field line, and the ball game was over.

Roy White, the man who had started in Reggie's place, had tied it. Jackson himself had won it and probably saved Billy Martin's job. Back in the locker room Reggie was uncommunicative. Depressed. "I can't say anything," he said finally. "If you were in my water for a week, you'd understand why."

On Saturday afternoon Mike Torrez was finally getting his start, a full week after he had been riddled for 13 hits and three home runs. He had promised at the time that the Red Sox were going to be made very uncomfortable the next time he pitched, and they were, although not the way he had seemed to imply. Torrez just kept his fast ball dipping low on the outside corner all day and put an end to the Red Sox home run jubilee, which had grown to 33 over 10 games.

The Yankees were 2½ games behind. The corpse was beginning to sit up. The final matchup was Don Gullett versus Reggie Cleveland. As the winning pitcher in the game that had featured the Martin-Jackson embroglio, Cleveland had run his record as a Yankee killer to 7–1.

As for Gullett, another free agent acquisition, if they weren't paying him $2 million to win this kind of game, what were they paying him for?

It was a World Series atmosphere: a crowd of 55,039, another "largest regular season attendance in reconstructed Yankee Stadium."

After trailing, 4–1, the Red Sox scored three runs in the ninth inning to tie the game. Bill Campbell came in to pitch, but the five innings he had thrown on Friday night were showing. He was able to retire Mickey Rivers on a ground ball, and that was the last good thing that was going to happen to him. Roy White worked him for a walk and scored the winning run on hits by Munson and Paul Blair, who had come into the game in the top of the inning for defensive purposes. Otherwise, it would have been Reggie Jackson up there with a chance to add to his heroics.

The sweep in Boston had been answered by a sweep in New York. It was a brand new season. "It isn't as easy as we were making it," Don Zimmer acknowledged.

"Baseball is no different than life," pronounced Billy Martin, the ol' philosopher. "You have your ups and your downs. You just hope people stick with you in the lows, because the highs are going to come."

There were 78 days to September, when they would meet again.

The Red Sox, who never seemed to recover from the shock of Roy White's home run, were into a losing streak that extended to nine games. Six days after the Red Sox left New York, and only 10 days after the Yankees had hit rock bottom, the Yankees were back in first place. They held onto the top spot exactly one week. By then the Sox had turned it around again, winning six of seven, and for the next three weeks the Red Sox and a resurgent Baltimore club passed the lead back and forth, never separated by more than a single game.

On August 23, in the 124th game of the season, the Yankees took over first place behind Torrez. They kept winning, and with 27 games left they had taken a 4½ game lead.

The five remaining games with the Red Sox didn't seem likely to mean much. But then the Yankees faltered just enough so that they did. It started when they lost both games of a Sunday double-header in Cleveland on "Yankee Hankies" Day, a promotion dreamed up by a local radio personality to allow all Yankee-haters to vent their spleen, for nothing more than the price of admission, by waving hankies on which was printed the fearsome device, "I Hate the Yankees." The Indians beat them twice in late-inning, hankie-waving rallies. As a note of reference, the pitcher in the second game was Rick Waits — the same Rick Waits who was going to knock off the Yankees in the final game a year later to force the play-off.

Back home, they were taking on the expansion Toronto Blue Jays. In 13 previous meetings the Blue Jays had scored a total of 12 runs against the Yankees and won exactly one game. Did somebody once say that baseball was a funny game? The same Blue Jays beat them, 19–3, the most runs scored in Yankee Stadium by an opposing team since June 17, 1925, when Ty Cobb, we can presume, was having himself a hell of a day for Detroit — although hardly as great as the immortal Roy Howell's five hits (including two home runs and two doubles) and nine runs batted in. In his previous 86 games, Howell had knocked in a total of 27 runs.

The Blue Jays' pitching staff was in such a sorry state that they had nobody to pitch the second game of the next day's double-header except Tom Murphy, a sore-armed relief pitcher who was making his first start in five years. When the game was over, Murphy had chalked up his second win of the year.

The pennant race was on again. The Red Sox, having won 10 out of 11, were coming into Yankee Stadium only a game and a half behind.

It wasn't to be a weekend series this time but a midweek series, starting on a Tuesday. Not only was the Stadium sold out for all three games, but the crowd surpassed the weekend total that had been set in June.

It had not been Billy Martin's intention to start Ron Guidry against the Red Sox. Nobody started left-handers against the Red Sox on purpose. Martin's original plan had been to pitch Guidry against Toronto with four days' rest and duck the test against the Sox. But a tough ten-inning game against Cleveland in which Guidry had thrown 154 pitches had made it necessary to give him another day's rest. Guidry was going to be the first left-hander to start against the Red Sox in more than three weeks. If he beat them, he would become the first left-hander to have done it in almost two months.

Facing the Red Sox for the first time as a starting pitcher, he opened by striking out the side on 10 pitches. In the second inning Yaz hit the very top of the center-field wall for a triple. A walk to Fisk, a wild pitch, and a single by Butch Hobson (his 100th RBI of the year), and the Red Sox had a 2–0 lead. They didn't score again. But that didn't mean that Guidry was anything close to overpowering.

On the contrary, it was a perfect illustration of the difference between pitching in Yankee Stadium and pitching in Fenway Park. Carlton Fisk hit three long shots. All of them would have been home runs in Fenway Park; two of them would have been home runs any place except Yankee Stadium. "This is a park for giants and rabbits," Fisk said afterwards. "You've got to be a giant to hit it out and a rabbit to catch it."

"I've been playing here for nine years," responded Thurman Munson in withering tones.

The same thing happened to Fisk and his teammates the following day, September 14. Mark it well, for this was the game that broke the Red Sox's back.

Ed Figueroa pitched a shutout. You could look it up. What was really happening was that the Red Sox were hammering everything he threw up and then going back out on the field, inning after inning, with nothing to show for it.

In the fifth inning they loaded the bases with nobody out. Fred Lynn hit the ball right back to Figueroa for an easy home-to-first double play. There were still runners on second and third with Yaz at bat. Given the green light on a 3–0 pitch, Yaz hit a wicked line drive up the middle for what looked like a sure two runs. But as Figueroa instinctively turned away, the ball hit him on the back of the thigh and dropped dead at his feet, and he was able to throw Yaz out.

There were Boston runners on base in every inning. Mickey Rivers was running down balls in deep left center, deep right center, and short everything.

It wasn't Mickey Rivers' day, though. It was Reggie Jackson's. Reggie, who had come in early to have a bruised knee worked on, had the best game of his life defensively. In the fourth inning, with Rice on base, George Scott boomed a line drive deep into his power alley in right-center. Reggie backed to the fence, timed his leap perfectly, and picked the ball out of the stands. In the seventh, with one out and a man on second, Bernie Carbo hit a soft line drive into short right-center. Reggie hesitated for the merest fraction of a second, then raced in and made a brilliant diving catch, just barely getting his glove under the ball before it landed.

And all the time Reggie Cleveland, the Yankee killer, was mowing the Yankees down through eight innings.

Then it was Munson and Jackson. Thurman Munson, who was driving toward his third straight .300–100 RBI year, singled to start the ninth. Martin wanted Jackson to sacrifice him to second. "What's percentage?" the master, Casey Stengel, used to ask. In other words, what's the sense of telling a man to bunt if he can't bunt? The Yankees didn't even have a bunt sign for Reggie Jackson. Dick Howser, the third-base coach, had to call time and go tell him the bunt was on. The first pitch was a ball. To no one's great surprise, Jax hit away on the next pitch and fouled it off.

The bunt was put back on. Howser didn't come down to tell him again. He went through the usual motions, and, as Jackson looked down at him, he said "Bunt" silently, just moving his lips. That was the Mickey Rivers sign. Another ball — a mistake for the Red Sox. When Jackson wants to bunt, maybe you ought to let him try. The count went to 3–2. Cleveland threw a hard sinker that dipped below the strike zone. If Reggie had taken the pitch, it would have been a walk. But Jackson was a low-ball hitter. The ball was gone from the moment it left his bat.

Reggie went dancing around the bases. He was mobbed at home plate, and Billy Martin was right in the middle of it, pounding him on the back. When they got back into the clubhouse, Billy said, "I'm sorry I gave you the bunt sign."

"I understood the situation well," Jax told him.

Outside, the fans didn't want to go home. They remained there screaming for Jackson. "Reggie . . . Reggie . . . Reggie!" Reggie was escorted out to take a bow and wave his hat. They still wouldn't leave, and he had to be escorted out again.

The Red Sox had come to town conceding that they had to win two out of three games to remain in contention. Now they had to win the third game to keep the last flicker of hope alive.

This was the game that the unsigned Torrez took himself out of with the score tied. Carlton Fisk, who had nothing to show for five 400-foot drives in the two previous games, knocked in the winning run with a ground ball that sneaked over second base.

The final series at Fenway Park had become close to an anticlimax. The Yankees were 4½ games ahead with only 12 to play. The Red Sox had to win both games to have a smell.

They did.

The final game was played on a cold, damp night after a day's layover because of rain. The delay was not unwelcome. Bill Campbell, fighting a sore arm, had been given a shot of cortisone before the opening game of the series, and although Zimmer had sent him out to the bullpen as a kind of decoy, he had known that Campbell would be out of action for at least two days.

Between them George Scott and Lou Piniella were involved in everything that happened all day — not only the runs that scored but also the runs that didn't.

It was Scott who had put Boston ahead, 3–2, in the sixth inning with a long home run into the bullpen. Both Yankee runs had been driven in by Piniella on a home run in the fifth and a line single off the fence in the sixth.

Once the Red Sox were in the lead, Campbell sent word to Zimmer that he was able to pitch. The rain had given him the extra day he needed. And although he wasn't great, he was good enough. George Scott saved him twice, and Campbell saved himself the other time.

The first batter he faced reached on an error. Mickey Rivers, always tough in the late innings of a close game, lashed a line drive toward right field. Scott, holding the man on, dove into the hole, caught the ball flat on his face, and scrambled back to first base on his hands and knees to double up the runner.

With one out in the eighth, Jackson got his second hit and Chris Chambliss followed with a double into the right-field corner. Out came Zimmer to find out whether Campbell would rather pitch to Nettles or Piniella. To everybody's surprise, Campbell preferred to stick to the righty-lefty percentage and walk Nettles, who wasn't hitting, and pitch to Piniella, who was hot. Piniella was hitting .336. He was 14 for his last 30 times at bat, and 4 for 5 in the series.

Campbell always came out a windmill of arms, kind of falling into the pitch. When he was right, he had a wicked curve that broke out and down. He got it breaking sharply on the outside corner for a strike. Then a ball. Then another breaking ball down on the outside corner, which Piniella, with his stiff-kneed swing, fouled back. Another ball, low and outside, and then Fisk called for a screwball, a pitch Campbell would normally throw only to a left-handed batter. It was a great call. Everything had been breaking sharply down and out; this one broke sharply in and down, catching the inside corner and leaving Piniella standing dumbfounded, and, it seemed, nodding to Campbell in appreciation as he walked away. No alibis for Sweet Lou.

In the ninth inning, with one out, Mickey Rivers slapped a ball into the hole between short and third. The man who ignited the Yankees was on first base, and Roy White, the man who had broken the Red Sox's heart, was coming to the plate. White lined the ball toward first, and in an almost exact duplication of the play he had made on Rivers, Scott dove for the ball, caught it flat on the ground, and scrambled back to first to double up Rivers and end the game.

The Red Sox won seven of the remaining 10 games. But it was too late. The Yankees won six in a row to clinch a tie. They clinched the tie by beating Cleveland, 10–0, with Don Gullett pitching the shutout and Reggie Jackson hitting a grand slam home run. The victory brought Gullett's season record to 14–4. The home run gave Reggie 109 runs batted in, more than any other Yankee player had been able to achieve since Mantle's 111 in 1964. It was also Reggie's twentieth game-winning hit.

It has become the custom, in recent years, to list Don Gullett among the high-priced free agents who failed. That's just not so.

Without Gullett, the Yankees couldn't possibly have won the pennant. Am I saying that one pennant was worth the outlay of $2 million? You bet I am.

If you want a truly remarkable pitching statistic, Gullett with his 14 victories won more games than any Red Sox pitcher. Bill Campbell, pitching entirely in relief, won more games — 13 — than any other Red Sox pitcher. (And that's not even counting Campbell's league-leading 31 saves.) The Sox starters were Tiant with 12, Rick Wise with 11, Cleveland with 11, Jenkins with 10, and Mike Paxton with 10.

In was, in fact, the overwhelming roles placed by Reggie Jackson, Don Gullett, and Bill Campbell in the 1977 pennant race that brought on the escalating bidding for the next year's crop of free agents.

Chapter Eighteen

1978:
The Boston Massacre

*Every time I come to Boston I get fired. Next year I'm going
to skip Boston and go straight to Detroit.*

— Billy Martin

I T would be impossible to match the 1977 season for such consistently dramatic games, but 1978 provided its own highlights.

• In 1977 the Yankees won 40 out of 50 games to beat the Red Sox
by 2½ games. In 1978 the Yankees put together a streak of 39 out
' of 53 to eat up a 14-game deficit. (If we include the end of the season,
it was 52 out of 73.)

• Gabe Paul had left the Yankee front office, but not before he had
talked George Steinbrenner into signing Rich Gossage in the second
running of the Reentry Sweepstakes.

• Reggie was tormented, and Martin was almost fired again after
the June series in Boston.

• The Yankee pitching staff was in even more of a shambles, except
for Ron Guidry, who had one of the great seasons in modern history,
going 24–3 and running his streak from the second half of the previous season to 34–5.

• The Boston Massacre of June 1977 disappeared into the dustbin
of history, to be replaced in the minds and memories of the fans of
both cities by the Boston Massacre of September 1978.

• Just before the All-Star break, Lou Piniella complained about the
lack of discipline in the clubhouse.

• In 1977 Steinbrenner prevailed on Martin to change his line-up.
In 1978 Steinbrenner took over the team and changed the line-up
himself.

• Don Gullett and Catfish Hunter went on and off the disabled list. But then — in one of the greatest miracles since Lazarus was last seen doing loop the loops over Jerusalem — Catfish Hunter came back from the dead.

• In 1977 the Red Sox did not have a starting pitcher who won more than 12 games. In 1978 they had a 20-game winner in Dennis Eckersley, and a 15-game winner in the all-purpose Bob Stanley.

• In 1977 there was a rained-out game in Boston that meant nothing. In 1978 there was a rained-out game that meant everything.

In the good old days of the 22-game schedule, the Yanks and Red Sox could be counted on either to open the season against each other or, at the very worst, to meet within shouting distance of Opening Day.

In 1978, the second year of juggling an unwieldy 12-team league, they did not meet on the field of battle until the sixty-fourth game of the season. "The new theory," said Haywood Sullivan, "was that Opening Day was a sellout anyway, so why waste it?"

With 15 games to deal out, the schedule makers split them up into two big packages. First, there were three series over 16 days opening on successive Mondays in June and July: three games in Boston, two in New York, and two more in Boston. Three successive Mondays meant three successive TV Games of the Week.

The second package opened up to reveal six games to be played on successive weekends in September.

Right in the middle, so the fans wouldn't forget they were around, two more games had been set down for New York in the first week of August.

In charting the ebb and flow of the pennant race, we find that the timing turned out to be positively uncanny.

On June 19 the Yankees took the field at Fenway Park, trailing by seven games. And it wasn't even that they had been playing that badly. Except for the Red Sox, who never seemed to lose, and the San Francisco Giants, the leaders in the National League, the Yankees had the best record in all of baseball. And this despite a horrific run of injuries that had put five of Billy Martin's pitchers on the disabled list and wiped out his entire middle defense. Willie Randolph's leg was in a splint, Mickey Rivers' hand was broken, Bucky Dent had a pulled hamstring, and Thurman Munson's leg was so bad that he shouldn't even have been playing.

Let it be recorded that on his first appearance at Fenway Park in

1978, Bucky Dent tried to play, felt the hamstring begin to go the first time he had to reach for a ball, and was back on the bench for another month.

The injuries Martin had been forced to contend with meant not a thing to George Steinbrenner. The tom-toms along the sports beat were carrying the word that Billy was about to be fired, not only — or even mostly — because his team was falling so far behind, but because he had committed the even more unforgivable sin of ridiculing George for having signed so many sore-armed, over-the-hill pitchers for huge amounts of money.

Steinbrenner was coming to Boston — always bad news — to let Martin know that if his pitchers were always getting hurt, it could only be because Art Fowler, his pitching coach, was mishandling them. As anyone familiar with the situation knew, this was a shot fired across Billy's bow, meant to remind him that a year earlier he had been allowed to bring in his buddy Fowler in return for certain promises to stop criticizing the front office.

Billy remembered those promises, all right. He had wanted Fowler, and George had wanted Lou Piniella in the line-up every day. Billy Martin's reaction, as anyone who knew him could have predicted, was to up the ante by benching Piniella. Made a helluva lot of sense: Piniella was only the second leading hitter in the American League at the moment, and Sweet Lou owned Fenway Park.

On Wednesday, with the series tied at one game each, Jim Beattie, a 23-year-old rookie who had been brought up from Tacoma a week earlier to give Billy a healthy arm, was belted out of the box in less than three innings. Barely had the rookie reached his locker before a hurricane named George came sweeping in to berate him as a gutless coward and ordered him to pack his stuff and grab the next plane back to Tacoma.

If you want to know why George III did those things, consult your local psychiatrist. George himself would say that it was because he owned the team — "I sign the checks," as he was fond of reminding everyone — and because he felt an obligation to toughen these kids up to face the fearsome pressure of playing in New York.

The significance of Steinbrenner's temper tantrum to his beleaguered manager was that when Billy was asked to comment about the humiliation that had been visited upon his rookie pitcher, he snorted, "The kid didn't have his good stuff, that's all. But he has all the guts in the world." And then he had a thing or two to say about his own precarious position. "My mother didn't raise any quitter," he said. "I remember last year I was going to get fired here. I'll show you the ring I got fired with. It says 'World Champions.' "

The world champions were going to Detroit for a weekend series, and then returning to New York to play Boston again — an exact rerun, you will note, of the most critical period for Billy in 1977. And, just as in 1977, Billy Martin came back from Detroit to face the first-place Red Sox with his job hanging by a thread. The trick for Steinbrenner was to fire him without bringing on riots in the street — or at least without flooding the switchboard at Yankee Stadium.

On Saturday, the day after the Yankees arrived in Detroit, Steinbrenner had Lee MacPhail, the league president, call Bill Veeck in Chicago to propose a trade of managers — Billy Martin for Bob Lemon.

Lemon had been the pitching coach of the Yankees' pennant-winning team in 1976, a man of infinite good nature and unfailing wit. ("I never took the ball game home with me," he said in his Hall of Fame induction speech. "I always left it in a bar along the way.") That was Bob Lemon. He also may well have been the first person to start calling Steinbrenner Boss. He was still calling him Boss, to George's delight, even though he was managing the White Sox.

And, not necessarily coincidentally, he had been a teammate and great friend of Al Rosen, the man who had succeeded Gabe Paul as president and general manager of the Yankees.

The deal didn't happen, but only because Veeck wanted the Yankees to throw a player into the deal. On Sunday, Steinbrenner called Al Rosen, who had accompanied the team to Detroit, and instructed him to tell Billy Martin that Fowler was going to be replaced. An utterly transparent stratagem. If Billy allowed his buddy to be fired in order to protect his own job, he would lose the sympathies of both his players and his fans. If he resigned in protest, so much the better.

In the course of a tearful meeting between Billy and his coaches, Billy vowed to fight for them all.

It was Monday, June 26, 1978. A year earlier, under roughly similar circumstances, a confident and defiant Billy Martin had been prepared to go down with his guns blazing: Billy the Kid in person. He had zapped his enemies Bill Lee and Reggie Jackson, shot his wad on Catfish Hunter, and gone on to pull out the victory that had turned the season around.

On June 26, 1978, a gaunt and haggard Billy Martin went into Steinbrenner's office for an "air-clearing" session and surrendered. Fowler was going to be allowed to stay on, sharing his duties with George's man, Clyde King. Billy Martin would continue as manager by becoming George Steinbrenner's lap dog.

It no longer seemed to matter, except perhaps to ABC television, that Dennis Eckersley beat the Yankees that night, in a listless 4–1 game, to extend the Red Sox lead to nine games.

One week later, on July 3, Eckersley did it again in Boston, his third victory over the Yankees in 12 days.

The seventh and final game of the three Monday series was scheduled for Tuesday, July 4. The Red Sox had Bill Lee (8–3) ready to pitch. The Yankees had no one.

So bereft were they of pitching that they were having a kid named Paul Semall drive up from their Double-A farm club in West Haven, Connecticut, so that Martin could take a look at him and decide whether he was good enough to start the game. The only other possibility was Don Gullett, who was trying to come back from his shoulder injury.

The game was rained out. "A gift from the heavens," Billy Martin said. "Christmas on the Fourth of July." It turned out to be exactly that. The game was rescheduled for the next Yankee visit in September. When it was finally played, the Yankees were the hottest team in baseball, and the Red Sox were barely ambulatory. The rescheduled game became part of the second Boston Massacre.

July 17 was the pivotal date. It was on that date, the day the Yankees fell 14 games behind Boston, that Reggie Jackson decided it would be a great idea to bunt, regardless of how the manager felt about it. Six days later, on the day of Jackson's return from his resultant suspension, the furies whipping around in Billy's psyche gave Martin a perfectly splendid rebuttal.

"They deserve each other," he said of Jackson and Steinbrenner. "One's a born liar and the other's convicted."

Almost as good as Reggie's "I'm the straw that stirs the drink," although not quite as original. Roy White had been saying the same thing, off the record, to friendly sports writers for more than a year. He wasn't referring to George Steinbrenner and Reggie Jackson, to be sure; he was referring to George Steinbrenner and Billy Martin.

· · ·

Bob Lemon, who had been fired by the White Sox three weeks earlier, had been alerted to stand by. Lemon came in, posted the lineup, and left the players alone.

No demons drove Bob Lemon. He had his own world in perfect perspective: "Baseball is a very simple game for children that we grownups have managed to screw up."

No problems of an undernourished or overnourished ego ate at him. He called a meeting and said, "I hope I don't screw up too bad. Go have some fun."

And when the writers asked him how it had gone, he said: "It went like every other clubhouse meeting. The manager talks and the players don't say a word. At least I wasn't booed."

And when the season was over, and he had led the team through its greatest comeback ever, the first thing he said was: "Don't forget that Billy Martin won the last five games he managed. This team was already on its way when I came in."

Give Bob Lemon all the credit. With the Red Sox in a tailspin, they came into the Stadium on August 2, with their lead cut to 6½ games. In the first game the Yankees took a 5–0 lead, but blew it in the ninth inning, and the game was eventually halted in the fourteenth inning by curfew. The next night the Red Sox scored two runs in the seventeenth inning to win that one, and went on to beat the Yankees in the regularly scheduled game.

Instead of being 4½ behind and back in the race, the Yankees were 8½ out with 40 games to play. After the game, some of the players — including the usually irrepressible Lou Piniella — were already saying that this was the day on which the Yankees lost the pennant.

Bob Lemon shrugged it off. "There are some games that you are not going to win no matter what you do," he said. "I believe that. There are some games you're not supposed to win."

Ten days later the Yankees scored five runs in the top of the seventh to wipe out a 3–0 Baltimore lead, and then the rains — and Earl Weaver — came along to wipe out the five runs. Weaver's contribution was to stall long enough so that the Orioles wouldn't be able to finish their half of the inning. If Billy Martin had still been around, they would have had to call out the National Guard. All Lemon said was, "That takes away the thrill of victory and gives you the agony of defeat."

.   .   .

It wasn't that simple, of course.

In the fifth game Lemon managed, the Yankees were finally able to field their starting line-up for the first time since the beginning of May, and they remained healthy for the rest of the year. Concurrently, plague, pestilence, and an occasional pulled hamstring struck the Red Sox. The team collapsed, no question about it, but their slide had begun in the last game before the All-Star break, when Rick Burleson sprained his ankle sliding into second. It was while Burleson was out that the Yankees had been able to pull up to 6½ behind.

Carlton Fisk, the other Red Sox indispensable, broke a couple of ribs and could hardly breathe. Everybody knew about Fisk's ribs; they didn't know that he also had bone chips in his elbow that made it very difficult for him to throw. The Red Sox were able to keep it a deep secret from everybody — except those base runners who were stealing on him almost at will. Yastrzemski, playing with a sore back and a sprained wrist, had lost his power. Dwight Evans, who was possibly the best all-around outfielder in baseball, was beaned badly and tried to come back too soon. Not only couldn't he hit, but he became dizzy when he had to look up at a fly ball. Butch Hobson, the third baseman, had floating bone chips in his elbow which were so big that the elbow would sometimes lock. They kept Hobson in there, and he set a world record for bad throws. Jerry Remy, the second baseman, broke his wrist. The center fielder, Fred Lynn, was playing on two bad ankles.

But what else does that tell you? Well, it tells you that putting together a strong bench is just as important as fielding a strong starting team. Steinbrenner's Yankees had been able to survive their early rash of injuries with their reserves. The Red Sox didn't have a strong enough bench.

And Catfish Hunter — never forget Catfish Hunter. The Cat had suffered through a year and a half of torture. No matter how hard he was hit — and his ability to give up home runs by the ton was almost laughable — he would insist that his arm felt good. "My control must be improving," he would say. "They're hitting them farther than ever."

No matter how badly he was going, the Cat wanted to pitch. "Winning isn't everything," he would say. "Wanting to win is." Every time he went out there, he thought he was going to win. And, just because he was the Cat, everybody else on the team felt the same way.

Catfish was playing out that first free-agent contract. If he couldn't pitch, he would drawl, he'd work it out washing George's boats. But whatever happened, it was his intention to go home to North Carolina when the contract was over, work on his farm, and watch his kids grow up. He was the old America, the old southern ballplayer. He knew who he was, and he knew where he came from.

In 1977 he had suffered pain and humiliation. When he was examined by Dr. Frank Jobe in Los Angeles, the club announced that he had been pronounced fit. Actually, Dr. Jobe had found that the rotor cuff on his shoulder was rubbing against the shelf of the shoulder every time he threw. In addition to the arm trouble, he had a pain in his groin. The Yankee doctor diagnosed it as a hernia, and it wasn't until the season was over that Catfish found out he had an inflammation of the bladder that could be treated with medication.

In 1978 he reported to camp wearing a silver medical alert wristband. On top of everything else, he was a diabetic. For the first half of the season it was 1977 all over again. In that game in Boston when Steinbrenner had stormed into the locker room to ship Jim Beattie back to Tacoma, it was Catfish Hunter, just off the disabled list, who had relieved him — and given up two quick home runs. The pain that day was so bad that there were tears in his eyes as he sat down on the bench. "I'll never pitch with that kind of pain again," he told his buddy Thurman Munson, and that was the first time anybody had ever heard Catfish Hunter complain.

And then, miracle of miracles, he had his arm manipulated under hypnosis, came back off the disabled list to start the game in which Reggie bunted, didn't look bad, kept pitching, and — who'd have thunk it — the Cat was back and throwing shutouts. He won six straight games — seven really, because he was leading, 12–0, in the fourth inning in Boston when the groin kicked up on him again, one inning short of the distance necessary to be credited with the win.

In all, Catfish won nine games out of 10 over the last two months, and that was the difference.

The Red Sox didn't collapse over the entire second half of the season; they collapsed in stages. When the Yankees were 14 games behind, there were 72 games to go. They had reduced it to 6½ with 57 games left, but were 8½ behind with 40 games remaining. Then they won 13 out of 15 to knock the lead down to four games when they went into Boston on September 7.

The *Herald American* had been running a front-page box in huge typeface charting the Red Sox's shrinking lead. The sports writers and radio commentators (and Boston is afloat in call-in sports pro-grams) were deep into recounting the inglorious history of blown leads and autumn swoons. "That wasn't us," the players would say. "I don't know anything about that."

By the time the press was through with them, they did know. By the time the Yankees left town, it *was* them.

A visiting club hopes to win two out of four in the home park of a contending ball club. If the Yankees didn't come into Boston feeling that they were going to sweep the series, it didn't take them long to get the idea.

They went in and reversed the Boston Massacre of 1977. Only more so. The scores were 15–3, 13–2, 7–0, and 7–4.

Here, once again, is the line score on the four games — runs, hits, and errors:

> Yankees   42–49–4
> Red Sox   9–16–11

In game one, Thurman Munson, batting third for the Yankees, had three hits before Boston's number nine batter, Butch Hobson, came up for the first time. (That was the game Hunter had to leave with a 12–0 lead. The easy victory was picked up by Ken Clay, who there-upon uttered a line that spoke for relief pitchers everywhere. "When the call came to the bullpen," said Clay, "there was a fistfight to see who was going to get the ball.")

In the second game it was Mickey Rivers, the lead-off man, who had three hits before the number eight batter George Scott, came to the plate.

That's how bad it was.

Looking back, you can find a certain theme of redemption and retribution. Or perhaps only an echo. The opposing pitchers in the opening game were Catfish Hunter and Mike Torrez. Go back to the opening game of what can now be called Boston Massacre I, and you will remember that the Cat had given up four home runs in the first inning. Go back to the opening game in Boston of the current season and you will find Clay being bawled out by Steinbrenner for not being able to hold on to an early lead.

The tone was set, fittingly enough, when Willie Randolph, the game's second batter, hit a one-hopper to Hobson. Hobson took a deep breath and bounced the ball into the dirt and through Scott's legs for his thirty-eighth error of the season. There had been a time when Scott would have handled that kind of throw blindfolded. Not only wasn't he fielding like he used to, but he had not had a hit in 30 times at bat. Munson and Jackson singled, and before the inning was over, the score was 2–0. In the second inning Torrez faced four batters and allowed four hits. The rout was on. The Yankees outhit the Red Sox, 21–8, and 16 of the hits were singles.

The second game marked the return of Jim Beattie. The rookie from Dartmouth had been brought back from Tacoma after he had presumably received a gut transplant. He had a three-hit shutout going into the ninth. He'd have had his shutout, too, if rookie catcher Mike Heath hadn't dropped Fisk's foul fly with two out. Heath was in there because Lemon had replaced everybody in the starting line-up except Beattie.

The game was over almost before it began. Rivers hit the first pitch past George Scott. On the second pitch he stole second and went on to third on Fisk's errant throw. Two pitches later Burleson booted Randolph's ground ball. Four pitches, two errors, and a run. By the end of the second inning, the score was 10–0.

The Red Sox made seven errors. Dwight Evans came in for an easy fly ball, grew dizzy, and dropped it. He took himself out of the game.

The first two games were slaughters. The last two provided the individual incidents for which the Massacre is best remembered.

In the third game Ron Guidry (20–2) and Dennis Eckersley (16–6) went head to head. The stoppers. Eckersley had already beaten the Yankees three times. The Red Sox were the only team Guidry had not defeated.

It was a pitcher's day, a day when a New England northwest wind was whipping around the field at 23 miles per hour, with gusts that were measured up to 32 miles per hour. Given the pitchers, and given the wind, Zimmer was predicting a 1–0 game. And so when Rick Burleson led off with a single, Zimmer, going against his general philosophy, had Fred Lynn bunt him to second. Jim Rice was given a hit when Bucky Dent fumbled his ground ball in the hole. Men on first and third with one out. And that was it for the day. The Red Sox did not get another hit.

The Yankees scored all seven of their runs in the fourth inning after two were out. The two outs had come in the high point of the series for Boston when Yaz made a leaping, twisting one-handed catch of Reggie Jackson's windblown fly in the left-field corner, bounced off the wall, and whipped the ball to first base to double up Munson. After the cheers would come the groans.

Chris Chambliss followed with a double to keep the inning alive. Zimmer, still playing as if he expected a 1–0 game, had Eckersley walk Graig Nettles and pitch to Lou Piniella. Good thinking. Piniella hit a routine fly ball into right-center. Routine, that is, until the wind grabbed hold of the ball, bounced it around, and carried it back toward the right-field foul line in the general direction of second baseman Frank Duffy. Fred Lynn came racing in from center. Burleson was still slanting over from short. Jim Rice sprinted in from right. Poor Duffy, trying to follow the flight of the ball, was looking straight up into the sun. The ball came back and landed in front of him, just inside the foul line. That was how the first run scored.

"It came back like a frisbee," Eckersley said. "It must have blown a hundred feet across the field."

Piniella said, "I thought I hit a fly ball to center field. I hit it pretty damn good. Then I saw what was happening and I started running hard."

Roy White was passed intentionally — the second intentional pass of the inning — to load the bases and bring up Bucky Dent.

Lou Piniella? Bucky Dent? Is a pattern beginning to develop here? Are coming events beginning to cast their shadow before?

Eckersley had always handled Dent with ease. He got ahead of him, 0–2, and then threw a hanging slider which Dent plunked into left. The score was 3–0.

"I lost the game with that 0–2 pitch to Dent," Eckersley said when the press began to jump all over Duffy. "Duffy didn't throw that pitch, I did."

Two more hits, a wild pitch, and a passed ball, and it was 7–0 before the inning was over.

The first run would have been enough. Ron Guidry, pitching 8⅔ innings of hitless ball, became the first left-hander to shut out the Red Sox in Fenway Park in four years.

As Joe Gergen wrote in *Newsday*, "The Yankees are a game behind and drawing away."

The panic was on.

The Red Sox were the butt of jokes, good and bad.

"The Black Sox looked better than the Red Sox."

"They're going to wear unlisted numbers on the back of their uniforms tomorrow."

Question: Are the Red Sox trying?

Answer: Very.

"They only beat us 7–0 this time. A squeaker."

And finally: "Don't throw in the towel — we've got Bobby Sprowl."

Bobby Sprowl represents the final chapter in the saga of Don Zimmer and Bill Lee. After the trading of Bernie Carbo, Lee had cleaned out his locker and gone slamming out of the park screaming about the stupidity of Zimmer and Haywood Sullivan and all the executives who did not believe that the players should have a say in the decisions that affect their lives.

A day later Sullivan called down to the manager's office to tell Zimmer that Lee had returned and was on his way down to the clubhouse. "I'll take him back," Zimmer said, "but I'm going to put a circle of men in the dressing room and I want to fight the sonofabitch. I'll let him come back on those conditions."

Bill Lee still says that Zimmer stopped using him as a direct result of the Carbo explosion. But time has a way of telescoping memory. As of June 15 Lee's record was 7–3, and he had been taking a childish delight in reminding Zimmer that he wouldn't be on the club if Zimmer had succeeded in getting him released.

Zimmer kept him in the rotation for two more months. On July 15 he ran his record to 10–3 by beating Milwaukee to end the Red Sox's three-game losing streak. He did not win another game. Given a little luck, he could have won a couple, though, most notably a 2–1 loss he took against Kansas City.

Zimmer's memory is that Lee was getting hit so hard that benching him became a matter of trying to save the season, and that's not entirely accurate either. At the time Lee was taken out of the rotation, the Red Sox held a seven-game lead, with only 37 games left.

Mike Torrez remembers that day well. Torrez was pitching the final game in Seattle, at the conclusion of a western swing. Before he went out to warm up, he was sitting on the bench between Zimmer and Lee. "I had already asked Lee what he was doing there, because Lee followed me in the rotation and the normal procedure is to send back the pitcher who is going to open at home a day or two early so that he will have some time to get over the jet lag.

"I'm sitting there, minding my own business, chatting with Zim. Bill Lee looks over around me and he says, 'Hey, Skip, is it all right if I do my running? I'm supposed to pitch the first game in Boston, right?'

"And Zimmer said, 'You're not pitching. We're bringing Bobby Sprowl from Pawtucket. You're pitching in the bullpen now.'

"I thought he meant they were going to pitch Sprowl for just one game. We had a big lead at the time, so it's no big deal. But I'm wondering what he's going to do that for. Bobby Sprowl never beat anybody."

Bobby Sprowl had a 9–3 record in Double-A ball, and a not-too-impressive 7–4 record, with a 4.15 ERA at Triple-A Pawtucket.

The Boston press had asked Pawtucket manager Joe Morgan about him when the Sox were down there for an exhibition game shortly after Sprowl had been brought up. He was a kind of jittery kid, Morgan told them, clearly not ready to pitch major league ball.

But Johnny Podres, Boston's minor league pitching coach, had been boosting Sprowl to Zimmer. Podres, a buddy from back in their playing days in Brooklyn, had recommended Mike Paxton and Don Aase in 1977. Zimmer had taken a chance on them, and the two rookies had kept the Red Sox in the race. "This kid's got ice water in his veins," Podres had told him in recommending Sprowl.

When the Red Sox started to lose, the three mainstays of the pitching staff, Torrez, Tiant, and Eckersley, talked about going to Zimmer as a delegation. "That would have been the smart thing to do, and we didn't do it," Torrez says. "We were going to tell him that we weren't going to win shit without Lee. Bill Lee missed six starts. If he won two of them, there wouldn't have been a play-off game. I said then and I say to this day, they can blame me all they want, but the reason we lost the pennant was because he took Bill Lee out of the rotation and never pitched him again."

Whether Sprowl was ready for the big leagues is one question. He was plainly not ready to pitch this kind of a game. He threw 25 pitches, and 16 of them were balls. He walked the first two batters, got only two men out, and was charged with three runs. Three of the six batters he faced walked.

The Yankees were leading, 6–0, in the sixth inning, before the Red Sox finally scored, and went on to win, 7–4.

Bobby Sprowl never recovered. The following year in spring training he couldn't get the ball near the plate. Some of his teammates ridiculed and taunted him. His career was destroyed.

A year later an apparently erroneous story got around that the Red Sox had just learned that Sprowl had only one eye.

When a massacre occurs, there has to be a body count. In baseball, the body count is called statistics:

• Bucky Dent knocked in seven runs. Add the three runs on The Home Run, and that amounts to 25 percent of his total RBIs for the year.

• Willie Randolph had eight hits and six walks and reached twice on errors. He was on base 16 of the 22 times he came to bat.

• Piniella had 10 hits in 16 at bats, walked twice, reached on an error, and scored eight times — one less than the total number of runs scored by the Red Sox.

• Reggie Jackson, at 5 for 17, was the only hitter who reached first base less than 33 percent of the time. This includes the combined total of the substitutes.

• As a team the Yankees hit .396, and had an on-base percentage of .508.

• The Red Sox hit .171 and had an on-base percentage of .265.

Even before the final game, Al Rosen was predicting the Yankees would be anywhere from five to 10 games ahead by the end of the season. "And when I say that," he added, rubbing it in, "I'm thinking of Milwaukee."

The Red Sox players were reduced to wondering whether they would be remembered like the 1964 Phillies as the team that had blown the pennant, with the Yankees — like the St. Louis Cardinals — being remembered as the team that had been the beneficiary of their collapse.

Carlton Fisk, for one, believed that his team would be remembered forever as the all-time loser. "What's wrong with us?" he kept asking. "How could this happen?"

Graig Nettles took the common-sense approach. "I think Boston fans will remember the collapse and New York fans will remember the comeback."

A stranger coming into town would have thought the Yankees had already clinched the pennant. They were tied. *Tied.* The Red Sox and Yankees were tied for first place.

"It's never easy to win a pennant," Carl Yastrzemski said. "We've got three weeks to play. We've got three games in Yankee Stadium next weekend. Anything can happen."

Rick Burleson, the resident hothead and cheerleader, was in despair. After the loss in the opening game, Burleson had expressed every confidence that the race would go down to the last couple of days. "No doubt about it in my mind." The humiliation of the Massacre left him so shell-shocked that he was now saying, "They may not have to win a game in New York. We might be through by then."

By the time the Red Sox arrived in New York, they were a game and a half behind. After two more losses, they were down by 3½.

It was their two big guys, Dennis Eckersley on the mound and Jim Rice at the plate, who got them back into a winning stride. Eckersley beat Beattie, 7–3. Jim Rice hit two home runs.

From there the Red Sox came back to pull out the tie in the last game. Even Bill Lee is ready to give all due credit to Don Zimmer for holding the team together. "He never gave up or allowed the players to give up. I've got to give him that."

The job Zimmer did in winning 97 and 99 games with those Red Sox teams has always been vastly underrated.

After losing the play-off game, Zimmer sat in his office and sighed, "I've won more games in these two years than any other manager in baseball, and those talk show hosts are going to run me right out of town."

Chapter Nineteen

Afterwards

"THE Bucky Dent home run festers," Lou Gorman says. Not quite an open wound but always there as a nagging reminder.

The play-off of 1978, like the final game of 1949, is classic in the way that the chariot race in *Ben Hur* is classic. Since then, the two teams have had their moments of heightened competition, but never again has it been the last game, last inning, last batter, wheel-sparking chariot race. Ben Hur, after all, only did it once.

Under George Steinbrenner, an almost pathological churning of managers and players set in. The Yankees won 103 games under Dick Howser in 1980, but when they were beaten in the play-offs by Kansas City, Howser was fired. Under Gene Michael and Bob Lemon, they won the league championship in the split season of 1981, then lost to the Dodgers in a Series which culminated with Steinbrenner either (a) beating up two Los Angeles rooters in the hotel elevator for bad-mouthing the great city of New York or (b) taking on the elevator wall in hand-to-hand combat and losing.

By the time George Steinbrenner was exited from baseball at the tip of Commissioner Fay Vincent's shoe, the most stable franchise in baseball had become the most erratic. Where there had once been a blur of World Series heroes, there was now only a blurring of managers and players. From Huggins to McCarthy to Stengel, the Yankees had had three managers in 42 years. During the reign of Steinbrenner, there were 18 managers in 18 years, and that's not counting Clyde King, who came in as an interim manager for two months at the end of 1982.

Ten days after Billy Martin resigned in tears, he was rehired. The subsequent career of Billy Martin deteriorated into a tragicomic progression of Roman numerals, as Billy II became Billy III and Billy IV and Billy V and was about to become Billy VI when he was killed in an automobile accident. There was Lemon I and Lemon II, Michael I and II, Piniella I and II. To be fired as a Yankee manager, it sometimes seemed, was prelude to being rehired.

Steinbrenner's greatest sin, perhaps, was that he imposed himself on the ball club. Imposed himself on the players. Imposed himself on the managers. Imposed himself on the game itself. Increasingly the story became not so much what had happened on the field as Steinbrenner's reaction to what had happened. What was happening on the field was not pretty. The Yankees dropped to fifth place in 1982 (under Lemon and Martin) and, despite vast expenditures of money for vastly underachieving free agents, were not able to win so much as a division title for the rest of the decade.

The Red Sox, relying primarily on home-grown players, won a pennant in 1986 and division championships in 1988 and 1990.

They also completed an invaluable trade with the Yankees in 1986 by swapping Mike Easler for Don Baylor, a left-handed designated hitter for a right-handed designated hitter. Baylor had forced the Yankees' hand by asking out of New York after Steinbrenner had handed down a ukase that the 37-year-old veteran was no longer capable of swinging against right-handed pitching.

It was the first trade between the Yankees and Red Sox since the Sparky Lyle deal 14 years earlier. And like the Lyle trade and the Elston Howard deal of 1967, it helped to produce a pennant.

Don Baylor had something that went beyond his well-proven ability to drive in runs. He had a commanding presence. Frank Cashen, in his first act as Baltimore general manager, had traded away Frank Robinson because room had to be made for Baylor. As prelude to the first reentry draft, Baylor had been traded to Oakland for Reggie Jackson in what was really an exchange of players who had already announced their intention to declare for free agency.

After his year with Oakland he had signed with California, won MVP in a knockout year of 1979, and had gone on to the Yankees via the free agent route four years later. Wherever he went, Don Baylor would install a Kangaroo Court with himself as the presiding judge, to levy small fines for minor infractions and mental errors. The courts served a dual purpose. They were a lot of fun, and they forced the players to become aware of their responsibilities. For the first year anyway. Especially when the judge was hitting 31 homers and knocking in important runs. (In his second year in Boston the Sox were a losing team, and some of the players were telling their favorite writers that Baylor and his persona were getting to be a real pain.)

More than anything else, though, 1986 was the year in which Roger Clemens became baseball's new superpitcher. With a blistering record of 24–4, Clemens was the winner of both the MVP Award and the Cy Young Award, and also picked up the MVP Award for the All-Star Game.

And finally there was a race for the batting title between Don Mattingly and Wade Boggs, the two premier hitters in baseball, that came down to the last game of the season. Or at least it would have if Boggs had bothered to show up.

As usual there were singular contributions from less celebrated players, most notably Joe Sambito, a left-handed relief pitcher with a reconstructed arm, and Al Nipper, an all-purpose right-hander who had managed to become a big league pitcher on a little bit of this and that and a lot of guts. Sambito had been a premier relief pitcher for Houston until he blew out a ligament in his elbow. In one of those bionic operations pioneered by Tommy John, a tendon had been transplanted from Sambito's right leg, leaving him with almost no feeling in his left hand. The Red Sox, always in need of a left-handed relief pitcher, had decided to give him a chance, and in two notable instances he came up big against the Yankees.

The championship season of 1986 began for all practical purposes on April 29 — in the twentieth game of the season — when Roger Clemens struck out 20 batters and excited the same kind of optimism that Billy Rohr's almost no-hitter had aroused in 1967.

The husky (6 feet 4 inches, 205 pounds) speedballer out of the University of Texas had been the Red Sox number one draft choice in 1983. The Sox were the nineteenth team to pick that year, which means that 18 other teams passed him by. Two years earlier the New York Mets had drafted him out of junior college and offered him a signing bonus of $20,000. Clemens wanted $25,000. The director of player personnel who had refused to go the extra $5,000 was Lou Gorman.

In 1986 Clemens was coming back from an off-season shoulder operation. He had already demonstrated that he was as good as ever by winning his first three games. Pitching against Seattle that night, he proved that he was even better. His fast ball was timed at a consistent 95 to 97 mph. His control was so sharp that he walked nobody and had two strikes on five of the seven hitters he didn't strike out. He also had two strikes on the two Seattle batters who reached him for base hits.

He had already chalked up six strikeouts when Spike Owen, the Seattle shortstop, led off the fourth by slicing an 0–2 curve ball into right field for a single.

Spike Owen had been the captain of the University of Texas baseball team in Clemens's freshman year, and he would become his teammate again before the 1986 season was over. In addition to breaking up the no-hitter, his single cost Clemens $5, the automatic fine in Don Baylor's Kangaroo Court for giving up a hit on an 0–2 count. First base was as far as Owen got. The next eight batters went down on strikes.

And yet, he could have lost the game. After Roger had struck out the first two batters in the seventh, Gorman Thomas crushed a 1–2 fast ball into the center-field bleachers to give the Mariners a 1–0 lead. Happily, Dwight Evans made things right again by hitting a three-run homer in the bottom of the seventh.

Like Billy Rohr, Clemens had to overcome some moments of physical discomfort along the way. During the seventh inning his legs had begun to cramp up on him. By the eighth they had tightened up so bad that after he struck out two more batters, he went back to the clubhouse and was preparing to take off his uniform when his buddy Al Nipper came running in to inform him that he needed only one more strikeout to tie the major league record.

So he came back out for the ninth and struck out Spike Owen to tie the record (which had been held jointly by Steve Carlton, Tom Seaver, and Nolan Ryan) and then blew three fast balls past Phil Bradley to establish a record of his own. The final batter was Ken Phelps, who had already struck out three times. Phelps hit a ground ball to short.

By the time of the first meeting with the Yankees in mid-June, Clemens had run his record to 11–0 and carried the Red Sox into first place. They had taken over from the Yankees on May 15. In the series opener at Yankee Stadium, Clemens was facing the no longer overpowering Ron Guidry. Guidry was unable to get past the third inning, and Clemens breezed to an easy 10–1 win. The headline on the back page of the *New York Post* screamed: HUMILIATION!

Ron Guidry wasn't the only ghostly echo from the 1978 season. Coaching at third base for the New York Yankees was Don Zimmer, and the former Red Sox manager was about to have a brainstorm that would hand the second game to the Sox.

The Red Sox had now pulled ahead by 3½ games, but if they were viewing the immediate future with something less than confidence, it was because their pitching had fallen apart. Bruce Hurst, just coming into his own, was out with a pulled groin, and among the other rotation pitchers only the unpredictable Oil Can Boyd was available for duty. "Clemens, Boyd, and an Empty Void" was the chant that was being heard in the Boston press box.

The Yankees, trailing 7–6 in the ninth, got three singles from their first three hitters, and had Rickey Henderson, Don Mattingly, and Dave Winfield coming to bat. Out of all that they got nothing because Zimmer had waved Butch Wynegar around third base after the third single, and the heavy-footed catcher was an easy out at the plate. Henderson walked to load the bases for Mattingly, and that was when Joe Sambito came in to retire Mattingly on a short fly to right and Winfield on a grounder to third.

Game three belonged to Don Baylor the way "Make my day" belongs to Clint Eastwood. Here is the scene, movie lovers: An early home run streak by Baylor had contributed mightily to Boston's surge into first place, but by the time of his return to New York he was in a deep slump. He comes to bat in the ninth inning of a 2–2 game with the bases loaded. Out on the mound stands the Yankees' ace right-handed relief pitcher, Brian Fisher. Up in the owner's suite watching every move is George Steinbrenner. The count goes to 3–2, and Baylor rips a double to left-center, clearing the bases.

As he pulls into second, the Red Sox players are up on the top step of the dugout, cheering. Baylor himself comes leaping to his feet at second base, pumping his fists in wild celebration.

"There were actually tears in my eyes," he said later. "I can't remember ever wanting a hit that bad."

Up in the owner's suite Steinbrenner had been entertaining Tip O'Neill, the Speaker of the House of Representatives and a lifelong Red Sox fan. "Baylor's bat will be dead by August," Steinbrenner, ever the gracious loser, growled.

The teams met again in Boston on June 23. Oil Can Boyd, who had been the winning pitcher in the Baylor game, was knocked out early in the first game. Whatever was left of their pitching staff was bombed in the second, and Rickey Henderson was predicting that if the Yankees swept the series, the Red Sox would go into another of their famous folds.

For what it was worth, the Red Sox did have a pitcher for the final game. They had been getting Al Nipper ready for the past two weeks.

Five weeks earlier Nipper's right knee had been sliced so badly on a play at the plate that 85 percent of one of the major muscles in his knee had been severed. Nipper was a tough little customer, though, and as one after another of the Sox pitchers had gone down, all the physical therapy and rehabilitation programs had been focused on getting him in shape to pitch this final game against the Yankees.

The first three batters reached him for base hits, but Nipper hung in and gave up only two runs. The Sox came right back with five in their half, and from there it became a matter of holding on. Nipper lasted until the seventh and left with a 5–4 lead. Sambito struck out the side in the eighth, but you can forget about that. His real contribution came in the ninth. Rickey Henderson, the greatest base stealer of all time, reached on an error with one out and went into his mocking, challenging dance at first base. Sambito threw over once . . . threw over twice . . . threw over at least six times before Henderson, having satisfied himself that he had Sambito's move down pat, took off for second too soon and was picked off.

To Dick Bresciani, the Red Sox publicity man, this was the game — both in Nipper's scrappy performance and in the picking-off of Rickey Henderson — that settled any doubts about whether the Red Sox had the stuff to go all the way. Their lead was up to 5½ games, and before the week was over Lou Gorman had closed a deal to bring Tom Seaver to Boston.

The second half of the season developed into a personal battle between Don Mattingly and Wade Boggs for the batting title.

The two best hitters in baseball had a couple of things in common. For starters, both had been drafted low. Boggs was a number seven draft out of high school in 1976. Mattingly was number nineteen in 1979, but that was only because the word had got around that he intended to go to college.

Another similarity was that they both could very easily have been lost. Boggs spent six years in Boston's minor league chain. "He could have been drafted by any team in the majors for twenty-five thousand dollars after the first three years," Eddie Kasko, the director of scouting, says. "We never protected him." More than once the Red Sox came close to releasing him. The rule in their player evaluation meetings — the old Branch Rickey rule — is that if one voice is raised to oppose the release of a player, he will be kept. There was always one small voice at the table that was raised in favor of giving Wade Boggs another chance.

Not that the guy couldn't hit. During his five years in the minors, Boggs was always among the leaders in batting average. But he was a singles hitter, and he was a poor fielder, and he couldn't run. There are five categories by which a player is judged: hit, hit with power, field, throw, and run. Major league ability in any three of those categories will guarantee a place on somebody's roster. Wade Boggs was clearly deficient in three.

After he had hit .305 for Pawtucket in the International League, he went to his manager, Joe Morgan, to ask what he had to do to get to the big leagues. He had to learn how to hit with more power, Morgan told him, and practice to improve his fielding at third base. Running was something that could not be improved.

And so Boggs went to work. The next year, under Morgan, he hit 41 doubles (his previous high had been 21) and five home runs (the most he'd ever had before was two). While he was about it, he batted .335 to lead the league.

He also came to the park early every day to have ground balls hit to him and became a consistently improving fielder. He still comes out early, every day, and he has become a great-fielding third baseman. "Greatly improved," the television announcers always say. No, not greatly improved. Great! In the world of baseball, a player can never completely overcome the first impression.

Fielding was never a problem for Don Mattingly. He has always been a magnificent first baseman. He hadn't shown the power expected of a first baseman in the minors, though, and the Yankees were ready to trade him to San Francisco. Not that he wasn't judged to be a potential major leaguer. The Yankees had two first basemen coming along in the minors, Don Mattingly and Steve Balboni. A decision had to be made on which one to keep, and Balboni was the kind of big, powerful guy that Steinbrenner liked. The deal on the table was Mattingly and Butch Wynegar for either Chili Davis or Jack Clark. Mickey Vernon, a two-time American League batting champion, had signed both Balboni and Mattingly for the Yankees, and

Vernon became the leading advocate for Mattingly. In his original report he had written, "This boy will win the batting championship some day." In the Yankee organization, however, there was only one voice that counted. While the talks were going on — and Mattingly's name had been tossed around in a few trades by then — Steinbrenner had him playing right field for the Yankees in order to hide his fielding ability from the fans.

The best trade, as the saying goes in baseball, is usually the one you don't make. The Mattingly deal was called off by the Giants after they had received a report from their scout that Mattingly was a singles hitter who was unlikely to ever develop any power.

"Even if he doesn't hit anything but singles and doubles," a greatly relieved Vernon told Steinbrenner, "I guarantee that he'll knock in 100 runs."

Frank Robinson was the manager of the Giants while the talks were going on. When Robinson came into the Baltimore front office a few years later, he told Doug Melvin, who had gone from assistant farm director of the Yankees to farm director for the Orioles, "If I'd had Mattingly, I'd still be in San Francisco."

By 1986 Boggs had led the league in batting in two of his three full seasons with the Red Sox, and was on his way to his fourth straight 200-hit season. Mattingly had led the league in 1984, his first full year, by beating out his teammate Dave Winfield on the last day of the season. While he was about it he had made a prophet out of Mickey Vernon by knocking in 110 runs to go with his 23 home runs and .343 batting average. The next year he hit 35 home runs, led the majors with 145 RBIs, and was voted the Most Valuable Player in the league.

In 1986 he was on his way to setting all-time Yankee records in base hits (238) and doubles (53) to go with his 31 homers and 113 RBIs. But he would not win another batting title. Not while Wade Boggs was around.

Boggs had been hitting .380 at the time of the first series with the Yankees. Before the second game he was called to the telephone and informed that his mother had been killed by a cement truck that had crushed her car after running through a red light. (That was the day on which Zimmer waved Wynegar home.) For a full month after he had returned from the funeral he batted under .250. And then he started to hit again.

With 11 games left he was still trailing Mattingly by seven points.

In the next seven games he went 17 for 31 and lifted his average from .346 to .357.

The season was going to be ending with a head-to-head competition between the two best hitters in the game. It ended instead with Mattingly chasing a ghost. Before the series began, the Red Sox announced that Boggs had aggravated a hamstring tear running from first to third during the pennant-clinching game in Baltimore and would sit out the rest of the season. Howls of derision came wafting out of the bowels of New York City, its immediate suburbs, and lovers of fair competition everywhere.

When he sat himself down, Boggs was leading Mattingly .357 to .350. In order to catch him, Mattingly was going to have to go 9 for 12.

Let's understand something. If the injury was legitimate, Boggs would have been a fool not to rest himself for the play-offs and World Series. But if it had been the other way around — if it had been Mattingly leading him — would he have played? That's an entirely different question, going to the tension between his personal ambitions and the best interests of the team. If Mattingly had pulled ahead of him with one game left, would Boggs have gone back into the line-up? What do you think?

This wasn't Rickey Henderson, after all. Wade Boggs doesn't make his living with his legs. The way Boggs runs it's hard to tell whether he's hurting or not.

Don Mattingly doesn't run very well either. Given his youth and his slender build, his slowness of foot always came as a surprise. Slow though he may be, he made some run at Boggs for the batting title in those final games in Fenway Park.

In the first game of the Saturday double-header, he went 3 for 5. In the second game he hit his thirtieth homer and became the first American League player to get 30 home runs, 100 RBIs, and 230 hits in a single season. The home run was his only hit in that game, however, and he finished the day at .351.

To catch Boggs on Sunday, he had to go 6 for 6. He homered on his first at bat but flied out on his second, and that was it. He finished with 2 for 5 on the day and a final batting average of .352.

When it came to the MVP voting, Mattingly was second to Clemens. Jim Rice was third. Wade Boggs finished seventh.

During those four great years — before he suffered a back injury — Mattingly was widely recognized as the best all-around player in baseball. And it infuriated Boggs. "What does he do better than me?" he would ask. "The only thing they can point to is his runs batted in, and if I were batting third I'd knock in 100 runs too."

The answer to that is obvious enough. If Wade Boggs hit with power he *would* be batting third. In 1987 he did hit 24 home runs, and if you wanted to make a case that he was out to prove something, you could. It would be closer to the truth, however, to say that the baseball was so hopped up in 1987 that it was flying out of ball parks everywhere. By the next year, Boggs was back to hitting his usual five home runs.

And yet, he *can* hit the long ball when he wants to. He hits so many balls out of the park during batting practice that the Red Sox always put him in home run contests along with the established home run hitters. In one such contest at Comiskey Park in Chicago, he put on such a fearsome display as to turn the affair into a one-man show. Roland Hemond was running the White Sox at the time. "He put everybody else to shame," Hemond remembers. "There's no question but that he can hit home runs. All you can say is that he seems to have committed himself to his batting average." The overwhelming feeling in baseball is that Boggs would be more valuable to his team if he were willing to swing for the fences at the sacrifice of 20 or 30 points off his batting average. But that is a sacrifice Boggs is clearly not willing to make.

Currently, his lifetime average ranks him fourth behind Ty Cobb, Rogers Hornsby, and Joe Jackson. That lifetime average, taken with the string of batting titles, will tell people who he was long after Mattingly has been forgotten.

In 1988 he hit .366 to win his fourth straight batting title — his fifth in six years — and became the first player to have 200 hits in six straight seasons. And if he was upstaged this time it wasn't by Mattingly, who was being troubled by that chronically sore back, but by his own manager, Joe Morgan.

Joe Morgan was 57 years old. He had managed in the minors for 16 years, nine of them in the Red Sox chain. During that time he had been Manager of the Year in four different leagues, and had still found it necessary to augment his minor league salary by working for the town of Walpole, Mass., over the winter as a snowplow driver, census taker, toll collector, substitute teacher, and bill collector.

He was on track to become manager of the Red Sox after Don

Zimmer, but when Zimmer left, the circumstances were judged to be all wrong. The ownership, which had been unsettled since the death of Tom Yawkey, was in turmoil, the club was about to lose Fisk, Lynn, and Burleson in a contract foul-up, and the press was growing more mutinous than ever. To bring an inexperienced, no-name manager into that kind of situation would have been disastrous, Haywood Sullivan felt. The need was for a manager like Ralph Houk who had the strength and stature to perform as an independent entity.

At the same time that Houk was being hired, the Red Sox — admittedly embarrassed — were recommending Morgan to a couple of other clubs that were looking for a manager, most notably San Francisco. The Giants narrowed the candidates down to three men: Frank Robinson, Jim Davenport, and Joe Morgan. The job went to Robinson, and four years later Davenport was hired to replace him. By that time Joe Morgan was no longer visible. The Red Sox had made a special-assignment scout out of him.

"It looked like he might be getting stale there," Haywood Sullivan explains, putting it as kindly as possible. Putting it somewhat less kindly, time had run out on him.

When John McNamara was hired to manage the Red Sox in 1985, he was asked to take Morgan on as a coach so that Joe could accumulate enough time to qualify for his major league pension. Joe spent his first year as the first-base coach, which is a job for a crony or more recently a black. The principal job of a first-base coach is to yell "Come back" on a pick-off attempt. In the hierarchy of the coaching staff only the bullpen coach ranks lower. The next year, Joe was the bullpen coach.

And then he caught a break. Rene Lachemann, the third-base coach, departed for Oakland, and Morgan became visible again.

And suddenly he was the right man in the right place at the right time. McNamara was fired in a last-minute decision, four hours before the Red Sox were to play their first game after the All-Star break.

Joe Morgan was hired on an interim basis, mostly because he was on the scene and he knew the players. Interim meaning "until we can look around and find the manager we really want."

Who could have dreamed that he would win his first 12 games and 19 out of his first 20? Who would have thought he'd take over a team that was nine games out of first place and carry them to the division title?

He managed by hunch and instinct. He made moves that some-times defied explanation. Morgan Magic, it was called.

The Red Sox won 24 straight games at Fenway Park (the first five under McNamara) to set an American League record.

After he had won six straight, he was given a new contract as the permanent manager.

"All 24 on the team are equal except for your paychecks," he told the players in his opening address. And he meant it. John McNamara had come out of the Joe McCarthy school of managing. The regulars were the regulars until they played themselves out of the line-up. Joe Morgan had a touch of the Stengel in him. He fit the player to the situation. He used the entire squad. During the most important se-ries of the year, the September series against the Yankees, he pinch-hit for Wade Boggs in the ninth inning with nobody out and the go-ahead run on third base. And while the pinch-hitter, a fellow named Jim Rice, did not get a base hit, he did hit a ground ball to bring in the run.

In the same series Carlos Quintana, who had never been to bat in the major leagues before, was used as a pinch-hitter for Jim Rice with the bases loaded and two out. Quintana walked on a 3-2 pitch and kept a game-winning rally alive.

As with Casey Stengel, Morgan's reading of the percentages was based on experience and observation. He almost never bunted in the eighth and ninth innings. The logic is pure Morgan: "The sacrifice bunt in the late innings is the worst play in baseball. You bunt the guy to second and the next two batters go out. I've seen it happen over and over. All you're doing is giving away an out at a time when you're running out of outs."

What he really means is that he never bunts in the late innings except when his team is a run ahead and he hears a voice that says, "Aw, let's take a shot . . ."

On his seventh day on the job, the same day on which he was signed to a new contract, he sent Spike Owen up to pinch-hit for Jim Rice in the eighth inning of a wild game against the Minnesota Twins with a runner on first and nobody out. The Red Sox were one run ahead, and Morgan had decided that if the lead-off man got on, he was going to bunt.

Rice, furious at being called back from the batter's circle, shoved Morgan as he was passing him on the bench, and Morgan — who had been one of the best hockey players ever to come out of New

England — went tearing into the runway to grab him by the elbow and shove him against the wall.

"I'm running this nine," he shouted, according to the players who were close enough to hear. "I made the move I wanted to make. I'm the skipper here now, and I'm the one who makes the decisions."

Rice was suspended for three games. In Rice's income bracket a three-day suspension goes for $30,000.

"No manager in my memory ever has made a greater statement," wrote Michael Madden of the *Globe*. "The Red Sox long have been divided into (a) the special few and (b) the rest of the crew. Morgan's pinch-hitting for Rice with Spike Owen (Spike Owen?) still boggles the mind."

"We couldn't believe Joe would pinch-hit for him like that with Spike Owen," one of the players was quoted as saying. "And we all got one message from it: that nobody is bigger than the team on this team."

The message was that the Red Sox caste system, the old line about 24 players going off in 24 different taxicabs, was no longer operative.

As for the strategy itself . . . well, Owen bunted the runner over to second and the next two batters went out. Just the way Morgan says it always happens. Minnesota tied the game in the ninth and then scored two runs in the tenth. So did the Red Sox. Minnesota went ahead 7–5 in the twelfth. Todd Benzinger, who had been inserted into the game for defensive purposes, came up and hit a three-run home run to win it. That's the way things were going for the Boston Red Sox under Joe Morgan.

In winning 19 out of 20, the Sox shot up into a tie with Detroit, fell back again, and finally took over first place a week before they were scheduled to play the Yankees for the first time under Joe Morgan. They were 4½ ahead with 17 games to play, which sounded like a safe enough lead, except that they were going to be playing seven of those games against New York.

The Yankees had led the league in the early going under Billy Martin (Billy V), forged back into first place for four days late in July, and had then been hit by a string of injuries to their pitching staff.

But just as the Yankees were being counted out, they won six out of seven under Lou Piniella, in his second tour of duty, to draw close enough to stir up memories of the Massacre of '78. Especially with Piniella on the scene.

"It's not the ghosts," Piniella insisted. "We're a good ball club and we're playing good baseball right now." He was, however, willing to concede that the Yankees reacted to the rivalry. "As a rivalry it's probably unparalleled. But it's the fans who make it. It's almost like a play-off championship atmosphere. Especially when it means something like it does now."

Joe Morgan, who was about to get his first crack at the rivalry he had grown up with, was quick to agree with him. "I can remember it from the time I was a kid," he said, "and they were always beating us." He was also in an unrivaled position to report that the series between the New York and Boston farm clubs had always brought forth the same kind of electricity.

The last time the two teams had met, the Yankees had given Clemens the worst drubbing of his life — 15 hits and nine runs in less than seven innings — and dropped the Sox to fifth place, 10 games behind the leader, the lowest they were going to be all year.

With Clemens down to pitch the opener, there seemed to be a remarkable unanimity of opinion that if the Red Sox didn't win with him this time, they were in trouble. And it made no sense at all. Roger had won two Cy Youngs in a row, and was rolling along with a smashing 15–4 record into August when the bottom suddenly fell out for him.

As he took the mound against the Yankees, he had lost five of his last six starts. When he left the field, amidst a gathering gloom, it was six out of seven.

The gloom was followed closely by intimations of doom and forebodings of another choke. "Sox Not Haunted By Fall of '78" read the headline for a *Boston Globe* story that went on to demonstrate rather conclusively that they were. "Boston baseball fans are like survivors of the great stock crash of 1929. . . . There is no true security."

The younger Red Sox players, like Todd Benzinger, were bewildered by the defeatist attitude that blanketed the city. What was 1978 to him, he wanted to know. In 1978 he had been playing for his junior high school team. "We're not all one big family. We didn't inherit any genes from those other teams."

Marty Barrett went even further. If they wanted to talk about blowing a 14-game lead, he said, they didn't have to go back to 1978.

The Red Sox had picked up 14½ games on the Yankees from the time they fell 10 games behind them in New York to the opening of the current series. Why, Marty asked, didn't they want to write about that?

Game two was the game where Morgan had Quintana pinch-hit.

The Yankees hopped off to a two-run lead. The Red Sox came back with two of their own in the third. In the fifth inning everything happened after the first two batters went out. Two runs were already in and the bases were loaded when Morgan had Quintana bat for Rice. Before the inning was over, the Red Sox had scored three more runs and put the game away. "No, it wasn't a hunch," Morgan says. "Steve Shields was the pitcher for the Yankees, and I knew that Quintana had always been able to hit him in the minors."

The Red Sox won the last three games of the series, got knocked off in Toronto, and arrived in New York with their lead back down to four games; dire things were predicted for the three games on the Yankees' home ground.

The opener was *the* game of the 1988 season. Bruce Hurst, coming in with an 18–5 record, had supplanted Clemens as the Red Sox money pitcher. Hurst took a 5–3 lead into the sixth and was sent to the showers trailing 9–5. Don Mattingly started him on his way by becoming the first left-handed batter to hit a home run off him all year, and Mike Pagliarulo finished him off by becoming the second. Sandwiched in between was a right-handed home run by Gary Ward.

The Red Sox closed to 9–7 in the eighth on a two-out double by Wade Boggs and a single by Marty Barrett. In the ninth, Jody Reed, the little rookie to whom Morgan had turned over the shortstop position, singled in a run, and Spike Owen, the man Reed had replaced, came in as a pinch-hitter with the bases loaded and slapped a ground ball that just barely squeezed through the middle of the diamond to make it 10–9. Owen, a switch-hitter, had been sent up to bat left-handed. Left-handed he was hitting .226.

It didn't matter that the Yankees pulled out a win the next day when, in a reversal of the first game, Jody Reed booted a double-play ball with the bases loaded to allow the winning run to score. This was the game in which Rice had given the Red Sox a ninth-inning lead batting for Boggs. Boggs was a week away from winning his fifth batting championship. He was hitting .362 to Rice's .264. Against left-handers he was hitting .329 to Rice's .296. With runners on third and less than two out, he had driven in 19 of 26 runners. But not lately. In the past few days Boggs had been doing nothing with the game on the line.

It didn't even seem to matter that much when Clemens won the odd game for Boston by pitching a shutout in the finale.

"We won it in that 10–9 game in New York," Morgan says.

"There were a lot of things that hurt us," Piniella said, after the season was over. "But we were still in it when we played those seven games with Boston in September, and we lost five of them. That was the pennant right there."

The series took its toll on the Red Sox, too. When they departed New York, there were seven games left in the season and their magic number was three. They lost six of the seven and backed into the pennant.

Lou Gorman: "We peaked in the Yankee series and then went flat. When we lost the first game with Clemens, everybody was saying 'Choke again.' After the Yankees, we stopped hitting completely and lost four straight to Oakland in the play-off series."

The Yankees didn't do much better. They picked up a couple of games on the Red Sox but were swept by Detroit in their last three games. Although the Yankees were only 3½ games behind the Red Sox at the finish, they were in fifth place, behind Detroit, Toronto, and Milwaukee. Five days after the season was over, Piniella was fired.

To those who may have begun to wonder whether the rivalry was losing its luster, the four games in Boston drew a total attendance of 140,743. The three-game series in Yankee Stadium drew 157,677 and helped the Yankees set a new season attendance record.

Lou Gorman finds it remarkable that in the face of the complete upheaval that has taken place in baseball the rivalry hasn't gone the way of so many other traditions. "With all the money they're making, and the union giving them a common interest, and the movement of players so that nobody plays out a career in one city, I'm always amazed at how they get caught up in it. They catch it from the fans. It's contagious. There's still that undercurrent of excitement when the band strikes up 'The Star-Spangled Banner' before a Red Sox–Yankee game that's unlike anything else. I live for it. I love it. It's still the only rivalry in sports for me."

APPENDIX

INDEX

Season Series, 1903–1990
Boston Red Sox vs. New York Yankees

Year	Red Sox	Yankees	Year	Red Sox	Yankees
1903	13	7	1948	14	8
1904	12	10	1949	9	13
1905	13	8	1950	9	13
1906	5	17	1951	11	11
1907	8	12	1952	8	14
1908	12	10	1953	10	11
1909	13	9	1954	9	13
1910	9	13	1955	8	14
1911	12	10	1956	8	14
1912	19	2	1957	8	14
1913	14	6	1958	9	13
1914	11	11	1959	13	9
1915	10	12	1960	7	15
1916	11	11	1961	5	13
1917	13	9	1962	6	12
1918	6	11	1963	6	12
1919	10	9	1964	9	9
1920	9	13	1965	9	9
1921	7	15	1966	8	10
1922	13	9	1967	12	6
1923	8	14	1968	10	8
1924	5	17	1969	11	7
1925	9	13	1970	10	8
1926	5	17	1971	7	11
1927	4	18	1972	9	9
1928	6	16	1973	14	4
1929	5	17	1974	11	7
1930	6	16	1975	11	5
1931	6	16	1976	7	11
1932	5	17	1977	8	7
1933	8	14	1978	7	9
1934	10	12	1979	5	8
1935	9	12	1980	3	10
1936	7	15	1981	3	3
1937	7	15	1982	7	6
1938	11	11	1983	7	6
1939	11	8	1984	7	6
1940	9	13	1985	5	8
1941	9	13	1986	5	8
1942	12	10	1987	7	6
1943	5	17	1988	9	4
1944	11	11	1989	7	6
1945	6	16	1990	9	4
1946	14	8		774	947
1947	9	13			

Babe Ruth as Pitcher Against Yankees

			Score		Season Record	Season W/L
1914	H	Oct. 2	(11–5)	W	(2–1)	1–0
1915	A	May 6	(3–4)	L	(1–1)	
	A	June 2	(7–1)	W	(2–4)	
	H	June 25	(5–4)	W	(5–4)	
	H	June 29	(4–3)	W	(6–4)	
	H	Sept. 6	(2–5)	L	(14–7)	
	A	*Oct. 6	(4–2)	W	(18–8)	4–2
1916	A	April 25	(4–3)	W	(4–0)	
	H	May 5	no decision, left with one out in 9th leading 4–3			
	A	May 27	(2–4)	L	(6–3)	
	H	June 22	(1–0)	W	(10–4)	
	A	Sept. 4	(7–1)	W	(18–11)	
	H	Sept. 29	(3–0)	W	(23–11)	4–1
1917	A	**April 11	(10–3)	W	(1–0)	
	H	April 21	(6–4)	W	(3–0)	
	A	June 20	(3–1)	W	(12–4)	
		June 28	missed start when suspended after punching umpire Brick Owens			
	H	Sept. 4	(4–2)	W	(21–10)	
	A	***Sept. 15	(8–3)	W	(22–11)	5–0
1918	H	April 19	(9–5)	W	(2–0)	
	A	May 4	(4–5)	L	(3–2)	
	H	Aug. 12	(1–2)	L	(10–6)	1–2
1919	H	May 3	(3–2)	W	(1–0)	
	H	July 25	(8–6)	W	(7–5)	2–0

* pennant clincher
** pitched opening day
*** gave up 3 runs in 9th to entertain soldiers

Ruth vs. Gehrig: The Home Run Derby of 1927

Ruth		Pitcher	Gehrig	
April 15	(1)	Howard Ehmke *Phila.*		
			(1, 2)	April 17
			(3)	April 21
April 23	(2)	*Rube Walberg *Phila.*	(4)	April 23
April 24	(3)	Hollis Thurston *Wash.*		
April 29	(4)	**Slim Harriss Boston**		
May 1	(5)	Jack Quinn *Phila.*	(5)	May 1
May 1	(6)	*Rube Walberg *Phila.*		
			(6)	May 4
			(7)	May 7
May 10	(7)	Milt Gaston *St. Louis*		
May 11	(8)	Ernie Nevers *St. Louis*		
			(8)	May 16
May 17	(9)	Harry Collins *Detroit*		
			(9)	May 19
May 22	(10)	Benn Karr *Cleve.*		
May 23	(11)	Hollis Thurston *Wash.*	(10)	May 23
			(11)	May 27
May 28	(12)	Hollis Thurston *Wash.*		
May 29	(13)	**Danny MacFayden Boston**		
May 30	(14)	*Rube Walberg *Phila.*		
May 31	(15)	Jack Quinn *Phila.*		
May 31	(16)	Howard Ehmke *Phila.*	(12)	May 31
			(13)	June 3
June 5	(17)	*Earl Whitehill *Detroit*		
June 7	(18)	Tommy Thomas *Chicago*	(14)	June 7
June 11	(19)	*Garland Buckeye *Cleve.*		
June 11	(20)	*Garland Buckeye *Cleve.*		
June 12	(21)	George Uhle *Cleve.*		
June 16	(22)	*Tom Zachary *St. Louis*	(15)	June 16
			(16, 17)	June 18
			(18)	June 21
June 22	(23)	***Hal Wiltse Boston**		
June 22	(24)	***Hal Wiltse Boston**		
			(19, 20, 21)	June 23
			(22)	June 26
			(23)	June 28
			(24)	June 29
June 30	(25)	**Slim Harriss Boston**	(25)	
June 30				
			(26)	July 1
July 3	(26)	Hod Lisenbee *Wash.*		
			(27, 28)	July 4
July 8	(27)	*Earl Whitehill *Detroit*		
July 9	(28)	Ken Holloway *Detroit*		
July 9	(29)	Ken Holloway *Detroit*		
			(29)	July 11

*left-handed pitcher

Ruth vs. Gehrig: The Home Run Derby of 1927

Ruth		Pitcher	Gehrig	
July 12	(30)	*Joe Shaute *Cleve.*		
			(30)	July 17
			(31)	July 18
July 24	(31)	Tommy Thomas *Detroit*		
July 26	(32)	Milt Gaston *St. Louis*		
July 26	(33)	Milt Gaston *St. Louis*		
			(32)	July 26
			(33)	July 27
July 28	(34)	*Walter Stewart *St. Louis*		
			(34, 35)	July 30
			(36, 37)	Aug. 3
Aug. 5	(35)	George Smith *Detroit*		
			(38)	Aug. 9
Aug. 10	(36)	*Tom Zachary *Wash.*		
Aug. 16	(37)	Tommy Thomas *Chicago*		
Aug. 17	(38)	George Connally *Chicago*		
			(39)	Aug. 19
Aug. 20	(39)	*Walter Miller *Cleve.*		
Aug. 22	(40)	*Joe Shaute *Cleve.*		
			(40)	Aug. 25
Aug. 27	(41)	Ernie Nevers *St. Louis*		
Aug. 28	(42)	*Ernie Wingard *St. Louis*		
			(41)	Aug. 29
Aug. 31	(43)	**Tony Welzer Boston**		
Sept. 2	(44)	*Rube Walberg *Phila.*		
			(42, 43)	Sept. 2
			(44)	Sept. 5
Sept. 6	(45)	**Tony Welzer Boston**	(45)	
Sept. 6	(46)	**Tony Welzer Boston**		
Sept. 6	(47)	**Jack Russell Boston**		
Sept. 7	(48)	**Danny MacFayden Boston**		
Sept. 7	(49)	**Slim Harriss Boston**		
Sept. 11	(50)	Milt Gaston *St. Louis*		
Sept. 13	(51)	Willis Hudlin *Cleve.*		
Sept. 13	(52)	*Joe Shaute *Cleve.*		
Sept. 16	(53)	Ted Blankenship *Chicago*		
Sept. 18	(54)	Ted Lyons *Chicago*		
Sept. 21	(55)	Sam Gibson *Detroit*		
Sept. 22	(56)	Ken Holloway *Detroit*		
Sept. 27	(57)	Lefty Grove *Phila.*	(46)	Sept. 27
Sept. 29	(58)	Hod Lisenbee *Wash.*		
Sept. 29	(59)	Paul Hopkins *Wash.*		
Sept. 30	(60)	*Tom Zachary *Wash.*		
			(47)	Oct. 1

*left-handed pitcher

DiMaggio vs. Williams During DiMag's 56-Game Streak

Date	Score		Opposing Pitcher & Club	Joe DiMaggio							Ted Williams						
				AB	R	H	RBI	HR	Streak Avg.	Season Avg.	AB	R	H	RBI	HR	Streak Avg.	Season Avg.
May 15	1–13	L	Smith, Chicago	4	0	1	1	0	.250	.304	3	2	1	0	0	.333	.339
May 16	6–5	W	Lee, Chicago	4	2	2	1	1	.375	.310	4	1	1	0	0	.286	.333
May 17	2–3	L	Rigney, Chicago	3	1	1	0	0	.364	.311	5	1	3	2	0	.416	.353
May 18	12–2	W	Harris (2), Niggeling (1), St. Louis	3	3	3	1	1	.500	.328	4	0	1	0	0	.375	.347
May 19	1–5	L	Galehouse, St. Louis	3	0	1	0	0	.411	.328	4	1	1	2	1	.350	.342
May 20	10–9	W	Auker, St. Louis	5	1	1	1	0	.409	.323	3	1	1	0	0	.348	.341
May 21	5–4	W	Rowe (1), Benton (1), St. Louis	5	0	2	1	0	.407	.326	5	0	4	1	0	.428	.369
May 22	6–5	W	McKain, Detroit	4	0	1	1	0	.387	.324	4	0	2	0	0	.438	.371
May 23	9–9	T	Newsome, Boston	5	0	1	2	0	.361	.319	3	0	1	3	0	.429	.374
May 24	7–6	W	Johnson, Boston	4	2	1	2	0	.350	.318	3	3	2	0	0	.447	.383
May 25	3–10	L	Grove, Boston	4	0	1	0	0	.341	.316	5	2	4	2	0	.488	.404
May 27	10–8	W	Chase (1), Anderson (2), Carrasquel (1), Wash.	5	3	4	3	1	.388	.331	6	1	2	2	0	.469	.400
May 28	6–5	W	Hudson, Wash. (night)	4	1	1	0	0	.377	.329	5	1	3	0	1	.481	.409
May 29	2–2	T	Sundra, Wash.	3	1	1	0	0	.375	.329	4	2	3	2	0	.500	.421
May 30	4–3	W	Johnson, Boston	2	1	1	0	0	.379	.331	5	4	3	1	1	.510	.429
May 30	0–13	L	Harris, Boston	3	0	1	0	0	.377	.331							
June 1	2–0	W	Milnar, Cleve.	4	1	1	0	0	.369	.329	9	4	4	4	1	.500	.430
June 1	5–3	W	Harder, Cleve.	4	0	2	0	0	.362	.329							
June 2	5–7	L	Feller, Cleve.	4	2	1	0	0	.376	.331	4	2	1	1	0	.487	.426
June 3	2–4	L	Trout, Detroit	4	1	1	1	1	.364	.330	4	4	3	3	1	.500	.436
June 5	4–5	L	Newhouser, Detroit	5	1	1	1	0	.354	.326	4	2	2	2	1	.500	.438
June 6			Rained Out														
June 7	11–7	W	Muncrief (1), Allen (1), Caster (1), St. Louis	5	2	3	1	0	.368	.333	4	1	1	0	0	.487	.433

DiMaggio vs. Williams During DiMag's 56-Game Streak

Ted Williams					Streak Avg.	Season Avg.	Date			Opposing Pitcher & Club	Joe DiMaggio					Streak Avg.	Season Avg.
AB	R	H	RBI	HR							AB	R	H	RBI	HR		
5	1	0	1	0	.462	.418	June 8	W	9–3	Auker, St. Louis	4	3	2	4	2	.374	.337
Rained Out							June 8	W	8–3	Caster (1), Kramer (1), St. Louis	4	1	2	3	1	.379	.340
7	1	2	2	1	.450	.412	June 10	W	8–3	Rigney, Chicago	5	1	1	0	0	.370	.337
5	0	3	0	0	.457	.418	June 12	W	3–2	Lee, Chicago (night)	4	1	2	1	1	.375	.340
6	4	4	2	1	.468	.427	June 14	W	4–1	Feller, Cleve.	2	0	1	1	0	.377	.341
Off Day							June 15	W	3–2	Bagby, Cleve.	3	1	1	1	1	.376	.341
5	3	2	2	1	.465	.426	June 16	W	6–4	Milnar, Cleve.	5	0	1	0	0	.368	.338
3	0	0	0	0	.454	.419	June 17	L	7–8	Rigney, Chicago	4	1	1	0	0	.364	.336
3	0	1	2	0	.451	.417	June 18	L	2–3	Lee, Chicago	3	0	1	0	0	.364	.336
3	1	2	2	0	.456	.421	June 19	W	7–2	Smith (1), Ross (2), Chicago	3	2	3	2	1	.379	.349
2	1	0	0	0	.449	.417	June 20	W	14–4	Newsom (2), McKain (2), Detroit	5	3	4	1	0	.395	.354
6	1	1	2	0	.436	.409	June 21	L	2–7	Trout, Detroit	4	0	1	1	0	.391	.352
							June 22	W	5–4	Newhouser (1), Newsome (1), Detroit	5	1	2	2	1	.391	.354
2	2	0	0	0	.430	.404	June 24	W	9–1	Muncrief, St. Louis	4	1	1	0	0	.387	.352
3	2	2	2	1	.435	.408	June 25	W	7–5	Galehouse, St. Louis	4	1	1	3	1	.384	.350
5	2	3	1	0	.440	.413	June 26	W	4–1	Auker, St. Louis	4	0	1	1	0	.380	.349
3	0	1	0	0	.438	.412	June 27	L	6–7	Dean, Phila.	3	1	2	2	1	.386	.352
3	0	1	0	0	.436	.411	June 28	W	7–4	Babich (10), Harris (7), Phila.	5	1	2	0	0	.386	.353
							June 29	W	9–4	Leonard, Wash.	4	1	1	0	0	.383	.352
							June 29	W	7–5	Anderson, Wash.	5	1	1	1	0	.377	.349
8	2	2	0	1	.427	.405	July 1	W	7–2	Harris (1), Ryba (1), Boston	4	0	2	1	0	.380	.351

DiMaggio vs. Williams During DiMag's 56-Game Streak

Ted Williams								Date		Opposing Pitcher & Club	Joe DiMaggio						
AB	**R**	**H**	**RBI**	**HR**	**Streak Avg.**	**Season Avg.**					**AB**	**R**	**H**	**RBI**	**HR**	**Streak Avg.**	**Season Avg.**
6	1	2	0	0	.423	.403	W	July 1	9–2	Wilson, Boston	3	1	1	1	0	.379	.351
3	1	1	0	0	.421	.402	W	July 2	8–4	Newsome, Boston	5	1	1	3	1	.374	.348
4	2	2	2	1	.422	.404		July 3									
3	1	1	1	0	.423	.403	W	July 5	10–5	Marchildon, Phila.	4	2	1	2	1	.372	.347
8	2	4	3	0	.425	.406	W	July 6	8–4	Babich (1), Hadley (3), St. Louis	5	2	4	2	0	.383	.355
							W	July 6	3–1	Knott, Phila.	4	0	2	2	0	.385	.357
All Star Break																	
Rain																	
4	0	0	0	0	.416	.399	W	July 10	1–0	Niggeling, St. Louis	2	0	1	0	0	.387	.358
1	2	0	0	0	.414	.397	W	July 11	6–2	Harris (3), Kramer (1), St. Louis	5	1	4	2	1	.397	.365
0	0	0	0	0	.414	.397	W	July 12	7–5	Auker (1), Muncrief (1), St. Louis	5	1	2	1	0	.397	.365
x							W	July 13	8–1	Lyons (2), Hallett (1), Chicago	4	2	3	0	0	.404	.370
x							W	July 13	1–0	Lee, Chicago	4	0	1	0	0	.401	.369
x							L	July 14	1–7	Rigney, Chicago	3	0	1	0	0	.400	.368
							W	July 15	5–4	Smith, Chicago	4	1	2	2	0	.402	.370
1	0	0	1	0	.412	.395	W	July 16	10–3	Milnar (2), Krakauskas (1), Cleve.	4	3	3	0	0	.408	.375
187	**62**	**77**	**49**	**12**				**Totals**			**223**	**56**	**91**	**55**	**15**		

x Sidelined with ankle injury

Carl Yastrzemski's Contributions, 1967 Season

Date	Opponent	What He Did	Final Score	Position After Win
April 14	At New York	Made spectacular 2-out, 9th-inning catch off Tom Tresh to temporarily preserve Bill Rohr no-hitter 2 for 4 at plate	3–0	2nd (tie)
April 22	New York	3 hits for 3 RBIs, including homer. Set up 4th run with stolen base	5–4	4th (tie)
April 29	Kansas City	Threw out potential winning run in 12th inning, as Sox went on to win in 15th (Repoz trying to score from 3rd)	11–10	1st (tie)
May 9 (2nd game)	At Kansas City	Bases-loaded double in 9th inning to climax 5-run inning after Sox trailed 2–0	5–2	5th
May 31	Minn.	Hit 2 home runs, got 3 of team's total of 7 hits	3–2	3rd
June 2	At Cleveland	2-run homer for only RBIs of game. Was 3rd in last eight at bats	2–1	3rd
June 8 (2nd game)	At Chicago	3 singles, 1 homer, 2 RBIs, fantastic catch in outfield. 6 for 9 in double-header following Stanky remark that he was "All-Star from the neck on down."	7–3	4th (tie)
June 9	Washington	2-run homer to break 6–6 tie, second homer to put Sox ahead, 3 RBIs	8–7	4th
June 21	At New York	3 for 4, 3 RBIs	8–1	3rd (tie)
July 14	Baltimore	3 for 4, 2 RBIs, homer	11–5	5th
July 17	Detroit	Homer and double, 3 RBIs	7–1	3rd
July 26	California	Bases-loaded double in 7th as Red Sox come from behind 1–4 to win, 3 RBIs. 6-run inning	9–6	2nd
July 27	California	Made game-saving running catch off Skowron in 10th		

Carl Yastrzemski's Contributions, 1967 Season

Date	Opponent	What He Did	Final Score	Position After Win
		with score tied after Sox rallied from behind in 9th. Also threw out Don Mincher at plate with potential tying run. Sox won in 10th	6–5	2nd
July 31	Minnesota	3-run homer	4–0	2nd
August 3	Kansas City	Threw out Hershberger at plate with A's leading 3–2. Sox got two in bottom of that inning. 2 for 5 at bat	5–3	2nd
August 19	California	4 hits, including 2-run homer to put club ahead 7–6 after trailing 6–5	12–11	3rd
August 20 (2nd game)	California	3 RBIs, homer in 5th, as Sox rally from 0–8 deficit to sweep double-header and 4-game series	9–8	3rd
August 22 (1st game)	Washington	Faked catch in left field to hold runner at 2nd with bases loaded and preventing run from scoring	2–1	3rd
August 25 (1st game)	At Chicago	3 for 4 at bat	7–1	1st
August 27 (1st game)	At Chicago	Two homers	4–3	1st (tie)
August 28	At New York	Drove in only run needed with sacrifice fly	3–0	1st (tie)
August 30	At New York	After going 0 for 16 and being sat down for rest, came in as pinch-hitter and with score tied 1–1 in 13th, hit homer to win it. Had played every inning of previous night's double-header with 2nd game going 20 innings. *This was probably biggest* must *game for club to date.*	2–1	1st
September 5	At Washington	Insisted on playing though manager wanted to rest him.		

Carl Yastrzemski's Contributions, 1967 Season

Date	Opponent	What He Did	Final Score	Position After Win
		Responded with 3 hits, including two home runs and 4 RBIs	8–2	2nd
September 18	At Detroit	Tied score in 9th with homer, also had another RBI, 3 hits. Big win needed after losing 3 straight	6–5	1st (tie)
September 19	At Detroit	Scored go-ahead run on wild pitch after coaxing walk in 9th when club rallied from behind. Also made great catch off Wert in bottom of 9th with men on base	4–2	1st (tie)
September 20	At Cleveland	4 hits, including home run, scored winning run	5–4	1st (tie)
September 30	Minnesota	3 for 4, including three-run homer which proved difference. 4 RBIs	6–4	1st (tie)
October 1	Minnesota	4 for 4, 2 RBIs. Got hit which tied game after Sox trailed 2–0 in 6th. Also threw out Bob Allison at 2nd base to snuff rally	5–3	1st (AL Champions)

Boston Massacre I, June 17–19, 1977

	AB	R	H	RBI	Pct.	HR	Total Bases	Slugging Pct.
Burleson	13	4	5	1	.385	1	8	.615
Lynn	12	4	4	3	.333	1	7	.583
Rice	13	2	7	2	.538	1	11	.846
Yaz	14	4	9	8	.643	4	21	1.500
Fisk	12	4	4	2	.333	2	10	.833
Scott	13	4	5	3	.385	3	14	1.077
Carbo	9	3	4	3	.444	3	13	1.444
Hobson	12	2	2	1	.167		2	.167
Doyle	11	3	4	5	.364	1	9	.818
Red Sox Totals	109	30	44	28	.404	16	95	.872
Yankees Totals	104	9	28	7	.269	0	35	.337

Boston Massacre II, Sept. 7–10, 1978

	AB	Hits	W	Reached on Error	HBP	On Base	Runs	RBI
Rivers	15	5	2	0	0	7 of 17	5	3
Randolph	16	8	6	2	0	16 of 22	5	6
Munson	16	8	2	0	2	12 of 20	2	2
Jackson	16	4	1	0	0	5 of 17	2	6
Chambliss	18	4	1	2	0	7 of 19	5	2
Piniella	16	10	2	1	0	13 of 18	8	5
Nettles	18	6	2	1	0	9 of 20	2	3
White	15	8	2	1	0	11 of 17	6	3
Dent	20	7	0	0	0	7 of 20	4	7
Substitutes	19	7	1	0	1	9 of 21	3	4
Yankees Totals	169 .396 avg.	67	19	7	3	98 of 193 .508 pct.	42	41
Red Sox Totals	123 .171 avg.	21	12	2	1	36 of 136 .265 pct.	9	8

Index

firing/rehiring of, 24, 303, 306, 318–19

and Reggie Jackson, 13, 278, 282, 286–88, 290, 291, 293, 300, 306

and Bill Lee, xvi, 24, 280, 292–93, 306

and Mantle, 247

as Minnesota coach, 272, 274

and 1977 season, 290–91, 292–93, 295, 296, 297, 298

and 1978 season, 303, 305, 305–6, 308

and 1988 season, 330

and Stengel, 237, 238

trading of, 239

Martin, Boris ("Babe"), 199–200, 205–6

Mathewson, Christy, 44

Mattingly, Don, xxii, 47, 320, 322, 323, 324–27, 332

Mauch, Gus, 215

May, Carlos, 283

Mays, Carl, 80–83, 85, 90, 91, 92, 138

Melvin, Doug, 325

Meusel, Bob, 53, 54, 56, 88–89, 94, 112

Michael, Gene, xvii–xviii, 318, 319

Milnar, Al, 151

Miranda, Willie, 236

Mitchell, Dale, 203

Mize, Johnny, xix, 236

Mogridge, George, 74

Monahan, Gene, 9, 22

Montgomery, Paul, 288

Moore, Billy, 111, 112

Moore, Gerry, 194

Moore, Jimmy, 120–21

Moore, Wilcy, 91, 111

Morgan, Joe (manager), 201, 315, 324, 327–30, 331, 332, 333

Mulligan, Dick, 163

Mumpton, Roy, 167, 210, 223–24

Muncrief, Bob, 152–53

Munson, Thurman, xi, xvii, 24

and Fisk, xvi–xviii, 24, 298

and Catfish Hunter, 310

and Reggie Jackson, 279–80, 282, 284, 286, 288

and Martin-Jackson dugout battle, 286, 288, 290, 291

and 1977 season, 150, 282, 283–84, 294, 296, 299

and 1978 play-off, 8, 11–12, 22

and 1978 season, 3, 304, 311, 312

Murphy, Johnny, 160

Murphy, Tom, 298

Myatt, Bobby, 168

Myer, Buddy, 112, 125, 126

Nack, Bill, 1

Negron, Ray, 5, 28

Nekola, Bots, 256–57

Nettles, Graig, xi, xvii, xviii, 22, 24, 28, 283, 290, 295, 301, 313, 316

Neuer, Tex, 261–62

Newsom, Buck, 157, 158

Newsome, Heber ("Dick"), 156, 159

New York Highlanders, 32

New York Yankees, xi–xii, xviii–xix, xix

beginning of, x, 32–33, 35–36

and DiMaggio/Williams, 168

dynasties of, 233, 234

sale of to CBS, 266–67

under Steinbrenner, 318–19

Niggeling, Johnny, 162

Nipper, Al, 320, 321, 323

Noren, Irv, 236

O'Connell, Dick, 250–52, 253, 265, 266, 267, 268

O'Leary, James C., 101, 113

Oliva, Tony, 273

O'Neill, Steve, 181

O'Neill, Tip, 322

Orlando, Johnny, 195

Orr, Jack, 171

Ostermueller, Fritz, 135, 139, 140

Owen, George, 205

Owen, Spike, 321, 329, 330, 332

Owens, Brick, 50–51, 338

Page, Joe, xi, 174, 176–79, 185, 206–7, 214, 216, 217, 220, 221, 231, 235, 238

Pagliarulo, Mike, 332

Paparella, Art, 212

Parent, Freddy, 37, 43, 62

Parnell, Mel, xi, 184, 193, 195–96, 198, 199, 200, 201, 202, 203, 208–9, 213–14, 219–20, 221, 228, 231

Patterson, Red, 244

Paxton, Mike, 302, 315

Paul, Gabe, 278, 290, 291–92, 293, 303, 306